Accountability for War Crimes in the Policy of the Polish Government-in-Exile

Legal History Library

VOLUME 85

Studies in the History of International Law

VOLUME 32

The titles published in this series are listed at *brill.com/shil*

Accountability for War Crimes in the Policy of the Polish Government-in-Exile

A Legal and Historical Analysis

By

Dominika Uczkiewicz

Translated from Polish by

Łukasz Gos

BRILL | NIJHOFF

This project was co-financed from the state budget funds granted by the Minister of Education and Science within the framework of the Excellent Science II (Doskonała nauka II).

Doskonała Nauka II

Ministry of Science and Higher Education Republic of Poland

Translated from the original Polish edition *Problem odpowiedzialności karnej za zbrodnie wojenne w pracach rządu polskiego na emigracji. 1939–1945* (Wydawnictwo Naukowe Scholar, Instytut Pileckiego, 2022).

This book is available as an open access publication via https://www.degruyterbrill.com.

Copy-editing by Ian Stephenson

ISSN 1874-1793
ISBN 978-90-04-75869-8
ISBN 978-90-04-75901-5(PDF)
DOI https://doi.org/10.1163/9789004759015

Library of Congress Control Number: 2026906422

Brill Nijhoff and Koninklijke Brill BV are part of De Gruyter Brill.
www.degruyterbrill.com.

Questions about General Product Safety Regulation: productsafety@degruyterbrill.com.

Cover illustration: Joint meeting of the Polish government-in-exile and the National Council, 1940, including Gen. Józef Haller, Ignacy Schwarzbart, Stanisław Kot, Henryk Strasburger, Premier Władysław Sikorski, and Stanisław Mikołajczyk. Source: Narodowe Archiwum Cyfrowe, photographed by Czesław Datka.

... jest nie do pomyślenia przypuszczenie, że sprawiedliwość miałaby być odmówiona właśnie Polsce, krajowi, który dla sprawy alianckiej i dla wolności świata poniósł ofiary bez wątpienia największe (...). Odmówienie sprawiedliwości Polsce byłoby niegodne ładu, dla którego walczymy.[1]

It is, therefore, an unthinkable supposition that justice be denied to Poland out of all countries, a country having suffered for the Allied cause and the freedom of the world doubtless the greatest sacrifices. (...) Denial of justice to Poland would be unworthy of the [*world*] *order for which we are fighting.*

---

1 *O sprawiedliwość dla Polski* ('For justice for Poland'). Speech given by Wacław Komarnicki, Minister of Justice in Polish Government-in-Exile, in a conference of Allied lawyers held by the Belgian Minister of Justice, Antoine Delfosse, *La leçon de quatre années de guerre*, 27 September 1943. IPMS Kol. 38/7.

Contents

Charts and Tables

Charts

Tables

Introduction

On 8 August 1945, the governments of the United Kingdom, United States of America, and Union of Soviet Socialist Republics, as well as the Interim Government of the French Republic, made an Agreement for the prosecution and punishment of the major war criminals of the European Axis (London Agreement). It incorporated as its integral part the Charter of the International Military Tribunal and outlined the legal bases for the Nuremberg Trials. Neither the drafters of the London Agreement nor the judges and prosecutors of the Tribunal included representatives of the occupied European states, who had suffered the greatest losses and mass crimes, as was the case of Poland. Nevertheless, representatives of the occupied states, including those from East Central Europe, had made significant contributions to the wartime development of Allied war-crimes policy projects, although these were often minimized and marginalized.[1] A unique role in that process was played by the Polish Government-in-Exile.

Faced with an unprecedented scale of persecution of the civilian population of Poland, the government began to press the matter of individual responsibility of perpetrators of war crimes even during the first months of the war. It was as soon as in those initial months, between the end of 1939 and the start of 1940, that the main directions of Polish war-crimes policy took shape. These were:

1) creating a system for documenting the crimes committed by the police, administrative, and military apparatus of the German Reich;
2) conducting an international campaign of information and propaganda about the total nature of the German occupation, with a view to
3) obtaining declarations from the Allied states in condemnation of the German atrocities and insisting on the criminal responsibility of their perpetrators; and
4) developing legal bases for future criminal trials.

These works were carried on consistently, though with varying intensity, throughout the entire duration of the war.

The Government-in-Exile's programmatic declaration of 24 February 1942 made advocacy for the punishment of Nazi war criminals and compensation

1 Mark Drumbl, 'The Supreme National Tribunal of Poland and the History of International Criminal Law', in Morten Bergsmo, Cheah Wui Ling and Yi Ping (eds.), *Historical Origins of International Criminal Law*, vol. 2 (Brussels: Torkel Opsahl Academic Epublisher 2014).

for their victims one of the main political goals of General Sikorski's cabinet, alongside the paramount question of the restoration of national sovereignty:[2]

> The Government will insist on the complete and effective disarmament of the aggressors, precluding any future aggression, and the strict punishment of those guilty of the present war – Germany and its allies. For the wrongs done by them, for the crimes committed and for the destruction [inflicted], they must suffer the deserved punishment, giving at the same time to the victims complete material and moral redress. This is a command of basic historical justice, which must prevail in international relations.[3]

The Polish Government-in-Exile's desire for justice for the crimes committed by the occupation forces and the personal responsibility of the individuals culpable was directed against the perpetrators of both German (Nazi) and Soviet crimes. The elements of war-crimes policy specified above referred also, especially in the initial months of the war, to crimes committed on Polish prisoners-of-war held in Soviet captivity and on the civilian population inhabiting the eastern territories of the Second Polish Republic annexed by the Soviet Union. While instructions issued with regard to the documentation of crimes committed by the occupying forces concerned themselves with crimes committed by both occupying states, as did government publications relating to the circumstances of the Polish population, winning international support for the prosecution of Soviet crimes became a practical impossibility after the Soviets joined the Allied side in the summer of 1941. This was confirmed by the failure of initiatives undertaken in the spring and summer of 1943 to establish the responsibility of the perpetrators of the Katyń Massacre of Polish officers executed in spring 1940, which was later incorporated as one of the counts in the Soviet indictment submitted to the International Military Tribunal in Nuremberg.[4]

---

2 Adam Jankiewicz, *W poszukiwaniu idei państwa prawa. Koncepcje Komisji Prac Ustawodawczych Rządu RP (1942–1945)* (Warszawa: Wydawnictwo Sejmowe 1992), 58–65.

3 Declaration of the Government of National Unity, 24 February 1942, Dz.U.RP 1943.8.40.

4 Concerning this topic, see: Józef Mackiewicz, *The Katyn Woods Murders* (London: Hollis&-Carter 1951); *Idem* (ed.),Władysław Anders (preface), *The crime of Katyn: facts & documents* (London: Polish Cultural Foundation 1965), Tadeusz Wolsza, *„Katyń to już zawsze katy i katowani". W „polskim Londynie" o sowieckiej zbrodni w Katyniu (1940–1956)*, (Warszawa: IH PAN 2008) 12ff; Adam Basak, *Historia pewnej mistyfikacji: zbrodnia katyńska przed Trybunałem Norymberskim* (Wrocław: Wydawnictwo Uniwersytetu Wrocławskiego 1993), Tadeusz Wolsza, *Encounter with Katyn: The Wartime and Postwar Story of Poles Who Saw the Katyn*

Although justice for the crimes committed by the Red Army and Soviet administrative authorities in the eastern territories of the Second Polish Republic had been a focal point of the Polish government's attention since the very beginning of the war, the international situation and the Western Allies' conservative position with regard to accountability for international crimes had an impact on the concepts of war-crimes policy developed by the Government-in-Exile in 1939–1945. The problem of Nazi (German) crimes came to the foreground. This is emphatically illustrated by the language of Article 1 of the Decree of the President of the Republic of Poland on Criminal Responsibility for War Crimes of 30 March 1943, restricting its applicability to crimes committed by 'persons belonging to the German Reich or to states allied thereto or collaborating therewith and other persons acting for the benefit of the German Reich'. This, too, falls within the subject-matter of the present book.

Despite the pride of place given to war-crimes policy among the war objectives of the Polish Government-in-Exile, and despite the involvement of almost the entire government structure in pertinent works, as well as Polish political émigrés' contributions to the promotion and development of the concept of penal sanctions and individual responsibility for war crimes during the years of the Second World War, there has been no comprehensive study devoted to these issues.

Due to the lack of access to foreign archives and to the dispersion of sources, as well as to the political situation, opportunities for studying the legacy of the Polish Government-in-Exile were limited in Poland under the communist regime. The contributions made by the Polish émigré authorities to the preparation of the war criminals' trials remained either at the margins of the spectrum of study pursued by Polish academics in the first decades after the war or completely outside it.[5] The role played by the Polish Government-in-Exile in the development of Allied policy on justice for the crimes of the Second World War era was partially described by Tadeusz Cyprian and Jerzy Sawicki in their 1948 monograph titled *Prawo norymberskie. Bilans i perspektywy* ('Nuremberg law. An accounting and perspectives').[6] In what was essentially an annotated compilation of source materials relating to the Nuremberg Trial, they emphasized the key role played by Polish authorities in the events leading up to the

Site in 1943 (Durham: Carolina Academic Press 2018); Paul Allen, *Katyń: the untold story of Stalin's Polish massacre* (New York: C. Scribner's Sons 1991).

5 Leszek Kubicki, *Zbrodnie wojenne w świetle prawa polskiego* (Warszawa: PWN 1963) 29ff; Franciszek Ryszka, *Norymberga. Prehistoria i ciąg dalszy* (Warszawa: Czytelnik 1982), 6.

6 Tadeusz Cyprian and Jerzy Sawicki, *Prawo norymberskie. Bilans i perspektywy* (Warszawa 1948).

inter-allied declaration on criminal responsibility for war crimes of 13 January 1942 (the Declaration of St James's Palace) and cited the most important examples from the Polish informational campaign on war crimes committed by the occupying powers. A breakthrough came with Franciszek Ryszka's monograph *Norymberga. Prehistoria i ciąg dalszy*[7] ('Nuremberg. Prehistory and continuation') (1982). Ryszka noted the comprehensive nature of the Government-in-Exile's war-crimes policy and described the broader historical-legal context. In an article published in 1981, *Kwestia ukarania zbrodni niemieckich na łamach „Biuletynu Informacyjnego" Armii Krajowej (1940–1945)* ('The topic of punishment for German crimes on the pages of the Home Army's "Information Bulletin" (1940–1945)'),[8] the legal historian Adam Basak discussed the Polish public's expectations of the Government-in-Exile and the opinions of Polish society in occupied Poland as to the manner in which the Nazis should be brought to account for their deeds. His findings relating to Polish émigré authorities' efforts in the field of documentation of war crimes were elaborated further by Elżbieta Kobierska-Motas,[9] who published a selection of a few source documents from the archives of the Polish War Crimes Office that to this day constitutes the sole thematic collection of materials developed by the Government-in-Exile with a view to war-crimes trials. Individual documents can be found in source editions highlighting the Polish government's activities during the years of the Second World War.[10] The nature of such publications, however, is but fragmentary given the scarcity of source studies into the documents originating from the highest echelons of the émi-

---

7 Franciszek. Ryszka, *Norymberga. Prehistoria i ciąg dalszy* (Warszawa: Czytelnik 1982); *idem, U progu Norymbergi. Ściganie zbrodni wojennych w projektach polskich władz emigracyjnych.* Czasopismo Prawno-Historyczne 30 (1978), 155–186.

8 Adam Basak, 'Kwestia ukarania zbrodni niemieckich na łamach *Biuletynu Informacyjnego* Armii Krajowej (1940–1945)'. *Acta Universitatis Wratislaviensis* 543 (1981), 59–84.

9 Elżbieta Kobierska-Motas, *Ekstradycja zbrodniarzy wojennych do Polski z czterech stref okupacyjnych Niemiec 1946–1950*, vol. 1 (Warszawa: GKBZPNP 1991); *eadem*, Rząd polski na emigracji wobec problemu dokumentowania niemieckich przestępstw wojennych, *Pamięć i Sprawiedliwość*, 38 (1995).

10 Waldemar Grabowski (ed.), *Protokoły posiedzeń Komitetu Ministrów dla Spraw Kraju, cz. 1: 1939–1941* (hereinafter: *Protokoły posiedzeń KSK*); Magdalena Hułas (ed.), *Polskie Dokumenty Dyplomatyczne 1940* (Warszawa: Polski Instytut Spraw Międzynarodowych 2010); Andrzej Krzysztof Kunert (ed.), *Rzeczpospolita Polska czasu wojny: Dziennik Ustaw RP i Monitor Polski 1939–1945* (Warszawa: Kopia 1995); Wojciech Rojek (ed.), *Polskie dokumenty dyplomatyczne wrzesień–grudzień 1939* (Warszawa: PISM 2007). Marian Zgórnia (ed.), *Protokoły Posiedzeń Rady Ministrów Rzeczypospolitej Polskiej*, vol. I-VIII (hereinafter 'PPRM').

gré authorities in 1939–1945[11] and the scarce number of monographs dealing with the structure and organization of the Government-in-Exile.[12] Official government publications from 1939–1945 in form of official reports, press releases, books and brochures relating to crimes committed in occupied Poland, which contain valuable information and documentation gathered during the war, have only seen limited use in the Polish academic literature on the subject. So far, only a fragmentary reconstruction of the London Government's documentation works has been achieved by Franciszek Ryszka and Elżbieta Kobierska-Motas. Neither the legislative works undertaken in preparation for post-war trials nor the contributions made by Polish legal minds to the international debate concerning the evolution of the concept of an international justice system have been explored in detail.[13] To date, the most studied aspect of the Polish Government-in-Exile's initiatives on behalf of the prosecution and punishment of the crimes of the Second World War era is its information policy on the crimes committed by the occupying powers,[14] and especially on the Shoah, as shown e.g. in the studies by Dariusz Stola, Adam Puławski, David Engel, and Michael Fleming.[15]

---

11 Waldemar Grabowski, 'Nieznany rząd Polski Walczącej 1939–1945. Przegląd badań'. *Dzieje Najnowsze* XLIV (2012), 153–156.

12 Ibidem.

13 Michael Fleming's *In the Shadow of the Holocaust. Poland, the United Nations War Crimes Commission and the Search for Justice*, published in 2022 after the submission of the typescript of the original Polish edition of this book, is illuminating on this topic. *Cf.* Fleming, *In the Shadow of the Holocaust. Poland, the United Nations War Crimes Commission and the Search for Justice* (Cambridge: Cambridge University Press 2022).

14 Henryk Batowski, *Walka dyplomacji hitlerowskiej przeciw Polsce 1939–1945* (Kraków-Wrocław 1984), 114ff; Tadeusz Dubicki and Andrzej Suchcitz, 'Walka dyplomacji polskiej z propagandą niemiecką w latach 1939–1945', in Waldemar Michowicz (ed.), *Historia dyplomacji polskiej (połowa X–XX w.)*, vol. V (Warszawa: PWN 1999), 640–665; Waldemar Grabowski, *Polska Agencja*, 240–265; Waldemar Grabowski, *Polska tajna*, 51–97; Rafał Habielski, 'Polityka informacyjna i propagandowa rządu RP na emigracji 1939–1945'. *Dzieje Najnowsze* XIX (1987), 53–73.

15 David Engel, *Facing a Holocaust. The Polish Government-in-Exile and the Jews, 1943–1945* (Chapel Hill & London: The University of North Carolina Press 1993), 79–167; Michael Fleming, *Auschwitz, the Allies and Censorship of the Holocaust* (New York: Cambridge University Press 2014); Walter Laqueur, *The Terrible Secret. An Investigation into the Suppression of Information about Hitler's "Final Solution"* (Boston: Little, Brown 1980); Adam Puławski, *W obliczu Zagłady. Rząd RP na uchodźstwie, Delegatura Rządu RP na Kraj, ZWZ-AK wobec deportacji Żydów do obozów zagłady (1941–1942)* (Lublin 2009); Adam Puławski, 'The Polish Government-in-exile in London, the Delegatura, the Union of Armed Struggle-Home Army and the Extermination of the Jews', in James Jordan, Jan Lanicek (eds.), *Governments-in-exile and the Jews during the Second World War* (Middlesex: Vallentine Mitchell 2013), 111–134; Piotr Wróbel, 'Dziennik Polski, the Official Daily

A whole new light has been shed on the Polish Government-in-Exile's information policy with regard to the Final Solution by the 2022 collection of sources edited by Piotr Długołęcki, *Confronting the Holocaust. Documents on the Polish Government-in-Exile's Policy Concerning Jews 1939–1945.*[16] The volume was published parallel to the Polish edition of the present book; therefore it has only been possible to use it for the English edition as an additional source base complementing the author's original findings. Another illuminating title, which was published only several months before the Polish edition of the present book, is Michael Fleming's monograph *In the Shadow of the Holocaust. Poland, the United Nations War Crimes Commission and the Search for Justice.*[17] Despite the similar research topic and in some cases examination of primary sources from the same archival records (in particular of the Polish UNWCC charges, official publications issued during the war on crimes committed in occupied Poland and documents of the Polish War Crimes Office from the archives of the Institute of National Remembrance), the two publications differ in structure, research questions, methodology, and chosen source base. Fleming's monograph focuses on the achievements of Polish diplomacy and information strategies in sustaining pressure on the Western Powers, influencing public opinion and political circles in the United Kingdom, and on the Polish contribution to international debates on punishing war criminals, in particular to the works of the UNWCC between 1943–1948, thus addressing also the cooperation between the communist government in Warsaw with the UNWCC. The focus of the present study is on the legal concepts and political strategies developed by the Polish Government-in-Exile in the years 1939–1945 to establish accountability for war crimes committed in the occupied territories and the contribution made by Polish lawyers during the Second World War in promoting the concept of the prosecution and punishment of war criminals. The timeframe of this analysis is limited by the withdrawal of the Polish Government-in-Exile's diplomatic recognition by the United Kingdom and the United States on 5 July 1945, but it includes also the interbellum years in order to trace the intellectual history and origins of

---

Organ of the Polish Government in Exile, and the Holocaust', in Robert Moses Shapiro (ed.), *Why Didn't the Press Shout? American & International Journalism During the Holocaust* (Yeshiva University Press 2003), 507–35; Dariusz Stola, 'Dyplomacja polska wobec zagłady Żydów', in Michowicz (ed.), *Historia dyplomacji, 666–689.* Idem, *Nadzieja i Zagłada: Ignacy Schwarzbart – żydowski przedstawiciel w Radzie Narodowej RP, 1940–1945* (Warszawa: Oficyna Naukowa 1995).

16 Piotr Długołęcki (ed.) et al., *Confronting the Holocaust. Documents on the Polish Government-in-Exile's policy Concerning Jews 1939–1945,* (Warszawa: PISM 2022).

17 Michael Fleming, *In the Shadow.*

concepts developed by Polish lawyers after 1939. Particular attention is paid to the international and domestic political factors influencing Polish accountability efforts and to the institutional framework and governmental structures developed by the authorities in exile to support this objective, with the systematic documentation of crimes and legislative works at the forefront.

For many years in the English- and German-language literature on the topic of justice for the war crimes of the Second World War era, including the history and legacy of the Nuremberg Trials, contributions made by jurists from the occupied countries and Central Eastern Europe to the development of the concept of international criminal accountability had mostly escaped notice. That has changed under the influence of the most recent studies into the United Nations War Crimes Commission (UNWCC) and into the pre-1945 history of the Allied justice project. Publications by Arieh Kochavi, Dan Plesch, Kerstin von Lingen, Daniel Marc Segesser, and Michael Fleming have emphasized the key role of the European governments-in-exile in the establishment and operations of the UNWCC and the essential involvement of legal experts from East Central Europe in defining the future principles of the IMT Charter.[18] As noted by Francine Hirsch in her monograph *The Soviet Judgment in Nuremberg,* the history of the Nuremberg Trial 'remains incompletely told' when interpreted through the lenses of Cold War politics that have erased the Soviet role in the IMT trial.[19] This books argues the search for a 'complete story' of Nuremberg requires a further step and a more comprehensive approach that would also recognize essential contributions to the Allied war-crimes trial programme made by actors excluded from the narrow circle of the signatories to the London Agreement.

A new light is also cast on the legacy of the Polish exiles by studies into the origins and evolution of the concept of penalization of war criminals in the years of the Second World War. These emphasize on the one hand biographical perspectives and cooperation between lawyers and intellectuals in the interbellum years and on the other hand the achievements of the science of

18 Arieh Kochavi, *Prelude to Nuremberg: allied War Crimes Policy and the Question of Punishment* (University of North California Press 1998); Daniel Plesch, *Human Rights after Hitler. The Lost History of Prosecuting Axis War Crimes* (Washington, D.C.: Georgetown University Press 2017) Kerstin v. Lingen, *"Crimes against Humanity". Eine Ideengeschichte der Zivilisierung von Kriegsgewalt 1864–1945* (Padeborn: Ferdinand Schöningh 2018); Daniel Marc Segesser, *Recht statt Rache oder Rache durch das Recht? Die Ahndung von Kriegsverbrechen in der internationalen wissenschaftlichen Debatte 1872–1945*, (Padeborn: Ferdinand Schöningh 2010); Fleming, *In the Shadow.*

19 Francine Hirsch, *Soviet Judgment at Nuremberg A New History of the International Military Tribunal after World War II* (New York: OUP 2020).

the law of nations and the development of international criminal law at the turn of the nineteenth and twentieth centuries.[20] In an attempt to construct a descriptive framework for this, Mark Lewis selected a timeline from 1919 to 1950 and coined the expression 'birth of the New Justice' in reference to the new concepts of regulation of international affairs through the use of instruments of international justice.[21] Lewis, similarly to other scholars,[22] has appreciated the unprecedented pivotal role played in that process by academic circles, legal experts, and international associations, as well as international political and humanitarian organizations such as the League of Nations the later United Nations, and the International Committee of the Red Cross. The debates held under their auspices in the interbellum years were largely kept alive during the years of the Second World War by the Allied émigré lawyers and jurists in the United Kingdom and United States, who according to Kerstin von Lingen formed an *epistemic community* by acting on a transnational scale and striving to establish 'new notions of justice as well as new forms of argumentation and new strategic goals.'[23] In recent years, the attention of scholars studying the development of the law of nations in inter-war Poland along with the continuation of that process during the Second World War and in its aftermath has mainly been focused on the life and legacy of Raphael Lemkin, who coined the term 'genocide' and co-authored the Convention on the Prevention and Punishment of the Crime of Genocide of 9 December 1948,[24] and on

---

20 Mark Mazower, *No Enchanted Place: The End of Empire and the Ideological Origins of the United Nations* (Princeton, 2009); Martti Koskenniemi, *The Gentle Civilizer of Nations The Rise and Fall of International Law 1870–1960* (Cambridge: Cambridge University Press 2001).

21 Mark Lewis, *The Birth of the New Justice. The Internationalization of Crime and Punishment 1919–1950*, (Oxford University Press 2014), 30.

22 See: Philippe Sands, *East West Street:* On the Origins of Genocide and Crimes Against Humanity (London: Orion Publishing 2017), Frédéric Mégret, Immi Tallgren (eds.), *The Dawn of a Discipline: International Criminal Justice and Its Early Exponents* (Cambridge: Cambridge University Press 2020); v. Lingen, "*Crimes against Humanity*"; and Segesser, *Recht statt.*

23 Kerstin von Lingen, 'Legal Flows: Contributions of Exiled Lawyers to the concept of crimes against humanity during the Second World War'. *Modern Intellectual History* 17 (2020), 508.

24 On this topic see, among others: Agnieszka Bieńczyk-Missala and Sławomir Dębski (eds.), *Rafał Lemkin: a hero of humankind,* (Warszawa: Polski Instytut Spraw Międzynarodowych 2010); Agnieszka Bieńczyk-Missala (ed.), *Civilians in Contemporary Armed Conflicts: Rafał Lemkin's Heritage* (Warszawa: Wydawnictwo Uniwersytetu Warszawskiego 2017); John Cooper, *Raphael Lemkin and the Struggle for the Genocide Convention*, Palgrave Macmillan 2008; Hilary Earl, 'Prosecuting Genocide before the Genocide Convention. Raphael Lemkin and the Nuremberg Trials, 1945–1949'. *Journal of Genocide Research* 15 (2013), 317–337; Marek Kornat, 'Barbarzyństwo – wandalizm – terroryzm – ludo-

Hersch Lauterpacht. The contributions made by other lawyers from Lemkin's generation still require further study.[25] Even though leading Polish legal scholars such as Wacław Komarnicki, Stefan Glaser, Bohdan Winiarski, Manfred Lachs, or Wiktor Sukiennicki participated in the works of the Government-in-Exile and international legal associations on the problem of accountability for war crimes, their post-war biographies ignore this angle almost entirely.[26] Important new findings in the field are presented by Patrycja Grzebyk, Bartłomiej Krzan, and Karolina Wierczyńska in their recent monograph *Polski dor-*

bójstwo: o Rafale Lemkinie i idei zdefiniowania zbrodni w obliczu prawa narodów'. Polski Przegląd Dyplomatyczny 3 (2008), 79–100; Marek Kornat, 'Rafał Lemkin (1900–1959) – studium biograficzne'. *Zeszyty Historyczne* 2004, 147 and 107–156; Raphael Lemkin, *Nieoficjalny: autobiografia Rafała Lemkina.* Translated by Hanna Jankowska and edited by Donna-Lee Frieze (Warszawa: Instytut Solidarności i Męczeństwa im. W. Pileckiego 2018); A. Dirk Moses, 'Raphael Lemkin, culture and the concept of genocide', in Donald Bloxham and A. Dirk Moses (eds.), *The Oxford handbook of genocide studies* (Oxford: Oxford University Press 2010) 19–41; Marco Odello (ed.) and Piotr Łubiński, *The Concept of Genocide in International Law. Developments after Lemkin* (New York, London: Routledge 2020); Philippe Sands, *East-West Street*; William A. Schabas, *Genocide in International Law: The Crime of Crimes* (Cambridge: Cambridge University Press 2010); Ryszard Szawłowski, 'R. Lemkin. Warszawski adwokat (1934–1939), twórca pojęcia „genocyd" i główny architekt konwencji z 9 grudnia 1948 r. (*Konwencji Lemkina*). W 55-lecie śmierci'. *Palestra* 9 (2014), 288–311.

25 New studies into the biographies of Lemkin's contemporaries among Polish lawyers – such as Ludwik Ehrlich, Stefan Glaser or Emil Stanisław Rappaport – have been published in the last several years; *cf.*, *inter alia*, Patrycja Grzebyk, 'Emil Stanisław Rappaport. His Road from Abolition to Prosecution of Nations', in Mégret and Tallgren (eds.), *The Dawn*, 93–117, and the literature cited therein; Patrycja Grzebyk and Rafał Tarnogórski (eds.), *Siła prawa zamiast prawa siły. Ludwik Ehrlich i jego wkład w rozwój nauki prawa międzynarodowego i stosunkach międzynarodowych* (Warszawa: PISM 2020); Karolina Wierczyńska and Grzegorz Wierczyński, 'Stefan Glaser: Polish lawyer, diplomat and scholar', in Mégret and Tallgren (eds.), *The Dawn*, 306–334.

26 See, among others: Krzysztof Skubiszewski, 'Bohdan Winiarski jako sędzia międzynarodowy'. *Ruch Prawniczy, Ekonomiczny i Socjologiczny* 3–4 (1999), 1–14; Jan Sandorski, 'Nauka prawa w życiu i działalności Bohdana Winiarskiego', *Ruch Prawniczy, Ekonomiczny i Socjologiczny* LXI (1999), 15–32; Paweł Sarnecki, 'Wacław Komarnicki', in: Wacław Komarnicki, *Polskie prawo polityczne (geneza i system)* (Warszawa: Wydawnictwo Sejmowe 2008). Reprint of Księgarnia F. Hoesicka edition of 1922, p. IX; Mikołaj Tarkowski, 'Prawo Publiczne na Uniwersytecie Stefana Batorego w Wilnie'. *Zeszyty Prawnicze* 9/1 (2009), 191–217. M. T. Góras, 'Profesor Wacław Komarnicki, poseł na sejm RP, jeniec obozu w Kozielsku, ocalony'. *Dzieje Najnowsze* LI (2019), 265–287; Stanisław Kilian, preface to: Wacław Komarnicki, *O ustroju państwa i konstytucji*, (Warszawa: Wydawnictwo Sejmowe 2000), 5–28.

obek w zakresie międzynarodowego prawa karnego w latach 1918–2018,[27] which emphasizes the achievements of Polish diplomacy, scholars, and the judiciary in the field of international criminal law.

By reference to the assumptions of the war-crimes policy pursued by the great powers and the model justice system developed for the London Agreement, the present book reconstructs and analyses the legal concepts and political strategies developed by the Polish Government-in-Exile in 1939–1945 towards the issue of accountability for international crimes committed during the Second World War. This study focuses on the period from the appointment of General Władysław Sikorski's cabinet on 30 September 1939 to the withdrawal of diplomatic recognition by the United Kingdom and United States on 5 July 1945. It attempts to offer a presentation of the Polish political émigrés' views and achievements relating to the popularization of the concept of responsibility for war crimes, as well as their contributions to Allied efforts in that field, to the works of the UNWCC, and to the development of international criminal law. It is based on the following research questions: Who were the authors of the Polish war crimes trials project and what was the origin of their views? What was the priority attached to the question of accountability for war crimes among the political goals of the Polish Government-in-Exile? Which factors shaped the Polish war crimes policy? How did it interfere with the Great Power's stance? What was the role played by the European governments-in-exile and lawyers associated with them in advancing the concepts of international justice and in formulating the war crimes policy of the Allies during the Second World War?

The present work will show that the problem of prosecution and punishment of war criminals was among the most important priorities of the Polish Government-in-Exile, which over the course of the five years of the war developed a complex political and legal framework to support this objective at the level of domestic and international policy. Thanks to the involvement in these works of legal scholars and experts in penal and international law, the assumptions of Polish war-crimes policy represented a critical development of selected aspects of the debate on the law of nations from the inter-war period and have resonated since in international legal debates. The comprehensive character of and early start on works concerning the post-war justice architecture significantly distinguishes the Polish approach from the conservative stance of Great Powers. This allows one to see the 'two dynamics' of the process of shaping the Allied war crimes trial programme during the Second World War. A catalytic role in that process was played by representatives

27 Patrycja Grzebyk, Bartłomiej Krzan, Karolina Wierczyńska *Polish Contributions to International Criminal Law* (Leiden-Boston: Brill 2025).

of small states – the European governments-in-exile and legal experts and scholars associated with them – who succeeded in advancing new concepts of justice in the international forum despite their less privileged position and despite the asymmetrical power relations among the Allies.

The book is presented in six chapters. The first chapter traces the development of international law and the various designs for an international justice system in the last decades of the nineteenth and first decades of the twentieth centuries, as well as the reception of that process in Poland and its influence on the concepts of penalization of war criminals formulated in Polish émigré legal circles in the years of the Second World War. The second chapter discusses the shaping of the Sikorski cabinet's war crimes policy, with an emphasis on its international informational campaign in 1939–1942 and on its creation of structures responsible for the implementation of that policy. The third chapter deals with the beginnings of inter-Allied cooperation on common directions in war crimes policy. This includes the works preceding the Declaration of St. James's Palace of 13 January 1942, along with its underlying principles and its significance to Allied policymaking on war crimes, especially its influence on the establishment of the United Nations War Crimes Commission in the autumn of 1943. The exiles' efforts beginning in January 1942 to bring the promises made in the Declaration of St James's Palace to fulfilment, juxtaposed with the Western Allies' marked distancing from the project from the initiative on, are used as an example to illustrate the differences in priorities between the great powers and the governments of the occupied states. This highlights the different dynamics in the processes of Allied policymaking on war crimes. The differences can be seen both in the context of a search for legal solutions and in the context of documentation work. Whereas Polish authorities had already commenced the gathering of evidence for future trials before the year 1939 was over, the first investigations under the auspices of the United Kingdom and United States through the Supreme Headquarters of Allied Expedition Forces (SHAEF) did not begin until the end of 1944. The fourth chapter discusses the documentation works undertaken by the Polish Government-in-Exile and the evolution of the responsible structures in 1941–1945. The fifth chapter discusses the legislative works of the Government-in-Exile's Ministry of Justice in preparation of post-war trials. It outlines the origin, background, and assumptions of the Decree on Criminal Responsibility for War Crimes of 30 March 1943, in the context of broader legislative works looking ahead to the post-war period and the draft Decree on the Punishment of Certain Criminal Offences Committed While Under Enemy Invasion prepared by the Government Delegation for Poland that emphasized the importance of punishing both crimes committed by the occupying forces and by individuals collaborating with them. It also discusses the activities of Polish émigré legal and academic associations on the topic of accountability and responsibility for war crimes. The last chapter deals with the results of those works in the context of the cooperation between the exiles and the UNWCC between 1943 and 1945, as well as the participation of Polish delegates in the Nuremberg Trial.

The research was based on archival sources that until now have been discussed in the literature on this subject only to a negligible extent. In particular the materials from the Modern Archives in Warsaw; archives of the Institute of National Remembrance in Warsaw; archives of the Polish Institute and Sikorski Museum in London; The National Archives in Kew; the Archive of the Polish Academy of Sciences; and the archives of the United Nations War Crimes Commission have been compiled and analysed.

The Polish edition of this book was published in 2022 by Wydawnictwo Naukowe Scholar and the Pilecki Institute. It was based on the author's doctoral dissertation *„O sprawiedliwość dla Polski". Problem odpowiedzialności karnej za zbrodnie wojenne w pracach rządu polskiego na emigracji (1939–1945 r.)* ('"For justice for Poland." The problem of criminal responsibility for war crimes in the works of the Polish Government-in-Exile (1939–1945)'),[28] carried out at the Willy Brandt Centre for German and European Studies of the University of Wrocław and defended at the Historical Institute of the Faculty of Historical and Pedagogical Sciences of the University of Wrocław in June 2020. My cordial thanks go to my tutor and reviewers – Professors Krzysztof Ruchniewicz, Marek Maciejewski, Paweł Machcewicz, and Piotr Madajczyk.

28 Financing for the studies of which the results are presented in this book was provided by scholarship grants from the Polish–German Foundation for Science, Stiftung Preußischer Kulturbesitz Foundation, and De Brzezie Lanckoroński Foundation.

CHAPTER 1

The History

1 The History

On 8 August 1945, the governments of the United Kingdom, United States of America, Union of Soviet Socialist Republics, and the Provisional Government of the French Republic entered into an Agreement for the prosecution and punishment of the major war criminals of the European Axis ('London Agreement').[1] The London Agreement narrowed the provisions agreed upon at the Yalta Conference and in the Protocols of the Potsdam Conference of 2 August 1945, pledging that war criminals and those involved in the planning or execution of Nazi extermination policies would be 'arrested and brought to judgment'.[2] The Agreement spelled out the principles of individual responsibility for international crimes and went on to establish an International Military Tribunal (IMT) 'for the trial of war criminals whose offenses ha[d] no particular geographical location'. The Tribunal's jurisdiction was limited to the major criminals, whose actions were not confined to a single state or could not be linked to any specific geographic territory, the consequence of the Moscow Declaration on German Atrocities of 30 October 1943. Therein, the governments of the United States, United Kingdom, and Soviet Union had announced that criminals responsible for offences committed in the territory of a given state would be extradited and remanded to the courts of that state. The declaration, however, was 'without prejudice to the case of the major criminals, whose offences ha[d] no particular geographical location'.[3] The

1 International agreement for the prosecution and punishment of the major criminals of the European Axis and Charter of the International Military Tribunal, London, 8 August 1945 (London Agreement) (82 U.N.T.C. 280).

2 Chapter III of the Potsdam Protocols defined goals and principles for the political reconstruction of Germany under the Allied Control Council. Section 5 addressed the responsibility of war criminals and Nazi leadership: 'War criminals and those who have participated in planning or carrying out Nazi enterprises involving or resulting in atrocities or war crimes shall be arrested and brought to judgment. Nazi leaders, influential Nazi supporters and high officials of Nazi organizations and institutions and any other persons dangerous to the occupation or its objectives shall be arrested and interned'. *Protocol of the Proceedings, Berlin, 2 August 1945.*

3 Moscow Declaration on atrocities, 1 November 1943. Cited after: *A Decade of American Foreign Policy: Basic Documents, 1941–1949. Prepared at the request of the Senate Committee on Foreign Relations by the Staff of the Committee and the Department of State* (Washington,

rules for that were laid down by the London Agreement and the annexed Charter of the IMT, defining its organization and procedure. The first decisions outlining the justice system for Nazi criminals were taken by the governments of the United Kingdom and of the United States in the spring of 1945; in the summer, the Charter of the IMT followed.

Initially, British authorities preferred to address the punishment of Nazi criminals through political decisions and the execution of key figures, rather than through judicial proceedings.[4] A similar stance prevailed in the US Departments of State and War from summer to winter 1944. It was modified under the influence of the plan drafted by the Secretary of the Treasury, Henry Morgenthau, for the post-war occupation of Germany, demilitarization, and decentralization of its economy, as well as re-education of its society, including the responsibility of Nazi criminals.[5] The Morgenthau Plan initially accounted for both possibilities: criminal trials and the execution of key Nazi leaders. Morgenthau's concept was replaced with proposals drafted by the Secretary of War, Henry L. Stimson, providing for the organization of a justice system for war criminals. The first drafts envisaging the establishment of an international military tribunal were created in the Personal Division G.I. of the War Department General Staff by Colonel Murray C. Bernays, the subsequent advisor to Robert H. Jackson, US Supreme Court justice appointed by President Truman in April 1945 to serve as Chief of Counsel for the Prosecution of Axis Criminality.[6] Bernays's proposal envisioned the creation of an international military tribunal to try major Axis criminals, as well as the criminal responsibility of members of criminal organizations and participants in conspiracies.[7]

The negotiations between the British, French, and Soviet governments in summer 1945 over the trials of major Nazi criminals were based on a report drafted by Robert H. Jackson in June 1945.[8] In accordance with the Moscow

---

D.C.: Government Printing Office, 1950), available at https://avalon.law.yale.edu/wwii/moscow.asp (accessed 7 May 2025).

4 Gary J. Bass, War Crimes and the Limits of Legalism, poprawić zapis, 2103.

5 Telford Taylor, *The Anatomy of the Nuremberg Trials. A personal Memoir* (New York: Skyhorse Publishing 2013), 30.

6 Kevin John Heller, *The Nuremberg Military Tribunals and the Origins of International Criminal Law* (Oxford: OUP 2011), 10.

7 Concerning this topic, see: Taylor, *The Anatomy*, 29–42, Kim Christian Priemel, *The Betrayal: The Nuremberg Trials and German Divergence* (New York: OUP 2016); 68–70; Smith, *The Road to*, 46–74, Kochavi, *Prelude*, 150ff.

8 Robert H. Jackson, Report to the President of the United States by Mr. Justice Robert Jackson, available at https://avalon.law.yale.edu/imt/jack08.asp (accessed 7 May 2025); see also: Priemel, *Betrayal*, 72–75; Bradley Smith, *The Road to Nuremberg* (New York: Basic Books 1981), 49–189; Tusa and Tusa, *The Nuremberg*, 50–115.

Declaration, the criminals responsible for offences committed in the territories of the various individual states were to be tried before domestic courts, whereas the London Conference saw the adoption of the Charter of the International Military Tribunal for the judgment of Nazi leaders. The Nuremberg Charter established individual criminal responsibility for violations of international law defined in Article 6:[9] crimes against peace, including the 'planning, preparation, initiation or waging of a war of aggression (…) or participation in a common plan or conspiracy for the accomplishment of any of the foregoing';[10] war crimes, i.e. 'violations of the laws and customs of war' and crimes against humanity, defined as:

> murder, extermination, enslavement, deportation, and other inhumane acts committed against any civilian population, before or during the war; or persecutions on political, racial or religious grounds in execution of or in connection with any crime within the jurisdiction of the Tribunal, whether or not in violation of the domestic law of the country where perpetrated.[11]

The Nuremberg Charter established criminal responsibility for direct perpetrators, instigators, accessories, accomplices, and members of conspiracies to commit any of these crimes, including the highest state or military officials, dispensing with the principle of sovereign immunity (Article 7), as well as responsibility of those acting pursuant to orders to commit the crimes defined in Article 6 (Article 8), and persons belonging to criminal organizations (Articles 9 and 10). Article 6 also established the criminal responsibility of those engaged in the making or execution of plans (conspiracies) to commit any of the crimes mentioned. The purpose of the provision was to enable the prosecution of Nazi leaders responsible for designing the principles of the Nazi extermination policy and plans of aggressive war, as well as members of organizations implementing the policy.[12] Moreover, in line with Jackson's concept, the conspiracy construct was pivotal to the extension of the Tribunal's jurisdiction to the new category of crimes of international law – crimes against humanity. The inclusion of this new definition in the Charter had the purpose of distinguishing a specific form of organized mass crime against the civilian population and persecution of a minority, irrespective of its nationality (the

9 Art. 6 of the Nuremberg Charter.
10 Art. 6(a) of the Nuremberg Charter.
11 Art. 6(c) of the Nuremberg Charter.
12 *Ibidem.*

Charter did not incorporate the concept of genocide, advocated in the London Conference by Raphael Lemkin, though it was relied upon by the prosecutors for the description of a specific form of crime against humanity).[13] That was to enable the possibility of putting Third Reich officials on trial for crimes committed against the citizens of their state, especially those against German Jews before 1 September 1939. During the drafting of the Nuremberg Charter, plans to create a tribunal to prosecute national and military leaders for violations of international law sparked significant controversy.[14] This was due to conflicts with the principle of *lex retro non agit*,[15] objections to so-called 'victor's justice', and challenges posed by doctrines of state sovereignty implying the jurisdictional immunity of heads of states and officials in the exercise of their office, as well as the doctrine of state immunity, meaning the jurisdictional immunity of a state as the entity having the exclusive jurisdiction over crimes committed in its territory.[16] To extend the Tribunal's jurisdiction to crimes committed by Axis state structures against their own nationals prior to the outbreak of the war, the legal construct adopted for the Charter foresaw charges of crime against humanity, subject to a nexus requirement with German preparations for a war of aggression and subsequent crimes in occupied territories. According to Jackson's concept, crimes against humanity committed against Axis nationals before 1 August 1939 were seen as part of a broader conspiracy and preparation for war in Europe, to be followed by war crimes and implementation of an extermination policy.[17] The IMT judgment did not uphold that interpretation, restricting its jurisdiction over crimes against humanity under Article 6 of the Charter, to crimes committed after 1 September 1939 and in

13 William A. Schabas, 'The Law and Genocide', in Donald Bloxham, Moses, *The Oxford Handbook*, 125 and 127.

14 Hans Kelsen, 'Will the Judgment in the Nuremberg Trial Constitute a Precedent in International Law?'. *International Law Quarterly* 1 (1947), 153–171.

15 Lawrence Douglas, 'Was damals Recht war… *Nulla Poena* and the Prosecution of Crimes against Humanity in Occupied Germany', in Elizabeth Edenberg and Larry May (eds.), *Ius Post Bellum and Transitional Justice* (Cambridge University Press 2013) 44–73, here: 47–50.

16 See Marcin Kałduński, 'Immunitet państwa w prawie międzynarodowym w kontekście zbrodni wojennych i zbrodni przeciwko ludzkości'. *Zeszyty prawnicze* 58 (2018), 67–95.

17 Report of Robert H. Jackson, United States Representative to the International Conference on Military Trials, London 1945, Minutes of Conference Session of July 23, 1945, https://avalon.law.yale.edu/imt/ (accessed 25 November 2023). For more on this topic, see: Devin O. Pendas, *Democracy, Nazi Trials and Transitional Justice in Germany* (Cambridge University Press 2020), 29–31; Kohavi, *Prelude…*, 155–158. Concerning the development of the concept of crimes against humanity, see: M. Cherif Bassiouni, *Crimes against Humanity: Historical Evolution and Contemporary Application* (Cambridge University Press 2011).

connection with the crime of aggressive war.[18] Furthermore, the charge of participation in conspiracy was of key importance to proving the criminal nature of the Nazi organizations covered by the indictment.[19]

On the basis of the provisions of the Charter, the first trial of international criminals in history was held from 20 November 1945 to 1 October 1946 in the Nuremberg Palace of Justice, with twenty-four political and military leaders of the Third Reich as defendants. The principles of international law expressed in the Nuremberg Charter and the IMT judgment of 1 October 1946 were adopted by the United Nations General Assembly on 11 December 1946[20] and later codified by the UN International Law Commission.[21] The Nuremberg principles enshrined individual responsibility for international crimes (principles I and II) and individual responsibility for international crimes committed by heads of states and high state officials (principle III); limitation of the justification from acting on the orders of a superior (principle IV); the right of those charged with crimes under international law to a fair trial (principle V); individual responsibility for crimes against the peace, war crimes, and crimes against humanity, in line with the definition in Article 6 of the Nuremberg Charter; and responsibility for conspiracy and complicity (principles VI and VII). Since their codification by the ILC in 1950, these principles have formed an integral part of international law, while the Nuremberg Trials and the establishment of the IMT are regarded as milestones in the evolution of international criminal law. Another key date was the adoption of the Rome Statute in 1998 and establishment of the International Criminal Court in The Hague.[22]

When analysing the origins and significance of accountability for the Second World War-era crimes, it is also necessary to consider the broader histor-

---

18 The IMT held: 'The Tribunal therefore cannot make a general' declaration that the acts before 1939 were Crimes against Humanity within the meaning of the Charter, but from the beginning of the war in 1939 war crimes were committed on a vast scale, which were also crimes against humanity; and insofar as the inhumane acts charged in the Indictment, and committed after the beginning of the war, did not constitute war crimes, they were all committed in execution of, or in connection with, the aggressive war, and therefore constituted crimes against humanity'. 'Judgment', Trial of the Major War Criminals, vol. 22, 426.

19 Taylor, *The Anatomy*, 36.

20 Unite Nations, General Assembly, Resolution 95 (I), 11 December 1946.

21 International Law Commission, 'Principles of International Law Recognized in the Charter of Nuremberg Tribunal and in the Judgment of the Tribunal'. *Yearbook of the International Law Commission* II (1950), par. 97.

22 Gerhard Werle, Florian Jessberger, *Principles of International Criminal Law, third edition* (Oxford University Press 2014), 5; Philippe Sands (ed.), *From Nuremberg to the Hague: The Future of International Criminal Justice* (Cambridge: Cambridge University Press 2003).

ical timeline of development of the law of armed conflicts and calls for sanctions for violations of the law of nations. The origins go back to the mid-nineteenth century,[23] with particular intensification in the aftermath of the First World War and the failure to implement the penal provisions of the Treaty of Versailles. In the light of the discussions held in the 1919–1939 period (and later in 1939–1945) on the evolution of the law of nations, definitions of 'war crimes' and 'crimes against humanity', as well as the need for the penalization of aggressive war and for the establishment of an international criminal justice system, the adoption of the IMT Charter can be viewed as an element, or the next stage of a lengthy and complex process.[24] The last stage of those developments before 1945 were the accountability efforts undertaken during the Second World War by the Allied governments by the UNWCC and by international legal organizations, with an important role blazed by the lawyers from the smaller states – representatives of the European governments in exile.

2 Development of International Criminal Law before 1939

The origins of international criminal law – defined as 'legal norms derived directly from international public law, regulating individual criminal responsibility and influencing principles of state responsibility'[25] – date back to the latter half of the nineteenth century. The results of the developments in military technology and tactics brought by the American Civil War, Crimean War and Franco-Prussian War sparked a debate among military and international law policymakers regarding the consequences of violating accepted customs of warfare, as well as the inclusion of humanitarian principles among the universally recognized foundations of *ius in bello* and the question of the limits of state sovereignty and 'military necessity' during armed conflict.[26] The first attempt at the codification of the rules of warfare was the Lieber Code of 1863, published after the end of the American Civil War (1861–1865). The Code introduced humanitarian principles into military conflict, defined the

---

23 David M. Crowe, *War Crimes, Genocide and Justice. A Global History* (Palgrave Macmillan 2014) 80–114.

24 Concerning this topic, see, among others: Segesser, *Recht*; Lewis, *The Birth*.

25 Tomasz Iwanek, *Zbrodnia ludobójstwa i zbrodnie przeciwko ludzkości* (Warszawa 2015) 63.

26 *Cf.* Michael N. Schmitt, 'Military Necessity and Humanity in International Humanitarian Law: Preserving the Delicate Balance'. *Virginia Journal of International Law* 50 (2010), 795–839.

status of belligerent parties, recognized the special status of prisoners of war, and emphasized the need to protect civilian populations.[27]

Numerous European proposals followed, aiming to regulate the rights and obligations of belligerents in armed conflicts. The Geneva Convention of 1864 guaranteed protection for sick and wounded soldiers, and recognized the neutrality of medical personnel and civilians assisting the wounded; the International Committee of the Red Cross was created in consequence. The Petersburg Declaration of 1868 prohibited the use of arms inflicting unnecessary suffering on enemy combatants. The Brussels Declaration of 1874, inspired by the Lieber Code, marked an attempt to systematize the principles governing an armed conflict, e.g. the scope of powers available to occupation authorities, treatment of prisoners-of-war, and definition of belligerent parties. Although not ultimately ratified, it laid the foundation for a Convention (II) with Respect to the Laws and Customs of War on Land during the Peace Conference in The Hague in 1899. The preamble affirmed the universal binding force of the laws of humanity in warfare, following the language of the Martens Clause formulated by the Russian diplomat, Friedrich Fromhold Martens. Until full codification of *ius in bello* could be achieved, it guaranteed civilian populations and belligerent parties, during warfare, the protection of international law, as derived from 'the usages established between civilized nations, the laws of humanity, and the dictates of public conscience'.[28] Thanks to the incorporation of the Martens Clause in The Hague Convention, the concept of 'crime against humanitarian principles' or 'against civilization' or 'against Christian morality' was applied to crimes committed during the Balkan Wars and the German crimes committed during the First World War.[29]

The question of how to enforce compliance with the law of nations remained unresolved. Neither The Hague Convention, amended in 1907, nor the prior codifications incorporated penal sanctions for violations of their provisions.

The proposal to create an international criminal court was, however, advanced as soon as the end of the 70s of the nineteenth century by the President of the International Committee of the Red Cross, Gustav Moynier, due to the violation of the provisions of the Geneva Convention and attacks on Red Cross hospital during the Franco-Prussian War (1870–1871). Lacking institutional

---

27 Crowe, *War Crimes*, 80–82.

28 Cited after: Crowe, *War Crimes*, 89.

29 Daniel M. Segesser, 'Die historischen Wurzel des Begriffs Verbrechen gegen die Menschlichkeit'. *Jahrbuch der Juristischen Zeitgeschichte* 8 (2006–2007), 83; see Antonio Cassese, 'The Martens Clause: Half a Loaf or Simply Pie in the Sky?'. European Journal of International Law 11 (2000), 187–216.

and political support, Moynier submitted a draft of a second Geneva Convention to the Institute of International Law for debate in 1894, envisaging criminal sanctions for violations of the 1864 Convention and the selection of courts competent to hear the disputes.[30] The question of the responsibility of states and individuals and the possibility of pursuing damages for violations of the law of nations were debated in reference to the Convention, respecting the Laws and Customs of War on Land and, especially its Article 3, stipulating the responsibility of a belligerent party for violations of the Convention by members of its armed forces:

> A belligerent party which violates the provisions of the said Regulations shall, if the case demands, be liable to pay compensation. It shall be responsible for all acts committed by persons forming part of its armed forces.[31]

The need to enforce sanctions for violations of The Hague Regulations once again gained momentum, following the outbreak of the First World War in the summer of 1914, in the face of mass-scale crimes being committed against the civilian populations of Belgium and France by the armed forces of the German Empire and violation of the neutrality of Belgium and Luxembourg by attacking them. In 1914–1915, Belgian, French, and British governments established special investigative commissions for the recording of German crimes. Responsibility for defining the principles governing the criminal liability of those who violated the laws and customs of war was assigned to the Commission on the Responsibility of the Authors of the War.[32] Its task was to determine the types of violations of international law committed by the Central Powers and their

30 Gustaw Roszkowski, *O sankcyi wykonawczej dla Konwencji genewskiej*. Copy from *Przegląd prawa i administracyi* (Lwów 1894). Gustaw Roszkowski (1847–1915), professor of the law of nations, from 1878 head of the chair of philosophy of law and international law at the University of Lviv, was an adherent and promoter of the concept of unification of international criminal law.

31 Art. 3, Convention respecting the Laws and Customs of War on Land. Second International Peace Conference, The Hague, Hague Convention (IV) Respecting the Laws and Customs of War on Land and Its Annex: Regulations Concerning the Laws and Customs of War on Land, 18 October 1907, available at https://www.refworld.org/legal/agreements/hague/1907/en/31788 (accessed 9 August 2024).

32 Commission on the Responsibility of the Authors of the War and on Enforcement of Penalties, 'Report presented to the preliminary peace conference'. *The American Journal of International Law* 14 (1920), 95–154. In the autumn of 1918, the UK Prime Minister, David Lloyd George, established within the Imperial War Cabinet a special team for the investigation of war crimes, under the leadership of Sir Frederick E. Smith, who recommended the creation of an international criminal court; see: Garry J. Bass, *Stay the Hand*

officials, the criminal responsibility for the authorship of the war, and to determine the procedure for the punishment of the criminals. The Commission's work product was a list of 32 war crimes,[33] along with rules for the prosecution of their perpetrators, subsequently included in Articles 227–230 of the Treaty of Versailles.

The decision was made to create an international tribunal to judge the former German Emperor, Wilhelm II: 'for a supreme offence against international morality and the sanctity of treaties' (Article 227 of the Treaty of Versailles), and to put those guilty of violations of the laws and customs of war on trial before the military tribunals of the Entente (Article 228). Simultaneously, the Treaty bound the German government to surrender the suspects to the Allied and Associated Powers (Article 229), along with the necessary evidence (Article 230).[34]

Analogous provisions were incorporated in the Treaty of Sèvres – Treaty of Peace between the Allied Powers and the Ottoman Empire.[35] Its Article 226–230 guaranteed the Allied and Associated Powers' right to hold criminally responsible the perpetrators of the Armenian Genocide committed in the Ottoman Empire in 1914–1917 and demand their extradition.[36]

Both of the Entente's efforts to bring violators of the laws and customs of war to justice, as outlined in the peace treaties following the First World War, ultimately proved futile. The Netherlands' grant of asylum to the former German Emperor, William II, closed the path to his being tried before an international tribunal. Because of the lack of consent from German State to the extradition of its citizens wanted by Entente, forty-five out nearly 900 accused individuals were put on trial before the German Supreme Court in Leipzig.[37]

---

of Vengeance: The Politics of War Crimes Trials (Princeton: Princeton University Press 2002), 70–74.

33 *Commission on the Responsibility of the Authors of the War*, 95ff.

34 Treaty of Peace between the Allied and Associated Powers and Germany, signed at Versailles, 28 June 28, [1919] UKTS 4 (Cmd. 153); [1920] ATS 1.

35 Crowe, *War Crimes*, 112–113.

36 The Armenian Genocide had been documented in multiple reports submitted by diplomats in 1915–1916, mentioning mass-scale 'crimes against humanity and civilization'. A note concerning the Entente's intention to 'hold personally responsible [for] these crimes all members of the Ottoman government and those of their agents who are implicated in such massacres' was forwarded to the Sublime Port already in the spring of 1915. See Viscount Bryce, *The Treatment of Armenians in the Ottoman Empire* (London: HMSO 1916), available at https://archive.org/details/treatmentofarmen001963mbp/page/n4 (accessed 20 October 2024); Bass, *Stay*, 114–117.

37 Gerd Hankel, *Die Leipziger Prozesse. Deutsche Kriegsverbrechen und ihre strafrechtliche Verfolgung nach dem Ersten Weltkrieg* (Hamburg: Hamburger Edition 2003); Bass, *Stay*, 58–105.

As most of the already limited number of cases were dismissed or ended in acquittals, the proceedings became known as the 'Leipzig farce'.[38] The show trials of criminals charged with the massacres of the Armenians also took place before Turkish courts in the summer of 1919, but the majority of cases were stayed or the suspects managed to flee,[39] and the Treaty of Sèvres itself was not ratified. In the Peace Treaty of Lausanne of 1923, containing revisions to the Treaty of Sèvres, criminal provisions relating to crimes against civilians and to the Armenian Genocide were no longer present.[40]

The failed attempt to punish perpetrators of mass crimes from the First World War era spurred intensified efforts to formulate principles of international criminal responsibility and creation of an international justice system.

A proposal of articles of an international criminal court was sponsored in the forum of the Advisory Committee of Jurists of the League of Nations by the Committee's president, Edouard Descamps.[41] In his draft, he referred to Article 14 of the Covenant of the League of Nations, providing for the establishment of the Permanent Court of International Justice (created in 1922),[42] which did not specify jurisdiction for criminal matters. Descamps emphasized the need to create a court with jurisdiction over 'violations of the international public order and of universal principles of the law of nations'.[43] In the aftermath of the criticism incurred by the penal provisions of the Treaty of Versailles just after the war, especially with regard to the violation of *lex retro non agit*, the ACJ did not back Descamps and his concept.[44] The following years saw blueprints of international criminal jurisdiction designed by international associations of legal professionals – International Law Association and *Association Internationale de Droit Pénal*. In 1926, the International Law Association

38 James Willis, *Prologue to Nuremberg: The Politics and Diplomacy of Punishing War Criminals of the First World war* (Westport: Greenwood Press 1982), 8–12; Hankel *Die Leipziger Prozesse*, 97–104.

39 Crowe, *War Crimes*, 112–113; Bass, *Stay*, 130–146.

40 Bass, *Stay*, 114

41 Segesser, *Recht statt*, 234–237.

42 Art. 14 of the Covenant of the League of Nations provided: 'The Council shall formulate and submit to the Members of the League for adoption plans for the establishment of a Permanent Court of International Justice. The Court shall be competent to hear and determine any dispute of an international character which the parties thereto submit to it. The Court may also give an advisory opinion upon any dispute or question referred to it by the Council or by the Assembly' – League of Nations, Covenant of the League of Nations, available at www.refworld.org/legal/constinstr/lon/1919/en/17145 (accessed 4 May 2024).

43 Cited after: Segesser, *Recht statt*, 235–236.

44 *Ibidem*, 236–237.

adopted the charter of a Permanent International Criminal Court, drafted by the secretary general, Hugh Bellot.[45] Polish lawyers were actively involved in the ILA's work and in 1923, established a Polish Branch, with Zygmunt Cybichowski, professor of state law and international law at the University of Warsaw as president and a diplomat, Ignacy Szebeko, as his deputy. In 1928, members of the Polish Branch hosted in Warsaw the 35th ILA conference that adopted two resolutions: 'Draft Convention on Extradition' and 'Rules for the Government of Territory Occupied'.[46]

A draft convention regulating the scope of and procedure for the exercise of international criminal jurisdiction was also compiled by the members of the *Association Internationale de Droit Pénal* (AIDP), created in 1924. In the autumn of 1928, the AIDP submitted to the League of Nations a draft to expand the jurisdiction of the Permanent Court of International Justice. The proposal included the establishment of the Criminal Chamber to determine cases involving violations of international law.[47] The final inter-war initiative to establish an international criminal court emerged in the late 1930s in connection with initiatives to penalize the crime of terrorism and the League of Nations Convention for the Prevention and Punishment of Terrorism of 1937.[48] The Convention obligated states to prosecute and extradite perpetrators of terrorist acts and was supplemented by an additional convention establishing an international criminal court. However, neither convention entered into force.[49]

The scope of the jurisdiction of the international justice system was an important element of the debate. The focus was on the need to define international crimes, including the problem – discussed already within the Commission for the Responsibility of the Authors of the War – of criminal responsibility for aggressive war and, in a broader sense, calls for the condemnation of warfare as a method of international dispute resolution. On 2 October 1924, the General Assembly of the League of Nations adopted the so-called 'Geneva Protocol', defining aggressive war as an 'international crime'.[50]

45 Daniel M. Segesser, 'Hugh H. L. Bellot: A Life in the Service of the Prevention and Punishment of War Crimes and Crimes Against Humanity', in Mégret and Tallgren (eds.), *The Dawn*, 24–48, here: 43–44.

46 K. Wierczyńska, Grzebyk et. al. *Polski dorobek*, 41.

47 Seggeser, *Recht statt*, 243–244 and 257–259; Rappaport, *Zagadnienie prawa karnego międzypaństwowego*, 22.

48 League of Nations Convention for the Prevention and Punishment of Terrorism, 16 November 1937, LN Doc. C.546.M.383.1937

49 Seggeser, *Recht statt*, 295–299.

50 League of Nations, *Protocol for the Pacific Settlement of International Disputes*, 2 October 1924, available at https://www.loc.gov/item/2021667896 (accessed 15 December 2024).

The penalization of aggressive war and war propaganda was also one of the fundamental demands advocated by the AIDP. In 1927, at the request of the Association's Vice-President, Emil Stanisław Rappaport, Polish scholar of criminal law and Secretary of the Codification Commission, the Assembly of the League of Nations adopted a resolution recognizing aggressive war as an international crime.[51] Nevertheless, the resolution was non-binding. The prohibition of the use of war as an instrument of dispute resolution and of national policy was incorporated in the Pact of Paris (Kellogg-Briand Pact) of 1928, leading to the conclusion of numerous non-aggression treaties, including the Polish–Soviet one of 1932[52] (extended to 1945 in 1934)[53] and Polish–German of 1934[54] (repudiated by the Third Reich in April 1939).[55]

The Kellogg–Briand Pact did not provide for penal sanctions, so already in 1928, the AIDP passed a resolution to narrow down the principles of responsibility for its violations. The problem was first addressed during the AIDP Conference in Warsaw in 1927. The Association's President and Romanian jurist specializing in criminal law, Vespasian Pella,[56] as well as the members, saw the opportunity for the creation of an effective system of international criminal law in reforms of the domestic legislation of European states, close international co-operation of legal circles, and unification of legal systems. In order to promote and develop upon those concepts, the AIDP organized annual congresses dedicated to the unification of criminal law and already in 1928, established the International Bureau for the Unification of Criminal Law.

In addition to Rappaport, other Polish members of the AIDP included Raphael Lemkin, who served as secretary, Wacław Makowski, Juliusz Makarewicz, Aleksander Mogilnicki, Stefan Glaser, Leon Rabinowicz, and Helena Wie-

---

51 Emil Stanisław Rappaport, *Zagadnienie unifikacji międzynarodowej prawa karnego* (Warszawa: Polski Związek Prawników Kresowców 1929) 114. Concerning this topic, see: Bohdan Winiarski, *Bezpieczeństwo, arbitraż rozbrojenie* (Poznań: Fiszer i Majewski 1928) 252–254.

52 Poland and Union of Soviet Socialist Republics – Pact of Non-aggression, with two Protocols of Signature. Signed at Moscow, July 25, 1932 [1933] LNTSer 7; 136 LNTS 41.

53 Poland and Union of Soviet Socialist Republics – Protocol renewing until December 31st, 1945, the Pact of Non-Aggression of July 25th, 1932, and Final Protocol. Signed at Moscow, May 5th, 1934 [1935] LNTSer 44; 157 LNTS 431

54 Dz.U.1934.16.124. A translation – *The British War Bluebook*. Text of German-Polish Agreement of Janurary 26, 1934 – is available via Avalon Project at: https://avalon.law.yale.edu/wwii/blbk01.asp

55 'The German Note to Poland'. *Bulletin of Internal News* 16 (1939), 13–15, available at https://www.jstor.org/stable/25642470

56 Andrei Mamolea 'Vespasian V. Pella: International Criminal Justice as a Safeguard of Peace, 1919–1952', in Mégret and Tallgren (eds.), *The Dawn*, 49–92.

wiórska.[57] At the AIDP Warsaw Conference in 1927, devoted to the issue of individual liability for international offences, universal jurisdiction, and unification of criminal law, a list of *delicta iuris gentium* was adopted, which included the following offences against the law of nations: piracy, counterfeiting of coins, bank notes and securities, trade in slaves, trade in women or children, intentional use of any instrument capable of producing a public danger [terrorism], trade in narcotics, and traffic in obscene publications.[58] Rappaport contributed to this discussion by presenting the concept of aggressive war as a crime of international law and by calling for the introduction of a prohibition against the propaganda of aggressive war in the criminal codes of European states. Through the instrumentality of Rappaport, who participated in the works of the Polish Codification Commission's Criminal Law Section, a provision to that effect was included as Article 113 of Polish Criminal Code.[59] Similar solutions made their way to the Romanian and Brazilian codes, drafted around the same time.

During the AIDP 5th Conference for the Unification of Criminal Law in Madrid in October 1933, Raphael Lemkin presented his concept of a 'new type of crime' that ought to be subjected to international repression, on behalf and in the interest of humanity as a whole. In his paper, Lemkin distinguished three crimes constituting *delicta iuris gentium* – acts of barbarity, acts of vandalism, and provocation of catastrophes in international communication – which should be covered by universal jurisdiction and recognized by an international convention ensuring their repression. The first two categories laid the foundation for the concept of the crime of genocide, developed by Lemkin in subsequent years. In 1933, he defined acts of barbarism and vandalism as 'attacks carried out against an individual as a member of a collective', as

57 Grzebyk et al., *Polish*, 25–33. Wierczyńska presents in this study an overview and summary of international congresses held by AIDP at Brussels (1926), Bucharest (1929), Palermo (1933) and Paris (1939) and highlights contributions provided by Polish delegates.

58 *Actes de la conférence internationale d'unification du droit pénal. publ. sous la dir. de Emil Stanisław Rappaport et avec le concours de Vespasien V. Pella par Michel Potulicki* (Paris: Librairie du Recueil Sirey 1929).

59 Art. 113 of the Polish Criminal Code provided:
(1) Whoever publicly calls for a war of aggression shall be liable to imprisonment for up to 5 years.
(2) The prosecution shall proceed only when the act set out in section 1 is penalized by the statutes of the state against which such calling is directed' – Regulation of the President of the Republic of Poland of 11 July 1932 – Criminal Code. Code of Criminal Law, Dz.U.1932.60.571 (hereinafter the 'Criminal Code of 1932' or 'CC') Concerning this topic see: Emil Stanisław Rappaport, 'Propaganda wojny zaczepnej jako *delictum iuris gentium*'. Copy from the *Gazeta Sądowa* (Warszawa 1929).

crimes aimed at the biological and cultural extermination of groups and their disintegration.[60] Acts of barbarism referred to the extermination and persecution of ethnic, religious, and social groups, while the acts of vandalism concerned the 'organized destruction of art and cultural heritage').[61] During the Second World War, Lemkin developed the term 'genocide' from these two concepts,[62] which became fundamental to shaping post-war justice, the codification of international criminal law, and the evolution of humanitarian law after 1945.

Raphael Lemkin's legacy constitutes the most famous and representative example of the way in which the involvement of the Polish jurists of the inter-war period influenced post-war concepts in the international debate on the development of criminal law and law of nations. Like Lemkin himself, many lived in exile. It is thanks to the co-operation of such protagonists of the practice and scholarship of the law of nations as Wacław Komarnicki, Stefan Glaser, Bohdan Winiarski, Wiktor Sukiennicki, and Władysław Kulski with the Polish Government-in-Exile that the assumptions of Polish war-crimes policy constituted a critical elaboration of selected aspects of the debate on the development of international law unfolding in the inter-war period.

3 In a Reborn Poland

Although detailed discussion of how international law and international criminal law were received and developed in Poland after the restoration of independence in 1918 exceeds the scope of this book, a brief outline is warranted. It should be noted that this reception included academic and research activities in law faculties, abundant publications in law reviews, and participation of Polish lawyers and jurists in the deliberations of numerous international organizations, as well as the Polish Codification Commission.

The traditions of Polish scholarship and teaching in the law of nations date back to the pre-partitioning era. The head of the Department of Philosophy of

---

60 Raphael Lemkin, 'Akte der Barberei und des Vandalismus als *delicta iuris gentium*'. *Internationalles Anwaltsblatt* 19 (1933). Jahrgang, Heft 6, S. 117–119; text of Lemkin's lecture delivered during the Madrid Conference: *Les actes constituant un danger général (interétatique) considérés comme delits de droit de gens* http://www.preventgenocide.org/fr/lemkin/madrid1933.html (accessed 27 May 2025).

61 *Ibidem.*

62 Raphael Lemkin, *Axis Rule in Occupied Europe: Laws of Occupation – Analysis of Government – Proposals for Redress* (Washington, D.C.: Carnegie Endowment for International Peace 1944).

Law and of the Law of Nations at Jagiellonian University in Cracow, since 1872, was Franciszek Ksawery Kasparek, who was followed in that position from 1902 by Michał Rostworowski. In Warsaw, the Polish university – Royal University of Warsaw – was closed down in 1831 amid repressions against the Polish population and reprisals for the November Uprising against Russia. The teaching of law by Polish academics resumed in 1863–1869 at the Faculty of Law and Administration of Warsaw Main School, and the teaching of international law in the Department of Political Skills and Public International Law, led by Professor Antoni Białecki.[63] After the liquidation of the Warsaw Main School and its replacement by the Russian Imperial University of Warsaw, Białecki led its Department of International Law until 1887.[64] At the University of Lviv, a dedicated Department of Philosophy of Law and the Law of Nations was led by Professor Gustaw Roszkowski from 1878.

The aspirations to regain independence at the turn of the twentieth century – and the eventual re-establishment of a sovereign Polish state after 1918 – were fundamental to the development of the Polish school of international law. In the late nineteenth century, Polish jurists actively contributed to international debates on the development of the law of nations,[65] publishing commentaries and studies and participating in organizations such as the Institute of International Law in Brussels. Those traditions were continued after Poland regained independence in 1918. Polish lawyers and jurists participated in The Hague Academy of International Law, the Permanent International Studies Conference of the League of Nations, the Paris Institute of Comparative Law, the Institute of International Law in Brussels, the International Law Association, and the *Association Internationale de Droit Pénal*. They also served as delegates of the Polish government to the Paris Peace Conference and to vari-

63 Marzenna Paszkowska, 'Wydział Prawa i Administracji Szkoły Głównej Warszawskiej (1862–1869)', in Grażyna Bałtruszajtys (ed.), *Zarys dziejów Wydziału Prawa i Administracji Uniwersytetu Warszawskiego* (Warszawa: Wolters Kluwer 2016) 69–70.

64 Adam Bosiacki, 'Wydział Prawa Cesarskiego Uniwersytetu Warszawskiego w latach 1869–1915', in Bałtruszajtys (ed.), *Zarys dziejów*, 106.

65 Among others, see: Gustaw Roszkowski, *O poselstwach dyplomatycznych i konsulatach*, Warszawa 1872; *idem*, *O azylach i ekstradycji* (Lwów 1881); *idem*, *O konwencji genewskiej* (Lwów 1887); Franciszek K. Kasparek, 'O wydawaniu przestępców'. *Przegląd sądowy i administracyjny* 1872; *idem*, 'O wydawaniu przestępców uchwały Akademii prawa międzynarodowego zapadłe w Oksfordzie we wrześniu 1881 r.'. *Przegląd Sądowy i Administracyjny* 1882; *idem*, *Udział polskich prawników w uprawie*, available at https://ruj.uj.edu.pl/xmlui/bitstream/handle/item/23634/szlachta_franciszek_ksawery_kasparek_2015.pdf?sequence=1&isAllowed=y

ous League of Nations agencies.[66] During the Paris Peace Conference, members of the Polish delegation Roman Dmowski, Ignacy Jan Paderewski and Stanisław Grabski participated in the negotiations on the recovery of territories lost as a result of the partitions by Prussia, Russian, and Austria, and on the delimitation of Polish boundaries (Art. 87 of the Treaty of Versailles). Polish representatives also contributed to the work of the Commission on Reparation of Damage (including Zygmunt Chamiec and Kazimierz Olszowski), as well to the proceedings of the Commission on the Responsibility of the Authors of the War and the Enforcement of Penalties (Konstanty Skirmunt, Leon Łubieński, and Kazimierz Rybiński). Polish delegates submitted to the Commission of Responsibilities, a report on violations of customary and international law on Polish Territory by Austrian and Prussian forces and participated in drafting Commission's final report, which included a list of 32 war crimes, defined principles of jurisdiction for violations of international law, and set out the rules, later adopted in articles 227–230 of the of the Treaty of Versailles.[67]

The inter-war period was a time of significant involvement of Polish experts in the debate on the developments of the law of nations following the Treaty of Versailles. Many studies and commentaries were devoted to the issue of state formation, in particular to the question of the restoration of Polish sovereignty, e.g. Wacław Komarnicki's *The formation of states from the position of state science and international law* of 1916 and *The origin of the territory of the Polish state from the position of the law of nations* of 1925; Michał Rostworowski's *War and peace treaty. How does a state form in our times?* of 1916, Cezary

66 Ehrlich, *Zarys historii*, 12. *Cf.* also: Cezary Berezowski, *Powstanie państwa polskiego w świetle prawa narodów* ('Formation of the Polish State in the light of the law of nations'), (Warszawa 1934); Zygmunt Cybichowski, 'Niepodległość Polski a Liga Narodów' ('Poland's independence and the League of Nations'). *Prawo* 4–5 (1929), (Warszawa 1929); Wacław Komarnicki, *Powstawanie państw ze stanowiska nauki o państwie i prawa Międzynarodowego* ('The formation of states from the position of state science and international law') (Warszawa: Gebethner i Wolf 1916); *idem*, *Geneza terytorium państwa Polski ze stanowiska prawa narodów* ('The origin of the territory of the Polish state from the position of the law of nations') (Wilno 1925); *idem*, *Polskie Prawo polityczne: geneza i system* ('Polish political law: history and system') (Warszawa: F. Hoesick 1922); Rada Głowna Opiekuńcza (Polish Welfare Council), *Likwidacja skutków wojny w dziedzinie stosunków prawnych i ekonomicznych w Polsce* ('Elimination of the consequences of the war in the field of legal and economic affairs in Poland') (Warszawa 1917: Rada Główna Opiekuńcza 1916–1920); Michał Rostworowski, *Wojna i traktat pokojowy. Jak powstaje państwo w naszych czasach?* ('War and peace treaty. How does a state form in our times?') (Kraków 1916).

67 Commission on the Responsibility of the Authors of the War and on Enforcement of penalties, 'Report'.

Berezowski's *Formation of the Polish State in the light of the law of nations* of 1934, or Zygmunt Cybichowski's *Poland's independence and the League of Nations*. Polish legal scholars also addressed issues such as the legal framework of the League of Nations, reparations, and international security, e.g. by Edward Borowski (*Evolution of Polish-Gdańsk relations in the context of decisions of League of Nations bodies*), Władysław Grzankowski (*The topic of international sanctions of the League of Nations*, 1930) Zygmunt Izdebski (*The advisory-opining function of the Permanent Court of International Justice*, 1936), Bohdan Winiarski, or Jerzy Waciórski (*Le terrorisme politique*, 1939). Many studies focused on public international law, international criminal law, and their relationship to domestic legislation. Zygmunt Cybichowski, Ludwig Ehrlich, and Julian Makowski authored the first textbooks on international law.[68] Expert studies were also devoted to diplomatic law, questions of state responsibility in international law, international judiciary, and extradition.[69] Emil Stanisław Rappaport, Stefan Glaser, Aleksander Mogilnicki, and Cezary Berezowski, among others, provided commentary on the incorporation of international criminal law into domestic legislation and on the Polish international law project, as reflected in the general provisions of the 1932 Criminal Code.[70]

68 Julian Makowski, *Rozwój i przyszłość prawa międzynarodowego. Przyczynek do teorii prawa narodów* ('Development and future of international law. A contribution to theory of the law of nations') (Warszawa 1926); Ludwik Ehrlich, *Prawo narodów* ('Law of nations'), (Lwów 1932), Zygmunt Cybichowski, *Prawo międzynarodowe publiczne i prywatne* (Lwów 1915).

69 Michał Rostworowski, *Prawo dyplomatyczne. Poprawione i uzupełnione na podstawie wykładów 1936–1937* ('Diplomatic law. Revised and supplemented on the basis of lectures 1936–1937') (Kraków 1938); Kazimierz Szwarcenberg-Czerny, *Immunitety dyplomatyczne i konsularne: zbiór norm prawnych z zakresu prawa międzynarodowego obowiązujących na obszarze Polski i Wolnego Miasta Gdańska* ('Diplomatic and consular immunities: collection of legal norms from the scope of international law in force in the territories of Poland and Free City of Gdańsk') (Warszawa 1935); Michał Król, 'Odpowiedzialność Państwa w Prawie Międzynarodowym' ('State responsibility in international law'). *Rocznik Prawniczy Wileński* (1932); *idem*, *Próby kodyfikacji zasad międzynarodowej odpowiedzialności państw* ('Attempts to codify the rules for international state responsibility') (Wilno 1936); Julian Makowski *Współczesne formy sądownictwa międzynarodowego* ('Modern forms of international justice') (Warszawa 1922); *Międzynarodowe prawo karne: kompetencja sądów do ścigania przestępstw zagranicznych* ('International criminal law: the courts' jurisdiction for foreign crimes') (1927); *L'uniformisation du droit d'extradition: rapport présenté au Congrès International de Droit Comparé à La Haye – 1932* (Warszawa 1932).

70 E. S. Rappaport, 'Prawo Karne międzynarodowe' ('International criminal law'). Copy from the *Encyklopedia Podręczna Prawa Karnego*, vol. XIV (Warszawa: Biblioteka Polska 1936); *idem*, 'Tendencje rozwojowe prawa karnego międzynarodowego' ('Development tendencies in international criminal law'). Copy from the *Ruch Prawniczy, Ekonomiczny i*

3.1 *The Makarewicz Code (1932)*

The new trends in the development of international criminal law and the debate on unifying criminal law through new drafts of domestic legislation, as seen within the AIDP, were reflected in the Polish Codification Commission's work on a new criminal code to cover the whole territory of Poland after reacquisition of independence.[71] This work began in the November of 1919; the Commission was tasked with drafting unified provisions of substantive and procedural criminal and civil law to replace the fragmented legislation inherited from the partitioning powers (Austria, Prussia, and Russia).[72] The Criminal Section of the Commission was chaired by Juliusz Makarewicz, a professor of criminal law at John Casimir University in Lviv and the founder of the Polish sociological school of criminal law. His deputy was a professor of criminal law from the University of Warsaw, Wacław Makowski. The position of secretary went to Rappaport. The result of the Criminal Section's work was the Criminal Code, promulgated in 1932,[73] colloquially known as the 'Makarewicz Code' (or 'Lex Makarewicz'), in recognition of the professor's central role in its conceptual development.[74]

The 1932 Criminal Code (CC) was regarded as a modern legislative achievement, noted for its concise language, logical structure,[75] and substantive content. Its solutions reconciled 'the classical bases of criminal liability with new tendencies in sentencing principles',[76] the latter stemming from the underpinnings of the sociological school of criminal law, emphasizing the purposive dimension of punishment. The Code enshrined the principles of equality before the law, legality (*nullum crimen sine lege, nulla poena sine lege*), and individualized criminal responsibility based on the perpetrator's personal culpability, including the personal responsibility of instigators and abettors,

Socjologiczny (1934); Cezary Berezowski, *O polskim projekcie międzynarodowego prawa karnego* ('Concerning the Polish design of international criminal law') (Warszawa 1927)

71 Rappaport, *Zagadnienie unifikacji*, 20.

72 The Codification Commission was established by the Act of 3 June 1919, DZ.PPP 1919.44.315.

73 Regulation of the President of the Republic of Poland of 11 July 1932 – Criminal Code, Dz. U.1932.60.571. Julian Makarewicz, *Kodeks Karny z Komentarzem* (Lwów 1935). Adam Lityński, *Wydział karny Komisji Kodyfikacyjnej II Rzeczypospolitej: dzieje prac nad częścią ogólną kodeksu karnego* (Katowice: Uniwersytet Śląski 1991).

74 See Alicja Grześkowiak (ed.), *Prawo karne w poglądach Juliusza Makarewicza* (Lublin: KUL 2005).

75 Józef Koredczuk, 'Znaczenie kodeksu karnego z 1932 r. dla rozwoju nauki i prawa karnego w Polsce w XX wieku'. *Zeszyty Prawnicze UKSW* 11.2 (2011), 45–60.

76 Tadeusz Bojarski, 'Tradycja i postęp w nowelizacji prawa karnego – od Makarewicza do stanu obecnego'. *Teka Komisji Prawniczej OL PAN* 2008, 8.

within the limits of their intent, thus rejecting the principles of collective and accessory liability. In its approach to sentencing, the Code introduced the principle of humanitarianism, emphasizing protective measures and reserving the death penalty for exceptional cases. The latter was permitted only for a few specific offences, such as assaults against the independence of the state, attacks on the life or health of the President of the Republic, or the participation of Polish citizens in a war against the Republic of Poland.[77] The above principles of the 1932 Code, and especially the principles of legality, subjectivization, and individualization of responsibility, as well as the issue of proportionality of the sentence to the degree of the perpetrator's culpability and the social harm in the act constituted the focal points of the debate on the legal bases of prosecution and punishment of war criminals in the Second World War era.

The Makarewicz Code also incorporated the principle of universal jurisdiction (Article 9) and grounds for prosecuting crimes committed by foreigners, outside Polish territory, among the provisions of the general part of the Code addressing its applicability. In line with Article 3(1) of the CC, Polish criminal legislation applied to any person 'having committed a criminal offence in the territory of the Polish state or Polish vessel or aircraft'. Article 5 expanded the applicability of the Code onto non-nationals having committed abroad a crime against the welfare or interests of the Polish state, of a Polish citizen or legal person, on condition of 'recognition (...) of the act as a criminal offence by the statute applicable at the place of commission' of the act (Article 6). Article 8 provided for the prosecution on the basis of Polish law, irrespective of the provisions applicable at the place of commission of the crime and nationality of the perpetrator, of crimes against the internal or external security of the Polish state, against the authorities or officials of the Polish state, or false testimony given before a Polish authority.

Article 9 elaborated the principle of universal jurisdiction, granting Polish courts competence over international crimes, regardless of where they were committed or the perpetrator's nationality.[78] The article listed certain crimes

---

77 Dariusz Makiłła, *Historia prawa w Polsce* (Warszawa: Wydawnictwo Naukowe PWN 2013), 496.

78 Art. 9 of the Criminal Code of 1932: Notwithstanding the provisions applicable at the place of commission of the offence, Polish criminal law shall apply to a Polish national or non-extradited foreigner having committed the following offences abroad:
(a) robbery at sea;
(b) counterfeiting of money, public securities or banknotes;
(c) slave trade;
(d) trafficking in women or children;

subject to universal jurisdiction, in accordance with international agreements ratified by Poland, though this was not an exhaustive list. According to commentators Stefan Glaser and Antoni Mogilnicki, Article 9 embodied the 'community of human interests' and the 'international solidarity of all civilized states in combating crimes of universal concern (*delicta iuris gentium*)'.[79] The principle of solidarity was also reflected in the specific provisions of the Code. Chapter XVIII (Articles 99–121) defined 'criminal offences against the security of the state and international relations', including the propaganda of aggressive war (Article 113). In the opinion of the commentators, the prohibition of the incitement of aggressive war manifested the international community's aspirations to peaceful dispute resolution (Kellogg–Briand Pact, Geneva Protocol), with resulting criminalization of not only aggressive war itself but also of acts of its propagation. This served as an example of applying the principle of protecting public order 'within the sphere of international order, which equally requires effective protection by criminal law'.[80] As Glaser and Mogilnicki emphasized in their commentary: 'Perhaps the clearest expression of the spirit of universal criminal-law protection in recent codifications can be seen in the new criminal codes and drafts of Central and Southeastern Europe, including the Polish Criminal Code of 1932'.[81]

3.2 *In the Universities of the Second Polish Republic*

International law was taught in all law faculties, as well as in specialized programmes for future civil servants and diplomats at the universities of the Second Polish Republic. From 1920, the law of nations became a mandatory course in all law faculties.[82]

After the re-establishment of the University of Warsaw in 1915, the Department of State Law and International Law was chaired by Zygmunt Cybichowski (1879–1946),[83] having previously taught the law of nations at the uni-

---

(e) use of a means capable of causing general danger with the intention of causing such danger;
(f) trafficking in narcotic drugs;
(g) trafficking in pornography;
(h) other offence provided for by international treaties concluded by the Polish State.

79 Stefan Glaser and Aleksander Mogilnicki, *Kodeks karny. Komentarz. Prawo o wykroczeniach. Przepisy wprowadzające, tezy orzeczeń Sądu Najwyższego* (Kraków 1934) 49.

80 *Ibidem*, 381.

81 *Ibidem*.

82 Ludwik Ehrlich, *Zarys historii nauki prawa narodów w Polsce*, in Ludwik Ehrlich and Stefan Langrod, *Zarys historii nauki prawa narodów*, 17.

83 Zygmunt Cybichowski, *Prawo międzynarodowe publiczne i prywatne*, (Warszawa 1928).

versity in Fribourg (and habilitated there on the basis of a dissertation titled *Das antike Völkerrecht. Zugleich ein Beitrag zur Konstruktion des modernen Völkerrechts*) and at the University of Lviv. Cybichowski was a member (and chair from 1925 to 1930) of the International Law Association, an honorary doctorate recipient from Columbia University, and the author of numerous works on the law of nations, including the textbook *Prawo narodów. System prawa międzynarodowego* ('Law of Nations: System of International Law').[84] Cybichowski's successor in the post, from 1933 onward, was Professor Wacław Makowski (1880–1942), simultaneously in charge of the University of Warsaw's department of criminal law. After the creation of two separate departments for state law and international law in 1935, the Department of International Law went on to be headed by Professor Cezary Berezowski (1898–1970), author of the habilitation dissertation titled *Powstanie Państwa Polskiego w świetle prawa narodów* ('Formation of the Polish State in the light of the law of nations') (1934), member of The Hague Academy of International Law and of the International Law Association.[85]

The founder of the Department of International Law at the University of Poznań in 1919 and its first chair was Professor Bohdan Winiarski (1884–1969). Winiarski, who served as legal advisor to the Polish delegation at the Paris Peace Conference, was a renowned expert in international fluvial law, a proponent of codifying international river law, and the author of numerous expert studies in the field, including the *Principes generaux du droit fluvial international* of 1934. He also addressed this topic in his 1933 lecture at The Hague Academy of International Law. Winiarski represented Poland in numerous committees of the League of Nations (e.g. in the Organisation for Communication and Transit). In Poland, he chaired the Liquidation Committee for German property in the western territories of the Second Polish Republic,[86] and was lecturer of the Polish School of Political Sciences (Polska Szkoła Nauk Politycznych) at Jagiellonian University. He wrote publications on the legal system of the League of Nations, international security, and international fluvial law, and compiled a selection of sources for international law.[87] During the Second World War, Winiarski joined the Government-in-

84 Hubert Izdebski, 'Zygmunt Klemens Cybichowski 1879–1946', in Grażyna Bałtruszajtys (ed.) *Profesorowie Wydziału Prawa i Administracji Uniwersytetu Warszawskiego 1808–2008* Warszawa: LexisNexis 2008, 99–100.

85 *Ibidem*; Karol Karski, 'Cezary Berezowski 1898–1970', in Bałtruszajtys (ed.), *Profesorowie Wydziału*, 158–161.

86 Sandorski, *Nauka prawa*, 16.

87 Bohdan Winiarski, *Rzeki polskie ze stanowiska prawa międzynarodowego* ('Polish rivers from the position of international law') (Poznań 1922); Bohdan Winiarski, *Principes gen-*

Exile, serving, among other roles, as President of the Bank of Poland, President of the Commission for the Investigation of Causes of September Defeat, and Polish delegate to the London International Assembly, in which he participated in the creation of the draft charter of an International Criminal Court.[88] After the war, he returned to the country and was sponsored by the government in Warsaw to become the Polish judge of the International Court of Justice in The Hague; in that capacity, he served until 1967, and in 1961–1964, as the President of the ICJ.

At Jagiellonian University, international law was taught at the Department of Political Law and Law of Nations, and at the Law Faculty of the School of Political Sciences which was established at the Jagiellonian University in 1920.[89] Connecting both institutions is Professor Michał Rostworowski (1864–1940), an eminent constitutionalist and expert in international law. Rostworowski continued the academic legacy of Franciszek Ksawery Kasparek, as a member of the Institute of International Law in The Hague and, from 1931, as a judge of the Permanent Court of International Justice as well as lecturer at the universities of Fribourg and Lviv, and in 1903–1931, as head of the Department of Political Law and Law of Nations of Jagiellonian University.[90] Between 1911 and 1914, he founded the Polish School of Political Sciences in Cracow, modelled on the Free School of Political Sciences in Paris, of which, he himself was a graduate (similarly to Bohdan Winiarski, his collaborator at the Polish School of Political Sciences).

The John Casimir University in Lviv (JCU) also made international law part of its base curriculum of legal studies, through the Department of the Law of Nations and State Science, as well as specialized preparatory studies for future diplomats.[91] Before his moving on to teach at the University of Warsaw, the

---

eraux du droit fluvial international (Paris 1934). Bohdan Winiarski, *Wybór źródeł do nauki prawa międzynarodowego* ('A selection of sources for the science of international law') (1938); Winiarski, *Bezpieczeństwo*; Bohdan Winiarski, *"Obrona konieczna" w prawie narodów* ('Self-defence" in the law of nations') (Lwów 1936).

88 London International Assembly, 'Reports of the Punishment of War Crimes', TNA LCO 2/2973, 324–339.

89 Concerning the establishment and curriculum of the School of Political Sciences in Cracow, see: Bartosz Włodarski, *Szkoła Nauk Politycznych Uniwersytetu Jagiellońskiego 1920–1949* (Kraków: Księgarnia Akademicka 2015).

90 Andrzej Zięba (ed.), *Jubileuszowa Księga Nauk Politycznych* (Kraków: Wydawnictwo Uniwersytetu Jagiellońskiego 2015), 113–123.

91 Adam Redzik, 'Ludwika Ehrlicha koncepcja kształcenia dyplomatów i jej realizacja – Studium Dyplomatyczne Uniwersytetu Jana Kazimierza we Lwowie', in Grzebyk and Tarnogórski, *Siła prawa*, 255–281, here: 261; Ehrlich, *Zarys historii*, 18; Adam Redzik, 'Lwowska szkoła dyplomatyczna. Zarys historii Studium Dyplomatycznego przy Wyd-

law of nations was taught at the JCU by Zygmunt Cybichowski, and was succeeded by Piotr Stebelski, a professor of criminal law, from 1919 to 1923.[92] In 1923–1939, the Department of the Law of Nations and State Science was chaired by Professor Ludwik Ehrlich (1889–1968), an expert in political law and law of nations, lecturer of political science at the University of California, Berkeley, in 1917–1920, and member of The Hague Academy of International Law in 1927–1928, and *ad hoc* judge of the Permanent Court of International Justice.[93] Thanks to Ehrlich's efforts, a specialized programme in international studies, the law of nations, and political science was established in 1930 at the JCU Faculty of Law – a three-year Diplomatic Studies programme offering a modern curriculum for future diplomats.[94] According to Ehrlich, the programme's concept was presented during meetings of the Permanent International Studies Conference of the League of Nations, where 'the Polish delegation was playing a leading role' in the works on the methods of teaching of international law and international relations.[95] Linked to the person of Ludwik Ehrlich and the Department of the Law of Nations and State Science were also Raphael Lemkin and Hersch Lauterpacht – two eminent legal scholars, whose definitions of international crimes made a key influence on the development of international criminal law and on the concepts adopted by the Great Powers for the Nuremberg Trials. Lemkin, who coined the term 'genocide' and later co-authored the Convention on the Prevention and Punishment of the Crime of Genocide was a student of Ehrlich's and a graduate of the law faculty of John Casimir University. Hersch Lauterpacht also began his legal studies in Lviv in 1915, and continued his legal career in Vienna, London and Cambridge, where in 1937, he took the chair of international law.[96] He coined the term 'crimes against humanity' and, in 1945, served as an advisor to the British government during the Nuremberg Trials. According to the recent research, two decades prior, in 1923, Lauterpacht had been Ludwik

---

ziale Prawa Uniwersytetu Jana Kazimierza we Lwowie (1930–1939)'. *Polski Przegląd Dyplomatyczny* 33 (2006), 121–149; Tomasz Pugacewicz, 'Nauka o stosunkach międzynarodowych w koncepcji Ludwika Ehrlicha'. *Stosunki Międzynarodowe – International Relations* 54 (2018), 231–266.

92 Adam Redzik, 'Wydział prawa', in Adam Redzik (ed.), *"Academia militans". Uniwersytet Jana Kazimierza we Lwowie* (Kraków: Wydawnictwo Wysoki Zamek 2015) 507–508.

93 Adam Redzik, 'Ludwik Ehrlich (1899–1968) – zarys życiorysu', in Grzebyk and Tarnogórski (eds.), *Siła prawa*, 339–362.

94 Ehrlich, *Zarys historii*, 18.

95 *Ibidem*, 19; Redzik, 'Ludwika Ehrlicha', 260.

96 Sands, *East West Street*, 146.

Ehrlich's competitor for the position of head of the Department of the Law of Nations at JCU.[97]

The Faculty of Law and Legal Sciences at Stephen Báthory University in Vilnius (SBU) did not have a dedicated department for the law of nations. Lectures and research in this field in 1919–1939 fell under the Department of State Law and State Science, headed by Professor Wacław Komarnicki (1889–1954).[98] Wacław Komarnicki was a professor of constitutional law, member of Parliament (elected in 1928 and 1930), graduate of the Institute of Higher International Studies in Paris, and member of numerous international academic organizations such as the Society of Comparative Legislation (*Société de Législation Comparée*) in Paris and the Permanent International Studies Conference.[99] Besides state law, his research ventured into topics of the law of nations, including the formation of states and the definition of an aggressor under international law.[100] At the 8th International Studies Conference in London in 1935, Komarnicki presented a memorandum on defining an aggressor in international law. His Hague lecture at the Academy of International Law in 1949, entitled *La définition de l'agresseur dans le droit international moderne* dealt with the same topic. Komarnicki's collaborators at the Department of State Law and State Science included authors of innovative works in the law of nations, such as Michał Król, whose doctoral and habilitation dissertations were dedicated to the problem of international responsibility of states.[101] Stanisław Kodź devoted his dissertation to the principle of nationality in international law,[102] Wiktor Sukiennicki defended a doctoral thesis on state sovereignty in modern international law in 1927 at the Sorbonne (*La souveraine te des etats en droit international moderne*)[103] and in 1929, submitted a habili-

---

97 Adam Redzik, *Stanisław Starzyński (1853–1935), a rozwój polskiej nauki prawa konstytucyjnego* (Warszawa-Kraków 2012) 55.

98 Michał Balcerzak, *O wileńskiej szkole prawa międzynarodowego (1919–1939)*, in Anna Przyborowska-Klimczak Anna et al. (eds.) *Polska nauka prawa międzynarodowego : dziedzictwo przeszłości i wyzwania współczesności* (Lubllin: Towarzystwo Naukowe KUL 2022) 177–208.

99 *Ibidem*, 4–5.

100 Wacław Komarnicki, *Geneza terytorium państwa Polski ze stanowiska prawa narodów* (Wilno 1925); Komarnicki, *Powstawanie państw*; *idem*, 'Określenie napastnika we współczesnym prawie narodów', in *Księga pamiątkowa ku czci Leona Pińskiego*, vol. I (Lwów 1936), 431–442. cf. Wacław Komarnicki, *La définition de l'agresseur dans le droit international moderne* (Paris: Académie de Droit International / Libraire du Recueil Sirey 1949).

101 Król, *Odpowiedzialność państwa*.

102 Stanisław Kodź, *Zasada narodowości w prawie międzynarodowym* ('Principle of nationality in international law'). *Rocznik Prawniczy Wileński* 6 (1933).

103 Wiktor Sukiennicki, *La souveraineté des états en droit international moderne* (Paris: A. Pedone 1927).

tation dissertation at Stephen Báthory University, titled *Podstawy obowiązywania prawa narodów. Studium prawnicze* ('Bases for the binding force of the law of nations. A legal study').[104] Following the establishment of the Academic-Research Institute for Eastern European Studies at the University of Vilnius in 1930, he led the Institute's Legal Section and was one of the founders of the Polish school of Soviet studies.[105]

In the days of the Second World War, three employees of the Department of State Law and State Science of the Faculty of Law and Social Sciences of SBU joined the Polish Government-in-Exile. Komarnicki served as the Minister of Justice from 1942 to 1944, co-authored the Polish policy on punishing war criminals,[106] and helped draft extradition convention, prepared by Allied ministers of justice. He was also the creator and lecturer of the Polish Law Faculty at the University of Oxford. Stanisław Kodź, in 1943–1945, led the Legislative Section of the Ministry of Justice. Following his release from a Soviet POW camp in the Krasnoyarsk region under the Sikorski-Mayski agreement, Wiktor Sukiennicki became a member of the émigré authorities, cooperated with the Ministry of Foreign Affairs in the USSR and in Tehran, and afterwards in London, where he wrote multiple analyses of the legal situation in occupied Poland, and war crimes committed under Soviet occupation, especially the Katyń Massacre. On behalf of the Government in exile, Sukiennicki supervised works of an inquiry commission investigating the Katyń massacre, collecting related documents in the early 1940s. The commission's work resulted in the report: *Facts and Documents Concerning Polish POWs captured in the USSR during the 1939 Campaign.*[107]

Among the academics of Stephen Báthory University who had been involved in the development of Polish scholarship in international law, joining

---

104 *Idem*, *Podstawy obowiązywania prawa narodów. Studium prawnicze* (Wilno-Warszawa: Księgarnia F. Hoesicka 1929).

105 Henryka Ilgiewicz, *Instytut Naukowo-Badawczy Europy Wschodniej oraz Szkoła Nauk Politycznych w Wilnie (1930–1939)* (Warszawa: Scholar 2019).

106 Komarnicki's legacy as Polish justice minister in exile is discussed exhaustively by Adam Jankiewicz. See Jankiewicz, *W poszukiwaniu idei.*

107 Wiktor Sukiennicki' biogram, IPMS, Kol. 214/2. Olga Kotulska, 'Z dziejów kłamstwa katyńskiego: o zasługach Wiktora Sukiennickiego (1901–1983) w odkrywaniu prawdy i paru niepewnych wynikach badań. Z badań archiwalnych w Instytucie Hoovera Uniwersytetu Stanforda w Kalifornii)'. *Bezpieczeństwo. Teoria i praktyka* 1 (2018), 185–206, here: 197–204; Committee Of Enquiry Into The Question Of The Polish Prisoners Of War Fom The 1939 Campaign Missing In The U.S.S.R., *Facts and Documents Concerning Polish POWs captured in the USSR during the 1939 Campaign* (London 1946), available at: https://www.szukajwarchiwach.gov.pl/jednostka?p_p_id=Jednostka&p_p_lifecycle=0&p_p_state=maximized&p_p_mode=view&_Jednostka_id_jednostki=29314064

the Polish authorities in exile and dealing with topics of responsibility for war crimes, particular attention must go to the person of Stefan Glaser (1895–1984).[108] Glaser was a professor of criminal law and criminal procedure at the SBU, expert in the criminal law of European states, as well as Polish criminal law of the Partitioning Era and after the reacquisition of independence. Although without formal ties to the teaching of the law of nations and the department headed by Komarnicki, in addition to his comparative and classical criminal law studies, Glaser's academic interests also encompassed international criminal law. Stefan Glaser was a member of numerous international organizations of legal professionals, including the AIDP, and an advocate for the unification of international criminal law.[109] His publications analysed problems such as political crimes, extradition, universal jurisdiction, temporal applicability of legal acts, or the effectiveness of international agreements penalizing selected international crimes.[110] Glaser joined General Władysław Sikorski's cabinet in autumn 1939 as head of the justice department, a post he held until becoming Polish envoy to the Belgian and Luxembourg governments in autumn 1941. He worked closely with Komarnicki and co-authored the conceptual framework of the Decree of the President of the Republic of Poland of 30 March 1943 on Criminal Responsibility for War Crimes 1943.[111] Stefan Glaser was Poland's first delegate to the UNWCC, presided over its Committee III and represented the Polish government in conferences held in preparation for the trials of Nazi criminals. In 1942, Glasser founded in London the Association of University Professors and Lecturers of the Allied Countries in Great Britain, and continued the activities of the Polish University Abroad in the United Kingdom and became the first dean of the Polish Law Faculty at the University of Oxford, which was established in 1944.

---

108 Wierczyńska and Wierczyński, 'Stefan Glaser', 306–334.

109 *Ibidem*, 316.

110 Stefan Glaser, *Zasada extradycji w odniesieniu do przestępców politycznych, Wykład inauguracyjny ogłoszony na USB 12 stycznia 1924* ('The principle of extradition with regard to political criminals. Inaugural lecture given at the SBU on 12 January 1924') (Wilno: Gebethner i Wolff 1924); *idem*, 'Geneza przestępstwa politycznego' ('The origin of a political crime'). *Palestra* 8 (1926), 345–356; *idem*, Międzynarodowe zwalczanie handlu żywym towarem a polski kodeks karny' ('The international fight against human trafficking in the context of the Polish Criminal Code'). *Gazeta Sądowa Warszawska* 9 (1938); *idem*, 'Nowe kierunki w międzynarodowem prawie karnem a ekstradycja' ('New directions in international criminal law in the context of extradition'). *Palestra* 5 (1929), 215–266; *Palestra* 6–7 (1929), 260–273; *Palestra* 12 (1929), 542–552; *Palestra* 6–7 (1930), 293–303; *Palestra* 8–9 (1930),; *idem, L'uniformisation du droit d'extradition: rapport présenté au Congrès International de Droit Comparé à La Haye – 1932* (Warszawa 1932).

111 Concerning this topic, see Chapter 5 of this book.

In addition to Bohdan Winiarski, Wacław Komarnicki, Stanisław Kodź, Wiktor Sukiennicki, and Stefan Glaser, several other Polish lawyers and jurists contributed significantly to shaping the Polish Government-in-Exile's policy on the prosecution and punishment of war criminals. Eugeniusz Jarra (1881–1973) was a professor of theory and philosophy of law; dean of the law faculty of the University of Warsaw in 1924–1928, and doctor *honoris causa* of the University of Lille. In emigration, he worked closely with Komarnicki, headed the Legislative Section and Legislative Works Commission of the Ministry of Justice (1942–1944), and was among the co-founders and lecturers of the Polish Law Faculty of the University of Oxford. Włodzimierz Moderow (1880–1970) was Poland's delegate to the League of Nations, and from 1938, headed the latter's subcommittee of lawyers. In 1921–1938, he served as counsel at the delegation of the General Counsel to the Republic of Poland in the Free City of Gdańsk (Danzig). From the autumn of 1939, Moderow worked for the justice department and later served as legal counsel to the Ministry of Treasury.[112] Ludwik Krajewski (1897–1969) was a scholar of state law, including the legal order of the German Reich, an editor of the Polish Journal of Laws, and since September 1937, Director of the Legal Bureau of the Praesidium of the Council of Ministers.[113] In London, Krajewski was employed by the Ministry of Justice, and from the autumn of 1942, he chaired the Legislative Works Commission's Section VI for Legislative Technique. Tadeusz Cyprian (1898–1979) was a pre-war Supreme Court prosecutor and head of the legal department of the Ministry of Foreign Affairs. In the Government-in-Exile, he served as a member of the Legislative Works Commission and Poland's representative to the UNWCC. He replaced Glaser as the government's delegate to that Commission in September 1944. He went on to take the same function in the autumn of 1945 on the appointment of the government in Warsaw, representing the Polish government as part of the delegation to the Nuremberg Trials.

Out of the many diplomats involved in Polish wartime efforts for the international recognition of demands for the punishment of war criminals, one should primarily note Władysław Kulski (1903–1989) and Michał Potulicki

112 Jankiewicz, *W poszukiwaniu idei*, 11.

113 Ludwik Krajewski, *Podstawy ustroju III Rzeszy* ('Foundations of the political system of the Third Reich') (Warszawa 1935); Ludwik Krajewski, 'Doktryna prawna hitleryzmu' ('The legal doctrines of Hitlerism'). *Biuletyn Urzędniczy* 1–2 (1939), 9–12; *Biuletyn Urzędniczy* 3–4 (1939), 4–7;, *idem, Z zagadnień techniki prawniczej: moc wsteczna prawa: początek obowiązywania prawa* ('From topics of legal technique: the retroactive force of law: the beginning of the applicability of law') (Warszawa: F. Hoesick 1934).

(1897–1984).[114] Władysław Kulski – a lawyer and diplomat – served as the legal advisor and secretary of the Polish Permanent Delegation to the League of Nations and head of the legal department of the Ministry of Foreign Affairs.115 While in exile, he helped initiate cooperation among the governments of occupied states concerning the prosecution of war criminals and co-authored the *Declaration of St James's Palace* of 13 January 1942. He is also the author of Polish white books and official editions of documents dealing with the situation in occupied Poland.[116] Kulski's close collaborator in London was Michał Potulicki, doctor of laws of the University of Geneva, who, from 1922, was employee of the Ministry of Foreign Affairs; Polish delegate to the International Labour Organization at the League of Nations; and from 1939, legal advisor of the Polish Embassy in London. He co-authored the Declaration of St James's Palace and served as secretary of the Inter-Allied Commission on War Crimes, established in 1942 at the initiative of the occupied states. He authored numerous expert reports on post-war reconstruction and German political movements in exile during the Second World War.

The next generation of lawyers included Manfred Lachs (1914–1993), who graduated from the Consular Academy in Vienna and obtained his doctorate in law from Jagiellonian University before the war. In 1938–1939, Lachs was in the course of supplementary studies in the United Kingdom, where the war found him. Working for the Government-in-Exile, he compiled numerous expert studies on the situation of Jews in occupied Poland and was a member

---

114 The most important of the aforementioned authors' works are: Stefan Glaser, *Przestępstwa polityczne a prawo ekstradycji* ('Political crimes and extradition law') (Lwów 1925); *idem*, *L'uniformisation*; Stefan Glaser and Przemysław Dąbkowski (eds.), *Okupacja niemiecka na Litwie w latach 1915–1918: stosunki prawne* ('German occupation in Lithuania in 1915–1918: legal affairs') (Lwów 1929); Wacław Komarnicki, 'La définition de l'agresseur', in *La sécurité collective. Mémoires présentés par le Comité Central des Institutions polonaises des Sciences Politiques à la VIII-e Conférence des Hautes Études Internationales à Londres, 3–8 juin 1935* (Lwów 1935) 73–84; Komarnicki, *Powstawanie państw*.

115 Kulski authored numerous publications in the law of nations, including: Władysław Kulski, *Przed I powszechną konferencją rozbrojeniową* ('Before the 1st World Disarmament Conference') (Warszawa 1931); Władysław Kulski, *Liga Narodów* ('The League of Nations') (Warszawa 1938); Władysław Kulski, *Odpowiedzialność międzynarodowa państw. Wykład Wygłoszony dnia 28 maja 1938 r. na kursie naukowym dla urzędników służby zagranicznej* ('International state responsibility. Lecture given on 28 May 1938 in an academic course for foreign-service officials'), (Warszawa: MSZ 1938); Władysław Kulski and Michał Potulicki (comps.), *Współczesna Europa polityczna: zbiór umów międzynarodowych 1919–1939* ('Contemporary political Europe: selection of international agreements 1919–1939'), (Warszawa: Księgarnia Powszechna 1939).

116 Concerning the Declaration of St. James's Palace, see Chapter 3 of this book.

of international legal organizations, as well as an employee of Polish War Crimes Office, on whose behalf, he represented Poland in the UNWCC.

A key strength of the Polish legal experts working to prosecute the occupying powers' crimes was their deep understanding of the political and legal systems of the German Reich and the Soviet Union. They also analysed the criminal law of the Third Reich and the USSR, particularly the legal reforms that departed from the principles of *nullum crimen sine lege and nulla poena sine lege*, allowing courts to convict by analogy. This was reflected in their analyses of the political and legal structures imposed on occupied Poland and the systematic violence against the civilian population. Publications in this area include Stefan Glaser's *Zarys polskiego procesu karnego wraz z ustrojem sądów powszechnych: przedstawienie porównawcze na tle ustawodawstwa austriackiego, niemieckiego i rosyjskiego* ('An outline of Polish criminal procedure and system of common courts: comparative presentation against the background of Austrian, German and Russian legislation'), Wacław Komarnicki's *Nowy ustrój państwowy Związku Sowietów* ('The new state system of the Soviet Union'), Ludwik Krajewski's *Podstawy ustroju Trzeciej Rzeszy* ('Foundations of the Third Reich's political system'), Marian Jedlicki's Przeobrażenia ustrojowe i polityczne dzisiejszych Niemiec ('The constitutional and political transformations of today's German'), and Wiktor Sukiennicki's *Ustrój radziecki a konstytucja stalinowska* ('The Soviet political system and the Stalinist Constitution').[117] Polish legal scholars' comparative studies on the legal and political systems of Nazi Germany and the USSR, as well as the critical reception of the development process of criminal law and international law in the inter-war period had a significant impact on the assumptions of the war-crimes policy of the Polish Government-in-Exile in 1939–1945.

117 Stefan Glaser, *Zarys polskiego procesu karnego wraz z ustrojem sądów powszechnych: przedstawienie porównawcze na tle ustawodawstwa austriackiego, niemieckiego i rosyjskiego* (Warszawa: Gazeta Administracji i Policji Państwowej 1929); Wacław Komarnicki, *Nowy ustrój państwowy Związku Sowietów* (Wilno 1938); Ludwik Krajewski, *Podstawy ustroju Trzeciej Rzeszy* (Warszawa: Księgarnia F. Hoesicka 1935); Marian Z. Jedlicki, *Przeobrażenia ustrojowe i polityczne dzisiejszych Niemiec* (Kraków: Koło Uczniów i Absolwentów Szkoły Nauk Politycznych 1939); Wiktor Sukiennicki, *Ustrój radziecki a konstytucja stalinowska* (Poznań: Rolnicza Drukarnia i Księgarnia Nakładowa 1937). See Marcin Maciejewski and Maciej Marszał (eds.), *Pod znakiem swastyki: polscy prawnicy wobec Trzeciej Rzeszy 1933–1939* (Kraków: Ośrodek Myśli Politycznej 2005); see also Marcin Maciejewski, 'Polscy uczeni prawnicy międzywojenni o ustroju i prawie Trzeciej Rzeszy' *Miscellanea Historico-Iuridica* 2 (XV) 2016, 85–126.

CHAPTER 2

The Early Making of the Government-in-Exile's War-Crimes Policy

On 1 September 1939, Poland was invaded by the Third Reich. Despite resisting the German blitzkrieg tactics for over a month, Polish forces waited in vain for an Allied offensive on the Western Front. Great Britain and France, both parties to mutual aid agreements with Poland, declared war on Germany on 3 September 1939, but never provided military support to the Polish troops fighting in the country. After the Soviet attack from the East on 17 September, the Polish Army had no chance of defeating both aggressors. The September Campaign ended with the lost final battle of Kock and cost the lives of over 66,000 Polish soldiers; the number of wounded on the Polish side was around 133,000; about 400,000 Polish soldiers were captured by Germany and around 250,000 by the USSR.[1] The end of hostilities marked the beginning of a brutal occupation of Poland by the Third Reich and the Soviet Union, following the German–Soviet Border and Friendship Treaty of 28 September 1939.[2]

The Treaty implemented the assumptions of the Molotov–Ribbentrop Pact of 23 August 1939 and its secret protocol with regard to cooperation between the two powers and division of the territories of the Second Polish Republic and neighbouring states into German and Soviet occupation zones. In line with the provisions of the Pact, the border between the two zones fell to the west of the San-Bug-Narew-Pisa river line, roughly along the proposed demarcation line between the Second Polish Republic and the USSR in 1919, the so-called 'Curzon line'. As a consequence of the German–Soviet collaboration and the capitulation of the last Polish regular forces in the field, on 6 October 1939, the territory of Poland came under German and Soviet occupation. In the weeks that followed, the two powers announced annexation of the majority

1 On the outbreak of the war in Poland and on the September Campaign, see: Roger Moorhouse, *First to Fight: The Polish War 1939* (Vintage Publishing 2019).

2 German-Soviet Boundary and Friendship Treaty of 28 September 1939; Raymond J. Sontag, James S. Beddie (eds.), *Nazi-Soviet Relations 1939–1941: Documents from the Archives of the German Foreign Office* (Washington: U.S. Department of State 1948), 105. Concerning the cooperation between the USSR and the Third Reich immediately before World War II and during its initial years, as well as the significance of Molotov-Ribbentrop Pact, see: Roger Moorhouse, *The Devils' Alliance: Hitler's Pact with Stalin, 1939–1941* (New York: Basic Books 2014).

of pre-war territory of the Polish state. By decree of Adolf Hitler of 8 October 1939, central and western provinces of Poland and the Free City of Gdańsk (Danzig) were annexed to the German Reich. Two new administrative areas established for them: The Reichsgau Wartheland (Warthegau) and Gdańsk, together with West Prussia and part of Mazovia, were incorporated to the East Prussia province of Germany; the territories of Upper Silesia (Górny Śląsk), along with the western part of Lesser Poland (Małopolska), were incorporated into the Silesia province of Germany, as a subdivision called Regierungsbezirk Kattowitz ('Katowice Government District'). These territories covered ca. 94,000 square kilometres (nearly a quarter of Poland's pre-war territory) with 10 million inhabitants. For the territories of central Poland not incorporated to the Reich, the so-called General Government (German: *Generalgouvernement*) with a population of about 12 million people was created on 12 October 1939. Soviet occupation extended to more than 51% of the territory of the pre-war Polish state – the so-called Eastern Borderlands (Kresy Wschodnie), with Vilnius and Lviv, were annexed to the USSR.[3] The occupations led to immense material losses, organized persecution of civilians, deportations to concentration camps, as well as Soviet and Nazi forced-labour camps, societal disintegration, and, most tragically, the deaths of millions of civilians.[4]

Appeals to the international public to stop the policy of terror in occupied Poland and to punish the perpetrators of crimes committed during and after the German and Soviet invasion were directed by Polish authorities from the beginning of the war and became one of the core political postulates of the Polish government-in exile.

Immediately after the Soviet aggression, Polish military and political authorities decided to evacuate to France through the territory of Romania, with which Poland had a defensive alliance. Nevertheless, Romanian authorities denied the Poles the *droit de passage*. President Ignacy Mościcki, Prime Minister Felicjan Sławoj-Składkowski, and Commander-in-Chief Edward Rydz Śmigły – the three principal leaders of the *Sanacja* camp, which continued the policies of the late Marshal Józef Piłsudski – were interned and prevented from carrying out their duties.[5] President Mościcki resorted to Articles 13 and 24 of

3 Jan Garliński, *Poland in The Second World War*, (Houndmills Basingstoke: Macmillan 1985) 26–37, David G. Williamson, *Poland Betrayed. The Nazi-Soviet Invasions 1939* (Pen&Sword Military 2009), 151–170; Martin Winstone, *The Dark Heart of Hitler's Europe: Nazi Rule in Poland under the General Government* (London: L.B. Tauris & Co. Ltd 2015).

4 Garliński, *Poland*, 27–46.

5 T. Wyrwa, 'Odbudowa władz Rzeczypospolitej w Paryżu i Angers wrzesień 1939-czerwiec 1940', in: Zygmunt Błażyński (ed), *Władze RP na obczyźnie podczas II wojny światowej, 1939–1945* (Londyn: Polskie Towarzystwo Naukowe na Obczyźnie 1994), 9–11. About the

the Constitution of 23 April 1935, empowering him to nominate a successor in a time of war. Having appointed Władysław Raczkiewicz, President of the World Union of Poles Abroad and former Speaker of the Senate, Mościcki resigned during the night of 29 and 30 September 1939. On the same day, Władysław Sikorski, who escaped Poland to France in September 1939, where he formed and commanded the Polish Army in France, was appointed Prime Minister. Sikorski was a divisional general of the Polish Army and former prime minister of 1922–1923, Minister of War, and co-founder in 1936 of the Front Morges alliance of centrist parties opposed to the Sanacja camp. The plan was for his cabinet to be a 'Government of National Unity',[6] bringing together the representatives of all political parties (Labour Faction – *Stronnictwo Pracy*; Polish Socialist Party – *Polska Partia Socjalistyczna*; People's Party – *Stronnictwo Ludowe*; and National Party – *Stronnictwo Narodowe*), in both Front Morges and *Sanacja* camps.

The formation of the cabinet was the outcome of the so-called Paris Agreement[7] concluded between Sikorski and Raczkiewicz on 30 August 1939, which allowed the formation of a cabinet-in-exile on the basis of the Polish Constitution of 1935. The agreement preserved the continuity of constitutional governance while imposing some limitations on the Article 13 prerogative powers, stipulated by Article 13, which had enabled the presidency to exercise centralized authoritarian rule in the years immediately preceding the war. By contrast, the President was now to wield executive power not independently but in a close consultation with the cabinet headed by the Prime Minister. This solution was intended to uphold the legality of the authorities in exile and the continuity of the Government acting within the constitutional mandate.[8]

Sikorski's first cabinet was sworn in on 30 September 1939 in Paris, where its first headquarters were located before the move south-west to Angers (department of Maine-et-Loire) in November 1939. At the beginning of October 1939, it was recognized as the legal continuation of the previous government of the

---

establishment of the Polish Government-in-Exile see: Evan McGilvary, *A Military Government in Exile: The Polish Government in Exile 1939–1945. A Study of Discontent* (Helion Studies in Military History 2013).

6 Hułas, *Goście*, 74–76.

7 Michał Kwiatkowski, *Rząd i Rada Narodowa R.P. W świetle faktów i dokumentów od września 1939 do lutego 1942 r.* ('The Cabinet and National Council of the Republic of Poland. In the light of documents from September 1939 to February 1942') (London 1942), 17; Dariusz Górecki, *Polskie naczelne władze państwowe w latach 1939–1990* (Warszawa: Wydawnictwo Sejmowe 2002), 25–26; Władysław Rostocki, *Stosowanie konstytucji kwietniowej w okresie drugiej wojny światowej. 1939–1945* (Lublin: Wydawnictwo KUL 1988).

8 Piotr S. Wandycz, *The United States and Poland* (Harvard University Press 1980), 236.

Republic of Poland by the United States (2 October) and the United Kingdom (4 October). Following the French defeat in June 1940, the Polish authorities evacuated to London, where the official headquarters would remain until 5 July 1945, which is when the Government-in-Exile lost its diplomatic recognition by the Western Powers.

The recovery of independent statehood, restoration of democratic rule, preservation of Poland's pre-war borders, and victory against the Third Reich and Soviet Union were the principal goals of the Government-in-Exile. The path to the achievement of those goals led through the participation of Polish Armed Forces in the West (France and United Kingdom), formed in France from September 1939 onward, as well as Polish Armed Forces in the East and Polish air-force officers in the RAF in the Allied war effort.[9] In General Sikorski's own words, Poland participated in the war 'as an ally of France and Great Britain on terms of full parity of statehood and unwavering freedom, as well as close co-operation and consensus, both in the conduct of the war and determination of its goals, as well as the making of peace'.[10]

From the very first weeks of the war, the Polish Government-in-Exile pressed the issue of violations of the laws and customs of war committed by the German Reich and by the USSR during their invasions of Poland. On 23 November 1939, General Sikorski delivered a radio speech on German atrocities and promised the punishment of perpetrators of the 'German cruelty exceeding, in the slaughter of innocents, the darkest memories'.[11] He noted that the information arriving from the homeland on crimes committed during the Polish Defensive War of 1939 ('September Campaign') had shaken the international opinion and would be published in the form of official government reports. Justice for crimes perpetrated by the Third Reich during the hostilities and subsequent occupation of Poland was the promise of one of the first resolutions passed by the Government-in-Exile on 15 December 1939:

> In view of the monstrous mass executions of Polish patriots which have taken place and which continue to occur by order of German author-

---

9 Minutes of the meeting of the Council of Ministers, 6 October 1939, PPRM vol. I, 4–5. Concerning the Polish contribution to the Allied war effort, see Michael A. Peszke, *The Polish Underground Army, the Western Allies, and the Failure of Strategic Unity in World War II* (Jefferson: McFarland 2009), *The Armed Forces of Poland in the West, 1939–1946 Strategic Concepts, Planning, Limited Success But No Victory!* (West Midlands: Helion 2015).

10 *Ibidem.* See also: Wandycz, *The United States*, 236 ff.

11 Radio speech of Prime Minister Sikorski, 23 November 1939, cited after Stefania Stanisławska (comp),*Sprawa polska w czasie drugiej wojny światowej na arenie międzynarodowej. Zbiór dokumentów* (Warszawa: PWN 1965), 123–124.

> ities, especially in the western provinces illegally incorporated into the Reich, the Polish government is obliged to make the following declaration:
>
> After the victorious war, the Polish state will apply to the Germans, and, especially to their leaders responsible for the deaths of so many innocent victims, reprisals which they justly merit.[12]

From autumn 1939 onward, declarations calling for punishment of war criminals accelerated the development of Władysław Sikorski's cabinet's war-crimes policy and the expansion of the relevant government structures.[13] The main directions of that policy included:

- organizing international informational campaigns about the atrocities committed in Poland and Europe;
- documenting the crimes;
- winning Allied support for calls for punishment for perpetrators of violations of international law;
- determining the legal bases for future criminal trials; legislative works.

1 The German and Soviet Crimes

Appeals for Allied intervention, condemnation of the aggression against Poland, and for humanitarian aid, were made in the form of diplomatic notes and protest campaigns and through international media. Especially during the first months of the war, care was taken to highlight the problem of the crimes being committed under German and Soviet occupation and to document the repressions and violations of international law engaged in by both occupying powers. The beginnings of the Polish government's protest and information campaign as well as efforts to secure Allied declarations condemning the terror in occupied Poland were relayed in the first issue of the Information Bulletin of the Cabinet Committee for Home Affairs (*Biuletyn Informacyjny Komi-*

---

12 Resolution of the Council of Ministers of the Republic of Poland of 15 December 1939, cited after *Lubbock Avalanche-Journal*, 24 December 1939, Lubbock, Texas, 3, https://www.newspapers.com/article/lubbock-avalanche-journal/10390419/ (accessed 5 May 2024); *Altoona Mirror*, 23 December 1939, Altoona, Pennsylvania, https://newspaperarchive.com/altoona-mirror-dec-23-1939-p-1/ (accessed 5 May 2024) *Cf.* Kwiatkowski, *Rząd i Rada Narodowa*, 24

13 Concerning the formation of the Polish Government-in-Exile and the shaping of the government structure, *cf.*: Błażyński, *Władze RP*.

tetu Ministrów dla Spraw Kraju) of 15 January 1940, having political and military conspirators as its target audience:

> The Polish Government strongly protested to friendly and neutral governments against the methods of bloody terror and unlawful torture and imprisonment of numerous Polish citizens, irrespective of age, sex and creed, used by the Germans and the Bolsheviks alike. (…) The inhumanity of the conquerors' conduct will be documented in the form of a book of atrocities committed by the occupying powers in Polish territories.[14]

The information campaign about the activities of the Red Army, security services, and administrative bodies in the eastern provinces of the Second Polish Republic, such as expulsions and forced deportations of civilians, forced labour in gulags, persecution of Polish culture and identity, and imprisonment of thousands of military officers, public servants, and intelligentsia failed to yield the expected results and to cause the condemnation by the Western Allies of the Soviet policy. Although the Soviet Union joined the Allied coalition only after the German aggression of June 1941, not even in 1939–1941, the Polish authorities were unable to secure British support in condemning the Soviet crimes.[15] The clauses guaranteeing protection in the event of third-party aggression in the mutual-assistance treaty between the United Kingdom and Poland, of 25 August 1939,[16] were – according to Article 1(a) of the annexed Secret Protocol – applicable only to invasion by the German Reich. This clause allowed the United Kingdom to avoid being at war simultaneously with Germany and the Soviet Union and to maintain correct relations with the USSR.[17] This also significantly influenced the direction of the war-crimes policy pursued by Polish authorities between 1939 and 1945. Its success, notwithstanding key actions in the sphere of home affairs, such as documenting the crimes and drafting the necessary legislation, hinged on the ability to win the support of

14 'Akcja przeciwko bezprawiom i krwawemu terrorowi okupanta'. *Biuletyn Informacyjny* 1 (1940).

15 The problem was discussed *inter alia* in the meeting of the Council of Ministers on 23 November 1939, cf. Minutes of the meeting of Council of Ministers on 23 November 1939, PPRM, vol.1, 100–101. Agreement of Mutual Assistance between the United Kingdom and Poland.-London, August 25, 1939, https://avalon.law.yale.edu/wwii/blbk19.asp (accessed 1 August 2024).

16 Agreement of Mutual Assistance between the United Kingdom and Poland.-London, 25 August 1939, available at https://avalon.law.yale.edu/wwii/blbk19.asp.

17 Concerning this topic see: Ernest L. Woodward, *British Foreign Policy in the Second World War vol. 1* (London: H.M. Stationery Office 1962), 6–8.

the Great Powers. Thus, in the international arena, Polish authorities focused on crimes committed by the military and administrative apparatus of the German Reich.

A major turning point in Polish efforts to expose wartime atrocities came in the spring of 1943 with the discovery of mass graves containing thousands of Polish officers near Katyń. The mass graves of former prisoners in the Soviet prisoner-of-war camps in Starobielsk, Kozielsk, and Ostaszkow were discovered by German troops and excavated by an international medical commission, appointed at the request of the Reich's cabinet. The investigation proved that the killings occurred in 1940 and established the responsibility of the Soviet forces. In response to the discoveries, Polish authorities submitted a petition to the International Committee of the Red Cross to investigate the circumstances of the victims' deaths.[18] This led to Soviet accusations of Sikorski's collaboration with the government of the Third Reich. Under pressure from the British and American governments, General Sikorski withdrew the petition from the ICRC 'proclaiming the whole affair as a slander of German propaganda'.[19] The Polish government's accusations against the USSR of the mass murder of Polish officers – along with multiple attempts to reach the international public opinion with the 'truth of Katyń' – resulted in the cutting of diplomatic ties by the USSR and in the weakening of the Governments international position of the Government-in-Exile.[20] Fearing Soviet displeasure, the Western Allies did not weigh in their support for the Polish stance against the USSR and Polish efforts to identify the perpetrators of the Katyń Massacre and hold them accountable.[21] In the early years of the war, the very idea of putting war criminals on trial was met with considerable scepticism, even in a 'narrowed formula' limited to German perpetrators.

An additional difficulty faced by the Polish diplomatic strategy, particularly during the initial years of war, was the British and American authorities' reserve towards information about the scale and ruthlessness of crimes committed in occupied Poland. The news and reports on Nazi atrocities were frequently disbelieved, and Polish accounts of 'German barbarity' perceived as attempts to justify or conceal true motivations such as a 'thirst for revenge' and bloody retaliation. The objections to the credibility of the reports on atrocities and to the validity of Polish demands to punish the perpetrators were in many cases caused – and certainly fuelled – by Nazi propaganda.

18 Mackiewicz, *The Katyn.*
19 *Ibidem,* 102.
20 Mackiewicz, *The Crime,* 101–110.
21 A. Bliss Lane, Foreword, in: *The Katyn Woods,* v.

The narratives on goals and means of the Nazi military efforts established by the Reich's Ministry of Public Enlightenment and Propaganda were intended to justify the 'blood and soil' ideology, to cover up crimes committed by the Third Reich on its own citizens and in occupied Europe, but also to legitimize the German conduct of warfare. A good example shows the successes of Nazi propaganda claiming Polish provocations in the border zone (so-called Gleiwitz incident), persecution of the German minority in Poland, and murders of German nationals in September 1939. In that narration, the German policy of terror in the occupied territories came down to the prevention of and retaliation for the persecution of the Germans in Poland.[22] Under the banner of the 'Bloody Sunday' (*Bromberger Blutsonntag*) – in reference to the events playing out on 3 and 4 September 1939 in Bydgoszcz – the Third Reich's Ministry of Propaganda informed the global opinion about persecutions of the German population in Poland, allegedly justifying the German aggression and subsequent use of methods of terror and extermination.[23] The first edition of the Auswärtiges Amt's publication, titled *Die polnischen Graeueltaten an den Volksdeutschen in Polen* ('The Polish atrocities against the ethnic Germans in Poland')[24] of November 1939, gave the estimated number of casualties among the German civilian population at 5,437, and the revised edition of February 1940 specified ten times as many, viz. 58,000 victims of the incident in Bydgoszcz (whereas, the total number of German and Polish civilian casualties, combined, is estimated at approximately four hundred).[25] The publication circulated in 185,000 copies, out of which 40,000 in German, 20,000 in French, and 17,000 in English.[26] The year 1940 saw the publication of *Der Tod in Polen. Die volksdeutsche Passion*[27] ('Death in Poland. The passion of the ethnic Germans') and a third white book of the German government, as well as a selection of Polish official documents: *Polnische*

---

22 Henryk Batowski, *Walka dyplomacji hitlerowskiej przeciw Polsce 1939–1945* (Kraków-Wrocław: 1984).

23 *Cf.* Andrzej Krzysztof Kunert, Zygmunt Walkowski, *Kronika kampanii wrześniowej 1939* (Warszawa: Edipress 2005) 35. Concerning this topic, see: Tomasz Chinciński and Paweł Machcewicz (eds.), *Bydgoszcz 3–4 września 1939: studia i dokumenty* (Warszawa: IPN 2008).

24 *Die polnischen Greueltaten an den Volksdeutschen in Polen* (Berlin: Auswärtiges Amt 1939).

25 Markus Krzoska, '*Der Bromberger Blutsonntag* Kontroverse und Forschungsergebnisse', in *Vierteljahreshefte für Zeitgeschichte*, H.2 (60), April 2012, 237–248, here: 248.

26 Janusz Sobczak, *Polska w propagandzie III Rzeszy w latach 1939–1945*, (Poznań: Instytut Zachodni 1998), 302.

27 Edwin E. Dwinger, *Der Tod in Polen. Die volksdeutsche Passion* (Jena: E. Diederichs 1940).

Dokumente zur Vorgeschichte des Krieges ('Polish documents from the prehistory of the war').[28]

The Polish Government-in-Exile was aware about the effectiveness of the German propaganda. In a letter to the Ministry of Information and Documentation – dated 2 April 1940 – the Consul General of the Republic of Poland in Uzhhorod, Mieczysław Grabiński, emphasized the necessity of:

> gathering authentic material about Bydgoszcz, determining the factual course of events. (…) The German propaganda, disseminated in the press, through special brochures (…) and conversations with foreigners endeavour[ed] to prove that the attitude of military and civil authorities towards Poles during the military campaign [wa]s merely retaliation for Polish 'crimes' committed previously and currently being committed against Germans. (…) Every German brochure, every conversation with a foreigner beg[an] with a tendentious and false presentation of the events in Bydgoszcz, (…) supposed to justify a further German response.[29]

Responding to the Nazi disinformation, conducting a diplomatic informational campaign on the German atrocities and identifying the suspects demanded reliable evidence. Already in autumn 1939, specialized units were formed within the government structure, responsible for gathering and processing information from occupied Poland. From November 1939 to April 1940, detailed instructions were written concerning the documentation of the occupying powers' crimes and of the activities of those suspected of collaboration. Securing competent evidence was part of preparation for post-war criminal trials but also an instrument for the achievement of current goals of informing the public opinion worldwide of the crimes committed by the German Reich and winning Allied support for calls for the punishment of the offenders.

28 Auswärtiges Amt, *Polnische Dokumente zur Vorgeschichte des Krieges* (Berlin 1940).

29 Letter from Mieczysław Grabiński, 2 April 1940, Polish Consul General in Uzhorod, IPMS, Kol. 183.

2 First Protest Notes and Attempts to Win Allied Support for the Polish Proposals

From autumn 1939 onward, the diplomatic informational campaign led by Polish authorities had the goal of demonstrating the scale and organized, systemic nature of the crimes being committed in Polish territories, as well as violations of international law and of treaties binding on the German Reich.[30] The collection of evidence and witness accounts documenting the large-scale crimes against civilians was accompanied by expert discussions on new types of crimes targeted against civilians or specific groups or perpetrated on political, racial, or discriminatory grounds. In the later years, those evolved into debates on new definitions of international crimes – crimes against humanity and genocide. The goal was to secure from the Great Powers, declarations condemning the German methods of warfare and occupation, and to develop a joint position of the Allied states on the German policy of terror. Of particular importance, in this regard, was the cooperation of smaller states, initiated in 1940 by the governments of Poland and Czechoslovakia. Those shared many political aims for the post-war period, including a common interest in security and balance of power, but also the punishment of criminals responsible for war-time sufferings and damages, along with the compensation of victims.

In the early months of the war, the Government-in-Exile did not focus on the specifics of organizing a post-war justice system for war crimes (the respective works commenced in autumn 1941). Nevertheless, in the declarations and protest notes, the crimes committed in occupied Poland were classified according to terms and categories of the applicable domestic and international legal provisions. Emphasis was placed on the grounding of the Nazi German systemic violence in the applicable provisions of German law. The lack of norms imposing sanctions for violations of The Hague Convention and the failure of the implementation of the penal provisions of the Treaty of Versailles following the First World War had a significant impact on the formulation of Polish demands for bringing war criminals to justice. The priority treatment of the issue of documentation was also prompted by the French and Belgian experience of the months following the end of the First World War, when it became impossible to secure the evidence of the crimes committed by the German armed forces during the war or to identify the culprits.

In addition to the extensive and systematic documentation of Nazi crimes, a core principle of Polish war-crimes policy was campaigning for the creation of an effective justice system based on domestic legal provisions, as well as

30 *The German Invasion of Poland*, 11.

norms and principles of international law. This was also meant to recognize the binding force of international custom and unwritten sources of the law of nations, such as international morality and humanitarian principles. The protest notes and reports on the situation in occupied Poland highlighted the violations of specific treaties or norms of substantive international law, especially those arising from The Hague Convention (IV) of 1907; Geneva Convention, relative to the Treatment of Prisoners of War of 1929; and Kellogg-Briand Pact of 1927, underlining the responsibility of Germany for aggressive war and for 'starting the war'.[31]

On the day General Sikorski's cabinet was formed – 30 September 1939 – the Polish government issued a protest note to the governments of the Allied and neutral states against the provisions of the German–Soviet Boundary and Friendship Treaty made on 28 September 1939.

On 27 October 1939, the Polish government issued a protest note to the League of Nations against the provisions of the German–Soviet Treaty, challenging the legality of the territorial changes transacted by the USSR and the Third Reich.[32] This intervention emphasized both of the aggressors' violation of bilateral non-aggression treaties with Poland and of the provisions of The Hague Convention (IV) concerning the situation of civilians and prisoners-of-war and the duties of the administration of occupied territories.[33] Attention was especially drawn to the usurpation of sovereignty in the territory of the Polish state by the German Reich and the Soviet Union. Polish authorities did not recognize the annexation of Polish territory by either state, and emphasized the obligations under The Hague Convention incumbent on the occupying forces during their temporary administration. The illegality of the actions taken in violation of *inter alia* Articles 42, 46, and 55 of The Hague Convention (IV) was underscored.[34] Article 43 of the Convention bound the occupying power to 'ensure (…) public order and safety, while respecting, unless absolutely prevented, the laws in force in the country' (emphasis added). Article 46 of the Convention guaranteed the protection of human life and private prop-

---

31 See Letter from the MFA to the Ambassador in London, containing the text of the protest lodged by the Council of Ministers against the violation of the Hague Convention by Germany, 5 March 1940, IPMS, Ambasada Londyn, A.1249/WB/17, reprinted in Magdalena Hułas (ed.), *Polskie Dokumenty Dyplomatyczne 1940* (Warszawa: PISM 2010), 117.

32 See Marek K. Kamiński, 'Zarys Polityki Zagranicznej Rządu RP na Obczyźnie 1939–1945', in Błażyński (ed.), *Władze RP*, 643.

33 *Ibidem*, 645.

34 Art. 42 of the Hague Convention (IV) Respecting the Laws and Customs of War on Land, of 18 October 1907, available at https://www.refworld.org/legal/agreements/hague/1907/en/31788 (accessed 6 May 2024).

erty under occupation, and Article 55 imposed limits on the administration of the public property of the occupied state, exercised by the occupying power, which 'must safeguard the capital of these properties, and administer them in accordance with the rules of usufruct'.[35] The annexation of the territories of the Polish state not only entailed profound changes in the administrative system but also interfered with the legal order and individual rights of the civilian population. Through the implementation of Nazi laws, Polish society was subjected to systemic violence, including confiscation of public and private property, forced labour, limitation of civil rights, Germanization, demolition of Polish courts, introduction of German political and legal institutions, and of a special system of criminal courts, as well as legislative acts serving as instruments of a policy of racial discrimination, terror, and extermination.[36] The texts of decrees and special laws enacted by the occupation powers were sourced and subsequently reprinted by Polish authorities in official publications, thus bringing the legal aspects of Nazi violence to the foreground of the information campaign.[37] On 30 November 1939, the Journal of Laws (*Dziennik Ustaw*) published a special Decree of the President of the Republic of Poland on the Nullity of the Occupation Authorities' Legal Acts. Article 1 of the Decree provided:

> any legal acts and ordinances of the authorities occupying the territory of the Polish State, if exceeding the limits of temporary administration of occupied territory, shall, in line with the provisions of Hague Convention (IV) on the Laws and Customs of War on Land, of 1907, be null and void.[38]

The purpose of the Decree was to create a regulatory framework to address the Nazi policy of Germanisation in the occupied territories by means of legal tools, which also included organized expropriations or theft of public and

35 *Ibidem*, Article 55.

36 The German Occupation of Poland. Extract of a note addressed to the Governments of the Allied and Neutral Powers on May 3 (London: The Cornwall Press Limited: post-1941), 1, 4. A systematic overview of Nazi legislation in occupied Poland with commentaries in English provide volumes edited by Karol M. Pospieszalski (ed) , *Nazi occupation "law" in Poland, Selected Documents*, Part I: The incorporated territories (vol.V); Part II: The Government General (vol VI)(Poznań: Instytut Zachodni 2019).

37 See, e.g. Polish Ministry of Information, The persecution of Jews in German-occupied Poland (London: 1940), 9–12; Polish Information Centre, *German Organisation of Courts in General Government of Poland* (New York: 1941); J. Bloch, *Justice outlawed. Administration of law in German-occupied territories* (London: 1944).

38 Decree of the President of the Republic of 30 November 1939 on the Nullity of the Legal Acts of the Occupying Powers, Dz.U.1939.102.1006.

private property, including works of art.[39] The decree also problematized the acts of discrimination and systemic violence against the population of the occupied territories, deeming null and void 'also the legal acts and ordinances of the authorities occupying the territory of the Polish State (…) where arising from the implementation of an exterminatory ethnic policy'.[40]

At the same time, the pressure and expectations from the Polish resistance to gain Allied support for the campaign on accountability was growing. The government body responsible for constant contact with the homeland was the Cabinet Committee for Home Affairs (*Komitet Ministrów do Spraw Kraju*, CHA).[41] Besides diplomatic posts and military–intelligence channels, it is through the CHA that the Polish authorities in Paris and Angers received the first reports from occupied Poland.

By a resolution of 21 November 1939, the Cabinet Committee for Home Affairs recommended that the government take co-ordinated actions to 'make the global opinion aware of the atrocities of the occupying powers and of the material situation of the population in the occupied territories, and on that path create the foundations for a broad protest action and benefit action for the war victims in Poland'.[42] Notice was made that the lack of vigorous efforts in that area could lead to 'painful moral dissonance between the government and the public opinion in the Homeland'.[43] Another CAHs resolution of December 1939 voiced the:

> definite demand of the political circles in Warsaw, transmitted through persons arriving from the country, [that] there should be made every effort to induce the Allied Governments to make official declarations, protesting against the systematic attempts at extermination and against the not less systemic cruelties perpetrated by the Germans on the Polish population, especially on its educated class, throughout the incorporated and occupied territories.[44]

39 *Ibidem.*

40 Art. 2(2), *Decree of the President of the Republic of 30 November 1939.*

41 Duraczyński, *Kontrowersje*, 80.

42 Conclusions regarding the organization of aid for the population in the homeland passed in the meeting of the MCHA, 21 November 1939, IPMS, PRM-K., 102/7, 26–27, PPRM vol.1, 101–102.

43 *Ibidem.*

44 Petition from the Homeland for CHA meeting, December 1939, *Protokoły Posiedzeń KSK*, 113–114, Anna Pachowicz, *Komitet Ministrów dla Spraw Kraju 1939–1945* (Warszawa: DiG 2010), 229.

It was emphasized that the declarations should promise 'that those guilty of cruelties and of committing acts of extermination [would] be held personally responsible by the allied Governments after the victorious conclusion of the war'.[45] The resolution recommended entrusting its own implementation to the Deputy Prime Minister and Minister of Information and Documentation Stanisław Stroński, Foreign Minister August Zaleski and Prime Minister General Sikorski. The latter was requested to approach the French Prime Minister, Edouard Daladier, concerning a joint Allied declaration 'and to address a letter on the same subject to Mr. Chamberlain'.

The issues of persecutions directed against the civilian population, Poland's wartime losses, and necessary response from the Allies were raised by General Sikorski and the Minister of Foreign Affairs, August Zaleski, during their visit to London on 14–20 November 1939. In talks with the United Kingdom's Secretary of State for Foreign Affairs, Viscount Halifax (as he then was), the Polish Prime Minister insisted that 'in connection with the repressions applied to Poland (...) the Germans be made clearly to understand that their crimes [would] be avenged in the future'.[46] While Sikorski obtained assurances that the suggestion would be considered, the British side took no concrete actions.[47] General Sikorski's visit to the United Kingdom marked the beginning of Polish diplomacy's initiative to secure a joint declaration from the prime ministers of France, the United Kingdom, and Poland condemning German crimes and vowing to punish the culprits. Negotiations with the French were led by Feliks Frankowski, chargé d'affaires of Polish Embassy to France, and Minister of Foreign Affairs August Zaleski. Talks with British authorities were handled by Polish Ambassador Edward Raczyński.[48]

In parallel to talks with the continental Allies in spring 1940, Polish diplomats vied for support from the United States government. On 9 March 1940 in Paris, Sikorski met Undersecretary of State Sumner Welles and warned him that the continuation of hostilities would lead to massive civilian casualties and extensive material damage.[49] He appealed for an intervention and for the creation of a neutral commission investigating Nazi crimes in Europe:

---

45 IPMS A.12.44/WB/18, leaves 1 and 2. Document according to a copy registered as IPMS, PRM-K 79.8, leaf 58.

46 PPRM vol.1, p. 96.

47 *Ibidem.*

48 IPMS A.12.44/WB/18.

49 Following the meeting, a memorial titled 'The Polish Territory occupied by Germans' was delivered to the US officials. IPMS, PRM 10/2, leaves 49–162. Available at http://pism.co.uk/PRM/PRM10.pdf (accessed 20 March 2025).

> If the Germans and Russians [are allowed to] continue with impunity, the oppression of Poles will through executions, resettlements, famine, destitution and diseases entail the destruction of many-million people. Only one thing could stay the Germans' hand, if it were to be communicated to the German public opinion, namely the establishment of a neutral investigative commission. The initiative could only be brought by such a power as the United States, which are not afraid of a direct threat from Germany. The commission would be authorized to investigate the travesties of which not only Poles but also other nations oppressed by the Germans are complaining. It could, if deeming it appropriate, impose moral sanctions.[50]

The extermination of the civilian population by the occupying powers and the casualties suffered daily by Polish society were also emphasized by Ambassador Edward Raczyński in his communication with the British Foreign Office concerning the text of the resolution of three prime ministers. He stressed that a promise of future punishment for war criminals and complete reparation for all suffering and losses inflicted could induce the perpetrators to restrain, and first and foremost give the necessary moral support to the population of occupied Poland.[51] The Polish side proposed to include the following passage (the last sentence is a literal translation from the French by the Foreign Office):

> H.M. Government in the United Kingdom, the French Government and the Polish Government desire to make a formal and public protest to the conscience of the world against the action of the German Government, whom they must hold responsible for these crimes, which cannot remain unpunished. They declare, moreover, that all the wrongs thus inflicted by Germany in violation of international law must be integrally repaired.

The intention of putting on trial before Polish courts such war criminals as were to be found in Polish jurisdiction, after the war, was also met with understanding by the Britons. Nevertheless, they categorically objected to the inclusion of anticipated criminal sanctions for war crimes in the text of the declaration.[52]

---

50 Note from the meeting of General Sikorski with the US Undersecretary of State, B. Sumner Welles, 9 March 1940 in Paris, IPMS, PRM 10/2, p. 9.

51 Proposed Allied Declaration regarding German atrocities, 26 February 1940, TNA/FO 371.24422/; 8 March 1940 TNA/FO 371.24422/C 3040. C 3612; C 3040.

52 TNA/FO 371.24422/ C 3040.

The stated reasons for the British scepticism were the lack of penal provisions for violations of The Hague Convention (IV) of 1907, failure to implement in 1919 the extradition procedure stipulated by Article 228 of the Treaty of Versailles, and the 'farce' of the criminal trials held before the German Supreme Court in Leipzig.[53] From Zaleski's account of the negotiations on the break of February and March 1940: 'The English do not want to agree to a passage providing for a sanction, explaining (…) that the Germans could make a mockery of any threats of sanction by pointing out the disuse of the sanctions provided by the Treaty of Versailles'.[54] Protracted negotiations over a revision after revision of the text, arising from the British disagreement with the inclusion of a passage addressing the individual responsibility of perpetrators (or, at a later stage, statement that the German crimes could not be 'left unpunished'), provoked impatience and 'delay in publishing the declaration [was] leading to dismay in the homeland and benefiting the German propaganda'.[55]

In the end, the declaration published on 20 April 1940 by Prime Ministers Neville Chamberlain, Paul Reynaud, and Władysław Sikorski omitted the penal sanctions that the Polish side had strongly advocated. Neither did it refer to integral reparation. The passage concerning aggression against Poland on 1 September 1939 was replaced with the statement that 'the German government (…) [had] opened the war by brutal attacks upon the civilian population in defiance of the accepted principles of international law'.[56] The states signatories condemned the 'most ruthless barbarity' of the German atrocities, the persecution of the Jewish population, and 'deliberate policy aiming at the complete destruction of the Polish nation', affirming German responsibility for the crimes and reaffirmed their determination to right the wrongs inflicted on the Polish people.

Despite the failure to succeed on all Polish proposals, the announcement of the declaration was welcomed as a success of Polish diplomacy and as an impulse for the continuation of its informational campaign on German crimes

---

53 Willis, *Prologue*, 8–12; Hankel, *Die Leipziger*, 97–104.
Zaleski reported on the negotiations in a meeting of the Council of Ministers on 1 March 1940. Minutes of the meeting of Council of Ministers, 1 March 1940, IPMS PRM-K. 102/18, reprinted in PPRM vol. 1, 216.

54 *Ibidem*. Minutes of the meeting of the Council of Ministers of 16 March 1940, PPRM vol. 1, 227.

55 *Ibidem*.

56 Reprinted text of the Declaration of the Governments of Poland, United Kingdom and France of 20 April 1940 condemning the methods of the German occupying power, in Stanisławska (comp.), *Sprawa polska*, doc. no. 95, 162. See Kochavi, *Prelude*, 7–9.

in Poland. The exact day of the three prime ministers' declaration – 20 April – also saw the release of the Polish white book titled *L'Invasion Allemande en Pologne*[57] in General Sikorski's press conference. It was published in English as *The German Invasion of Poland* in May 1940, in a volume of 10,000 copies. On 10 May 1940, Polish authorities issued another protest note against the induction of Polish citizens into German armed forces and the introduction of a statute on military service in the territories annexed to the German Reich. In connection with the declaration of the three prime ministers and publication of the white books, Polish authorities were looking forward to continued development of international cooperation on documenting the German crimes and holding the offenders accountable.

In April 1940, Polish authorities decided to press for the creation of an 'international commission to investigate the German atrocities in Poland'.[58] Apart from the investigation of Nazi crimes, the intention was for the commission to work out the legal aspects of a jurisdiction for war criminals and for the 'setting of a ground for the establishment of a criminal-justice system to decide, after the war, upon the individual acts of German violations'.[59] Polish authorities initiated consultations on the creation of such a Commission with the governments of Belgium, the Netherlands, and the United States. However, after the capitulation of France in May 1940, the initiative was suspended, as Polish authorities had to evacuate to the United Kingdom.

During its first weeks in the United Kingdom, the Polish government attempted to strengthen the Polish–British alliance based on principles of the 'closest understanding and co-operation'[60] and garner support for Polish demands concerning both the Soviet Union – thus 'restoring the Polish-Soviet border from before September 1939' – and the German Reich, i.e. defeating the aggressor and achieving an 'ultimate victory of law and justice'.[61] Despite Poland's adamant position on the country's eastern borders, British authorities continued in their efforts to stabilize Polish–Soviet relations. On 5 August 1940, a Polish–British Military Agreement was signed to the effect that the formation of Polish Armed Forces in the United Kingdom could begin.[62]

---

57 Édouard Herriot (preface), *L'invasion allemande en Pologne: documents, témoignages authentifiés et photographies / recueillis par le Centre d'Information et de Documentation du Gouvernement Polonais* (Paris: Flammarion 1940).

58 Note by Michał Potulicki, 9 October 1941, Hoover Institution Archives, 800/42/0/-/104 (collection of Polish Ministry of Foreign Affairs), leaf 693.

59 *Ibidem.*

60 Cabinet Political Committee, Main theses of Polish foreign policy, 24 August 1940; Minutes of the meeting of the Council of Ministers, 26 August 1940, PPRM vol. 2, 102–103.

61 *Ibidem.*

62 Peszke, *The Polish Underground,* 188–195.

The Polish government submitted to the British Minister of Labour, Ernest Bevin, a memorandum on the German question, which also contained some Polish demands and proposals for the post-war period. The document stressed the existence of a 'solidarity of interests between the United Kingdom and the continental nations, endangered by Germany's constant aspiration to hegemony', as well as the necessity of maintaining the European balance of power through the creation of regional political alliances of lesser powers. In particular, a close cooperation among the central and eastern European states was to guarantee their independence from Berlin and Moscow and to avert future threats to their security. The prevention of future German aggression, a post-war 'occupation of all German territory', and territorial changes benefiting the nations neighbouring the German Reich, which would weaken Germany strategically and economically, were of fundamental importance to the European balance of power. The memorandum also provided for the payment of reparations 'to states injured by Germany's war of aggression'.[63] The creation of a strong political alliance of smaller central-eastern European states based on Polish–Czechoslovak cooperation that could significantly reshape the geopolitical system in post-war Europe was an important goal of Sikorski's policy and won the approval of the US and British governments. Sikorski initiated talks on the future Polish–Czechoslovak confederation with Edward Beneš and other Czechoslovak leaders in exile, in autumn 1939. Negotiations of the principles of a bilateral agreement intensified after the establishment and international recognition of the Czechoslovak interim government in exile, in July 1940,[64] and their initial phase was concluded by a declaration of 11 November 1940. In this statement, the Polish and Czechoslovak governments declared their will to 'join after the war ends as independent and sovereign states, into a closer political and economic association, which would become the basis for a new order in Central Europe and guarantee of its stability'.[65] The declaration emphasized that the two governments were resolved 'to cooperate closely for the defense of their common interest' and united by the common goal of defeating the German aggressor. The declaration condemned

63 Memorandum from Polish Government to the British Minister of Labour, Ernest Bevin, IPMS, PRM 20/31 For more on this subject, see Magdalena Hułas, *Rząd gen. Władysława Sikorskiego czerwiec 1940-lipiec 1943*, in Błażyński (ed.), *Władze*, 172–173.

64 Concerning this topic, see Piotr S. Wandycz, *Czechoslovak-Polish Confederation and the Great Powers 1940–1943* (Indiana University Publications: 1956).

65 Joint Declaration of the Polish and Czechoslovak Governments favoring Closer Political and Economic Association of 11 November 1940, reprinted in Wandycz, *Czechoslovak-Polish*, 128–129.

> in the gravest terms the cynical farce which the leaders of Nazi Germany [were] endeavouring to stage by proclaiming themselves the builders of a New European Order'. (…) The violence and cruelty to which [the] two nations [were] being subjected, the expulsion of the native populations from immense areas of [their] secular homelands, the banishing of hundreds of thousands of men and women to the interior of Germany as forced labor, mass executions and deportations to concentration camps, the plundering of public and private property, the extermination of the intellectual class and of all manifestations of cultural life, the spoliation of the treasure of science and art and the persecution of all religious beliefs – are unparalleled in human history. They offer a striking example of the spirit and methods of the Germanic new order.[66]

The announcement of the November Declaration opened the path to cooperation between the Polish and Czechoslovak governments on the project of a central-European union, which would also include a common defence and military policy. Despite the enthusiasm and commitment on both sides, after over two years of negotiations, the plan to establish the Polish–Czechoslovak Confederation failed due to the differences in their policies towards the USSR and due to the Soviets' critical view of a Polish–Czechoslovak rapprochement. With strengthening Czechoslovak security against future German aggression in mind, a good relationship with USSR was Beneš's priority and also the reason for his gradual withdrawal from the talks on the bilateral agreement. Czechoslovakia definitively abandoned negotiations in May 1943, after USSR cut diplomatic ties with Poland.

It is worth noting that the Polish–Czechoslovak Confederation plans, developed in 1940–1943, have been discussed in numerous publications, exploring not only the political framework of the 'predecessor of the European Union' but also the political obstacles that stood in its way. Little attention was paid to the success of the Polish–Czechoslovak cooperation of that time and to the question of accountability for Nazi crimes, which both governments identified as a shared priority in the Declaration of 11 November. As a result of this close cooperation between Beneš's and Sikorski's administrations from 1940 to 1942, the issue of Nazi persecution in occupied countries received increased attention on the international stage.

66 *Ibidem.* Also: Leften Stavros Stavrianos, *Balkan Federation: A History of the Movement toward Balkan Unity in Modern Times*, Part 2, 1944 (Northampton, Mass., Dept. of History of Smith College) https://archive.org/stream/BalkanFederation.AHistoryOfTheMovementTowardBalkanUnityInModern_535/balkan7_djvu.txt (accessed 7 May 2024).

On 12 November 1940, *The Times* published a portion of the Polish–Czechoslovak declaration containing a list of Nazi crimes, condemning the organized atrocities visited on the civilian population.[67] In summer 1941, both governments took it upon themselves to persuade the Allied governments to issue a joint declaration condemning the German system of terror and promising to put war criminals on trial. The draft declaration compiled by Polish and Czechoslovak lawyers was submitted to the Foreign Office in October 1941.[68] In the face of the British authorities' withdrawal from plans of a joint resolution, the Polish-Czechoslovak draft become the basis for a declaration of representatives of nine Governments-in-Exile that those guilty of violations of international law would be held criminally responsible. Leaders of the European Governments-in-Exile published the declaration on 13 January 1942 at St James's Palace in London, hence its name – the Declaration of St James's Palace.[69]

3 Official Reports and the Information Campaign

From the onset of the war, the axis of Polish effort to win international support for the demand to punish war criminals was the government's information policy directed to the political partners, certain intellectual circles, and the general public. At the beginning of December 1939, there already existed several government departments responsible for the registration and processing of the information on German crimes forwarded from Poland and found in German press and official publications. The Ministry of Foreign Affairs had a special section preparing white books for publication. The Cabinet Committee for Home Affairs received reports from occupied Poland on a continual basis.[70] Under the Praesidum of the Council of Ministers, Witold Czerwiński and Fr. Franciszek Forecki established a documentation commission and archive.[71] In the Centre for Information and Documentation, the works were

67 UNWCC, *History of the United Nations War Crimes Commission and the Development of the Laws of War* (London: His Majesty's Stationery Office, 1948) (hereinafter 'History of the UNWCC'), 87.

68 TNA/ FO 371 36540/ C11442, C11518/267/18.

69 For more on this subject, see Chapter 3 of this book.

70 *Protokoły Posiedzeń KSK*, 393–394; Janusz Gmitruk and Jerzy Mazurek, *Działalność władz okupacyjnych na terytorium Rzeczypospolitej w okresie od 1 IX 1939–1931 XI 1939. Raport z archiwum politycznego prof. Stanisława Kota* (Warszawa: Muzeum Historii Polskiego Ruchu Ludowego 1999).

71 Minutes of the CHA's 6th meeting, 12 December 1939, in *Protokoły posiedzeń KSK*, 90.

co-ordinated by the Information Section (Press–Political Section) headed by Marian Seyda and Documentation Section headed by Stanisław Stroński,[72] as well as the Polish Research Centre in London, dating from November 1939.[73]

Polish diplomatic missions as well as cultural and academic institutions and diaspora circles served as important conduits for news from Poland, which proved invaluable to the informational and protest campaigns. In autumn 1939, a protest campaign was initiated against the arrests of the professors of Jagiellonian University carried out on 6 November (so-called *Sonderaktion Krakau*) as part of the German *Intelligenzaktion* – persecution of Polish intellectuals and socials leaders. The arrests and imprisonment in concentration camps of 184 lecturers of the Jagiellonian University and the Minor Academy in Kraków gained support of members of the academic circles of the United Kingdom, France, United States, and Canada.[74] Towards the end of December, a protest campaign against the closing down of Stephen Báthory University in Vilnius on 15 December 1939 followed.[75] In 1940–1941, in the wake of another wave of persecution of Polish intellectuals, Stefan Glaser implored the academic circles of the Allied powers to condemn the Nazi crimes and persecutions of cultural and academic life. His efforts intensified in summer 1941 and afterwards, following the murder of professors of the University of Lviv and their family members at Wzgórza Wuleckie in July 1941 by the Einsatzkommando under the command of Karl Eberhard Schöngarth just after the German invasion of the Soviet Union. During the first half of 1941, British academic circles, the International Law Association, and the Grotius Society, as well as the International Alliance of Women for Suffrage and Equal Citizenship joined the Polish informational campaign about the Nazi persecution of intellectuals and social leaders.[76]

The Polish government published the first edition of materials on the German occupation in December 1939.[77] Several weeks later, a 127-page long memorial titled 'The Polish Territory occupied by Germans', originally pre-

72 Minutes of the meeting of the Council of Ministers on 8 November 1939, IPMS, PRM-K. 102/6, Kol. 1–10, PPRM vol. 1, pp. 62–68, here: 66.

73 Hułas, *Goście*, 193.

74 Polish Ministry of Information, *Martydrom of Polish Professors* (London: 1942).

75 Minutes of CHA meeting on 28 December 1939, *Protokoły posiedzeń*, 106.

76 See International Alliance of Women for Suffrage and Equal Citizenship, Protest, 10 July 1941, AIH, 800/42/0/-/104, scan 318. The attempts of Polish diplomacy to engage women's organisations and influence female public opinion in the United Kingdom and the leading role of Ma discusses more extensively M. Fleming, see Fleming, *In the Shadow*, 80–86.

77 Unsigned study of methods used by the Germans in Poland and the response from society, 20 December 1939, in Polish Diplomatic Documents, doc.454, pp. 553–558; TNA FO 371 23137, C20664/123/55.

pared by the Centre for Information and Documentation for government use, was made available to the general public.[78] The report contained eleven chapters: I. Massacres and executions; II. Ill-treatment and torture of the Polish population; III. Concentration camps, prisons, prisoners-of-war, forced labour; IV. Inhuman treatment of prisoners-of-war; V. Mass expulsions of Poles; VI. Pillaging of public and private property; VII. Destruction of Polish culture; VIII. Persecutions of the Church; IX. Abasement of the Polish population; X. Persecutions of Jews; XI. Extermination.[79] Under the influence of the first reports and accounts from Poland, arriving in January and February 1940, the Parliament of the United Kingdom deliberated on the need for the British government to publish a full list of atrocities and violations of international law committed by German armed forces and civilian administration in the occupied territories. During his visit in London in January 1940, August Zaleski informed Lord Halifax about the official White Book being prepared by Polish authorities at the time, which supposedly influenced the UK authorities to abandon the idea of a separate publication.[80]

The first Polish White Books were published on 16 March 1940 simultaneously in Paris and London, with a selection – compiled by Polish MFA – of diplomatic documents on Polish-German and Polish–Soviet relations in 1933–1939 – *The Polish White Book: Official Documents concerning Polish-German and Polish-Soviet Relations.*[81] In late March 1940, with negotiations on the text of Polish–British–French declaration nearing the end, Kazimierz Sosnkowski made a radio address to the occupied homeland, offering assurances that the occupying powers' crimes would be brought to justice.[82] In an emotional speech, the CHA leader vowed full compensation for injuries suffered and expressed his recognition of the Polish population's resistance against the occupying power, emphasizing that 'every moral or physical suffering [was] a service rendered to humanity in the fight against barbarism'.[83]

On 17 April 1940, the Polish Embassy in Paris hosted a meeting between Minister Stanisław Stroński – in charge of the works of the Centre for Informa-

---

78 'The Polish Territory occupied by Germans' (memorandum), IPMS, PRM 10/2, leaves 49–162.

79 *Ibidem*, leaf 50.

80 Parliamentary inquiries by Captain Plugge, 6 February 1940, and Mr Joel, 14 February 1940, TNA FO 371/24422/ C 2026; C2530.

81 Concerning this topic, see Suchcitz, Dubicki, *Walka dyplomacji*, 651.

82 Radio speech by General Sosnkowski from Paris to the Homeland, of 30 March 1940. Text published on 20 April 1940 in the *Monitor Polski* no. 85–94, 30–31. Reprinted in *Protokoły posiedzeń KSK*, 223–235.

83 *Ibidem*.

tion and Documentation – with French journalists, during which the announcement was made of the Government-in-Exile's first publication titled *L'Invasion Allemande en Pologne.*[84] It contained reports from the German invasion in September 1939, witness accounts and rich photographic material depicting the scale of the destruction, including photographs taken by the American documentarian, Julien Bryan.[85] The official première of *L'Invasion Allemande en Pologne* took place on 20 April 1940.

The book highlighted the German Reich's 'methods of total war consisting in the systematic use of violence and terror against the civilian population'.[86] It presented the most important facts concerning the Defensive War of September 1939, gave the list of towns and lists of civilian casualties of Luftwaffe air strikes, as well as witness accounts of bombing attacks against civilians, hospitals, churches and settlements; bombardments of Warsaw, persecutions of the Jewish population (the mass murder of Jews in Przemyśl on 26 September 1939), and arrests of the employees of the Polish Consulate in the Free City of Gdańsk (Danzig). The White Book outlined key messages of Polish wartime propaganda on German crimes. It emphasized Germany's violations of international law – including unprovoked aggression (Article 1, Hague Convention (III));[87] bombardment of civilian areas (Article 25, Hague Convention (II)), and a deliberate policy of total war and terror against the civilian population. In addition to the rich photographic materials and witness testimony, the publication also featured eyewitness accounts from foreigners in Poland during the September Campaign. Among these was the testimony of British teacher Lucy Baker Bell on the events in Bydgoszcz and the extermination of the Polish population in Pomerania in autumn 1939.[88] In London, *The German invasion of Poland: Polish Black Book containing documents, authenticated reports and photographs* released on 25 May 1940. The circulation was 10,000 copies.[89] Polish authorities sought to raise the profile of their campaign by involving prominent British and French public figures. The preface to the French edition was written by the President of the French Chamber of Deputies, Édouard Herriot, and to the English one by the Archbishop of York, William Ebor (Temple).

---

84 Herriot, *L'invasion.*

85 Zygmunt Sawicki and Tomasz Stempowski, *Oblężenie Warszawy w fotografii Juliena Bryana / Siege of Warsaw in the photographs of Julien Bryan* (Warszawa: IPN 2010).

86 *Ibidem*, 13.

87 Dz.U.RP.1927.21.159.

88 *The German Invasion of Poland: Polish Black Book Containing Documents, Authenticated Reports and Photographs* (London–Melbourne: Hutchinson & Co. LTD, 1940), 40–43.

89 *Ibidem.*

On 10 May 1940, another protest note was published by Polish authorities against the German occupation policy. It dealt with matters such as the forcible drafting of Polish citizens into the German military, as well as the introduction of a statute on military service in the territories annexed to the German Reich, in violation of the Hague Convention. On 20 December 1940, General Sikorski's cabinet published a declaration addressing the German policy of denationalizing the Polish population and forcibly inducting inhabitants of the annexed territories on the Deutsche Volksliste, as well as Germanization of the residents of the General Government.[90] This colonial approach aiming at the elimination of non-German culture and identity had a basis in the laws and regulations issued by the occupation authorities: *Erlass für die Überprüfung und Aussonderung der Bevölkerung in den eingegliederten Ostgebieten*, of 12 September 1940, and *Bescheinigung über die Nichtzugehörigkeit zum polnischen Volke. Rund-Erlass des Reichsministers des Innern*, of 14 November 1940.[91] A regulation of the Reich's Minister of the Interior of November 1940 laid down the rules for determining the German affiliation of residents of Silesia and Gdańsk–West Prussia circuits, irrespective of their actual origin and ethnicity, on account of cultural ties to 'Germandom' (*Deutschtum*). In a protest note, the Polish government emphatically denounced the provisions legitimizing the denationalization as incompatible with the principles of international law and Articles 43 and 45 of The Hague Convention:[92]

> All the measures applied by the German Government against Poland and the Poles, from the first day of the war down to the present time, constitute one long chain of physical and moral violence directed towards the destruction of the Polish nation.[93]

On 3 May 1941, the Polish Government submitted a diplomatic note to the governments of Allied and neutral states, detailing Nazi crimes in occupied Poland. It was bolstered with victim lists and texts of laws and regulations enacted by the occupation authorities.[94] The document gave a rundown of the German Reich's violations of international law, especially of the provisions

90 Polish Ministry of Information, *The German New Order*, 424.

91 *Ministerialblatt des Reichs- und Preussischen Ministerium des Innern* 1940, p. 2111, Deutsche Justiz 1940, cited after Pospiszalski, *Documenta Occupationis*, vol. V, 162ff.

92 Art. 45 of the Hague Convention: 'It is forbidden to compel the inhabitants of occupied territory to swear allegiance to the hostile Power'.

93 Polish Ministry of Information, *The German New Order*, 424. Minutes of the meeting of the Council of Ministers on 20 December 1940, PPRM vol. 2, pp. 229–230.

94 *The German Occupation*, Cyprian and Sawicki, *Prawo norymberskie*, 78–79.

of The Hague Convention (IV) and the Geneva Convention, relative to the Treatment of the Prisoners of War, of 1929. Supplementing the publication was a digest of the special provisions enacted for the General Government and those territories administratively annexed to the Reich. Those served as an illustration of the legal violence applied by the occupation authorities – both civilian and military – especially with regard to the new administrative subdivision of the occupied territories and German colonization, organization of the justice system, and retroactive application of criminal provisions to Polish citizens; judicial crimes committed against Poles and Jews; economic violence; persecution of the Jews; and mass deportations. The Black Book underscored the organized mass-scale brutality against the civil population, intentional 'violations of the most elementary principles of human rights' by the occupying authorities, as well as the use of 'measures which surpass each other in inhumanity and in their negation of the rules of international law and morality, and which are in fact designed to reduce the population to virtual slavery and ultimately to exterminate the Polish nation'.[95] When it came to judicial repressions in criminal matters, the note stressed the accountability of German civilian authorities for the wide use of collective responsibility and for resorting to mass executions of the civilian population by the police and the SS as retaliatory measures, as well as:

> execution of Polish citizens on the basis of the judgments of special military courts, police courts and special courts. (…) It is scarcely necessary to add that they do not observe any procedure laid out in advance; the guarantees represented by defence are lacking, and the grounds of judgments are not published.[96]

The end of 1941 saw the publication of another white book, titled *The German New Order in Poland*,[97] illustrating the policies of the German occupation from autumn 1939 to mid-1941. Spanning more than six-hundred pages, the document counts nine chapters: Massacres and torture of the civilian population; Forced resettlements; Persecution of Jews, and ghettoes; Pillaging of public and private property; Economic exploitation in occupied Polish territories; Persecution of religion; Abasement of the Polish nation; Destruction of Polish culture; and Acts of violation of international law by the German Reich.[98]

95 *The German Occupation*, 1
96 *Ibidem*, 16.
97 Polish Ministry of Information, *The German New Order.*
98 *Ibidem.*

Because of its size, resulting from the inclusion of abundant source materials, and due to media campaign surrounding its publication, coinciding with the declaration published on 13 January 1942 by the governments of the occupied states, *The German New Order in Poland* attracted significant interest from the international public opinion.[99]

Nevertheless, the list of the Polish Government-in-Exile publications dealing with the German policy of terror in occupied Poland was significantly longer. These included two key series: 'Documents Relating to the Nazi and Soviet Occupation of Poland' by the Ministry of Information and Documentation,[100] and 'Studies and Sketches'. The later included: *The Polish Spirit of Freedom* Olgierd Górka, Konstanty Jezioranski, and Paweł Skwarzyński; *The quest for German blood: policy of Germanization in Poland*; *The legal position of Jews in Poland* (1942); *The Protestant church in Poland*; *Martyrdom of Polish Professors*,[101] and (among many others): *The German Fifth Column in Poland* (1940), *Poland's martyrdom: the German invasion in photographs and facts* (1940), *L'Occupation Allemande et Sovietique de la Pologne* (1941), *The Ghetto of Warsaw* (1942/1943), *The Mass Extermination of Jews in German Occupied Poland* (1942), *Obrona Warszawy* ('The defence of Warsaw') (1942), *Poland and Germany and the Post-War Reconstruction of Europe* (1942); *Justice outlawed. Administration of law in German-occupied territories* (1944). In 1944 and 1945, two extensive volumes documenting losses of Polish cultural heritage were published by the Ministry of Preparatory Works: *Cultural losses of Poland: index of Polish cultural losses during the German Occupation, 1939–1944* and by the Ministry of Information and Documentation: *The Nazi Kultur in Poland* and by the Ministry of Preparatory Works.[102]

---

99 Puławski, *W obliczu Zagłady*, 185–203.

100 Polish Ministry of Information, *The persecution of Jews in German-occupied Poland* (London 1940); Polish Ministry of Information, *German destruction of cultural life in Poland* (Chicago 1940); Polish Ministry of Information, *Poland after one year of war* (London 1940).

101 Olgierd Górka, Konstanty Jeziorański and Paweł Skwarzyński, *The Polish Spirit of Freedom* (London: Polish Ministry of Information 1942); *The quest for German blood: policy of Germanization in Poland* (London: Polish Ministry of Information 1943); *The legal position of Jews in Poland* (London 1942: Polish Ministry of Information); *The Protestant church in Poland; Martyrdom of Polish Professors* (London: Polish Ministry of Information 1942).

102 Polish Ministry of Information, *The Nazi Kultur in Poland* (London: Hutchinson 1945), Karol Estreicher (ed.), *Cultural losses of Poland: index of Polish cultural losses during the German Occupation, 1939–1944* Some of the titles provided in this section are discussed extensively and commented by Michael Fleming, see: Fleming, *In the Shadow*, 24–46.

Series of special editions dealing with the situation in occupied Poland and Polish–German relations were also published by the Polish Information Centre (PIC) in New York and the Polish Research Centre in London. In 1941, the Polish Information Centre published nine items in a series titled *Documents Relating to the Administration of Occupied Countries in Eastern Europe*: *German Exploitation of Polish Forests, German Destruction of Cultural Life in Poland, German Organisation of Distribution in Poland* (No. 3), *German persecution of religious Life in Poland, The Soviet Occupation of Poland* (No. 5), *German Organisation of Courts in General Government of Poland, German Iron and Steel Policies* (No. 7), *Extermination of the Polish People and Colonisation by German Nationals* (Nos. 8 and 9). From mid-1941 onward, in cooperation with the PIC in New York, the Polish Labor Group, linked to the Polish Socialist Party, published an English-language periodical titled *Poland Fights*. Circulating 22,000 copies, the magazine featured news from occupied Poland, as well as reports and witness accounts of crimes against civilians, extermination of Jews, concentration camps, forced labour, and mass resettlements. It also made appeals to American society for solidarity with the population of the occupied territories.[103]

Among items published by the Polish Research Centre in London were: Józef Winiewicz, *Aims and Failures of the German New Order* (1943); *German withdrawal in the East: a study in vital German and Polish statistics* (1941); *Upper Silesia* (1941); *Poland and Danzig* (1941); *Eastern Poland* (1941); *The Story of Wilno* (1942); *The Protestant Churches in Poland* (1944); *Poland and the USSR, 1921–1941* (1941); *The Orthodox Eastern Church in Poland. Past and present* (1942); and *German Failures in Poland. Natural obstacles to Nazi population policy* (1942). In 1943, the efforts of the Middle East Information Centre saw the publication of *Underground Struggle in Poland*.[104]

---

103 For a more extensive account of the publishing activities of the *Polish Labor Group* and the informational policy of the Polish Government-in-Exile in the United States, see: Iwona Drąg-Korga, 'The Information Policy of the Polish Government-in-Exile Toward the American Public During World War II'. *Polish American Studies* 64 (2007), 27–45; Krzysztof Groniowski, 'Poland Fights (1941–1946)'. *Kwartalnik Historii Prasy Polskiej*, XXIX (1990), 67–93.

104 *Inter alia* Józef Winiewicz, *Aims and Failures of the German New Order* (London: Polish Research Centre 1943); *German withdrawal in the East: a study in vital German and Polish statistics* (London: Polish Research Centre 1941); *Upper Silesia* (1941); *Poland and Danzig* (1941); *Eastern Poland* (1941); *The Story of Wilno* (London: Polish Research Centre 1942), *The Protestant Churches in Poland* (London: Polish Research Centre 1944); *Poland and the USSR, 1921–1941* (London: Polish Research Centre 1941); *The Orthodox Eastern Church in Poland. Past and present* (London: Polish Research Centre 1942); *German Failures in Poland. Natural obstacles to Nazi population policy* (London: Polish Research Centre

4 The Government Structures Responsible for the Implementation of Polish War-crimes Policy

The complexity and breadth of Sikorski cabinet's efforts in the field of war-crimes policy find reflection in the organizational structure of the Polish Government-in-Exile. The main hubs responsible for the making and co-ordination of Polish war-crimes policy were ministries outlining the principal directions of that policy – documentation of the crimes, conduct of the international informational campaign, as well as legislative works and preparations for the criminal trials anticipated to follow in the aftermath of the war. For the most part, those were the Ministry of the Interior, Ministry of Foreign Affairs, Ministry of Information and Documentation, and Ministry of Justice. Although their responsibilities were distributed according to portfolios, it must be noted that the works were frequently handled by specialized sections from different resorts acting in a complementary manner.

Initially, the works of the government-in-exile focused on gathering and processing information about the occupying authorities' acts of violation of international law; the responsible departments were the Cabinet Committee for Home Affairs, Centre for Information and Documentation (Ministry), Ministry of Foreign Affairs with a network of diplomatic outposts, and the Homeland (Social) Department (*Wydział Krajowy* (*Społeczny*)) under the Praesidium of the Council of Ministers. As the government structure expanded, specialized units were created under the different ministries. The evacuation of Polish authorities to the United Kingdom in February 1940 led to a reshuffle of General Sikorski's cabinet.[105] Near the end of July, Sikorski tabled a motion in the Council of Ministers to transform the departments of the Praesidium of the Council of Ministers responsible for home affairs and contacts with occupied Poland into a Ministry of the Interior.[106] August 1940 saw the creation of a Bureau of Political, Economic, and Legal Works tasked with the 'development

---

1942). Apart from publications dealing strictly with the German and Soviet occupation of Poland, books and brochures detailing the works of the Polish Government-in-Exile, as well as Polish history and culture and the political system and business life in Poland in 1918–1939 were also published for the purposes of the Polish diplomatic campaign. Among those were: *Poland after one Year of War* (London: George Allen and Unwin Limited 1940); Jan Jankowski and Antoni Serafiński, *Polska w liczbach* (London: Stowarzyszenie Prawników Polskich w Zjednoczonym Królestwie 1941); *The Truth about Poland.* (New York: Polish Government Information Centre, 1944). See also Fleming, *In the Shadow.*

105 Hułas, *Goście*, 83–95.

106 Minutes of the meeting of the Council of Ministers on 29 July 1940, PPRM, vol. 2, 51–59.

of a reclamation programme and Polish aspirations for after the war'.[107] In September 1940, the Centre for Information and Documentation led by Stanisław Stroński was reconstituted into a Ministry of Information and Documentation to gather information from occupied Poland and prepare publications needed in current activities.

4.1 *Cabinet Committee for Home Affairs*

A key challenge for the Government-in-Exile was quickly establishing secure channels of communication and co-operation with occupied Poland. On 6 October 1939, the Council of Ministers commissioned Aleksander Ładoś to 'establish confidential contact with the Homeland'.[108] General Kazimierz Sosnkowski, however, took over soon after his arrival in Paris and was appointed the inaugural president of the Cabinet Committee for Home Affairs,[109] established on 13 November 1939.[110] Its core responsibilities were: 'care of all matters relating to the Homeland, to the conspirational efforts of the Nation, aspiring to free the Republic from enemy occupation'.[111] This included maintenance of constant contact with the occupied territories; preparation of updates on the war situation; the policy and goals of the Polish government; and formulation of government guidelines for the organization of life in occupied Poland. Despite the lack of regularity of the Committee's works starting from the latter half of 1940, its activities – especially during the initial months of the war – were of considerable importance to the development of the Government-in-Exile's stance on the occupying power's policy of extermination. The Committee

---

107 *Ibidem*, 193.

108 Minutes of the meeting of the Council of Ministers on 6 October 1939, IPMS, PRM-K. 102/2, leaves 1–6. PPRM vol. 1, p. 7.

109 Kazimierz Sosnkowski chaired the CHA until January 1941. In 1939–1940, Sosnkowski acted as the Supreme Commandant of the Union of Armed Struggle (Związek Walki Zbrojnej), and in 1939–1941 was the appointed successor to the President of the Republic (in the event of a vacancy arising before the conclusion of peace, according to Art. 24(1) of the Constitution of 1935). The first members of the CHA were Aleksander Ładoś, Marian Seyda, Jan Stańczyk and General Marian Kukiel. Stanisław Kot, Jan Stańczyk Tadeusz Bielecki and Stanisław Mikołajczyk participated from January 1940 onwards. Subsequent presidents of the CHA were Stanisław Kot (1941), Stanisław Mikołajczyk (1942–1944) and Tomasz Arciszewski (1944–1945). The CHA's composition is discussed in detail by Pachowicz, *Komitet Ministrów*, p. 26–46.

110 Duraczyński, *Kontrowersje*, 80.

111 Reprinted in *Sprawa polska w II wojnie światowej*, doc. 74, p. 118; *Armia Krajowa w dokumentach 1939–1945*, vol. I, *Wrzesień 1939–czerwiec 1941, London 1970, doc. no. 3, pp. 4–5; Referat i wnioski gen. Sosnkowskiego w sprawie organizacji łączności z krajem* ('General Sosnkowski's paper and conclusions on the organization of communication with the homeland'), of 11 November 1939, PPRM vol. 1, 71–77.

organized humanitarian assistance for the Polish population,[112] developed and publicized – in the international forum – reports on the atrocities committed by the occupying forces in Poland, and endeavoured to win Western-Allied support for the idea of penal repression against war criminals. Among the important elements of the CHA's first instructions concerning the organization of social life in occupied Poland were detailed guidelines on the documentation of the crimes committed by the occupying powers. Materials forwarded from occupied Poland were leveraged for the purposes of the government's international informational campaign, which had been a significant component of the diplomatic activities of General Sikorski's cabinet since its first days in office.[113]

4.2 *The Ministry of Information and Documentation* (*Centre for Information and Documentation*)

The agency, founded in autumn 1939, as the Centre for Information and Documentation was transformed into a full-fledged ministry (MiID) one year later.[114] It comprised two sections – Information (Press and Politics), led by Minister Marian Seyda, and Documentation, led by Stanisław Stroński. The Information section gathered press reports and monitored foreign – especially German – media and news from foreign outposts,[115] and collected testimonies from persons arriving from occupied Poland. It also kept radio watch. Materials obtained in this manner provided the basis for a daily bulletin titled 'Report from the Centre for Information and Documentation' and for propaganda contents used by press agencies and diplomatic outposts, including the Bulletin of the Polish Press Office in London – *News from Poland*.[116] The Docu-

112 The CHA resolution of 15 November 1939 proclaimed: 'according to the consonant witness of compatriots and foreigners, in the closest time the population in the territory of the German occupation is threatened with famine, destitution and epidemics. The Committee addresses to the whole of the cabinet the request that each of the ministers advance the cause of the organization of aid for the German occupation as the most urgent (…) matter for his ministry'. In a resolution of 21 November 1939, the CHA defined precise recommendations in respect of humanitarian aid for occupied Poland, coordinated by the Minister of Labour and Welfare and by Ludwik Rajchmann, Government Delegate to the USA for assistance to Poland and Polish refugees. See Conclusions regarding the organization of aid for the population in the homeland passed in the meeting of the CHA, 21 November 1939, IPMS, PRM-K., 102/7, leaves 26–27, PPRM vol. 1, pp. 101–102.

113 Wyrwa, *Odbudowa*, 43

114 The Ministry of Information and Documentation was established by the presidential decree of 11 September 1940; see Hułas, *Goście*, 168.

115 IPMS A.10.2/24, IMPS A.10.2/2, IPMS A.10.5/23–27.

116 Minutes of the meeting of the Council of Ministers on 8 November 1939, IPMS, PRM-K. 102/6, Kol. 1–10, PPRM vol.1, 62–68.

mentation Section was responsible for the 'publication and circulation of brochures and publications' and for the gathering of 'academic/political information'. An academic/political subsection dealt with the problems of academic and intellectual circles, legal, political, economic, and social topics, and kept a general archive documenting German and Russian atrocities.[117] The aforementioned task load was ultimately divided between the Documentation Section and the War Goals Bureau, the latter of which was transformed in August 1940 into the Bureau of Political, Economic and Legal Works, and later Ministry of Preparatory Works. Beforehand, the Centre for Information and Documentation comprised a War Goals Bureau, including a Bureau of Political, Economic and Legal Works. The autumn of 1939 saw the creation of the Polish Research Centre in London as a unit subordinate to the Legal Bureau. The Centre was an important hub for Polish informational–diplomatic campaigning in the United Kingdom, in an institutional cooperation with the Royal Institute of International Affairs (Chatham House) from spring 1940 onward.[118] From November 1939, the Polish Research Centre was led by Professor Adam Żółtowski. It comprised three sections: 1. Section for the gathering of materials and information and for political studies; 2. Section for educational assistance and cultural activities; 3. Educational section. In the Centre for Information and Documentation, the archive of the occupying power's crimes was kept by the Documentation Section headed by Witold Czerwiński from 1940 to 1945. Near the end of 1939, special sections responsible for gathering information from occupied Poland also functioned under the Praesidium of the Council of Ministers and under the Ministry of Foreign Affairs.[119]

Following the establishment of the Ministry of Information and Documentation (MIaD) in September 1940, the Polish Telegraphic Agency (PTA) – previously under the Political Office of the Praesidium of the Council of Ministers – also was subordinated to the Information Section led by Juliusz Skowski.[120] In 1940, the network of the PTA's foreign outposts included branch offices in New York, Rio de Janeiro, London, Rome, Brussels, Helsinki, Bucharest, Budapest, Bern, Stockholm, Athens, and Ankara.[121] Moreover, towards the end of 1939, the PTA Headquarters came into contact with outposts in Warsaw, Cracow, Lublin, Lviv, and Vilnius, gaining access to information coming dir-

117 *Ibidem*, 66.
118 Concerning this topic, see Hułas, *Goście*, 191–196.
119 Minutes of the 6th meeting of the CHA on 12 December 1939, in Grabowski (comp.), *Protokoły posiedzeń KSK*, 90. See also footnotes c and 2 in the cited minutes
120 Grabowski, *Polska Agencja*, 240.
121 *Ibidem*, 246–253.

ectly from the occupied territories.[122] As the war progressed, field outposts of the Ministry of Information and Documentation were created in Jerusalem, Cairo, Beirut, Tehran, Lisbon, Madrid, Istanbul, Bern, Stockholm, Athens, Belgrade, Dublin, Paris, Brussels, Amsterdam, Rome, Nairobi, Montreal, Quebec, Winnipeg, Vancouver, and Algiers, as well as numerous outposts in the United Kingdom.[123]

The Ministry's foreign agencies included the Polish Information Centre in New York – established in 1940 and led by Stefan Gotfryd Ropp – as well as the MIaD Information Centre in the East, established in Jerusalem in 1942.[124] A special section at the ministerial headquarters in London, tasked with the preparation of informational materials about the activities of the German occupation forces and expert studies on the future of Polish–German relations, was known as the German Office (*referat niemiecki*), presided over by Tadeusz Katelbach. Works relating to documentation of German crimes in the anticipation of a post-war accounting were also done at the Ethnic Section (*Dział Narodowościowy*) ('Nationalities Department' in some sources), under the leadership of Olgierd Górka. Its responsibilities included gathering intelligence on the conditions of the Jews in occupied Poland and compiling specialized reports on that topic.[125] Its rapporteurs for Jewish matters were L. Sokołow and Dr. Marceli Dogilewski, the latter of whom, from 1944 onward, worked with Manfred Lachs in the Jewish section of the Polish War Crimes Office.[126] In July 1943, the Ethnic Section was moved from the MiAD to the Ministry of the Interior.[127]

In its information campaign about the situation in occupied Poland, the Ministry of Information and Documentation relied on the aforementioned book publications and also on the media controlled by the MIaD – a film bureau;[128] the Polish Radio; a Polish broadcast aired by the BBC already from September 1939; the Polish Government-in-Exile's official Polish Journal (*Dziennik Polski*); and the English-language biweeklies Polish Fortnightly Review and Free Europe.[129]

---

122 *Ibidem.*

123 Grabowski, *Polska tajna*, 277–278.

124 *Ibidem.*

125 IPMS A.10.3/2.

126 The works of the Jewish Section of the War Crimes Office and of the PWCO as a whole are discussed in Chapter 4.

127 Hułas, *Goście*, 169.

128 Grabowski, *Polska Agencja*, 258.

129 Concerning Polish émigré press in the World War II era see: Jerzy Jarowiecki, Jerzy Myśliński, Andrzej Notkowski (eds.) *Prasa polska w latach 1939–1945* (Warszawa 1980); Habielski, 'Polityka'.

4.3 *Ministry of the Interior*

In December 1939, home affairs, including communication with the occupied territories,[130] were made the responsibility of Stanisław Kot's Political Section of the Praesidium of the Council of Ministers. Its structures provided the organizational cornerstone for the future Ministry of the Interior, created in August 1940.[131] Also in 1939, the Internal Affairs Office (*Referat Spraw Wewnętrznych*) was established under the Praesidium of the Council of Ministers, and later transformed into the Political Section of the Ministry of the Interior, headed by Paweł Kopocz and his deputy, Tadeusz Ullman. The spring of 1940 saw the establishment of a Homeland (Social) Section reporting to the Praesidium of the Council of Ministers. The Section's inaugural head was Władysław Banaczyk, followed from autumn 1940 to the end of 1944 by Paweł Siudak.[132] The Homeland Section, subsequently transformed into the Ministry of the Interior's Social Section, was a 'government organ maintaining contact with the civilian hubs of the underground conspiracy, namely the factions and subsequently the Government Delegate (receiving and dispatching emissaries and couriers, sending instructions, and receiving and sending dispatches and reports)'.[133] The Social Section of the Ministry of the Interior was in contact with the Government Delegate for Poland and the Ministry of the Interior's foreign outposts through couriers and emissaries, diplomatic mail, and, from mid-1941, via radio transmissions.[134]

The Social Section of the Ministry of the Interior served as the main hub for gathering and processing information about all aspects of life under the occupation. It also transcribed interviews with persons arriving from Poland who

---

130 Guidelines regulating contacts with the homeland were drafted in November 1939 by Aleksander Ładoś. The contacts were to be routed through political outposts established under the authority of Polish diplomatic missions in neutral countries. The first such outposts were created in Budapest, Bucharest and Rome, and later in Belgrade, Bern, Jerusalem, Cairo, Kuybyshev, Lisbon, Madrid, Sofia, Stockholm, Tehran, the United States and Vichy. Concerning this topic, see: Grabowski, *Polska Tajna*, 57–83.

131 Hułas, *Goście*, 155.

132 Grabowski, *Polska Tajna*, 51–60.

133 Andrzej Friszke, 'Rząd na Obczyźnie wobec Państwa Podziemnego w Kraju', in Błażyński (ed.), *Władze*, 562.

134 The first station for radio communications with occupied Poland was launched by the Ministry of the Interior in July 1941, and a second one in mid-1942. In autumn 1942, the Social Section of the Ministry of the Interior launched a radio station called *Świt* ('Dawn'). Concerning this topic, see Janusz Laskowski, 'Radiostacja *Świt*'. *Zeszyty Historyczne* 9 (1966), 101–130. Independently from civilian channels of communication with the homeland, military authorities maintained radio communication with the Supreme Headquarters of the Union of Armed Struggle/Home Army through Section VI of the Headquarters of the Commander-in-Chief.

had been witnesses or victims of persecution.[135] In September 1941, a new special section responsible for information arriving from the homeland was formed under the leadership of Józef Kisielewski. The materials gathered in the Social Section's archive provided the main source material for the Polish authorities' first list of war criminals, completed at the beginning of 1942. It comprised more than 2000 names at the time. In autumn 1943, the files would be transformed into a Polish War Crimes Office responsible for co-ordinating the Polish government's cooperation with the United Nations War Crimes Commission. More than fifty studies were compiled on the basis of materials gathered by the Ministry of the Interior documenting the Third Reich's extermination policy in occupied Poland. Those include: *Zasada odpowiedzialności zbiorowej na podstawie raportów polskich z kraju* ('The principle of collective responsibility according to Polish reports from the homeland'), *Skorowidz materiałów do niemieckich obozów koncentracyjnych* ('Index of materials for German concentration camps'), 'The Prosecution of Polish Women' (published under this title in English), and *Niemiecka akcja przesiedleńcza na ziemiach polskich* ('The German resettlement campaign in Polish territories').[136]

In November 1941, a German Section was created in the Ministry of the Interior's Political Department, with subunits for German war crimes, archival records, and the issue of the German minority in Poland.[137] It was first led by Dr. Jan Wagner, until summer 1943, and afterwards by Jerzy Litawski. On 1 November 1943, the German Section ('German Archive') of the Ministry of the Interior was transformed into the Polish War Crimes Office.[138] The latter kept the archive, prepared Polish charges in war-crime cases, interrogated witnesses, co-operated with Allied states on the documentation of Nazi crimes, and represented Poland in the UNWCC.[139]

Matters relating to the situation of ethnic minorities in occupied Poland, including persecutions of the Jewish population, fell in the purview of the Ministry of the Interior's Department of Ethnicities and Denominations (*Dział Narodowościowo-Wyznaniowy*). It was established in spring 1942 and

135 Situation reports from the homeland, reports submitted by the Government Delegate, dispatches and relations from occupied territories in 1939–1945 gathered by the Ministry of the Interior's Social Section can be found in the collections of the Sikorski Institute in London. *Cf.* IPMS A.9.III.2a/ 1–59. (Ministry of the Interior. Social Section. Office for the Processing of Homeland Materials).

136 IPMS A.9III/2b-2c.

137 Hułas, *Goście*, 157.

138 The activities of the German Section and of the Polish War Crimes Office are discussed in Chapter 4 of this book.

139 Note on the activities of the War Crimes Office, 9 December 1943, AIPN GK 159.1, leaves 297–298.

headed by Antoni Serafiński.[140] It commissioned multiple expert studies on the problems of ethnic minorities in Poland and also legal, political, and social aspects of the German occupation. For example, from 1944: *Ziemia Czerwińska pod okupacją niemiecką* ('Czerwińsk District under German occupation'); *Przegląd stosunków niemiecko- ukraińskich na terenie państwa polskiego pod okupacją niemiecką* ('Overview of German-Ukrainian relations in the territory of the Polish state under German occupation'); *Okupacja niemiecka na Białej Rusi* ('German Occupation in the White Rus', i.e. in Belarus); *Polityka narodowościowa niemieckich władz okupacyjnych na terenie Generalnego Komisariatu Białoruś i okręgu administracyjnego Białystok/ zagadnienie białoruskie* ('German occupation authorities' ethnic policy in the General Commissariat Belarus and Białystok administrative district / Belarusian question'); *Ukraińska polityka narodowościowa niemieckich władz okupacyjnych na terenach okupowanych, zamieszkałych przez ludność ukraińską* ('Ukrainian ethnic policy of German occupation authorities in occupied territories inhabited by Ukrainian population'); and *Polityka narodowościowa niemieckich władz okupacyjnych na terenie Reichskomissariat, ze szczególnym uwzględnieniem Wołynia* ('German occupation authorities in the territory of the Reichskomissariat, with emphasis on Volhynia') by Dr Józef Rudnicki; *Przewarstwowienie ludności żydowskiej w Polsce* ('Restratification of Jewish population in Poland') and *Zagadnienie obywatelstwa Żydów polskich* ('The question of nationality of Polish Jews') by Manfred Lachs; *Rozładowanie przymusowych skupień ludności żydowskiej w Polsce* ('Discharging the forced concentration of Jewish population in Poland') by Leon Feit; and *Współżycie żydowsko-polskie na terenie Palestyny w okresie wojny i jego wpływ na okres powojenny* ('Jewish-Polish co-existence in Palestine during the war and its influence on the post-war period') by Dawid Bauer.[141]

From autumn 1940, the competences of the Ministry of the Interior also included the supervision of intelligence, propaganda, and sabotage activities among the Polish diaspora worldwide under the so-called 'Continental Action' (*Akcja Kontynentalna*), conceived and directed by Jan Librach.[142] The purpose of the Continental Action was to engage in 'conspiratorial warfare against the enemy by all means except open armed warfare', keep alive 'the spirit of resistance to the Germans', and gather political and economic information in western-European states and neutral states concerning the states of the Axis and

140 Minutes of the meeting of the Council of Ministers on 12 March 1942, PPRM vol. IV, 168–169

141 List of papers commissioned by the Department of Ethnicities of the Ministry of the Interior for the year 1944 IPMS, A.9.V/80.

142 Jan Librach, 'Nota o „Akcji Kontynentalnej"'. *Zeszyty Historyczne* 23 (1973), 159–171; Biegański et al., *Polish Resistance*, 201–207.

the situation in occupied territories. The key hubs of the Continental Action's intelligence and propaganda activities were Lisbon and Paris, whence numerous reports of Nazi crimes in Poland and Europe were dispatched to the Polish authorities in London.[143] Foreign delegations of the Ministry – in Tehran, Cairo, Bern, New York, Brussels, and Stockholm – also contributed to its documentation and information efforts.

4.4 *Ministry of Foreign Affairs*

A prominent place in the structures of the Polish Government-in-Exile involved in the policymaking on accountability for crimes committed in occupied Poland belongs to the Ministry of Foreign Affairs, established on 30 September 1939. Its inaugural head, until his dismissal in July 1941, was August Zaleski. Zaleski's duties were temporarily assigned in August 1941 to Edward Raczyński, the Polish Ambassador to the United Kingdom. Raczyński was officially appointed Minister of Foreign Affairs in June 1942. In the cabinet chaired by Stanisław Mikołajczyk (14 July 1943 – 29 November 1944), the position was held by Tadeusz Romer, and in that of Tomasz Arciszewski (29 November 1944 – 5 July 1945), by Adam Tarnowski. The Ministry of Foreign Affairs was the main co-ordination centre for the international informational campaign on the occupying powers' crimes. It publicized political information and reports on the situation in occupied Poland through Polish diplomatic missions worldwide[144] and sourced information from foreign media. It also received reports and dispatches from couriers and interviewed refugees on their routes of escape from the country. On the basis of studies prepared by the Centre for Information and Documentation, Polish diplomatic posts issued information bulletins for local press, titled *Polska pod okupacją niemiecką* ('Poland under German occupation').[145]

Diplomatic and consular posts were furthermore responsible for organizing humanitarian aid for refugees and for civilians in occupied territories; they also participated in measures taken to save the Jewish population. The most recent research has highlighted the systemic nature and massive scale of the relief efforts undertaken by Polish diplomatic and consular services throughout the war. In the words of Piotr Długołęcki: 'it would probably not be an

143 *Ibidem.*

144 The organization of Polish diplomatic service in the World War II era is covered in detail by Waldemar Michowicz, 'Organizacja polskiej służby dyplomatycznej w okresie II wojny światowej', in Michowicz (ed.), *Historia dyplomacji*, 9–105, here: 26–93. See also: Długołęcki, *Confronting*, 29–33.

145 See IPMS A.9.III.2d/23.

exaggeration to state that the Polish diplomatic and consular service took part in one of the largest assistance actions to help Jews carried out during World War II'.[146] The most publicized example of Polish diplomats' activities in this regard is the 'passport campaign' – an unofficial support action organized by the 'Ładoś group' in 1941–1943 by employees of the Polish Legation in Bern – e.g. Aleksander Ładoś, Juliusz Kühl, Konstanty Rokicki, and Stefan Ryniewicz. In order to save the Jewish people from deportations to concentration camps and enable their escape from Europe, Polish diplomats illegally issued passports and citizenship certificates of South and Central American states: Paraguay, Honduras, Haiti, and Peru.[147] According to recent estimates, during this rescue campaign, 4 000 – 5 000 passports were issued.

Polish diplomats also delivered protest notes against the deportation of European Jews to death camps.[148] In summer 1942, Stanisław Zabiełło, head of the Directorate of Polish Bureaux in France, intervened with the Vichy Government to halt deportations of Jews from France (the Bureaux were unofficial diplomatic outposts maintained by the Polish government in Vichy France).[149] Later, Edward Raczyński instructed Polish outposts at the Vatican, in Switzerland, Sweden, Canada, and South America to demand that 'the governments thereof intervene with Vichy in the name of humanitarian principles against the surrender of Polish nationals to the Germans'.[150] The Polish Bureaux in France were created to replace the Polish consulates closed down by Vichy in September 1940. After the French defeat, there were approximately 10 thousand Polish refugees in France, as well as approximately 15 thousand Polish soldiers and officers, who, in autumn 1940, were incorporated into French labour companies. Stanisław Zabiełło wrote numerous reports to the Polish

146 Długołęcki, *Confronting*.

147 Jakub Kumoch (ed.), *The Ładoś List,* transl. by Julia Niedzielko, Ian Stephenson (Warszawa: Instytut Pileckiego 2020); Danuta Drywa, *Poselstwo RP w Bernie. Przemilczana historia* (Warszawa-Oświęcim: MKIDN 2020); Roger Moorhouse, *The Forgers. The Forgotten Story of the Holocaust's Most Audacious Rescue Operation* (London: Vintage Digital 2023).

148 Dariusz Stola, 'Dyplomacja polska', 695, 'Dyplomacja polska wobec zagłady Żydów', in *Historia dyplomacji polskiej*, 695, and the literature cited in the article: David Engel, 'The Polish Government-in-Exile and the Deportation of Polish Jews from France in 1942'. *Yad Vashem Studies* XV (1983).

149 Polish Diplomatic Documents, '9 September 1942. Cable from the Government representative in Vichy on the need to submit a protest note regarding the deportation of Jews from France' (doc. no. 240, p. 450). '15 August 1942. Cable from the Government Representative in Vichy on the deportation of persons of Jewish descent from France' (doc. no 228, p. 415).

150 *Ibidem*, doc. no. 244–246.

government in London on Nazi crimes committed in France and elsewhere in Western Europe, as well as Vichy preparations to deport Jews out of France on a massive scale.[151]

A special unit was established by the Ministry of Foreign Affairs near the end of 1939, responsible for gathering information about the occupying powers' crimes from Polish consulates and embassies and for the compilation of white books. Heads of diplomatic missions in London, Washington, D.C., and, until mid-1940, also Paris, advocated – in their contacts with Western Allies – for reprisals against the German Reich for crimes committed in the occupied territories and for the punishment of the criminals; they spearheaded international cooperation and liaised with Allied legal circles and politicians. The Ministry of Foreign Affairs also had a special German Section in place, which was directed by Józef Marlewski.

One of the results of such initiatives was the aforementioned British–French–Polish Declaration of 20 April 1940, followed near the end of 1942 (17 December) by the *Declaration of the United Nations on the Persecution of the Jews*.[152] Polish diplomats – Edward Raczyński, Polish Ambassador in London; Władysław Kulski, legal advisor to the Polish Embassy in London; and Michał Potulicki, Head of the Legal Department of the Ministry of Foreign Affairs – made key contributions to establishing cooperation among the governments of the occupied states around a joint war-crimes policy and were co-authors of the theses of the Declaration of St James's Palace (which were compiled by Władysław Kulski). The signing of the Declaration led, in February 1942, to the creation of an Inter-Allied Commission on the Punishment of War Crimes and Conference of Ministers of Foreign Affairs of the Occupied States.[153]

4.5 *Inter-ministerial Commissions for German Affairs*

A special form of works on topics of Polish policy towards Germany (both current and post-war) was pursued by the Inter-Ministerial Commission on German Affairs. The Commission served as a cooperative platform for multiple ministries, dealing also with the topic of justice for Nazi crimes. Its deliberations were continued jointly by the Ministry of Foreign Affairs and the

151 Stanisław Zabiełło, *Na posterunku we Francji* (Warszawa: Pax 1967).

152 Republic of Poland. Ministry of Foreign Affairs, *The mass extermination of Jews in German occupied Poland: note addressed to the Governments of the United Nations on December 17th, 1942, and other documents* (New York: Hutchinson & Co., 1943).

153 For more on this subject, see Chapter 3 of this book.

Ministry of Internal Affairs into spring 1945.[154] Participants included representatives of the Ministry of Foreign Affairs (Stefan Lalicki, chairing most of the meetings; Mirosław Arciszewski, Michał Potulicki, Adam Kuratowski, and Adam Lisiewicz); Ministry of the Interior (Jan Wagner, Józef Kisielewski, and Jan Librach); Ministry of the Treasury; Ministry of Information and Documentation (Tadeusz Katelbach, Bernard Ziffer, and Witold Czerwiński); Ministry of Preparatory Works (Józef Winiewicz and Józef Weyers); Ministry of Labour and Social Policy (Ludwik Grossfeld); Ministry of Industry, Commerce and Navigation (Tytus Łychowski); Ministry of National Defence (Colonel Marian Ogórkiewicz); and Headquarters of the Commander-in-Chief (Major Leśniak and Lieutenant Lipski).

The Commission discussed the fate of the population in occupied territories, the development of Western Allies' and neutral states' policy towards the German Reich, directions of the Polish informational campaign on crimes committed by the occupying powers, as well as the political and economic situation of the German Reich and losses incurred by the Germans, the problem of post-war Polish-German relations, and the contextually crucial issue of reparations.[155] The problem of bringing those guilty of the crimes committed in occupied Poland to justice was discussed, together with the topic of Polish demands from Germany and the terms of the peace, which – according to the Polish concept – should guarantee the extradition of war criminals and surrender of the evidence and information needed for criminal trials.[156]

A central issue for the Inter-Ministerial Commission in 1942–1944 was the growing activity of German pro-democratic exiles – a key factor in shaping the Polish government's evolving policy toward Germany.[157] German expatriate circles were making a powerful influence on the public opinion in the United Kingdom and United States, focused on the catchphrase of 'Good Germany' (or 'Good Germans') in opposition to the policies of the National Socialist regime, so as to shape a positive post-war image of Germany. The success of those efforts was brought to the attention of the Inter-Ministerial Commission on German Affairs in May 1942 by Michał Potulicki,[158] who analysed the activities

154 MFA. *German affairs. Notes from Inter-Ministerial Commissions on German Affairs*, IPMS AXII 1.88D pt I, IPMS AXII 1.88D pt II.

155 *Ibidem.*

156 *Cf.* Ministry of Preparatory Works, 'Principles of preliminary settlement concerning relations with Germany after the end of Hostilities', IPMS A XII 1.88E, pt 1, leaves 115–119.

157 More on that topic see: Anthony Glees, *Exile Politics During the Second World War: German Social Democrats in Britain* (Oxford: Clarendon Press 1982).

158 Note from the inter-ministerial conference at the MFA on German threats, 8 May 1942, IPMS A.9 II/10.

of the German diaspora in the international sphere within the Inter-Allied Commission on the Punishment and Reconstruction established by the governments of the occupied states. Tadeusz Katelbach and Józef Winiewicz,[159] on the other hand, simultaneously emphasized the need for a positive message in Polish policy towards Germany and for distancing from the extreme anti-German positions, popularized in the United Kingdom by circles linked to Lord Robert Vansittart, including the Win the Peace Movement or the Never Again Association.[160] In one of the Commission's meetings, Winiewicz observed:

> too vehement action on our part against the German nation will reinforce among the British the belief that we are an obstacle to the better ordering of the future. Our goal should be to explain to the English that Poles do indeed fear the German threat but have no hatred of the Germans as such.[161]

The departure, especially in 1943–1944, of Allied states from a completely negative view of the Germans and belief in the moral responsibility of German society as a whole for Nazi crimes posed a difficulty for the Polish informational campaign on German crimes. The development of a positive Polish policy towards Germany, in parallel with plans of pursuing justice for the crimes committed during the war, became an important item on the agenda of the Inter-Ministerial Commission on German Affairs. The most active participants of its works were the head of the German Office at the MIaD, Tadeusz Katelbach, and the head of the German Office at the Ministry of Preparatory Works, Józef Winiewicz.

---

159 Note from the inter-ministerial conference at the MFA on German threats, 1 April 1942, and 8 May 1942, IPMS A.9 II/10; Note from the inter-ministerial commission for German affairs, 2 April 1942, IPMS A.11.AXII 1.88D pt 1, leaves 57–66.

160 Lord Robert Vansittart (1881–1957) was a British diplomat; during World War II he stood at the helm of anti-German organizations Win the Peace Movement, Never Again Association and The Prisoners of War Relations Association. Lord Vansittart's movement warned against the threat posed by the Germany to European peace, lobbied for demanding the unconditional capitulation of the German Reich and strict justice for Nazi crimes, as well as demobilization and prolonged occupation of Germany after the war and payment of complete restitution to the occupied states. See Aaron Goldman, 'Germans and Nazis: The Controversy over "Vansittartism" in Britain during the Second World War.' *Journal of Contemporary History*, 1 (1979), 155–191; Robert G. Vansittart, *Black Record: Germans past and Present* (London: Hamish Hamilton 1941).

161 Note from the meeting of the inter-ministerial commission for German affairs of 2 April 1942, IPMS A.11.AXII 1.88D pt 1, leaf 66.

4.6 *The Ministry of Justice*

The legal aspects of the pursuit of justice for crimes committed during the Second World War in Poland and elimination of the consequences of the war became central to the work of the Ministry of Justice. Although the Ministry had been created in autumn 1939 on the basis of the resolution of the Council of Ministers 'concerning the organization of the head authorities and the scope of activities of the Ministry of Justice',[162] its portfolio during the first two years of its existence was significantly limited. At first, matters under the jurisdiction of the Ministry of Justice had been incorporated into the tasks of the Legal Department of the Praesidium of the Council of Ministers, with General Władysław Sikorski as the inaugural head, simultaneously serving as Prime Minister, Minister of Military Affairs, Minister of the Interior, Commander-in-Chief, and Inspector General of the Armed Forces. From December 1939 to September 1941, the Ministry of Justice was led by Stefan Glaser, who later became the Polish minister to the Belgian government.[163]

During the first months of the ministry's existence as a rather provisional part of the cabinet, its responsibilities included legislative drafting, advising other ministries and the Polish National Council on legal issues, as well as leading the works of the Legal Department of the Praesidium of the Council of Ministers and General Counsel to the Republic of Poland (*Prokuratoria Generalna* RP – exchequer lawyers).[164] After the office of the Minister of Justice was taken in July 1940 by Marian Seyda of the National Alliance (*Stronnictwo Narodowe*) political faction, simultaneously leading the Bureau of Political, Economic and Legal Works, and later Ministry of Preparatory Works, an interim organizational charter was adopted for the ministry.[165] The ministry's responsibilities included tasks delegated to it by statute, the care of the formal legal aspects of draft legislation, publication of the Journal of Laws of the Republic of Poland, preparation of drafts of decrees and legal opinions on matters being in the competence of other ministries or of the

162 Jankiewicz, *W poszukiwaniu*, 9.

163 *Ibidem*, 10–11.

164 *Ibidem*. During the ministry's first months of existence, its collaborators included Włodzimierz Moderow, Counsellor of the General Counsel to the Republic of Poland and Polish Delegate to the League of Nations; Bronisław Hełczyński, professor of Jagiellonian University, First President of the Supreme Administrative Court and President of the World Association of Poles Abroad, as well as lawyers and jurists Stanisław Karboński, Kazimierz Gielniewski and Kazimierz Schwarzenberg-Czerny.

165 Hułas, *Goście*, 177ff; Resolution of the Council of Ministers of 28 August 1940 concerning the interim organization of the Ministry of Justice, AAN, 2/133/0/6// 90, leaves 1–3; Jankiewicz, *W poszukiwaniu*, chapter 1, fn. 58.

General Counsel, liaisons with foreign legal organizations, and maintenance of records of the laws and regulations issued for Polish territories by the occupying powers.

The necessity of strengthening the position of the Ministry of Justice in the government structure was appreciated by Seyda's successor, the legal practitioner from Cracow, socialist activist and Deputy President of the National Council of the Republic of Poland, Herman Lieberman. Lieberman announced the expansion of ministerial structures and establishment of a commission of experts responsible for preparing and opining on the government's legislative drafts. His intention was for the ministry's substantive work to focus on a programme of reconstruction of a democratic legal system in post-war Poland, as well as designs of a reform of the justice system guaranteeing the independence of the judiciary.[166] The minister's sudden decease in October 1941 prevented those plans from seeing fruition, and a reform of the ministry along lines similar to Lieberman's was prepared and carried out by the eminent constitutionalist, expert in international law, and professor of state law at the Stephen Báthory University in Vilnius – Wacław Komarnicki, after he took over as the next minister.[167]

Komarnicki's intention was for the Ministry of Justice to become the main hub for the preparation and consultation of legislative drafts, as well as constitutional reforms for post-war Poland. That was in keeping with the government's programmatic guidelines taken from the February Declaration, drafted by Komarnicki himself, together with Stanisław Grabski. The ministry's interim charter, devised by Komarnicki in February 1942,[168] established several new organizational units – Administrative Department, Legislative Department, Secretariat, and Legislative Works Commission. The responsibilities of the Administrative Department included personnel and budgetary matters, publication of the Journal of Laws, issue of replacement civil-registration documents, and tasks mandated by the Decree of the President of the Polish Repub-

---

166 Jankiewicz, *W poszukiwaniu*, 12.

167 From November 1941 to the appointment of Komarnicki on 21 January 1942, the ministry was led by Karol Popiel, leader of the Labour Alliance and later Minister of Reconstruction of Public Administration. During that time, a unit for legal and administrative studies was being created at St Andrews University in Scotland in co-operation with the ministry, on the initiative of the Polish Lawyers' Association in the United Kingdom. Additionally, Polish Admiralty Courts were established in 1942 in the United Kingdom. See: Jarosław Rabiński, *Stronnictwo Pracy we władzach naczelnych Rzeczypospolitej Polskiej na Uchodźstwie w latach 1939–1945* (Lublin: KUL 2012), 390ff.

168 The staffing of the Ministry of Justice and the expansion of its structures is discussed in detail in Jankiewicz, *W poszukiwaniu*, 29–39.

lic on Gathering and Securing the Evidence in Cases of Common Crimes.[169] The Minister's Secretariat also was placed under the Administrative Department. The tasks of the Legislative Department included preparing legislative drafts, liaising with the Commission for Constitutional Affairs under the President of the Council of Ministers, and seeing to the formal–legal aspects of all legislative and regulatory drafts. It was, moreover, responsible for revisions to pre-war Polish legislation, especially the legal changes introduced by the Sanacja government, and for the gathering and processing of laws and regulations issued in Poland by the occupying powers.[170] Until 25 January 1943, the Department was headed by Komarnicki's close collaborator, legal philosopher, and theorist and professor of University of Warsaw – Eugeniusz Jarra. With Jarra in the position of Secretary General of the Ministry of Justice, the Legislative Department came to be led by the international-law expert, Stanisław Kodź.[171]

An institution of unique importance from the perspective of planning constitutional reforms and pursuing the current political goals of the Polish Government-in-Exile was the Legislative Works Commission established on Komarnicki's initiative in spring 1942. It served as the ministry's advisory body, composed of leading academics and practitioners responsible for the preparation and assessment of legal drafts. Its responsibilities included revision of the system of common courts, criminal law, and 'other decrees and statutes concerning the administration of justice issued during a period of dominance of authoritarian tendencies in the life of the state', as well as the drafting of transitional provisions for the post-war period. Among the latter were substantive and procedural provisions governing the occupying powers' criminal responsibility for crimes against the Polish state and nation.[172]

The Commission's Section V for Criminal Law and Procedure and the Corrections System, led by Glaser, saw to the drafting in 1942 of the Decree of the President of the Republic of Poland on Criminal Responsibility for War Crimes, published in the Journal of Laws of the Republic of Poland on

169 Decree of 29 April 1940, Dz.U.1940.9.23, Decree on the Appointment of a Commission in Connection with the Outcome of the Defensive War in 1939, Dz.U.1940.10.27. *Cf.* Jankiewicz, *W poszukiwaniu*, 31.

170 Art. 3(3)(2) of the Interim Charter of the Ministry of Justice enacted by the Council of Ministers on 9 February and 12 March 1942, AAN 2/133/0/6/90. Text reprinted in Jankiewicz, *W poszukiwaniu*, 47–49.

171 Jankiewicz, *W poszukiwaniu*, 25.

172 Komarnicki's speech during the inauguration of the works of the LWC on 27 March 1942; cited after Jankiewicz, *W poszukiwaniu*, 75.

31 March 1943.[173] Key points of the ministry's agenda with regard to the principles of the criminal responsibility for war crimes were discussed in interministerial conferences organized in April 1942 and June 1945 by Wacław Komarnicki and his successor in the post of Minister of Justice, Bronisław Kuśnierz.[174]

Apart from legislative works intended for post-war criminal trials, the ministry provided ongoing supervision for investigations in cases of crimes committed in occupied Poland. October 1942 saw the creation of a Criminal-Judicial Office (*Referat Karno-Sądowy*), headed by admiralty prosecutor Jerzy Jaczynowski, who was appointed in December 1944 to the position of delegate of the Ministry of Justice in France. The responsibilities of his unit included 'securing evidence in the judicial sense in the case of German crimes on the basis of accounts and testimonies of persons arriving from the homeland'.[175]

Outside of the borders of the United Kingdom, the investigative tasks of the Ministry of Justice were carried out through its special agencies – the Investigative Commissions of the Ministry of Justice created under the provisions of the Decree of the President of the Polish Republic on Gathering and Securing the Evidence in Cases of Common Crimes.[176] The task load of the Investigative Commissions functioning in Istanbul, Jerusalem, Tehran, Nairobi, Paris and Stockholm focused primarily on interrogating Polish nationals, conducting investigations, and co-ordinating cases relating to the administration of justice in foreign hubs with large Polish populations. This included investigating war crimes. A foreign agency of the Ministry of Justice created solely for the purpose of 'determining and securing (...) the evidence of war crimes committed by the Germans against the Polish Nation and State'[177] was the Investigative Commission in Stockholm, established for the interrogation of Polish prisoners evacuated to Sweden from death camps in 1945.[178]

4.7 *Ministry of Preparatory Works*

One ministry closely cooperating with all other ministries involved in the development of the government's war-crimes policy was the Ministry of Pre-

173 Decree of the President of the Republic of Poland on Criminal Responsibility for War Crimes, 30 March 1943, Dz.U.RP.1943.3.6. For more on this subject, see Chapter 5 of this book.

174 AAN 2/133/0/6/69, leaf 1, AIPN GK 159.2, 204–205.

175 Cited after: Jankiewicz, *W poszukiwaniu*, 33.

176 For more on the works of the Investigative Commissions of the Ministry of Justice, see Chapter 4 of this book.

177 Minutes of the meeting of the Council of Ministers of 25 May 1945, RRRM vol. VIII, 512.

178 *Ibidem.*

paratory Works to Peace Conference, created on 6 July 1942. Its predecessor was the Bureau of Political, Economic and Legal Works, established in August 1940 under the Centre for Information and Documentation.[179] The ministry's task was:

> preparation of political, economic and legal topics relating to the future peace conference, and in particular the development, for the Government, of a programme of reclamation and of aspirations Poland intends to realize in the aftermath of the pending war, with a supporting rationale[180]

The ministry's assessments related to Poland's wartime losses, indemnities to be claimed, as well as guidelines for Polish war-crimes policy, including matters of extradition.[181] Within the ministry, these works involved the German Office at the Political Department (headed by Józef Winiewicz) and the Legal Department, the latter of which had a unit for international law and treaty law under the leadership of Roman Piotrowski, a professor of civil law at the University of Warsaw.

One of the Legal Department's subdivisions was the Bureau for the Recovery of Cultural Losses, led by the art historian from the Jagiellonian University, Karol Estreicher. Already early into the war, in April 1940,[182] a Commission for the Registration and Recovery of Cultural Material was created at the Centre for Information and Documentation under his leadership. Its task included keeping records of Poland's cultural losses, the pillaging of works of art, archives and libraries, in cooperation with the underground conspiratorial structures.[183] Estreicher's associates in this office were: Czesława Chowaniec, M. Dienstl-Dąbrowa, Maciej Loret, Danuta Marsówna, Janina Urbańska, and Jerzy Żarnecki. After the establishment of the Ministry of Preparatory Works, this unit was transformed into the Bureau for the Recovery of Cultural Losses.

---

179 Concerning this topic, see: Hułas, *Goście*, 191–196.

180 Motion for the Council of Ministers concerning an organizational charter for the Office of the Minister of Preparatory Works, 2 July 1942, PPRM vol. IV, 359.

181 *Cf.* Ministry of Preparatory Works, *Principles of preliminary settlement concerning relations with Germany after the end of Hostilities,* IPMS A XII_1_88 Pt 1, leaves 115–119.

182 Dariusz Matelski, *Karol Estreicher jr 1906–1984: biografia wielkiego Polaka* (Kraków: Pałac Sztuki Towarzystwa Przyjaciół Sztuk Pięknych), 355.

183 In the civilian structures of Polish underground conspiracy, the unit responsible for the keeping of records of losses sustained by Polish culture was the Culture Section of the Department for the Eliminations of the Consequences of the War, led by Dr Stanisław Lorentz. See Matelski, *Karol*, 391.

Estreicher and his collaborators played a key role in inter-Allied co-operation on the protection of cultural property and recovery of property looted during the war. As a member of the international committee of the Central Institute of Art and Design –established in London in 1939 – Estreicher strongly advocated for the cultural reconstruction of Europe and for addressing the destruction of cultural heritage under German occupation and the question of restitution of looted artworks. He raised the same demands in the memorandum *The destruction and plunder by the Germans of works of art and the necessary cultural revindication resulting from it*, presented during his study visit to the United States between autumn 1942 and spring 1943.[184] Estreicher's appeals resonated in the American academic and political environment. In January 1943, the American Council of Learned Societies established the ACLS Committee on the Protection of Cultural Treasures in War Areas, which aimed at guiding 'the Allied Forces in the protection and recovery of art, monuments, and other treasured cultural heritage threatened by the ongoing conflict';[185] in the summer of that year, President Roosevelt appointed the American Commission for the Protection and Salvage of Artistic and Historic Monuments in Europe (so-called Roberts Commission).[186] On 5 January 1943, on the initiative of the representatives of the occupied countries, the Inter-Allied Declaration against Acts of Dispossession committed in Territories under Enemy Occupation or Control was released.[187] As a member of the Conference of Allied Ministers of Education, Karol Estreicher co-initiated the Inter-Allied Commission for the Protection and Restitution of Cultural Material (Vaucher Commission, 1944), which prepared restitution requests for Allied states and compiled lists of individuals suspected of looting works of art and destroying monuments during the war. The Polish Government-in-Exile had already been in constant touch with the Restitution Commission headed by Harold Macmillan, to which it submitted in 1942 a general report on cultural losses and expected indemnities (*Zagadnienie strat i odszkodowań kulturalnych. Zagadnienia ogólne*).[188] Apart from maintaining records of the losses and the photographic documentation of the damage inflicted by the German and Soviet occupations,

---

184 Wojciech Kowalski, 'Udział Karola Estreichera w alianckich przygotowaniach do restytucji dzieł sztuki zagrabionych w czasie II wojny światowej.' *Muzealnictwo* 30 (1986), 30–31.

185 American Council of Learned Societies, 'ACLS and the Monuments Men', https://www.acls.org/acls-and-the-monuments-men/.

186 Ibidem, Matelski, *Karol*, 392.

187 Fleming, *In the Shadow*, 132.

188 *Ibidem*, 395.

the Bureau for the Recovery of Cultural Losses established personal files for those guilty of destruction and looting of works of art, spanning 2,000 names, out of which 600 were forwarded by the Polish authorities to the Vaucher Commission. In 1944, Estreicher's office prepared an extensive report titled 'Cultural losses of Poland: Index of Polish Cultural Loses during the German Occupation, 1939–1944'.[189] The report was subsequently relied upon in the preparation of Polish charges for the UNWCC, Polish indictment presented to the International Military Tribunal in Nuremberg,[190] and Polish claims for war reparations from Germany.

In summer 1945, Estreicher described the works of the Bureau for the Recovery of Cultural Losses in the following words:

> When in the spring of 1944 the restitution cases went into motion in the international arena, Poland was the only country to have had materials prepared and a method established. There exist three directories forming the basis for the Bureau's operations: 1 Directory of localities, in which the losses [sustained by] our institutions are discussed according to location. 2 Directory of items, in which the individual items are recorded according to their kind. 3. Personal directory comprising the names of the Germans who had been pillaging in Poland and who are now being arrested and interrogated.[191]

The Ministry of Preparatory Works commissioned numerous expert studies covering not only the scope of destruction and damage inflicted on Polish culture and science but also war losses, indemnities, and responsibility for war crimes. The above included: *Projekt tez w sprawie odszkodowań gospodarczych od Niemiec* ('Draft theses on economic indemnities from Germany'), *Podstawy prawne karania zbrodni wojennych* ('Legal bases for the punishment of war crimes') and *Ujęcie prawne szkód wojennych oraz podstawy prawne roszczeń odszkodowawczych Polski* ('Legal overview of war damage and legal grounds for Poland's claims for indemnities') by Roman Piotrowski;[192] *Projekt rozwiązania sprawy odszkodowań wojennych od Niemiec* ('Draft solution to the matter of war reparations from Germany') by Witold Łęgowski; *Prawo odszko-*

---

189 Estreicher, *Cultural losses.*

190 For more on this subject, see Chapter 6 of this book.

191 Estreicher's letter to Stanisław Lorentz, 14 June 1945 – Karol Estreicher, *Dziennik wypadków.* Vol. 1, 1939–1945, Anna Maria Joniak (ed.) (Kraków: Pałac Sztuki Towarzystwa Przyjaciół Sztuk Pięknych 2001), 779.

192 IPMS, A.XII/1/88E, pt II.

dowań we Francji w związku z wojną lat 1914–1918 ('Law of indemnities in France in connection with the war of 1914–1918') by Edward Muszalski; and an expertise by Paweł Minowski, *Problem odszkodowań wojennych na tle doświadczeń reparacyjnych z ubiegłej wojny* ('Problem of war indemnities against the backdrop of reparation experience from the past war').[193]

---

193 IPMS, A.21.1/48: List of studies compiled by the Praesidium of the Council of Ministers, no pagination.

CHAPTER 3

The Agency of Small States: Declaration of St. James's Palace of 13 January 1942

The key initiative of Polish government policy on bringing war criminals to justice was to initiate the cooperation of Allied governments and lawyers on the development of proper legal frameworks and justice structures, and see to its intensification. Already during the negotiations on the text of the joint declaration of prime ministers of Poland, France, and the United Kingdom in early 1940, Polish authorities advocated for the inclusion of a provision that those guilty of violations of the laws and customs of war would be put on trial before a court of law. Sikorski cabinet's first efforts on behalf of the establishment of an international expert commission to investigate Nazi crimes in Poland and deal with the legal aspects of post-war criminal trials date back to April 1940.[1] As initiatives of this kind were initially not met with support from the Western Allies, Polish authorities addressed themselves through the official channels to the European governments-in-exile of the occupied states, but also, by means of 'soft diplomacy',[2] to the international academic circles and civil-society organizations in the United Kingdom. The close cooperation of governments-in-exile and their representatives in various official and unofficial networks around the question of accountability for war crimes and designs of post-war justice began to bear fruit as early as January 1942, with the adoption of the Declaration of St. James's Palace. The joint statement of representatives of the nine exiled governments was expected to move the British and American public opinion, inspire change in the so-far sceptical approach taken by the governments of the USA and United Kingdom, and enable Allied governments to define guidelines for a common policy on war crimes. While developing principles for the effective punishment of war criminals, the small states also coordinated their information strategies and diplomatic campaigns, thus creating a political forum and tools of influence independently from the constraints of power politics.

1 AIH, 800/42/0/-/104 Potulicki papers, 693.
2 Fleming, *In the Shadow*, 79.

1 The Draft Joint Declaration of the British Government and Governments of Occupied States

A path for a close cooperation of the governments-in-exile around the questions of post-war order that included accountability for war crimes was paved by Poland and Czechoslovakia with the Declaration of November 1940. In the summer of the following year, both governments commenced works on the text of a joint declaration condemning German atrocities, anticipating the accession of all of the governments of occupied states. The first draft was submitted to the Foreign Office by Władysław Kulski and Adolf Procházka, the latter in charge of the legal department of Czechoslovak MFA mid-October 1941.[3] In response, the British government advised about its own works on a statement that it intended to publish jointly with the other Allied states. Due to the necessity of consultations and agreement on a final text, the recommendation was to put the Polish-Czechoslovak initiative on hold for the time being.[4]

The matter of the British authorities' publication of an official statement condemning German methods of war was the subject of a debate in Parliament and in government circles in the summer of 1941. The debate was initiated under the influence of the informational campaign led by the governments-in-exile, also in connection with the German aggression against the USSR in June 1941 followed by a new wave of mass-scale crimes being committed on the Eastern Front.[5] In a parliamentary inquiry posed on 8 July 1941 to Anthony Eden, a conservative MP by name of Captain William Frederick Strickland asked whether records were kept of names of Axis criminals and those from states allied to the Axis who were responsible for acts of violation of the law of nations and for atrocities against the defenceless population of the occupied territories, in anticipation of putting them on trial after the war.[6] On 29 September, the acting justice minister of the French National Committee, Maurice Dejean, approached the British authorities about the publication of a joint Allied resolution condemning the German system of terror and promising retaliation against the culprits.[7] In his letter to Eden of 25 September 1941, the UK Minister of Economic Warfare, Hugh Dalton (subsequently

3 TNA/ FO 371 36540/ C11442.

4 TNA/ FO 371 36540/ C11518/267/18.

5 Alex J. Kay, Jeff Rutherford, David Stahel, *Nazi policy on the Eastern Front, 1941: total war, genocide, and radicalization* (Rochester, NY: University of Rochester Press 2012).

6 TNA/ FO 371 36540/ C11518/267/18.

7 TNA / FO 371. 36540/ C11111.

Lord Dalton), articulated the need for a British response to the reports of numerous executions of prisoners-of-war in German captivity, and for a message that those guilty would be brought to justice. In Dalton's opinion, such a declaration by the British government would be favourably received both in the United Kingdom and in the United States of America, and provide the inhabitants of the occupied territories with an impulse to document the crimes and record the perpetrators' personal information.[8] He did not find much support from the Foreign Office, largely because of the futility of Allied attempts to prosecute war criminals in the aftermath of the First World War.[9] In his memorandum titled 'Action of the German Authorities in Occupied Territory', Anthony Eden admitted:

> my feeling is that the commitment to hunt down and try many thousands of Germans after the war may be as embarrassing as, for example, a commitment in favour of any particular frontier. (…) I am doubtful of the efficiency of threats and propaganda, at least until there is some immediate prospect of being able to carry them out.[10]

On 5 October 1941, the text of the memorandum was submitted to the War Office in the company of a draft declaration condemning the German war crimes and was subsequently forwarded for consultation to Belgian, Czechoslovak, Greek, Dutch, Yugoslavian, Luxembourgian, Norwegian, and Polish governments and to representatives of the Free French.[11] In a letter attached to the draft, Eden emphasized that the means of repression used by the German authorities in the occupied territories called for a formal note from HM Government and possibly a joint declaration by Allied states. He especially noted the increasingly frequent executions of prisoners-of-war under the guise of retaliation for acts of sabotage and resistance. The British government, however, did not deem it expedient for any specific manner of retaliation to be mentioned in the text of such a document.[12] The draft contained four points. The first three described the methods of terror and repression employed by the German Reich in the occupied territories, and the fourth dealt with the matter of punishment of the offenders:

---

8 TNA / FO 371. 36540/ C10982/267/18.

9 Kochavi, *Prelude*, 12.

10 Anthony Eden, 'Action of the German Authorities in Occupied Territory' (memorandum), 5 October 1941, TNA / FO 371. 36540/ C11112/278/18.

11 Kochavi, *Prelude*, 15.

12 TNA / FO 371. 36540, C 11518/287/16.

> We, therefore, publicly declare that the brutalities which are being committed in the occupied countries are contrary to the dictates of humanity; are reversion to barbarism; and will meet with sure retribution. To this end we are united in our resolve to win the freedom of the oppressed people and to execute justice. When these things are known, world opinion will not allow the criminals to escape just punishment for their crimes. Careful record is being kept of this facts so that in the due time the world may pronounce its judgment. With victory will come retribution.[13]

Eden notified the American embassy of the plans of publishing a joint declaration with the governments-in-exile on 21 October 1941, and a meeting of Allied representatives was scheduled to follow in the last days of October.[14] On 25 October, Harold Shantz, the first secretary of US embassy to the United Kingdom, forwarded to the Foreign Office a communication from the American government to the effect that President Roosevelt had the intention of issuing his own statement on German crimes against prisoners-of-war. In FDR's words:

> The practice of executing scores of innocent hostages in reprisal for isolated attacks on Germans in countries temporarily under the Nazi heel revolts a world already inured to suffering and brutality. Civilized peoples long ago adopted the basic principle that no man should be punished for the deed of another. Unable to apprehend the persons involved in these attacks, the Nazi characteristically slaughter fifty or a hundred innocent persons. Those who would 'collaborate' with Hitler and try to appease him cannot ignore this ghastly warning.
>
> The Nazis might have learned from the last war the impossibility of breaking men's spirit by terrorism. Instead, they develop their lebensraum and new order by depths of frightfulness which even they have never approached before. These are the acts of desperate men who know in their hearts that they cannot win. Frightfulness can never bring peace to Europe. It only sows the seeds of hatred which will one day bring frightful retribution.[15]

---

13 TNA/ FO 371.36540/ C11518/287/18.

14 TNA/ FO 371. 36540/C11829/287/18

15 *History of the UNWCC*, 88.

On the same day, Winston Churchill extended his official support to the US President's declaration. In the conclusion, he stated: 'Retribution for these crimes must take its place among the major purposes of the war'.[16] In consequence, British authorities abandoned the works on a joint resolution of Allied states drawing the basic outline of a common war-crimes policy.[17]

Winston Churchill's and Franklin D. Roosevelt's respective addresses of 25 October 1941 did not pass without a response from the Soviet Union. Following Ivan Mikhailovich Maisky's urging for a joint protest in condemnation of German crimes by the Allied governments,[18] the Foreign Office advised the Soviet government to issue a separate statement. On 7 November 1941, the People's Commissar for Foreign Affairs of the USSR, Vyacheslav Molotov, published a note of the Soviet government concerning the German crimes.[19]

2 Conferences of Governments of Occupied States and Works on the Text of a Joint Declaration on German Crimes

The October declarations of President Roosevelt and Winston Churchill inspired the governments-in-exile to work on more precise guidelines for the punishment of war criminals. A series of conferences devoted to this issue were organized by the Polish Ministry of Foreign Affairs in November 1941 and January 1942, resulting in the publication of the Declaration of St. James's Palace on 13 January 1942. The first session of deliberations among the exiled governments took place in the Polish MFA's building at Queen's Gate 70 in London, on 5 November 1941. A total of seven conferences took place from 5 November 1941 to 2 January 1942.[20] Attendees included representatives of Belgium (Paul Tschoffen, cabinet head at the Ministry of Justice), Czechoslo-

16 TNA/ FO 371. 36540/ C11829/287/18, leaf 243.

17 TNA/ FO 371. 36540/ C11960/287/18; TNA/ FO 371. 36540/ C11960/287/18, TNA/ FO 371. 36540/ C11955/287/18

18 Frank Roberts, 'Proposed protest against German cruelties in occupied territories' (note), 14 November 1941, TNA/ FO 371.36540/ C12747/287/18.

19 The Molotov Notes on German Atrocities. Notes sent by V. M. Molotov, People's Commissar for Foreign Affairs, to all Governments which the U.S.S.R. has diplomatic relations. Issued on behalf of the Embassy of the U.S.S.R. in London. (H.M. Stationery Office 1941).

20 Minutes of the conference: 'Conférence des représentants des pays occupés par l'enemi tenue à Londres du 5 au 21 Novembre au Ministère des Affairs Etrangères de la Republique de Pologne'; 'Procès-Verbel de la 7-*ème seance* [*de la* Conférence des représentants des pays occupés par l'enemi] *du 2 janvier, 1942* à *16 heures, au Ministere des Affaires Etrangères de la Pologne'*, IPMS, A.10.3/3.

vakia (Dr. Černy and Adolf Prohäzka, head of the MFA's legal services), France (Maurice Dejean, Raymond Offroy), Greece (Romanos, legal advisor to Greek government), Luxembourg (Victor Bodson, Minister of Justice), Norway (Hans Berg, chargé d'affairs to Polish Government, E.A. Colban), the Netherlands (Star Busmann, director of the MFA Legal Bureau), Poland (Edward Raczyński, Michał Potulicki, Władysław Kulski), and Yugoslavia (Vladimir Milanović).

The conference opened with a presentation of the Polish-Czechoslovak draft declaration. The preamble stated that the German Reich had pursued in the occupied territories, under the guise of lawful activities, methods of extermination contrary to the elementary principles and customs of humanitarian law, such as executions and imprisonment of the civilian population, concentration camps, mass deportations, and labour camps. Emphasis was placed on that the persecution of civilians, the looting of property and destruction of spiritual life, cultural legacy, and the economy of the occupied countries constituted a crime without precedent in the history of European civilization. In the body of the text, the states signatory declared as follows (translation from the French minutes of the conference):

(a) the German Reich bears full responsibility for the crimes mentioned;
(b) all Germans guilty of committing in the occupied territories criminal offences defined by the domestic penal legislation of the states concerned or by international law will be punished – both the issuers and executors of orders;
(c) all those guilty will be remanded to the justice systems of the interested states so that they do not avoid their deserved punishment.[21]

Furthermore, the parties promised to keep records of perpetrators with a view to securing their extradition and announced that the acts would not be regarded as political crimes justifying the grant of asylum by a third state. Compensation for all harm done by the German Reich in the occupied territories was recognized as one of the principal goals of the war, and the announcement of the declaration was in itself intended as a manifestation of the firm solidarity existing among the governments of the occupied states. That solidarity was to become the foundation of the peaceful ordering of international relations and security in Europe after the war.[22]

Edward Raczyński, who chaired the discussion, emphasized in his speech the attempts of the Polish government to date to establish international

21 *Ibidem*, 5.

22 *Ibidem*, « L'unite morale de l'Europe est realisee. Elle survivra au temps des epreuves. Elle permettra l'etablissement d'une paix stable, assurant a l'Europe la securite centre une npuvelle meance allemande, et un avenir prospere. »

cooperation against the German Reich's policy of extermination and violations of international law. He stressed that the need for formal cooperation among the governments of the occupied states in that respect had become all the more urgent given Britain's withdrawal from the effort to issue a joint statement with the governments-in-exile. Raczyński highlighted the need to establish principles governing the prosecution and punishment of those guilty of crimes committed in the occupied territories and to create an effective system of international justice, which could not have been achieved after the First World War. The drafters' ambition was not only to condemn the crimes committed by the German Reich but also to 'create expressis verbis a system of international jurisdiction that, for many reasons, remained an empty letter after [World War I]'.[23]

The representatives of Czechoslovakia and Belgium, who focused on the scope of the domestic and international jurisdiction, supported this position. As emphasized by Adolf Procházka, Czechoslovak authorities placed special importance on the matter of keeping records of the crimes and their perpetrators, and the concept of putting the latter on trial before the domestic courts of the state in whose territory the crimes had been committed. He attributed the failure of the plans laid out in the Treaty of Versailles for the prosecution of war criminals to the flawed reliance on the principle of international jurisdiction. Consequently, he believed that remanding the offenders for judgment by the domestic courts of the states concerned was the only solution capable of bringing 'satisfactory results'. Simultaneously, he insisted that what his government sought was not revenge against the Germans but justice and compensation for the victims.

The weaknesses of the system adopted in 1919 for the punishment of the war criminals of the First World War were also discussed by the representative of the Belgian government, Paul Tschoffen. The lack of provisions for extradition and Germany's failure to comply with its obligation to deliver the perpetrators effectively prevented their trials by the courts of the Entente. The Belgian authorities viewed the declaration as an opportunity for the precise definition of principles of criminal responsibility for crimes committed during the war, as well as terms of international cooperation in respect of the extradition of suspects. Tschoffen referred to the provisions of Hague Convention (IV), to which Germany was also party, especially its Article 43, obliging the occupation authorities to comply with the law of the occupied state 'unless absolutely prevented', and Article 46, guaranteeing the protection of private

---

23 Conférence des représentants... IPMS, A.10.3/3, 3.

life, family life, and private property in occupied territories.[24] Stressing the media aspect of the related problems and the importance of the judgement of the public opinion, he proposed that – in lieu of language to the effect of delivering the criminals to each of the interested countries – the declaration should make the promise that all those guilty would be brought to justice.[25] During the conference at Polish MFA, Tschoffen recommended that all acts incompatible with the provisions of general criminal law and international law regulating the rules of warfare be deemed liable to penal repression. Such acts were to be treated as criminal offences under the generally applicable law, liable to prosecution, with the effect of considerably facilitating the extradition procedure.[26] The representative of Belgium regarded the joint declaration as an opportunity for the establishment of an effective system of sanctions for international crimes

The French representatives – Maurice Dejean and Raymond Offroy – took a more balanced view on the declaration's legal and political objectives and opted for imbuing it with a political tone. In Dejean's opinion, the main task of the declaration was to enhance the exiled governments' informational campaign on Nazi crimes and to show the public opinion in the neutral states the true face of German occupation. The promise of punishment for the criminals and the hope that it would deter future atrocities were key elements. The remarks submitted by the Free French were of purely editorial nature and reducible to the deletion of a passage on war indemnities and political crimes. Raymond Offroy emphasized that the declaration should serve a political purpose and highlight the solidarity of the governments of the occupied states in the fight against the Nazi barbarism along with the investigative and documentation works.[27]

The representative of Yugoslavia, Vladimir Milanović, argued along similar lines. He was firmly in favour of publishing the declaration and simultaneously giving it more of a political tone. In his opinion, the Allies' foremost objective had to be the prevention of further crimes. He also noted the necessity of addressing the declaration to a much broader audience, so that rather than the Germans alone, it should also apply to their allies – Hungary, Italy, and Bulgaria. The draft was accepted with similar reservations by the governments of Greece and Luxembourg, of which the latter saw the need for precise description of the acts defined as offences, which would strengthen the deter-

24 *Ibidem*, 9.

25 *Ibidem*, 10

26 *Ibidem*, 20–21.

27 *Ibidem*, 19.

rent effect of the declaration.[28] Determined support for the expansion of the applicability of the declaration onto all of the states of the Axis came from Ambassador Raczyński. According to him, because of the responsibility for the military aggression and implementation of a system of terror throughout Europe, the German Reich was culpable in the greatest degree (L'Allemagne est le criminelle No.1), without diminishing the crimes attributable to its allies.[29] Raczyński's comments are of especial significance in the context of the discussion surrounding the treatment of German aggression against Poland (and other European states) as a crime sui generis. The latter idea, distinctly resounding in internal discussions, was rarely voiced by Polish representatives in the international arena.

The most neutral position on the Polish-Czechoslovak draft was that of the Netherlands. The Dutch representative, Edouard Star Busmann, viewed it as inexpedient to prejudge at the then-stage of the war the legal solutions for the prosecution of war criminals in its aftermath. He agreed with the concept of a joint declaration by governments of occupied states but advised caution and recommended going no further than condemning the German Reich's violations of international law and expressing support for Churchill and Roosevelt's statements of 25 October 1941. The government of Norway also took a conservative stance, mindful of the legal problems with the post-war implementation of legislation adopted by governments-in-exile, especially in the area of criminal law. The Norwegian representative, Hans Berg, regarded the principle of criminal responsibility of the executors of orders as something calling for precise definition, followed by narrowing down of the definition of a 'political crime' – something Norwegian law clearly defined as an act committed with a political goal in mind. Both of the topics – similarly to the problem of the retroactive force of the penal provisions intended for application to war criminals – were hotly debated during the meetings at Polish MFA and reflected the diversity of expectations placed on the joint declaration of the governments of the occupied states.

All the representatives ultimately agreed on the idea of issuing a declaration condemning the German crimes and promising to hold the perpetrators criminally responsible. The proposal, put forward by the governments of Poland, Czechoslovakia, and Belgium, to give the declaration a legal character – in an attempt to define more narrowly the relevant points of international law[30] – was nevertheless received as premature by a significant part of those

28 *Ibidem*, 13.
29 *Ibidem*, 29.
30 *Ibidem*, 16.

in attendance. Representatives of the majority of the occupied states decided to frame the declaration in political terms, using it as a platform to manifest 'moral solidarity' and as an impulse for closer cooperation on the documentation of German crimes and on the international informational campaign. The fruit borne by the November conference at Polish MFA was the adoption of a resolution by representatives of nine governments on keeping records of the crimes committed by the occupation forces[31] and the announcement, on 13 January 1942, at St. James's Palace in London, of a declaration foreboding the punishment of war criminals.

3 The Declaration of St. James's Palace

The solemn conference during which the declaration of the governments-in-exile was signed was held by the Foreign Office on 13 January 1942 at St. James's Palace in London and chaired by General Władysław Sikorski. The conference was attended by representatives of the states signatory, and, in guest capacity, representatives of the United Kingdom, USSR, India, China, Canada, Australia, New Zealand, and Union of South Africa.[32]

The declaration condemned the system of terror implemented by the German Reich and its allies in the occupied territories in the aftermath of the German aggression. The signatories proclaimed that punishing the criminals 'in a spirit of international solidarity' was necessary for the satisfaction of the sense of justice of the civilized world and avoidance of acts of vengeance from the wronged societies. Calling upon the Provisions of the Hague Convention of

31 *Ibidem*, 36.

32 Participants included: for Belgium – Prime Minister Hubert Perlot and Minister of Foreign Affairs Paul Henri Spaak; Czechoslovakia – Prime Minister Jan Šrámek and Minister of State Hubert Ripka; Greece – Prime Minister Emmanuel Tsouderos and Minister of Justice S. Dimitrakakis; Yugoslavia – Prime Minister Slobodan Jovanović and Minister of Foreign Affairs Momčilo Ninčić; Luxembourg – Minister of Foreign Affairs Joseph Bech and Minister of Justice Victor Bodson; the Netherlands – Prime Minister Pieter Sjoerds Gerbrandy and minister without portfolio M. J. Michelis van Verduynen; Norway – Minister of Foreign Affairs Trygve Lie and Minister of Justice Terje Wold; Poland – Prime Minister General Władysław Sikorski and Minister of Foreign Affairs Count Edward Raczyński. The guests included representatives of the United Kingdom (Anthony Eden), Australia (Stanley Bruce, High Commissioner to the UK), New Zealand (Bill Jordan, High Commissioner to the UK), Canada (Vincent Massey, High Commissioner to the UK), USA (Anthony Drexel Biddle, ambassador and minister to multiple Allied states), India, USSR (Alexander Bogomolov, diplomatic representative to multiple governments-in-exile), China (Wunz King, diplomatic official), and Union of South Africa (Sydney Waterson, High Commissioner to the UK).

1907, prohibiting 'belligerents in Occupied countries to commit acts of violence against civilians, to disregard the laws in force, or to overthrow national institutions', the states signatory resolved to:

(1) affirm that acts of violence thus inflicted upon the civilian populations have nothing in common with the conceptions of an act of war or a political crime as understood by civilised nations,

(2) take note of the declarations made in this respect on 25 October 1941,by the President of the United States of America and by the British Prime Minister,

(3) place among their principal war aims the punishment, through the channel of organized justice, of those guilty of or responsible for th[o]se crimes, whether they ha[d] ordered them, perpetrated them or participated in them,

(4) resolve to see to it in a spirit of international solidarity that (a) those guilty or responsible, whatever their nationality, [we]re sought out, handed over to justice and judged, (b) that the sentences pronounced [we]re carried out.[33]

The majority of participants in the conference distinctly emphasized the legal significance of the Declaration. In his speech, Władysław Sikorski noted:

> As can be seen, the Declaration resolutely turns International Law in a new direction without, however, establishing all the details. It expresses the principle of the united repression of acts which normally would be considered crimes against common law if they had been committed in peace time, and which will not rest unpunished on the pretext that they have been committed in war time.[34]

Belgian Prime Minister Hubert Pierlot emphasized that the resolution marked a key stage in the effort to establish legal penalties. In his opinion, violations of the fundamental principles of the law of nations by the occupation forces ought to be regarded as criminal offences in common law.[35] Edward Raczyński concurred: 'the wrongs committed against the civilian population will be treated as offences against the common law with all the law's severity'.[36] The need for the legal solutions proposed by the declaration to be adopted by

33 Punishment for War Crimes. The Inter-Allied Declaration Signed at St, James's Palace London on 13th January 1942 and Relative Documents, document issued by the Inter-Allied Information Centre (London: 1942), 3–4.

34 *Punishment for War Crimes*, 7.

35 *Ibidem*.

36 *Ibidem*, 16. *Cf.*

'all the civilized nations' with the consequence of enabling the arrest and judgment of war criminals, was emphasized by the Prime Minister of Czechoslovakia, Jan Šrámek. According to him, the crimes committed by the Axis states could not be regarded as either political crimes or military operations justified by military necessity. General de Gaulle, in turn, appreciated that the declaration called out the German aggression in a singular manner:

> In signing this Joint Declaration to-day, we mean (...) to declare solemnly that Germany alone is responsible for the outbreak of this war and that she shares with her allies and accomplices responsibility for all the atrocities that proceed from it. We demonstrate our firm intention to see to it that all the guilty parties and men who are responsible in any way should not be allowed to evade just punishment as did those of the other war'.[37]

The Prime Minister of Greece, Emmanuel Tsouderos, noted the formulation of a new principle of international criminal law, establishing the individual criminal responsibility of both the issuers and the executors of orders. As underlined by Joseph Bech, the Minister of Foreign Affairs of Luxembourg, the declaration condemned in a particular manner the incompatibility of the legislation of the German Reich – legitimizing the actions of its armed forces and administration in the occupied territories – with the accepted principles of international law and universally accepted moral rules. He emphasized that those guilty would be judged according to the laws of the countries in which they had committed their crimes, and 'if need be (...) national legislative systems must be adapted to the aims laid down in [the] Declaration', as well as appropriate mechanisms created on the international level.[38] The Prime Minister of Yugoslavia, Slobodan Jovanović, expressed on behalf of this government the following hope 'that the solidarity shown to-day w [ould] serve to form a moral juridical basis of a really new order, wherein no possibility w[ould] be left for the repetition of such returns to barbarism'.[39]

The Chinese government, too, voiced its support for the Declaration of St. James's Palace. By a note of 9 January 1942, delegate Wunz King communicated his government's agreement with the principles expounded in the Declaration, firmly condemning the crimes committed by the occupiers and anticipating their individual criminal liability. Chinese authorities announced the applica-

37 *Punishment for War Crimes*, 9.

38 *Ibidem*, 11.

39 *Ibidem*, 14.

tion of the principles of the Declaration of St. James's Palace to the Japanese occupation forces.[40]

International Jewish organizations also expressed their interest in acceding to the Declaration. On 12 January 1942, the Joint Foreign Committee of the Board of Deputies of British Jews and the Anglo-Jewish Association addressed a letter to the Allied governments, promising to supply the signatories with the documentation of the persecutions and extermination of European Jews, stressing the need for the Declaration's tenets to be extended also to them.[41] The World Jewish Congress spoke on the matter near the end of November. In a letter to the signatories of the Declaration, its representatives voiced the conviction that 'the nine Governments participating in the Conference of St. James had had in mind the recognition of the many crimes against the Jews committed by the Nazis and their accomplices and also their belief in the necessity for the text of the Declaration to include reference to anti-Semitic crimes, as well as a clear promise of prosecution of those guilty of crimes committed against the Jews in the occupied territories'.[42]

The Declaration of St. James's Palace marked a key turning point in the development of Allied war-crimes policy of the Second World War era. It constituted the first official communication from Allied states on the subject of punishment for those guilty of violations of international law, the German policy of extermination, and organized mass-scale violence against civilians. Its publication preceded by one week the conference of the government of the German Reich and SS leadership at Wannsee on 20 January 1942, in which the Nazi elites decided on the means for the 'final solution to the Jewish question'. The principles set out in the Declaration found reflection in the Western Allies' decisions concerning the organization of the justice system for the criminals of the Axis, including the intention to prevent lynching or other acts of vengeance and refrain from addressing the issue through political fiat. The purpose of the Declaration was to proclaim the principles of individual responsibility of the perpetrators of war crimes – accountability of both the issuer and the executor of an unlawful order accountable, as well as the aider and abettor; establishment of a procedure for the extradition of war criminals; and exclusion of the treatment of crimes committed during the

40 *Ibidem*, 15–16.

41 Letter from the Joint Foreign Committee of the Board of Deputies of British Jews and Anglo-Jewish Association, 12 January 1942, TNA, FO 371/30914 / C487/61/18.

42 Letter from S. Silverman, N. Barou, A. Eastermann and A. Cohen to the states-signatories of the Declaration of St. James's Palace, 18 February 1942, TNA, FO 371/30914 / C2009/61/18. See also: Lewis, *The Birth*, 153–154

hostilities as political crimes, which would otherwise allow perpetrators to claim political asylum.

Despite the attempts to emphasize the 'community of goals' among the governments of the occupied states and the Western powers, the Declaration of St. James's Palace and subsequent initiatives of its signatories were met with significant reserve from the Great Powers. The United Kingdom and the USA did not accede, which highlighted the differences in their outlook on the problem of prosecution and punishment of war criminals. Already during the works on the text of the Declaration, British authorities approached with considerable scepticism its core demand for international collaboration on keeping records of the crimes and their perpetrators with a view to post-war trials.[43] Their scepticism about reports from the occupied territories stemmed from, on the one hand, the dearth of options to confirm the veracity of the accounts, and on the other, suspicions of exaggeration or fact-twisting by the governments of the occupied states.[44]

The intensely sceptical attitude changed in the summer of 1942, with Winston Churchill's positive opinion on plans of establishment of a United Nations Commission of Atrocities. In July 1942, the British government decided to prepare guidelines on the treatment of war criminals.[45] Both during the drafting of the Declaration of St. James's Palace and after its publication, British authorities approved of the cooperation among the representatives of small states in London but emphasized its independence from the policy of the Great Powers.[46] The latter took their first joint decisions regarding the organization of trials for war criminals no sooner than the spring of 1945.

The works on the text of the Declaration of St. James's Palace set the wheels in motion for closer cooperation among the European governments-in-exile,

---

43 Note by Frank Roberts, 7 November 1941, TNA FO 371/36540/ C11999/287/18.

44 Frank Roberts had the following to say in his note of 7 November 1941, upon the withdrawal of British authorities from plans of publishing a joint declaration with the governments-in-exile in condemnation of Nazi crimes: 'Since we have contracted out of this declaration and are not ourselves committed to the principle of keeping lists of offenders, it seems to me that it may be a little awkward to ask the Allies to supply us with particulars. They would (…) regard such a request as indicating that we were prepared to act as a sort of clearing office, and they might well consider that we had thereby accepted some responsibility for ensuring the punishment of offenders in all the "well-authenticated" cases brought to our notice. This might well prove extremely embarrassing after the war.' *Ibidem*.

45 Anthony Eden, 'Treatment of War Criminals' (memorandum), 22 June 1942, TNA PRO, PREM1/100/10; see also Kochavi, *Prelude*, 28.

46 Strang's report on his meeting with Retinger on 4 February 1942, TNA FO 371/30871/ C1544/ 1543/62.

resulting in their greater integration around plans of developing a common war-crimes policy. The cooperation unfolded both on the political plane – with joint statements issued by heads of governments, conferences of ministers of justice and foreign affairs – and on the plane of expert debate. The discussions on the development of international criminal law and establishment of an effective justice system for war criminals initiated during the works leading up to the Declaration of St. James's Palace subsequently continued in association meetings and informal gatherings of lawyers and jurists. Examples of the latter include the London International Assembly, International Commission for Penal Reconstruction and Development,[47] Inter-Allied Commission on the Punishment of War Crimes,[48] and United Nations War Crimes Commission, as well as a draft extradition convention agreed by ministers of justice of the occupied states in autumn 1943.[49]

The Declaration of St. James's Palace also impressed its mark on the internal and foreign policy of Polish government-in-exile. It was viewed as a success for General Sikorski's cabinet and in particular for the Polish diplomats – Edward Raczyński, Władysław Kulski, and Michał Potulicki – whose efforts led to the signing of the Declaration. The ability to win international support for, and co-ordinate the works on, a declaration on what was a matter of key importance to the Polish government strengthened its position among the other governments-in-exile. The adoption of the Declaration resulted in the intensification of Poland's informational and propaganda campaign on German crimes and in the incorporation of demands for the punishment of war criminals in an official government programme titled 'Declaration of the Government of National Unity'[50] (*Deklaracja Rządu Jedności Narodowej*). It also provided the impulse for the commencement of works on a domestic statute regulating the substantive and procedural bases for the prosecution of suspects in war crimes. The first draft of the Decree of the President of the Republic of Poland on Responsibility for War Crimes was finished in spring 1942, and the promulgation of the final text in the Journal of Laws of the Republic of Poland (Dz.U.RP) followed on 31 March 1943.[51]

---

47 On this topic see: *History of the UNWCC*, 95.

48 *Ibidem*, 89.

49 'Draft Convention for the surrender of war criminals drawn up by the Ministers of Justice of certain of the occupied countries', United States, Department of State: Foreign Relations of the United States: Diplomatic Papers, vol. 1, 1354ff.

50 Republic of Poland, Government declaration of 24 February 1942, Dz.U.RP.1943.8.77.

51 The works on the text of the decree and the accompanying debates and discussions are the subject of the fourth chapter of this book.

4 A Tightening of Cooperation among Governments of Occupied States

The first initiative of tightening the cooperation among the signatories of the Declaration of St. James's Palace was the proposal put forward by General Sikorski's cabinet on 29 January 1942, of continued co-operation after the war. Polish authorities came up with a draft Eight Power Declaration (France was not participating) designed to lay down the principles of post-war international relations in Europe in respect of the states occupied by the German Reich and its allies. The Declaration anticipated continued cooperation with the UK, USA, USSR, and China, and sought to establish principles for post-war relations and economic ties with Germany. The intention behind co-ordinating the policies of the interested states on political, economic, social and military planes was to reshape the balance of power in Europe, guarantee peace and security in post-war Europe, and strengthen the position of the small states.[52] The principles of Christian morality, self-determination of nations, democracy, and social justice were to be the pillars of that cooperation. As noted by Magdalena Hułas, besides the assurance of severe punishment for the crimes and of a stronger position of the occupied states in relation to Germany, another important aspect was the 'creation of an allied bloc as a sort of counterbalance to the USSR'.[53] The idea achieved partial approval. The governments of Norway, Belgium, and the Netherlands showed enthusiasm for the project,[54] while the Czechoslovak government, concerned over Moscow's response to independent initiatives of the governments-in-exile and rapprochement between Poland and Czechoslovakia, took a conservative stance.[55]

The Polish government's designs also contemplated the establishment of expert committees working on various problems concerning international relations and balance of power in post-war Europe.[56] The committees were

52 Minutes of the meeting of the Council of Ministers, 28 February and 3 March 1942, IPMS PRM-K. 102/43d, leaves 48–49. PPRM, vol. IV, 161–162. *Cf.* Draft declaration sent by Władysław Kulski to William Strang, 3 March 1942, TNA FO 371/30871/C2529.

53 *Ibidem*, 291.

54 Note by William Strang from his meeting with Władysław Kulski, 9 February 1942, TNA FO/371/30871/C1544/1543/62; note by William Strang from his conversation with Józef Retinger, 4 February 1942, TNA FO/371/30871/C1544/1543/62.

55 Hułas, *Goście*, 93. Concerning this topic, see: Eugeniusz Duraczyński, 'ZSRR wobec projektów konfederacji polsko-czechosłowackiej (1940–1943)', 3(29) *Dzieje Najnowsze* 1997, 129–153, here: 135–137.

56 To Sikorski, the establishment of 'eight-power co-operation committees' was a source of hope that a space could be created for the promotion of the Polish position in the

intended to include representatives of the governments-in-exile alongside British delegates.[57] The British side took a reserved approach – there were fears, on the one hand, of the governments of the occupied states developing such political goals with regard to Germany and the USSR as would be unacceptable to the Brits, and on the other hand, of the weakening of the United Kingdom's position as the leader of the Allied states.[58] In a meeting on 3 March 1942, Anthony Eden told Władysław Sikorski that an additional obstacle was coming from the distrust felt by the Soviet government and fears 'that the government of the USSR could view the declaration as anti-Soviet and the Brits as its animators'.[59] That, in turn, could harm the negotiations of a British-Soviet alliance already in progress.[60] A negative reaction from the USSR to plans of a declaration of governments-in-exile setting forth the principles of their post-war cooperation was also anticipated by some in the Polish government and by representatives of other governments-in-exile. The Prime Minister of Greece, Emmanouil Tsouderos, termed General Sikorski's plans 'anti-Soviet' and voiced concerns of a possible withdrawal of the Great Powers' support in the view of such a concerted policy of the émigré governments.[61] He recommended that the Brits put a halt to the Polish initiative and organize a platform for communication among Allied states under their own auspices. Sikorski resumed his initiatives of an eight-power declaration in the summer and autumn of 1942 but his goal never materialized.[62] Sikorski's firm

---

international forum. In the meeting of the Council of Ministers on 28 February 1942, he argued: 'The Declaration (…) anticipates the establishment of eight-power co-operation committees. Poland will through those committees be able to promote her theses as to the future reconstruction of Europe. Such problems as the German one, the reconstruction and economic development of the continent, improvement of the living standard of the working masses (…) will be for the committees to work on. The proposed solutions will have broad publicity and influence on the position of England and America, as they will be backed by the authority of eight Allied states'. See Minutes of the meeting of the Council of Ministers on 28 February and 3 March 1942, IPMS PRM-K. 102/43d, leaves 48–49. PPRM, vol. IV, 157.

57 *Ibidem.*

58 TNA, FO/371/30871/C1544/1543/62.

59 Hułas, *Goście*, 295.

60 Made on 26 May 1942, the Twenty-Year Mutual Assistance Agreement Between the United Kingdom and the Union of Soviet Socialist Republics was a consequence of the British-Soviet Agreement of 12 February 1941 and accession of the USSR to the anti-Nazi coalition; https://avalon.law.yale.edu/wwii/brsov42.asp (accessed 5 May 2024).

61 TNA, FO/371/30871/C1544/1543/62.

62 In May 1942, General Sikorski asked Raczyński to contact Allied governments once again about a joint declaration. In a meeting with Anthony Eden on 16 July 1942, Sikorski

stance against USSR and on the issue of the Polish borders, which never gained strong support from the USA, caused diplomatic tensions with the USSR. The fear of being suspected of pursuing an anti-Soviet policy ultimately brought the demise of General Sikorski's concept of 'political unification of continental Allies'.[63,64]

Despite the ultimate failure of the plans of a joint political declaration by the occupied states, the cooperation initiated around the concept proved to be important in the establishment of closer ties among the governments-in-exile in London in the longer term. In a modified form, the assumptions of the contemplated eight-power declaration were adopted by the émigré governments in May 1943, with the creation of an *Entente des Parlaments des Pays Occupés* – Union of Deputies of the Occupied Countries in London.[65] The goals of that assembly included fostering cooperation for the benefit of post-war reconstruction of Europe on economic, social and political planes, as well

---

proposed the establishment of a committee composed of delegates of governments-in-exile, without any representatives of the United Kingdom, USSR, or the USA. The committee would be working on tasks relating to post-war economic planning. That proposal, too, failed to win the approval of the Foreign Office. On 18 August 1942, Józef Retinger, together with Kulski and Raczyński, held a breakfast for representatives of the governments of Greece, Belgium, the Netherlands, and Yugoslavia. During that meeting, the decision was made to resume the works on a declaration by the occupied states with regard to the terms of their post-war cooperation and that working meetings among Allied prime ministers and ministers of foreign affairs were to be the preferred form of contact. Hułas, *Goście*, 296–297.

63 Hułas, *Goście*, 302.

64 More on that topic see: Milan Hodža, *Federation in Central Europe. Reflections and reminiscences* (London: Jarrolds 1942), Piotr Wandycz, *Czechoslovak-Polish Confederation and the Great Powers, 1940–1943* (Westport: Greenwood Press 1979), Ivan Štovíček, Jaroslav Valenta (eds.), *Czechoslovak-Polish Confederation of the Estabilishment of Confederation and Alliance* (Prague: The Institute of History, Academy of Sciences of the Czech Republic 1995).

65 The *Entente des Parlaments des Pays Occupés* was the initiative of the President of the Belgian Senate, Robert Gillon. The committee held its first meeting on 3 May 1943, attended by representatives of Belgium, Czechoslovakia, French National Committee, Yugoslavia, Luxembourg, the Netherlands, and Norway. Greece and Poland acceded in June 1943. Members on behalf of the Polish government were: Władysław Raczkiewicz, Stanisław Mikołajczyk, Wacław Komarnicki, General Józef Haller, Jan Stańczyk, Jan Kwapiński, Karol Popiel, Marian Seyda, Stanisław Grabski, Fr Kaczyński, Adam Pragier, Adam Ciołkosz, Bohdan Winiarski, Stanisław Stroński, Tadeusz Bielecki, Edward Dubanowicz, Adam Żółtowski, August Zaleski, and Bronisław Kuśnierz. *Cf.* Note by Godfrey, 16 June 1943, TNA FO 371.34399/ C6951, *List of members of Entente des Parlamentaires des Pays Occupés* TNA FO 371/34399/ C7673/553/62.

as re-establishment of democratic rule in the states occupied by the Third Reich, and guarantees of political rights and freedoms for their citizens.[66]

The tightening of cooperation among the governments-in-exile led to the establishment of numerous expert bodies working on topics linked to a broad spectrum of issues relating to post-war reconstruction, war-crimes policy, and their joint informational campaign in the United Kingdom and Unites States on Nazi crimes and situation in occupied territories.

The spring of 1942 saw the creation of an Inter-Allied Commission on the Punishment of War Crimes. In April 1942, the Polish government hosted a conference of nine occupied states for a discussion of instruments by which to implement the Declaration of St. James's Palace.[67] In August 1942, the Inter-Allied Committee for the Study of German Activities was established with Michal Potulicki as secretary. The Committee's focus was on analysing German influence in neutral and Allied states, in particular the opponents to the Nazi regime, the exiled 'Good Germans' and their political agenda. During the first weeks, the representatives of Czechoslovakia compiled a report on the activities of nineteen German refugee organizations, and the Belgians one on German émigré publications.[68] The analyses also studied British and American organizations and media sympathetic to the German cause.[69] Identifying and countering German influence and preventing its possible dominant role in Europe after the war were essential aspects of cooperation in this forum. The matter was also discussed in a meeting of prime ministers and ministers of foreign affairs organized by the Belgian government on 15 October 1942, with Anthony Eden also in attendance. The agenda included material aid for occupied countries, proceedings of the Leith-Ross committee, and terms of a future peace treaty with Germany. Particular attention was given to the problem of the German crimes in the occupied territories. General Sikorski stressed the mass-scale extermination of the Jews in Poland, giving the number of casualties at 10,000 daily. The Polish government appealed to the Great Powers for retaliatory measures such as retorsions against German nationals present in the territory of the United States.[70] However, the lack of support doomed the project to failure.[71] The British took up the question of 'two Germanys' and

66 Resolution of the Union of Deputies of the Occupied Countries, 3 May 1943, TNA FO 371.34399/ C6951/553/62.

67 Note by Makins following his meeting with George Kaeckenbeck, 8 April 1942, TNA, FO. 371/30915/ C3773.

68 IPMS, AXII.88D, leaf 287.

69 Fleming, *In the Shadow*, 109.

70 Note by Athony Eden, 15 October 1942, TNA, FO/371/30871/C9942/2279/G.

71 *Ibidem.*

inclusion of German liberal and democratic circles – especially those active in the United States and in the United Kingdom – in Allied propaganda efforts to counterbalance the negative image of Germany as a nation morally burdened with the guilt of Nazi crimes and accountability for them.[72]

In order to improve the co-ordination of different expert groups and cyclical meetings among the prime ministers and ministers of foreign affairs of the occupied states, a Committee of Ministers of Foreign Affairs was formed in autumn 1942. It was deemed expedient for the cooperation of the governments-in-exile to continue, especially the information campaign.[73] The Committee of Ministers of Foreign Affairs inaugurated its works on 23 October 1942 with Edward Raczyński chairing[74] and Władysław Kulski as secretary. Raczyński's intention was for the Committee's works to include the co-ordination of the activities of all of the working groups of governments of occupied states, as well as designs of the economic reconstruction of Europe, the common informational campaigns of the governments-in-exile, and retaliatory measures against states 'guilty of war crimes'.[75]

The Polish ambassador's proposal was accepted, though some questioned the need of an Economic Committee, given the existence of a Committee of Treasury Ministers under the auspices of the British government. The decision was made for the Committee of Ministers of Foreign Affairs to proceed in subcommittees for topics relating to the war (working groups).[76] A *Comité Interallié pour l'étude de l'Armistice* – Inter-Allied Committee for Armistice Terms – was created to address problems linked to the 'evacuation of occupied territories, repatriation of prisoners-of-war, political prisoners, forced labourers, (…) restitution of property confiscated by the occupiers',[77] demilitarization of Germany, and its division into occupation zones.[78] Moreover, the existing Inter-Allied Committee for the Study of German Activities and Inter-Allied Committee for the Suppression of War Crimes were incorporated into the Committee of Ministers of Foreign Affairs. There were also plans for add-

72 *Ibidem.*

73 Report from a meeting of Prime Ministers and Ministers of Foreign Affairs of continental Allies, IPMS PRM 81. 6/1.

74 In another meeting, on 4 November 1942, the Committee – at Raczyński's motion – adopted the principle that its president would be elected every three months on a rotating basis. Minutes of the meeting of the Committee of Allied Ministers of Foreign Affairs, 4 November 1942, IPMS, PRM 81/6/2.

75 *Ibidem*, leaf 10.

76 *Ibidem*, leaves 7–9.

77 Hułas, *Goście*, 299.

78 TNA FO 371/34399/ C11553

itional three subcommittees for retorsions (retaliatory measures), propaganda, and the post-war economy.[79]

Closer cooperation among the Allied governments also led to the creation of the Inter-Allied Information Committee in 1942. It was a counterpart of the United Nations Information Board in New York, co-ordinated by the British Ministry of Information. The Committee's tasks included 'preparation of news an cables on Allied activities (…), arrangements for the world-wide publicity of special material (…), preparation, publication and distribution of Inter-Allied publications', as well as staging exhibitions on topics such as the situation in the occupied countries, and providing support for Allied states' media campaigns.[80]

5 The Inter-allied Commission on the Punishment of War Crimes

The first expert committee created by the states signatory of the Declaration of St. James's Palace, incorporated into the structures of the Committee of Ministers of Foreign Affairs in autumn 1942, was the Inter-Allied Commission on the Punishment of War Crimes (*Commission Interalliée pour la Répression des Crimes de Guerre*). The Commission was headed by Georges Kaeckelbeck, legal advisor to the Belgian Ministry of Justice, with Polish representative Michał Potulicki as secretary. Its members were: Victor Bodson, Minister of Justice of Luxembourg; Erik Colban, Secretary of the Ministry of Foreign Affairs of Norway; Georges Kaeckenbeck, legal advisor to the Ministry of Foreign Affairs of Belgium; Władysław Kulski; Raymond Offroy; Michał Potulicki; Adolf Procházka, legal advisor to the Czechoslovak MFA; Jean Romanos, Councillor of the Embassy of the Kingdom of Greece in London; Georges Schommer, Secretary General of the MFA of Luxembourg; Edouard Star-Bussman, Chief of the Justice Division in the Dutch MFA; and Charles Tschoffen.[81]

Because of the scope of its tasks and duties, Inter-Allied Commission on the Punishment of War Crimes is viewed as the prototype of the United Nations War Crimes Commission, subsequently created in the autumn of 1943. The Inter-Allied Commission began its works in the spring of 1942, and they con-

79 It could not be ascertained, however, whether the groups were in fact formed. Letter from William Strang to Oswald Scott, 30 March 1943, TNA FO 371/34399/ C3164.

80 Communicate of the Inter-Allied Information Committee; 15 April 1943, TNA FO 371/ 34399/ C4411.

81 List of members of the Inter-Allied Commission for War Crimes, TNA FO 371/34399/ C11553.

tinued until August 1943, which is when the governments of the United Kingdom and of the United States organized the works of the United Nations Commission for Investigation of War Crimes (later renamed to UNWCC).[82] Among other things, it was responsible for the documentation of the occupying powers' activities; joint statements by governments-in-exile stigmatizing German crimes; informational campaigns; initiatives to solicit the active involvement of the Great Powers in the works; and discussions on the legal aspects of the accountability for war crimes. The Commission's principal goal was to develop practical legal solutions for the implementation of the principles of the Declaration of St. James's Palace. A special questionnaire was designed to address the relevant issues, which included the question of law applicable in war crimes cases and limitations of the Hague Convention of 1907; liability of persons issuing and carrying out orders to commit a war crime; inclusion of the provisions concerning the arrest and trial of Germans in the armistice treaty; distinction between 'national traitors' (collaborators) and German criminals; extension of criminal liability to crimes committed not only against the Allied nationals but also against the German Jews, as well as technical aspects of investigating war crimes, collecting evidence, finding and arresting the accused, and bringing them to trial before a competent tribunal.[83]

In summer 1942, through the efforts of the Inter-Allied Commission, the text of the Declaration of St. James's Palace was released in print as part of a brochure published under the auspices of the British Ministry of Information under the title *Punishment for War Crimes. The Inter-Allied Declaration Signed at St. James's Palace London on 13th January 1942 and Relative Documents*. It was followed by a printed report titled *Situation dans les pays occupés par l'enemi*, documenting the intensifying German terror, crimes against civilians, and mass extermination of the Jews in countries occupied by the Third Reich.[84] The report, with diplomatic notes attached, was distributed to the governments of the United States, United Kingdom, USSR, and the Holy See, and

---

82 Minister Raczyński was notified of the termination of the Commission's works by Michał Potulicki: 'the American-[British] initiative in question [Fact Finding Commission] came to life as a result of the action of the Inter-Allied Committee of nine European states in London (St. James Palace Conference 1942), in the form of President Roosevelt's response to the appeal of the same states from August 1942. In the light of the contemplated expansion of the action in the matter of punishment for war criminals, so-called *Commission* Interalliée pour la Répression des Crimes de Guerre (…) has meanwhile terminated its works – anticipating further developments'. See Note for the Minister of Foreign Affairs, 30 July 1943, AIPN GK 159.1, leaf 361.

83 *History of the UNWCC*, 92.

84 'Situation dans les pays occupés par l'enemi', report, AAN 2/133/0/6//44, leaves 321–342.

pending the powers' position on the matter, its contents were not to be made public knowledge.[85] On 22 July 1942, the note to the British government was delivered by the ambassador of Norway and *chargé d'affairs* of Greece, and the one to the President of the United States on 30 July 1942 by the representatives of the Netherlands, Yugoslavia, and Luxembourg. The contents of the notes addressed to the Western Allies were nearly identical. Both mentioned reprisals:

> The invader's acts of oppression and terrorism have recently developed to such an extent and assumed such forms as to arouse the fear that, as the defeat of the enemy countries approaches, the regime of occupation will assume an ever more barbarous and merciless character, not excluding the extermination of whole groups of people.
>
> The signatories to the Inter-Allied Declaration of January 13th 1942 are therefore convinced that only very definite steps by the most powerful among the Allies can exert a deterrent influence.
>
> The Allied Ministers (…) express their firm hope that His Britannic Majesty's Government, whose Prime Minister, Mr. Winston Churchill, as early as October 25th 1941, included the punishment of war crimes among the principal war aims of the Allied countries, will take all measures, which they may consider timely in order to save innumerable innocent lives in the territories occupied by the enemy.[86]

On 23 July 1942, representatives of the French National Committee and Czechoslovakia appealed to Soviet authorities for a serious warning to war criminals:

> (…) the above-mentioned Governments, anxious to spare, as much as possible the population of invaded countries trials more terrible than those already endured, and relying on the spirit of solidarity of all the United Nations in the face of a menace which is in reality nothing else than an inhuman method of forcing nations, against their will, to contribute to the enemy war effort or of extorting acts of adhesion to the so-called " new order," have decided to send an urgent appeal to the President of the Council of the People's Commissars of the Union of Soviet Socialist Republics, to give a solemn warning to the guilty.[87]

85 Ibidem.
86 *History of the* UNWCC, 93.
87 *Ibidem.*

A pivotal element of the information campaign jointly pursued by the governments of the occupied states was the attempt to motivate the Great Powers to take action to restrain the occupying powers' policy of extermination and to order retorsions against the German Reich. Due to requests arriving from occupied Poland, Polish diplomats repeatedly raised the issue in their correspondence with British and American authorities in the first half of 1942.

General Sikorski's journey to the USA in spring 1942 provided an opportunity to renew appeals for an intervention of the Great Powers. In a meeting with Sumner Welles, the Polish Prime Minister informed the Undersecretary of Stat about 'demands of the Polish public opinion in the homeland for the [great] powers, and especially the United States, to use all measures to halt the wave of terror that the Germans ha[d] released with redoubled force in Polish territories. The Poles expect[ed] the United States to opt for reprisals as the most effective measure'.[88]

In his letter to Winston Churchill, on 22 June 1942, Władysław Sikorski insisted that the protests and warnings of possible future retaliation against the perpetrators of the German crimes had not achieved their expected results. The Polish Prime Minister requested the United Nations to take all measures available to put a stop to the German atrocities and manifest the solidarity and determination of the Allied states in the implementation of the retaliatory measures mentioned in the warnings.[89] Demands for the immediate use of direct retaliation were also addressed to the British authorities, in June and July 1942, by President Edvard Beneš and Czechoslovak diplomats, as an indispensable response to the destruction of villages Lidice and Ležáky in June 1942 in retaliation for the assassination of Reinhard Heydrich, the Acting Reich Protector of Bohemia and Moravia.[90]

The pressure exerted by both governments resulted in Winston Churchill's raising of the topic of the accountability of war criminals during his visit to Washington, D.C., in June 1942, and in the establishment of the United Nations Commission on Atrocities.[91] In July 1942, a discussion was held in the British

88 IPMS, PRM 71, doc. 4, leaves 34–40. Report on General Sikorski's conversation with the Undersecretary of States, Sumner Welles, 25 March 1942, PPRM vol. IV, 233. *Cf.* Sumner Welles, 'Memorandum of Conversation, by the Acting Secretary of State', in G. Bernard Noble and E. R. Perkins (eds), *Foreign Relations of the United States: Diplomatic Papers, 1942, Europe*, Volume III (Washington, D.C.: 1961), 860C.002/3–2542, available through https://history.state.gov/historicaldocuments/frus1942v03/d117 (accessed 10 August 2024).

89 General Sikorski's letter to Anthony Eden, 22 June 1942, TNA PREM 4/100/13.

90 On 4 June 1942.

91 Note by Winston Churchill, 'Treatment of War Criminals', 1 July 1942, TNA PREM4/100/10, leaf 666.

War Office on guidelines for a British position on the matter of criminal responsibility for war crimes, and a Cabinet Committee on the Treatment of War Criminals was established under the leadership of Lord High Chancellor Simon.[92] These efforts failed to produce the hoped-for declaration of reprisals or accession to the Declaration of St. James's Palace. The leaders of the United Kingdom and of the Unites States clearly distanced themselves from such demands in their responses to the notes submitted by the governments-in-exile and reports prepared in the summer of 1942 by the Inter-Allied Commission on the Punishment of War Crimes.

The first response arrived from over the ocean. In his address of 21 August 1942, Franklin D. Roosevelt declared the US government's openness to all reports coming from credible sources, and that the government's goal after the war would be to 'make appropriate use of the information and evidence in respect to the barbaric crimes of the invaders, in Europe and Asia'. He concluded: 'It seems only fair that they shall have to stand in courts of law in the very countries they are now oppressing and answer for their acts'.[93] Speaking to the House of Commons on 8 September 1942, Winston Churchill referred to President Roosevelt's words in an emphatic address:

> I wish most particularly to identify the British Government and the House of Commons with the solemn words which have been lately used by the President of the United States, namely, that those who are guilty of the Nazi crimes will have to stand up before tribunals in every land where their atrocities have been committed, in order that an indelible warning may be given to future ages and that successive generations of men may say 'so perish all who do the like again'.[94]

The most resolute answer came from the USSR, in a note of 14 October 1942:

> The Soviet Government approves and shares the just desire expressed in the collective note received that those guilty of the crimes indicated shall be handed over to judicial courts and prosecuted, and that the sentence passed on them shall be put into execution. (...) The Soviet Government consider it essential to hand over without delay to the

92 Kochavi, *Prelude*, 31.

93 Cited after *History of the UNWCC*, 94. See also: *Punishment for War Crimes* (2) *Collective Notes presented to the Governments of Great Britain, the USSR and the USA* (London: 1942).

94 *History of the UNWCC*, 94.

> courts of the special international tribunal and to punish according to all the severity of the criminal code, any of the leaders of Fascist Germany who, in the course of the war, have fallen into the hands of States fighting against Hitlerite Germany.[95]

6 The Information Campaign of 1942: Towards a Common War-Crimes Policy of the Allies

The Declaration of St. James's Palace was to open the path to influencing not only the Western Allies' position on the problem of criminal responsibility for war crimes but also the international public opinion. That was of especial importance in the light of the expectation of the Polish conspiratorial resistance that General Sikorski's cabinet intervene to stop the progressive intensification of the German terror and the extermination of the Jews, of which the authorities in London had been receiving reports since late 1941.[96] According to Adam Puławski, in January 1942, the Information Division of the Bureau for Information and Propaganda of the Union of Armed Struggle/Home Army (ZWZ-AK) analysed British press reports on the situation in occupied Poland and took a critical view on the grounds of fragmentariness, lack of precise information on the numbers of the victims, the systemic nature of the German policy of extermination, mass persecutions of the Jews and murders of Soviet prisoners-of-war. In that connection, 'Propaganda Postulates' (*Postulaty w sprawie propagandy*) were forwarded to the Government-in-Exile in London.[97] Attempts to exert pressure on the Western powers to use reprisals against Nazi Germany intensified in the spring of 1942, when the consequences of Wannsee Conference had already become known. At the time, London received a flood of reports about Operation Reinhard, new extermination camps (Bełżec and Sobibór) in the Lublin region, deportations and mass killings of Poles and Jews, and renewed forcible induction in the German Armed Forces.[98]

In parallel with the intensification of media activities, the Polish government's works on the documentation of the war crimes, co-ordinated since 1941 by the 'German Division' ('German Archive'), set on a new course in early 1942. Stanisław Mikołajczyk, in charge of the Ministry of the Interior at

95 *Ibidem.*
96 Puławski, *W obliczu Zagłady*, 46–58.
97 *Ibidem*, 71–83.
98 *Ibidem*, 324–39.

the time, held regular meetings with Frank Savery from the British embassy to the Polish government and former consul general in Warsaw in 1939. Mikołajczyk provided Savery with reports and documentation materials from occupied Poland, such as the collection of shocking photographs from ghettoes in Poland, as well as prisoner-of-war camps for Soviet captives.[99] On the basis of materials received from Mikołajczyk, Savery compiled in June 1942 his own report on the situation in Poland, which the British ambassador, Cecil Dormer, forwarded to Anthony Eden on 13 June 1942.[100] Although Mikołajczyk consistently campaigned for the use of Polish materials in British media, information about the Nazi extermination policy in occupied territories was not always given proper attention. Some Polish reports, such as those presenting detailed facts on concentration camps, were rejected from publication by the British press.[101] As already mentioned, on 25 March 1942, during a visit to the United States, General Sikorski submitted to Sumner Welles (Undersecretary of State) a memorandum on the new wave of violence unleashed by the German occupation authorities in Poland. It expressed Polish society's hope 'for the United States to take all necessary steps to stop the renewed waves of German terror in Polish territories' and for the use of reprisals as the most effective measure.[102]

Near the end of May, Polish authorities received the reports of the Government Delegate for Poland, of 10 and 12 May 1942, concerning the new wave of terror in occupied Poland, as well as a letter from the Bund, the Jewish socialist party and one of the pillars of civil and military underground resistance in occupied Poland, concerning the persecution of the Jews, of 26 April 1942.[103]

---

99 In June 1942, a collection of photographs from ghettoes and prisoner-of-war camps for Soviet captives in occupied Poland reached London. The photographs depict, among others, mass graves, piles of corpses, and starved inhabitants of ghettoes. Photographs from prisoner-of-war camps were captioned with comments such as: 'Killing off of wounded fugitives from the Rembertów camp by German military police'; 'Carts arriving for the corpses of prisoners'; 'Woman hanged for guerrilla activities'; 'Corpses of Russian prisoners shot during [an alleged] attempt to escape'; 'German soldier treads on corpses of Soviet prisoners' – TNA FO.371.31097/C954, TNA FO.371.31097/C12243, TNA FO.371.31097/C12412; Report from the inter-ministerial conference for German affairs, IPMS A.XII.1/88D pt 1, leaf 16. According to the Ministry of the Interior's estimates, approximately half a million Soviet prisoners of war were being held in camps in occupied Poland at the beginning of 1942.

100 *Cf.* TNA FO.371.31097/C5951.

101 Fleming, *In the Shadow,* 74–77; Engel, *In the Shadow.*

102 IPMS, PRM 71, doc. 4, leaves 34–40. Report on General Sikorski's conversation with the Undersecretary of State, Sumner Welles, 25 March 1942, PPRM vol. IV, 233.

103 '26 April 1942. Letter from Bund politicians to the Polish authorities in London on the situation of Jews in occupied Poland' in Długołęcki (ed.), *Confronting,* 326–329. More extensively on the reports from Poland in 1942 topic see: Walter Laqueur *The terrible*

It outlined the stages and methods of liquidation of the Jews in occupied Polish territories from July 1941, and provided facts on extermination camps Auschwitz, Chełmno (Kulmhof), Sobibór, and Bełżec, putting the estimated number of victims at 700,000. The letter raised the alarm that '[m]illions of Polish citizens of Jewish nationality face[d] immediate annihilation', requesting Polish authorities to influence the Allied leaders with a view to the immediate use of reprisals against German citizens and against the 'fifth column' in Allied countries.[104] Expectations of a 'categorical demand of immediate cessation of the barbaric excesses of the Gestapo and German administration in the occupied territories' and '[promise of] as severe retorsions as possible, as provided by international law' were also voiced in the Delegate's letter of 12 May 1942.[105] In a letter of 1 February 1942, the Government Delegate for Poland, Cyryl Ratajski, sent to London a set of guidelines for propaganda activities to assist the homeland. Those included 'constant (…) condemnation of Gestapo bestiality' and promises of 'the strictest accounting for that with the Germans after the war'; communications in the press and radio to the effect that the names of the criminals and their superiors '[we]re being recorded, and, they w[ould] be punished with due severity after the war', as well as announcement of reprisals against German political prisoners in Allied countries.[106]

The response to the new wave of terror in Poland was discussed at meetings of the Ministers' Political Committee and of the National Council on 26 May 1942 and of the Council of Ministers on 6 and 4 June 1942.[107] The Council of Ministers tasked Minister Raczyński with 'seeing to the completion of the cam-

---

secret : suppression of the truth about Hilter's "final solution" (Boston: Little, Brown 1980), 104–117. Dariusz Stola, 'Early News of the Holocaust from Poland'. *Holocaust and Genocide Studies* 11, 1–27. Puławski, *The Polish Government.*

104 Letter from the Bund concerning the persecution of the Jews, 11 May 1942, IPMS Kol. 183/27, no pagination. Mentioned in Długołęcki (ed.), Confronting, 329, fn. 66: 'In this publication the letter from the Bund is published with the date of 26 April 1942, according to the date hand-written below the text of the document. There are, however, several other versions of it, at times dated 11 May 1942 or simply May 1942. The copies are kept, among other places, in Yad Vashem Archives, the Hoover Institution, as well as in the Central Archives of Modern Records in Warsaw (AAN), in the collection Delegatura Rządu RP na Kraj, 202/XV-2, where a handwritten annotation can be found on the document: "Letter from the Bund from 11 May 42 on the persecution of Jews, sent with the correspondence of 21 May, No. 37."'.

105 Letter from the Government Delegate for Poland, 12 May 1942, IPMS Kol. 183/27.

106 Letter from the Delegate of the Government for Poland, 1 February, 1942, IPMS Kol. 183/27, no pagination.

107 IPMS, PRM-K. 102/47, leaves 2–11: Minutes of the meeting of the Council of the Ministers, 6 June 1942, PPRM vol. IV, 330.

paign for a joint statement from all Allies on punishment for the guilty'.[108] An address of the National Council of 10 June implored European parliaments to condemn the Nazi crimes. At the same time, the Council of Ministers approved a protest note to Allied governments, highlighting the most egregious acts of oppression committed against the population of occupied Poland: compulsory drafting of Polish citizens into the German Armed Forces; growing number of death sentences passed by special courts; displacement of the Polish population from cities and settlement of German nationals there; persecution of the intellectual circles, arrests and kills of social and political leaders; mass killings in concentration camps; and extermination operations directed against the Jews. '[I]n cities such as Wilno [Vilnius], Lwów [Lviv], Kołomyja [Kolomya], Stanisławów [Ivano Frankivsk], Lublin, Rzeszów, Miechów, tens of thousands of Jews [we]re slaughtered'.[109] The note emphasized that the acts of terror constituted violations of international law and that their perpetrators had to be held criminally responsible – 'this principle should become the guiding principle of the Allied war policy[110]'. The appeal was made for the governments and the public opinion of Allied states to lend their support to the fight against the German terror and to the international informational campaign about the extermination of the population of the occupied territories:

> The public opinion of free nations must be alarmed anew by the German terror in Europe, while the retaliation on the part of the Allies should be once again brought to the fore and immediately applied, wherever possible. (…) The Germans and the Axis powers infected with their frenzy of terror must learn that their crimes shall not go unpunished. Otherwise, they are going to intensify the terror in the occupied countries. The awareness of the punishment for the crimes of terror must penetrate the opinion of the German people and their allies.[111]

General Sikorski presented the contents of the note in a radio address on 9 June 1942, of which an English translation was forwarded to the Allied gov-

108 Minutes of the meeting of the Council of Ministers, 6 June 1942, IPMS, PRM-K. 102/47, leaves 2–11 PPRM vol. IV, 331.

109 '2 June 1942 [?]. Draft of a Government note on the situation in occupied Poland' (doc. no. 190) in Długołęcki (ed), *Confronting*, 340. See fn. 73 on 341 concerning the date (2 June or 6 June). *Cf.* IPMS, PRM-K.102/47a, leaves 12–14. *Cf.* PPRM, vol. IV, 333–334.

110 *Ibidem*, 341.

111 *Ibidem*, 334.

ernments.[112] Polish President Władysław Raczkiewicz requested the British support on 10 June 1942 in a conversation with Ambassador Dormer. During a meeting between representatives of governments-in-exile and King George VI of the United Kingdom, on 14 June 1942, Edward Raczyński proposed that Allied air forces execute bombing raids in retaliation against the Reich. A special edition of the Polish Information Centre's bulletin in New York, published on 15 June 1942, presented the most up-to-date information taken from reports of the prosecution of the Jews and situation in ghettoes in occupied Poland.[113] The Polish message of the necessity of putting an end to the German terror and applying retorsions against Germany was reiterated by General Sikorski in his letters to Franklin D. Roosevelt and Winston Churchill of 22 June 1942, during the latter's visit to the United States.[114]

Reports from occupied Poland, including the Delegate's report of 12 May 1942, appealing for immediate retorsions against the German Reich, were forwarded by Raczyński to Eden on 17 and 27 June 1942. Supplementing Raczyński's own correspondence was a report titled 'Statement on German Crimes Committed against the Jewish Population in Poland', submitted by Ignacy Schwarzbart to the British chief diplomat on 30 June 1942, reiterating that '[o]nly immediate appropriate steps could deter Hitler from carrying on his criminal action' and protect Poland's population from destruction, in particular the Jews, exposed as they were to complete annihilation.[115] In a meeting of the National Council on 7 July, Stanisław Mikołajczyk rendered an extensive account of the situation in the homeland, including massacres of the Jews (putting the victim count at 200,000, thus below the Bund's estimate),[116] noting the organized and planned nature of the extermination. On the same day, the National Council passed a resolution to supplement the June address to the parliaments of the free nations with 'newly revealed facts of the systematic destruction of the vital strength of the Polish Nation and the planned murder

112 Anthony Eden, 'Treatment of'. Full text of Sikorski's speech reprinted in Polish Ministry of Information and Documentation, *Bestiality...unknown in any previous record of history*, London, Stratton House 1942, 31–35.

113 '15 June 1942. Bulletin by the Polish Information Center in New York: the situation in ghettos in occupied Poland (extract)' (doc. no. 196), in Długołęcki, Confronting, p.352.

114 22 June 1942, letter from Władysław Sikorski to Anthony Eden, TNA PREM 4/100/13.

115 Letter from Edward Raczyński to Anthony Eden, 27 June 1942, TNA FO 371/31097/ C6605, TNA; Ignacy Schwarzbart's report, 'Statement on German Crimes Committed against the Jewish Population in Poland', TNA FO 371/31097/ C7101. Also available at https://www.holocausthistoricalsociety.org.uk/contents/jewishaccounts/ignacyschwarzbart.html (accessed 9 August 2024).

116 On this topic, see Stola, *Nadzieja*, 160.

of almost the entire Jewish population' in Poland, and supported the Polish government's endeavours to ensure that the crimes would not go unpunished.[117]

The full texts of the resolution of the Polish National Council, General Sikorski's radio speech of 6 June 1942, and reports from occupied Poland were published in English in a special publication titled *Bestiality...unknown in any previous record of history*, issued on the occasion of the Polish government's press conference 'German Terror in Poland' at the British Ministry of Information on 9 July 1942.[118] Participants included the British Minister of Information, Brendan Bracken, and the director of the Ministry's news division, John Brebner, as well as representatives of Polish government: Stanisław Mikołaczyk, Stanisław Stroński, Witold Kulerski (Secretary of the Praesidium of the National Council), Fr. Marian Kaczyński, and Jewish deputies to the Council: Ignacy Schwarzbart and Szmul Zygielbojm. Mikołajczyk, Schwarzbart and Zygielbojm outlined the most important data on the progressively intensifying Nazi persecutions in Poland and planned extermination of the Jewish population, along with a list of cities, towns, and villages where mass pogroms and deportations took place. They also showed a map of Europe with the locations of twenty-three concentration camps, including information on the mass murders committed in the camps at Bełżec (Belzec) and Trawniki with the use of poisonous gasses.[119]

The 'German Terror in Poland' conference was among the many media addresses and protest campaigns hoped to stop the German extermination policy, which were pursued in the summer and autumn of 1942 together with other governments-in-exile, international Jewish organizations, members of the Inter-Allied Commission on the Punishment of War Crimes, and with a considerable support by the British Labour Party.[120] Reports dealing with the persecution of civilians throughout occupied Europe were published under the auspices of the Inter-Allied Information Committee in 1942 in a series of nine brochures titled 'Conditions in Occupied Territories': *The Axis system of hostages* (No. 1); *Rationing under Axis rule* (No. 2); *Religious persecution* (No. 3); *Axis oppression of education (No. 4); The penetration of German capital into*

117 '7 July 1942. Resolution of the National Council on the German activity in occupied territories' (doc. no. 210) in Długołęcki (ed.), *Confronting*, 379. *Cf.* IPMS PRM-K. 18/4

118 Polish Ministry of Information and Documentation, *Bestiality...unknown in any previous record of history* (London: Stratton House 1942)

119 *Ibidem*, 13.

120 Fleming, *In the Shadow of the Holocaust*, 95–97.

Europe (No. 5); *Persecution of the Jews* (No. 6); *Women under Axis rule* (No. 7); *Slave labour and deportation* (No. 8); and *The law* (No.9).[121]

An international campaign of information and protest on an enormous scale was organized in the summer of 1942 by the government of Czechoslovakia, with appeals for retorsions against the Germans for the mass killings and resettlements of the inhabitants of Lidice and Ležáky after the assassination of the (Acting) Reich Protector of Bohemia and Moravia, Reinhard Heydrich, on 4 June 1942.[122] One of the elements of the campaign was a successful fundraiser for the reconstruction of Lidice – *Lidice shall live.*[123]

Despite Polish government's constant contact with the staff at Foreign Office and constant exchange of information, as well as intensive media campaigning, the calls for retorsions and for the Western Allies to take steps to halt the German extermination policy were only met with a partial success. On the break of June and July 1942, the combination of the intensified informational campaign about German crimes, documentation works of the Inter-Allied Commission on the Punishment of War Crimes, and pressure from the exiled governments have influenced the British and American position on the necessity to coordinate the documentation and investigation of war crimes.

On 22 June 1942, Anthony Eden appraised the cabinet members of a memorandum titled 'Treatment of War Criminals', prepared by Crown lawyers on his orders.[124] It was an attempt at a response to the demands of the governments-in-exile and to General Sikorski's radio speech of 9 June 1942, in which the Polish Prime Minister had relayed reports on the intensification of German terror in Poland and insisted that the keeping of records on the criminals, promises of severe punishment and use of retorsions had to become the main guidelines of Allied policy.[125]

Winston Churchill, during his visit to the United States in June 1942 and talks with Franklin Delano Roosevelt, supported the establishment of the

121 Inter-Allied Information Committee, Conditions in Occupied Territories (London: HMSO, 1942).

122 See; 'Allied People and Retribution'. *Central European Observer* 19 (1942), 21–24; v. Lingen, Crimes against, 217.

123 *Lidice shall live* (London: Chechoslovak-British Friendship Club 1942); Alan Gerrard, *The Path to Lidice: And the Legacy of the Lidice Shall Live Campaign* (Independent Publishing Network 2022); Czechoslovak Ministry of Foreign Affairs Department of Information, *German Massacres in Occupied Czechoslovakia Following the Attack on Reinhard Heydrich* (London 1942), Jan Lanicek, '"To get a refusal would result in an unfortunate loss of prestige": The Czechoslovak Government-in-Exile and the Holocaust'. *Holocaust Studies: A Journal of Culture and History* 13 (2008), 119–141.

124 Anthony Eden, 'Treatment of'; see also: Kochavi, *Prelude*, 28.

125 Eden, 'Treatment'.

United Nations Commission on Atrocities.[126] On 1 July 1942, the British Prime Minister referred the memorandum on that subject prepared by Roosevelt's advisor, Harry Hopkins, to debate in the War Cabinet, advocating for the incorporation of its theses into the British government's official position.[127] The tasks placed before the United Nations Commission on Atrocities were similar to the scope of activities of the Inter-Allied Commission on the Punishment of War Crimes. This primarily means processing the evidence of atrocities in the occupied territories to inform the public opinion about the nature of the crimes and the identity of the perpetrators and to deter the perpetrators from committing further violations of international law. The plan was to appoint eminent legal scholars to the Commission and to task it with investigating war crimes, gathering the evidence, interrogating witness and submitting reports to the United Nations, including the names of the perpetrators.[128]

The War Cabinet discussed the proposal in meetings held on 1 and 6 July 1942. There was agreement as to the need for an international investigative commission to handle investigations into war crimes, but its responsibilities and powers were to be limited to the gathering of data and fact-finding (hence Fact-Finding Commission). The inclusion of tasks relating to substantive or procedural points of law in war-crime cases was opposed. The suggestions of Eden's memorandum of 22 June 1942 to abandon any plans of creation of an international justice system and instead to remand the war criminals to the jurisdiction of the respective states, in order to be judged on the basis of the existing provisions of domestic law, were also accepted.[129]

In line with Eden's concept, it was necessary to divide war criminals into two categories – 'enemy leaders', such as Adolf Hitler, Heinrich Himmler or Joseph Goebbels, of whom it could be said: 'the guilt of such individuals is so black, that they fall outside and go beyond the scope of any judicial process',[130] and their subordinates, the lower-rung criminals, to be judged by the domestic courts of the Allied states. Proposals to establish an international criminal court or to create new provisions of international criminal law for the purposes of post-war trials were firmly rejected. In Eden's opinion, pursuing that course of action would have delayed the whole procedure, whereas the British

126 Kochavi, *Prelude*, 28.

127 Note by Winston Churchill, 'Treatment of War Criminals', 1 July 1942, TNA PRO, PREM1/100/10, leaf 666.

128 'A United Nations Commission on Atrocities', memorandum TNA, PRO, PREM1/100/10.

129 Eden, 'Treatment of'.

130 *Ibidem*.

authorities' priority should be to ensure swift convictions in the immediate aftermath of the war.[131]

Lord Chancellor Simon was not completely on board with the War Cabinet's guidelines, noting that the abandonment of the idea of putting the 'enemy leaders' on trial would be a disappointment to the continental Allies.[132] He concurred with the view that, because of the number of states concerned and the volume of domestic criminal legislation to be heeded in such an undertaking, the establishment of an international criminal tribunal along with suitable legal codifications lacked viability for purely pragmatic reasons. He deemed it necessary to agree with the other Allied governments upon a set of procedures for the war criminals, without excluding the top echelon.[133]

The detailed concept of the United Nations Commission for Atrocities and guidelines of the British government's war-crimes policy were designed by Simon during the works of the Foreign Office War Cabinet Committee on Treatment of War Criminals, established on 6 July 1942. According to the guidelines, the Commission was to be responsible for the documentation of crimes committed against citizens of a United Nations member state (not Axis crimes in general) and for keeping lists of the criminals. Apart from the Four Great Powers – United Kingdom, United States, Soviet Union, and China – the continental Allies and the Dominions were to be represented in the Commission's proceedings. Along with Eden's Lord Chancellor's views, the establishment of an international criminal tribunal was not among the goals of the British policy.[134]

The principles drafted in July 1942 were presented to the governments of the occupied states by Anthony Eden and John Simon on 6 August 1942, in a special conference held by the Foreign Office. Plans of the establishment of a United Nations commission were not communicated in the meeting but only the recommendation of the British government that any information about crimes committed in the occupied territories be recorded.

A detailed discussion of the principles of the policy followed during the meeting of the Inter-Allied Commission on the Punishment of War Crimes on 20 August 1942. The meeting highlighted the differences between the theses of the British policy and the principles postulated by the signatories of the Declaration of St. James's Palace. The key importance of the problem of extradition of war criminals to the success of the trials was appreciated, and atten-

131 *Ibidem.*
132 Lord Simon's letter to Churchill, 6 July 1942, TNA, PRO, PREM1/100/10.
133 *Ibidem.*
134 Kochavi, *Prelude*, 32.

tion was drawn to the need for suitable international treaties and adaptation of domestic laws.[135] Speaking on behalf of the Czechoslovak government, Adolf Procházka argued for the necessity of new codifications with a view to post-war trials. He raised the problem of the lack of norms and sanctions applicable to war-crime cases in Czechoslovak law and the impossibility of compliance with *nullum crimen sine lege, nulla poena sine lege*.[136] He advocated for the development by the Allied states of core principles governing the punishment of war crimes – the definitions of crimes and the penalties to be imposed for them in all countries.[137] Władysław Kulski, in his own speech, drew attention to the one tenet of British policy that was in the closest alignment with the policies of the governments of the occupied states – that a provision for the surrender of war criminals should be included already in the armistice terms. Kulski advocated for requesting the United States, China, and USSR to adopt the principle of extradition of war criminals, citing the deterrent effect.[138] Kulski's suggestion was approved by Malkin and forwarded to the leadership of the Foreign Office.[139]

At the same time, requests for the British authorities to declare an official stance on war-crimes policy were addressed by members of the British Parliament and the intellectual circles and public opinion in the United Kingdom. Near the end of August 1942, Lord Maugham – former Lord Chancellor and member of the International London Assembly – impressed on the British government the urgency of the problem of punishment for war criminals.[140] Speaking in the Lords on 9 September 1942, he recommended specific solutions. Maugham's conclusions differed from the July theses of the War Cabinet. In the light of the practical failure of Articles 227–230 of the Treaty of Versailles and the lack of suitable domestic penal statutes, he stressed the necessity of an international agreement on the principles of the punishment of war crimes being concluded as soon as possible. He saw it as a critical task to come up with some principles concerning jurisdiction, especially with regard to criminals active in multiple countries, as well as German criminals having committed their acts within the territory of the German Reich and against its own citizens. He recommended extending the jurisdic-

---

135 Minutes of the meeting of the Inter-Allied Commission on the Punishment of War Crimes, 20 August 1942, AIPN BU 159.1, leaves 524ff.

136 *Ibidem*.

137 *Ibidem*.

138 Lord Maugham, *Punishment of War Criminals*, TNA FO 371/30918/ C8659/ 61/18.

139 William Malkin (note), 'Treatment of War Criminals', 20 August 1942, TNA FO 371/30918/ C8174/61/18.

140 Kochavi, *Prelude*, 35.

tion of Allied courts to crimes committed on the nationals of a given state also outside of its borders, for example in prisoner-of-war camps, labour camps, and concentration camps located either within the territory of the Third Reich or of an occupied state. Moreover, the Viscount emphasized the need to agree on terms of extradition of the criminals, especially from neutral states, and the necessity of establishing an International Criminal Tribunal for the judgment of the perpetrators of mass-scale crimes committed on nationals of multiple states in more than one country.[141] Due to the British authorities' unpreparedness to elucidate on guidelines and goals of war-crimes policy, and in the light of negotiations with the United States on a joint statement on the inclusion of extradition rules in the armistice terms, attempts were made to delay Maugham's proposed debate in the Lords.

The debate in the Lords on the tenets of the British authorities' war-crimes policy ultimately took place on 7 October 1942. Maugham opened by presenting his recommendations for the principles of responsibility and of an international investigative commission to gather documentation on the Nazi crimes. Lord Chancellor Simon outlined the guidelines of British policy[142] adopted on 30 September 1942 by the Committee for the Treatment of War Criminals – the intention to make a provision in the armistice terms for the surrender of listed war criminals and for the establishment of a United Nations Commission for the Investigation of War Crimes by the British government together with the governments of the United States and other Allied nations.[143] Lord Simon stressed that the Commission's responsibilities should include investigating war crimes committed against the nationals of any of the United Nations member states, the gathering of all available evidence, and the identification of the perpetrators. As he noted, the reason for the establishment of the Commission was not to justify lynching or executions of Axis nationals but, in documented cases, inflict punishment on persons guilty of crimes.[144] Also on 7 October 1942, an official position on the matter of Allied cooperation on war-crimes policy was communicated by Franklin Delano Roosevelt. The US President expressed support for both of the points conveyed by the Brits, as well as his government's readiness to cooperate with other Allies on the establishment of the United Nations Commission for the Investigation of War Crimes. He emphasized that it was not the intention of the

141 Lord Maugham, *Punishment of War Criminals*, TNA FO 371/30918/ C8659/ 61/18.

142 Minutes of the meeting of the War Cabinet Committee on Treatment of War Criminals, 30 September 1942, TNA FO 371/30918/ C9477/ 61/18.

143 *History of the UNWCC*, 111; Cyprian and Sawicki, *Prawo norymberskie*, 118.

144 *History of the UNWCC*, 110.

American or any other Allied authorities to 'resort to mass reprisals'; instead, the intention was to make sure that 'just and sure punishment [would] be meted out to the ringleaders responsible for the organised murder of thousands of innocent persons'.[145] In actuality, the Commission was not formally established until October 1943, with its works *de facto* starting in early 1944.

The unquestionable success of the Polish informational campaign of 1942 was the United Nations Declaration on the Prosecution of Jews, published on 17 December 1942. It marked a response to Jan Karski's report of the extermination of the Jews by the Third Reich, delivered to London in November 1942. Karski (real name Kozielewski) was an emissary of the Polish Government-in-Exile.[146] Since the beginning of the war, he had completed a total of four missions as a courier, personally delivering reports and information from occupied Poland to the government in London and back to the Underground conspiratorial structures. His last mission ended in November 1942, when he arrived in London[147] and presented to the Polish and British authorities a report detailing the situation of the Jews in occupied Poland, the Warsaw Ghetto, liquidation of the ghettoes, mass deportations, and extermination at death camps.[148] A set of documents on the situation in Poland and extermination of Jewish population prepared by Karski and the Polish Underground was delivered to London through intelligence channels in mid-November 1942 and used by the Polish government for the diplomatic campaign. A report issued on 24 November 1942[149] was commented by *The New York Times* on the following day.[150] On 27 November, the Polish National Council, referring to the 'most recent information from Poland', renewed its appeals to the inter-

145 *History of the UNWCC*, 111.

146 Polish Ministry of Foreign Affairs, *The mass extermination of Jews in German occupied Poland: note addressed to the Governments of the United Nations on December 17th, 1942, and other documents / Republic of Poland. Ministry of Foreign Affairs* (New York: 1943) 4–10.

147 Karski arrived in London on 25 November 1942, between 26 and 28 November; he was interrogated by section MI19 of the British Directorate of Military Intelligence (War Office), Fleming, *Auschwitz*, 151–152.

148 Jan Karski, *Story of a Secret State*, Boston 1944; E. Thomas Wood, Stanisław M. Jankowski, *Karski, How One Man Tried to Stop the Holocaust* (New York: John Wiley & Sons 1994); Martin Gilbert, *Auschwitz and the Allies* (London: Michael Joseph 1981), 88–93; *The Karski Report. Report on the attacks on the Jewish ghetto in Warsaw* TNA FO 371/30923 https://www.nationalarchives.gov.uk/education/resources/holocaust/karski-report/.

149 24 November 1942, 'Report by the Government on the situation of the Jewish population in occupied Poland', TNA FO 371/30923, reprinted in: Długołęcki (ed.), *Confronting*, 515–518.

150 Stola, 'Early News', 1; James MacDonald, 'Himmler Programm Kills Polish Jews', *New York Times*, 25 November 1942, 10.

national public for the condemnation of German atrocities and of the extermination of Jews. Upon arriving in the United Kingdom, Jan Karski met with Anthony Eden to acquaint him personally with the contents of his report. In summer 1943, the legendary courier moved to the United States, where he attended meetings with President Roosevelt and representatives of the American administration and gave numerous lectures. He implored the United States to intervene for the sake of saving the Jews from complete extermination, presenting reports from occupied Poland and discussing the activities of the Polish Underground State.[151]

In December 1942, Polish MFA published a diplomatic note based on Karski's report, providing the impulse for the works leading up to the United Nations Declaration on the Prosecution of Jews. The documents concerning those efforts, the text of the Declaration and parts of previous reports on the situation of the Jews in occupied Poland were published in a special MFA brochure titled: 'The mass extermination of Jews in German occupied Poland: note addressed to the Governments of the United Nations on December 17th, 1942, and other documents'.[152] The signatories of the December Declaration were the governments of Poland, Belgium, Czechoslovakia, Greece, the Netherlands, Yugoslavia, Norway, United States, United Kingdom, and USSR, as well as the Free French. They condemned the 'bestial policy of cold-blooded extermination' of European Jews, insisted that those responsible should not be able to escape punishment, and appealed for the 'the necessary practical measures'. The Declaration stated:

> The attention of the Governments (…) has been drawn to numerous reports from Europe that the German authorities, not content with denying to persons of Jewish race in all the territories over which their barbarous rule has been extended the most elementary human rights,

151 In 1944, in the United States, he published his book *Story of a Secret State* (Boston: Houghton Mifflin Co., 1944), describing his mission as the emissary of the Polish government, endeavours to win the Western Allies' support for efforts to protect the population of occupied Poland, including Polish Jews, and the functioning of the Polish Underground conspiracy during the war. Karski's lectures in the United States in 1944–1945 were also accompanied by a travelling exhibition depicting life in occupied Poland, the crimes committed by the Nazis, and the activities of the Polish resistance, titled *Poland's Underground State*, and prepared by the Polish embassy. See also: Thomas Wood, Jankowski, *Karski: how one man tried to stop the Holocaust* (Texas Tech University Press, Gihon River Press 2014); Eugeniusz Smolar (ed.), *Memory and Responsibility: the Legacy of Jan Karski* (Warszawa: Fundacja Edukacyjna Jana Karskiego, Polish History Museum 2015).

152 Ministry of Foreign Affairs, *The mass extermination.*

> are now carrying into effect Hitler's oft-repeated intention to exterminate the Jewish people in Europe. From all the occupied countries Jews are being transported, in conditions of appalling horror and brutality, to Eastern Europe. In Poland, which has been made the principal Nazi slaughter-house, the Ghettoes established by the German invaders are being systematically emptied of all Jews, except a few highly skilled workers required for war industries. (…).
>
> The above-mentioned Governments and the French National Committee condemn in the strongest possible terms this bestial policy of cold-blooded extermination. They declare that such events can only strengthen the resolve of all freedom-loving peoples to overthrow the barbarous Hitlerite tyranny. They reaffirm their solemn resolution to ensure that those responsible for these crimes shall not escape retribution, and to press on with the necessary practical measures to this end.

Following the Declaration, Edward Raczyński resumed his entreaties for retaliatory bombing raids and for retorsions to save the Jewish and Polish populations. During a meeting of the ministers of foreign affairs of Allied countries on 18 January 1942 at the Foreign Office, Raczyński underlined that the retaliatory bombings 'would largely contribute to the public exposure of the German lawlessness and decide of the powers to punish them.'[153] In a further communication he appealed to the British government 'to do all in their powers to prevent further murders' and mass extermination in occupied territories.[154] His efforts bore little result.[155] The informational campaign continued in the subsequent years of the war, especially the first half of 1943 – in connection with the liquidation of Warsaw Ghetto and the Ghetto Uprising,[156] and a new wave of deportations to the concentration camps – or in summer 1944, in the face of persecution and death of tens of thousands of civilians during the Warsaw Uprising. Nevertheless, even then it failed to achieve the anticipated response from the Western Allies. The first decisions concerning the organization of a justice system for war criminals were taken by the United

153 Note from a discussion at the meeting of ministers of foreign affairs of Allied European Countries in the Foreign Office upon invitation from Minister Eden on 18 January 1943, IPMS, A.12.49/141, Długołęcki (ed.), *Confronting*,

154 'Aide Memoire by the Polish Government for the Secretary of State for Foreign Affairs of Great Britain on German Crimes, London, August 5th, 1943', Długołęcki (ed.), *Confronting* (doc. no. 375), 696.

155 On this topic, see Stola, *Nadzieja*, 188–196.

156 Stola, *Nadzieja*; Gilbert, *Auschwitz*.

Kingdom and the United States only in the spring of 1945,[157] which is when the 'immediate retaliation' advocated for in 1942 was no longer a current possibility. The principles of the Wannsee Conference – the so-called Final Solution – had already been implemented, and by that point, most victims of Nazi crimes in Europe had already perished.

---

157 See Kochavi, *Prelude,* 218–222.

CHAPTER 4

Documenting the Crimes

Documentation of crimes committed in occupied Poland was a fundamental element of Sikorski cabinet's accountability strategy. Poland's war-crimes policy stood out due to its systematic approach. This included collecting evidence, developing communication channels with the homeland, consistently exchanging information between the government and representatives in occupied Poland from autumn 1939, and establishing specialized structures responsible for securing documentation. This was clearly illustrated by the intense information and media campaigns disclosing some of the evidence, and even more so after the establishment of the UNWCC in autumn 1943, when the member states were instructed to create special offices conducting war-crimes investigations and collecting relevant data.[1] In the case of Poland, it was the matter of adapting the already existing structures (creation of 'National Offices', as advised by the Commission) and sharing with other UNWCC members the experience and practices of processing war-crimes evidence gained over the four years of work.[2]

1 A Systematic Approach

The turn of 1939 and 1940 saw the establishment – within the structures of both the Government-in-Exile and the conspiracy in the homeland – of the first specialized sections tasked with the gathering and processing of documentation of all aspects of life under the occupation. The most important governmental bodies established to gather information on the occupiers' crimes were initially the Cabinet Committee for Home Affairs (*Komitet Ministrów dla Spraw Kraju*), Social Department (*Wydział Społeczny*) of the Praesidium of the Council of Ministers (*Prezydium Rady Ministrów*), and the Centre for Information and Documentation (*Centrala Informacji i Dokumentacji*),

1 Narrelle Morris, Aden Knaap 'When Institutional Design Is Flawed: Problems of Cooperation at the United Nations War Crimes Commission, 1943–1948'. *The European Journal of International Law* 28 (2017), 521–523.

2 Dominika Uczkiewicz, 'Transitional Justice before Nuremberg. The Polish Contribution to the Works of United Nations War Crimes Commission 1943–1945' in Wolfgang Form, Dominika Uczkiewicz (eds.), *Polish and German Perspectives on Transitional Justice. World War Two and its Aftermath* Wrocław: (CSNE 2021).

upgraded in September 1940 to a Ministry of Information and Documentation (*Ministerstwo Informacji i Dokumentacji*), as well as the Ministry of Foreign Affairs and diplomatic outposts throughout the world. The expansion of the government structure resulted in the creation of specialized cells providing cross-departmental co-ordination of the documentation works. Those were: the 'German Archive' (*kartoteka niemiecka*) of the Ministry of the Interior; the German Department of the Ministry of Foreign Affairs; the Bureau for the Recovery of Cultural Losses (*Biuro Rewindykacji Strat Kulturalnych*) of the Ministry of Preparatory Works; the German Department of the Ministry of Preparatory Works; the Section for Testimonies and Reports (*Dział Zeznań i Sprawozdań*) and German Office (*Referat Niemiecki*) of the Ministry of Information and Documentation; and the Criminal-Judicial Section (*Dział Karno-Sądowy*) and investigative commissions of the Ministry of Justice.

In occupied Poland, works in the scope of documentation of the crimes engaged both the civil and the military structures of the underground conspiracy.[3] Within the military structure, the Headquarters of the Supreme Commander of the Polish Victory Service – later the Union of Armed Struggle and Home Army – oversaw the documentation efforts. The relevant units included: (i) in the Bureau for Information and Propaganda: the Department of Information (*Wydział Informacji*), in which, in 1940, an ethnic unit was created, and in 1942 a subunit for Jewish affairs,[4] as well as Office W1 (*Referat W1*), dealing with the occupying power's policies, German propaganda and documentation of German acts of terror, as well as complication of weekly thematic reports titled 'Current Information' (*Informacja Bieżąca*); Department of Current Propaganda (*Wydział Propagandy Bieżącej*); Bureau of Military History (in charge of the Occupation Chronicle (*Kronika Okupacji*) and biweekly Appendices on Terror (*Aneksy o terrorze*), sent as the Supreme Commander's post to London; (ii) Section II of the Headquarters of the Commander-in-Chief (in it, the Department of Intelligence and Information). Within the civilian administration, the unit in charge of situation updates from the occupied Poland was the

3 Concerning this topic see: Grzegorz Mazur, *Biuro Informacji i Propagandy SZP-ZWZ-AK 1939–1945* (Warszawa: PAX 1987); Adam Puławski, 'Polityka informacyjna Polskiego Państwa Podziemnego w odniesieniu do Zagłady' in: Tomasz Chinciński (ed.), *Przemoc i dzień powszedni w okupowanej Polsce* (Gdańsk: Muzeum Drugiej Wojny Światowej 2011), 365–387; Janusz Gmitruk, Arkadiusz Indraszczyk and Adam Koseski (eds), *Pro memoria (1941–1944) Raporty Departamentu Informacji Delegatury Rządu RP na Kraj o zbrodniach na narodzie polskim* (Warszawa: Muzeum Historii Polskiego Ruchu Ludowego 2005); W. Biegański, M. Juchniewicz, P. Matusak, S. Okęcki (eds.), *Polish Resistance Movement in Poland and Abroad* (Warszawa: PWN 1987).

4 Puławski, *W obliczu Zagłady*, 25.

Department of Information of the Government Delegation for the Homeland, which edited *Pro memoria* reports on the occupying powers' crimes and the Department of Reports for the Government in London (Lo). Occupation legislation and judgments of German courts against Polish nationals were recorded and translated by the Department of Justice of the Government Delegation for the Homeland and subsequently forwarded to the authorities in London.[5]

The Polish government compiled detailed instructions concerning documentary works. On 23 November 1939, the Committee for Home Affairs adopted an Instruction no. 1 to Trustees in the Homeland (*Instrukcja numer 1 do Mężów Zaufania w Kraju*), drafted by Aleksander Ładoś, prescribing patterns of conduct towards the occupying power, the political organization of society, and operating rules of the military conspiracy.[6] The instruction called for a boycott of the occupation authorities and outlined permissible forms of resistance and contact with the German administration. The latter could include working in the education system or in the administration, as well as – 'in cases of absolute necessity' – cooperation 'to the extent of charitable activity, health-care and material care to alleviate the suffering of the population'.[7] The problem of the responsibility of those suspected of collaboration was also raised, along with recommendations to provide the Polish government with 'the fullest possible documentation of the occupying powers' repressions in Poland'.[8] The documentation was to include the names of persons who had been executed or imprisoned, summaries of special legislation and emergency ordinances, witness accounts, and photographic documentation. The information gathered was forwarded to the 'section for the registration of injuries, violations and atrocities committed by the occupying powers against the Pol-

---

5 *Ibidem.*

6 The instruction was drafted in the meeting of the CHA on 23 November 1939 and its final revision bears the date of 30 November 1939. *Cf. Protokoły posiedzeń KSK*, 69–75.

7 *Ibidem.*

8 CHA Instruction for Trustees, 23 November 1939, *Armia Krajowa w dokumentach*, vol. VI (London 1989) 1–2. Responsibility for crimes committed in wartime and for collaboration was addressed by the Instruction's sections e and f: '(e) the conviction must be imparted to the Polish Germans that any injury to the rest of the citizens for which they are culpable will be avenged. Polish communists must be reminded that if their activities in the occupied territories take the form of violence, that violence will be retributed (…); (f) spies and provocateurs, if their guilt is proved, will be punished with death'. This provision was debated in the CHA meeting on 23 November. In the amended text of the Instruction no. 1 to Trustees in the Homeland, of 30 November 1939, section III(2)(c) specified the following as one of the forms of activity of the military conspiracy 'within the directives formulated by the Polish government, use of repression against persons maintaining social, organizational and political ties with the occupying power, up to punishment in cases of public and manifest betrayal'. Grabowski, *Protokoły posiedzeń*, 74.

ish population' established already in 1939.[9] The CHA resolution of 12 December 1939 emphasized the need for diligent record-keeping for the purposes of future retaliation.[10] 'Acts of moral, physical and legal violence' were to be recorded with detailed descriptions of the incident and names of those guilty,[11] and documentation had to be as extensive as possible and kept in a systematic manner, including the culprits' names. The CHA's members believed that issuing an instruction determining the organizational principles for the documentation of the occupying power's crimes would lift the spirits of Polish society and provide a realistic promise of punishment for the criminals.[12]

The next Instruction, of 9 January 1940,[13] specified the method of registration of damage suffered and the purpose of collection of evidence. The documents, eyewitness accounts, and photographs were to be used as evidence of the barbarous methods of warfare 'incompatible with the most elementary principles of international law', such as the aerial bombings on 1 September and bombing of Polish cities and towns after 1 September 1939; massacres of the civilian population, attacks on traits; acts of violence against the civilian population by setting fire to settlements and use of violence; and destruction of temples, libraries, monuments, academic, scientific and cultural facilities, and hospitals. Moreover, the authorities requested 'accurate and detailed Polish accounts' of German attacks against the civilian population, 'destructive actions of the [German] air force against towns, villages, evacuation transports, people working in the fields, etc.',[14] as well as the diversionary actions and sabotage undertaken by the German population of Poland in September 1939 (ultimately, this category of documentation also came to cover the preceding months). The purpose of the latter was to oppose the Nazi propaganda accusations of crimes against the German minority in Poland.

The most detailed guidelines concerning the documentation of the crimes are found in the Draft Instruction from Committee for Home Affairs concerning the documentation of the occupying powers' activities on Poland, published on 21 April 1940 (originally intended to apply both to German and to

9 CHA resolution on the registration of injuries, 12 December 1939, *Protokoły posiedzeń KSK*, 90–91.

10 *Ibidem.*

11 *Ibidem*, 88.

12 *Ibidem*, 90.

13 Excerpts from Instruction no. 2 to Trustees in the Homeland from Prime Minister and Commander-in-Chief Władysław Sikorski and Supreme Commandant Kazimierz Sosnkowski, 9 January 1940; in *Armia Krajowa w dokumentach*, vol. 1, 133–134.

14 Instruction no. 2 to Trustees in the Homeland; in *Armia Krajowa w dokumentach*, vol. 1, 169.

Soviet crimes).[15] Compiled by Dr. Michał Potulicki, the document contained a sort of evaluation of the initial reports and accounts gathered from refugees after their departure from the country, as well as precise guidelines with regard to the manner of assembling the documentation of the occupying powers' crimes. However, Potulicki noted that the mental condition of the refugees, the hearsay, and the fragmentary nature of their accounts made much of the material useless for criminal litigation. The Instruction emphasized that the principal burden of the documentation works rested on the political and military structures in the occupied homeland. The accounts being forwarded from occupied Poland provided the main source of information used by Polish authorities and were anticipated to serve as the basis of indictments after the war.[16] The document stressed that the success of future criminal charges hinged on the probative value of evidence gathered.

Emphasis was placed on the quality and reliability of the evidence taken – the testimony of victims and witnesses was to be taken from those 'directly interested' at the place of commission of the crime. Information was to be gathered on methods of warfare or occupation incompatible with the 'principles of law and morality binding on civilized states' defined on the basis of the Hague Convention respecting the Laws and Customs of War on Land and the list of thirty-two war crimes compiled in 1919 by the 'Commission of Responsibilities' for the purposes of the Peace Conference in Versailles. Particular importance belonged to documentation concerning the German policy of hegemony, extermination of the Polish population, mass executions, concentration camps, labour camps, destruction of Poland's economy, persecution of the intelligentsia, the looting of works of art and libraries, and persecution of religion and of the Jewish population, including special legislation and regulations discriminating against the Jewish population of occupied Poland.[17] The recommendation was to gather legal or regulatory instruments, announcements and cutouts from German press and any such data as 'might localize and identify German troops or authorities (…) for the purpose of determination of the individual responsibilities of the [members of the occupying forces] (names, regimental insignia, types of uniforms, and other details noticed)'.[18]

---

15 Draft Instruction from Committee for Home Affairs concerning the documentation of the occupying powers' activities on Poland, 21 April 1940, IPMS, Kol. 183/53, reprinted in Grabowski (comp.), *Protokoły posiedzeń KSK*, 289–290.

16 *Ibidem.*

17 *Ibidem.*

18 *Ibidem.*

On 29 April 1940, the Journal of Laws promulgated the Decree of the President of the Polish Republic on Gathering and Securing the Evidence in Cases of Common Crimes, containing provisions applicable also to the gathering of evidence of the occupying powers' crimes in Poland. Article 1 of the decree enabled the Minister of Justice to authorize employees of the Ministry and members of Investigative Commissions subordinate to it – on condition of holding judicial qualifications – 'to perform outside of the borders of the state any and all activities with a view to gathering, determining and securing evidence in cases of common crimes'.[19]

2 The 'German Archive'

The principal point of contact with the homeland, and the main information hub, was the Social Section of the Praesidium of the Council of Ministers and, from August 1940, of the Ministry of the Interior. In October 1941, in an inter-ministerial conference on German affairs hosted by the MFA,[20] the decision was made to create a central file repository at the Ministry of the Interior for the documentation of German crimes, so-called German Archive. That archive became the Government-in-Exile's focal point for record-keeping on German crimes and for information about the suspects. In autumn1943, it was transformed into a Polish War Crimes Office (*Biuro do Spraw Zbrodni Wojennych*) as an element of the network of 'national offices' concentrated around the United Nations War Crimes Commission.

The creation of the 'German Archive' – also known as the 'German department' or 'German files' – in autumn 1941 was not coincidental. On the one hand, it stemmed from purely technical considerations, as well as the need for systematic organization of the materials so far retained by different cells within the Government-in-Exile, and for guidelines on further work to be done.[21] On the other hand, it was linked to the Polish authorities' initiative for a joint Allied declaration condemning German crimes and for a common Allied position on the documentation of the crimes needed for post-war criminal trials. General Sikorski published the decision to create the German Archive on 28 October 1941, which was three days after the announcement of

19 Decree of the President of the Polish Republic on Gathering and Securing the Evidence in Cases of Common Crimes (*Dekret Prezydenta Rzeczypospolitej z dnia 29 kwietnia 1940 r. o zbieraniu i zabezpieczaniu dowodów w sprawach o przestępstwa pospolite*), Dz. U.1940.9.23

20 AIPN GK 159.1, leaf 650.

21 *Cf.* note taken by Tadeusz Ullmann, 20 October 1941, AIPN 159.1, leaf 650.

Franklin D. Roosevelt's and Winston Churchill's statements condemning German crimes (25 October 1941) and just before the beginning of a conference of the governments of the occupied states on criminal responsibility for war crimes.[22] Winning at least partial support from the Allies strengthened the Poles' position. The adoption, on 21 November of 1941, by the representatives of the governments-in-exile, of a joint resolution on the documentation of the occupying powers' crimes and the adoption, on 13 January 1942, of the Declaration of St James's Palace, were two other factors to stimulate the works on the documentation of the crimes.[23]

On 28 October 1941, the Political Section (*Dział Polityczny*) of the Ministry of the Interior created files on 'individuals responsible for violence and murder perpetrated on citizens of Poland'.[24] In the care of Dr. Jan Wagner, they were accessible to all ministers of the Polish Government-in-Exile, as well as officials authorized by them.[25] In a government circular of 29 October, Sikorski requested the heads of the other ministries to forward all documents and information on 'Germans suspected of criminal activity against the Polish State and its nationals' to the new unit at the Ministry of the Interior. The request was reiterated on 22 November 1941 by Stanisław Mikołajczyk, then in charge of the Ministry of the Interior, in a letter enclosed with the aforementioned Guidelines.[26] Mikołajczyk stressed that the documentation sent from the homeland and collected by all the ministries concerned would in the future enable the 'identification of the German criminals and their apprehension either in Polish territory or by their country of refuge pursuant to an extradition request'. He emphasized that bringing the Germans to book 'for their criminal activities in Poland' required ongoing documentation of the perpetrators and their crimes, as well as witnesses and physical evidence.[27] It was Mikołajczyk's intention for

---

22 Concerning this topic, see Chapter 2 of this book.

23 Ministry of the Interior Guidelines on the submission of materials to the German files (*Wytyczne Ministerstwa Spraw Wewnętrznych w sprawie dostarczania materiałów do kartoteki niemieckiej*), AIPN GK 159.1, leaf 642.

24 Circular no. 1579/41 of 28 October 1941, AIPN GK 159.1, leaves 640–664.

25 *Ibidem.*

26 Ministry of the Interior Guidelines on the submission of materials to the German files, AIPN, 159/1, leaves 640–641. Reprinted in Kobierska-Motas, *Rząd polski*, 188. Prior to the publication, the Guidelines were discussed in an inter-ministerial conference on German affairs held by the MFA on 20 November 1941.

27 Note by Stanisław Mikołajczyk, *Odpowiedzialność Niemców za działalność przestępczą w Polsce* ('Responsibility of Germans for criminal activities in Poland') 22 November 1941, AIPN 159.1, leaf 642.

the files to include alphabetic lists of suspects, as well as a territorial register categorized by major cities and counties.[28]

The Guidelines of November 1941 defined the scope of tasks assigned to the files and the group of persons covered. Those were German, Polish, and other nationals who – because of acts committed after the German aggression against Poland on 1 September 1939 – could be suspects in 'criminal activity against the Polish State and its nationals'. Thus, both the givers and takers of orders, as well as persons acting on their own initiative, belonging to one of the following three groups:

> leaders of the Reich, playing a role in shaping German policy toward occupied Polish territories and their populations politically, militarily, economically and culturally;
>
> Germans staying in Poland or the Free City of Gdańsk (Danzig), playing or having played leading roles in the following fields in Polish territory: (a) armed forces; (b) police and Gestapo; (c) civil administration – general and self-government; (d) judiciary and prosecution service; (e) business associations and self-regulation bodies; state-owned, self-government or private enterprises (industry, commerce, agriculture or communication); (f) general and vocational education; (g) cultural life (libraries, museums and collections, theatres, cinema, radio); (h) National Socialist party organizations;
>
> all Germans of whose criminal activities against the Polish State and Polish citizens materials already existed in the various ministries.[29]

The recommendation concerning the first two groups was to gather information on all officials, whether or not they had been formally charged. For suspects from the third group, if evidence existed, the requirement was to 'specify precisely where and in whose care such evidence [was] held'.[30]

The documentation being assembled had to contain a reasonably detailed description of the act; names of the perpetrators and witnesses, and – if possible – whatever physical evidence could be secured. As was noted, one could only collect such evidence in close cooperation with the homeland, where the majority of the materials was located. The following was also emphasized:

28 *Ibidem.*

29 Ministry of the Interior Guidelines on the submission of materials, AIPN, 159/1, leaves 640–641.

30 *Ibidem.*

> while putting the Germans on the record, it is important to state their personal information with as much precision as possible, so as not to leave any doubts as to a person's identity. It is important, furthermore, to establish nationality, provided that the individual's citizenship held before 1 September 1939 is relevant, as one must anticipate the application of a different procedure to Germans [being] Polish citizens [than to those] holding the citizenship of the Reich or some other.[31]

The lack of direct access to the evidentiary material and lack of options for securing it at the crime scene presented a difficulty that was perfectly appreciated. The principal goal before the Ministry of the Interior was to compile accurate lists of the Reich's party and military leaders along with: 'all Germans whose criminal activity [was] particularly flagrant or mass-scale' – meaning commandants of concentration camps, members of the Gestapo, and presidents of special courts.

The first documents had been dispatched to the Ministry already at the beginning of November 1941.[32] In January 1942, on the wave of international interest in the problem of crimes committed under the German occupation inspired by the white book *The German New Order in Poland* and the Declaration of St. James's Palace, Polish authorities requested the assistance of the general public in the information gathering. On 14 January 1942, the *Dziennik Polski* ('Polish Daily') printed a communiqué from the Polish Telegraphic Agency, later reprinted by Polish diaspora press, concerning the records of 'German crimes committed in Polish territories', assembled and maintained by the Polish Ministry of the Interior. The article asked Polish nationals abroad to report any relevant information to the government via embassies and consulates. The materials were expected to identify the: (a) date and place of the crime; (b) type of crime; (c) perpetrator's name and rank; (d) names and addresses of the victims and (e) names of witnesses, if any.[33] On 28 January, Stanisław Mikołajczyk asked Ambassador Raczyński – as the official in charge of the MFA at the time – to instruct the heads of Polish diplomatic missions (and, through them, the investigative commissions of the Ministry of Justice)[34]

31 Stanisław Mikołajczyk's note *Odpowiedzialność Niemców za działalność przestępczą w Polsce* ('Responsibility of Germans for criminal activities in Poland'), 22 November 1941, AIPN 159.1, leaf 642.

32 *Cf.* Letter from Mirosław Arciszewski to Tadeusz Ullmann, 7 November 1941, AIPN GK 159.1, leaf 646.

33 *Dziennik Polski*, 14 January 1942.

34 Letter from Aleksander Robinson to Stanisław Mikołajczyk, 27 April 1942, AIPN GK 159.1/ leaves 504, 528 and 550–551.

to publish the PTA communiqué, keep records of the occupying powers' crimes, and forward the materials to London.[35] Mikołajczyk sent separate letters concerning the submission of data for the 'German Archive' to the Headquarters of the Commander-in-Chief (Commander-in-Chief's Staff) and Navy Command with requests for orders to be given that any service personnel being victims or witnesses of war crimes report on those crimes to the Ministry of the Interior through the military chain of command.[36] Mikołajczyk also approached Stanisław Szurlej – the president of Polish Lawyers' Association in the United Kingdom – to get in touch with those of the association's members who had already dealt with war crimes in general and specifically the documentation of the crimes committed by the occupying powers.[37] Sections I and VI of the Commander-in-Chief's Headquarters regularly submitted reports to the Ministry of the Interior for the 'German Archive' – a practice that had begun in early 1941. Additional materials came from Polish diplomatic missions and private individuals. As an example of incentive for becoming involved in the Polish government's campaign and of the expectations that were placed before the crime records, it will be expedient to quote a letter sent on 15 January 1942 by Sergeant Tadeusz Putz, serving with the RAF's No. 307 (Polish) Squadron, the day after the *Dziennik Polski* published the PTA communiqué:

> To the long list of Poles bestially murdered in concentration camps please add the name of my brother, the late Kazimierz Putz (...), who died on 20 July 1941 at the Conc[entration] Camp in Mauthausen. (...) As I belong to the combat personnel of Polish Air Forces, I do not therefore know whether it will be given to me to return happily to the homeland and there deal with the tormentors who caused my brother Kazimierz to be taken away, as well as my father Marian, counting 72 years [of age] today, in which camp (Dachau) he continues to remain. (...) As is known to me from the Minister's communiqués and radio speeches, all such crimes are now being recorded so that the guilty to be punished in the future, therefore please put on the record the matter of my family, residing at [illegible], county of Gniezno, for the future apprehension of the local culprits.[38]

35 AIPN GK 159.1, leaf 690.
36 AIPN GK 159.1, leaf 592.
37 AIPN GK 159.1, leaf 589.
38 Letter from Sergeant Tadeusz Putz, 15 January 1942, AIPN GK 159.9, leaves 277–278.

The inauguration of the 'German Archive' was an element of the Polish authorities' intensified diplomatic and informational campaign at the turn of 1941 and 1942 leading up to the Declaration of St. James's Palace. As the operator of the central archive for German crimes in occupied Poland, the Ministry of the Interior also participated actively in the current works on the domestic criminal legislation addressing personal responsibility for war crimes.[39] Mikołajczyk emphasized that his ministry was 'by nature of things' interested in the establishment of 'concrete legal norms on the basis of which individual Germans [would] in the future be held criminally liable – either before an international tribunal or before Polish courts'.[40] In discussions within the government concerning domestic laws and regulations to be applicable in war-crime trials, Mikołajczyk was a determined advocate of promulgating a suitable legal instrument as soon as possible and publicizing the names of individuals registered in the 'German Archive' under suspicions of the most flagrant violations of international law. In his view, those steps would both have a deterrent effect and satisfy Polish society's expectations of strict punishment for the crimes committed by the occupying power.

Since the beginning of 1942, the Ministry of the Interior leveraged the materials on an ongoing basis in the international informational campaign. Mikołajczyk regularly met with Frank Savery of the British Embassy to the Polish Government-in-Exile, former consul general in Warsaw in 1939, sharing with him reports and documentation forwarded from the homeland.[41] Those included a collection of shocking photographs from Polish ghettoes and prisoner-of-war camps for Soviet captives the minister had received in January 1942.[42] Mikołajczyk asked the authorities of the United Kingdom to condemn the Ger-

---

39 Letter from Stanisław Mikołajczyk, 16 April 1942, AIPN GK 159.1, leaf 580.

40 *Ibidem.*

41 On the basis of Mikołajczyk's materials, Frank Savery wrote in June 1942 his own report on the situation in Poland, which the British ambassador, Cecil Dormer, forwarded to Anthony Eden on 13 June 1942. TNA FO.371.31097/C5951.

42 In June 1942, a collection of photographs from ghettoes and camps for Soviet prisoners of war in occupied Poland reached London. The photographs depict – among others – mass graves, piles of corpses, and starved inhabitants of ghettoes. Photographs from prisoner-of-war camps were captioned with comments such as: 'Killing off of wounded fugitives from the Rembertów camp by German military police'; 'Carts arriving for the corpses of prisoners', 'Woman hanged for guerilla activities'; 'Corpses of Russian prisoners shot during [an alleged] attempt to escape'; and 'German soldier treads on corpses of Soviet prisoners' – TNA FO.371.31097/C954, TNA FO.371.31097/C12243, TNA FO.371.31097/C12412; Report from the inter-ministerial conference for German affairs, IPMS A.XII.1/88D pt. 1, leaf 16. According to the Ministry of the Interior's estimates, approximately half a million Soviet prisoners of war were being held in camps throughout occupied Poland at the beginning of 1942.

man crimes and, at a later stage, announce retorsions to be applied against the Reich.

In February 1942, Tadeusz Ullmann – who headed the Ministry's Political Department – together with Stefan Konar, who was in charge of the Ministry of Information and Documentation outpost in Scotland, launched the initiative of a 'Criminals of War' press conference, which was ultimately held by the Ministry of Information in Edinburgh, at St. Andrew's House, on 27 March 1942.[43] The head of the 'German Archive', Dr. Jan Wagner, outlined the scale of violations of international law committed by the occupying forces in Polish territories, including the policy of extermination, as well as the discriminatory laws and regulations issued against Poles and Jews, and marshalled support for the key points of the Declaration of St. James's Palace. Dr. Wagner attached special importance to the motive guiding the Declaration's drafters, which was not to confer legitimacy on acts of revenge for crimes committed in occupied territory but to follow the demands of justice and develop adequate legal provisions to that end (translating from the Polish text):

> Without a doubt, moral considerations demand that any acts of revenge be condemned. Equally, however, moral principles demand that criminal elements be neutralized. The legal order of any civilized state punishes and eradicates crime committed against society or individuals. (…) Every state punishes the criminal to neutralize them and to deter others from committing anti-social acts. No one – other than the criminal themselves – will call the judge's sentence an act of revenge. Is the meting out of justice to international criminals who under the pretence of a new order deprive the population of a conquered country of life, freedom, religion, language and property to bear all of a sudden the name of an act of revenge?
>
> On the contrary, it is high time that the international community treat acts directed against universally recognized principles of our civilization in the same manner as any nation treats criminal acts committed against its legal order. For the impunity of a criminal becomes to the criminal themselves an encouragement to repeat the crime and to others the encouragement to emulate them. It began in 1914 from the atrocities in Belgium and has come – so far – to the shooting of hostages in Poland, France and Yugoslavia, an incalculable number of crimes throughout the conquered Europe, and to the Japanese atrocities in Hong Kong. If we do not want for such methods to become the custom as a new sort of con-

43 Letter from Stefan Konar to Tadeusz Ullmann, 9 March 1942, AIPN GK 159.134, leaf 13.

> queror's right, we need to create a system that will bring the perpetrators of such crimes to justice according to the legal principles of the civilized world.[44]

Attempts were made to reach the public opinion in the United Kingdom and neutral states but also Germany with information about the occupying forces' policy of extermination and the necessity of punishment for the guilty. Near the end of 1941, the Ministry of the Interior and the Radio Section of the Ministry of Information and Documentation developed the script for a radio drama titled *Proces Franka* ('Frank's trial' or 'Frank on trial'), which was to be broadcast by the BBC's German-language outlets. The theme was a trial of Hans Frank, chief executive of the General Governorate before a Polish tribunal 'as the main [person] responsible for the German war crimes committed in the Gen[eral] Governorate'.[45] After several weeks of negotiations, the BBC – under influence from the Foreign Office – refused to air the broadcast 'because of a difference of opinion (…) in the matter of the responsibility of German war criminals between the British Government and Allied Governments'. Mikołajczyk requested Raczyński's intervention, emphasizing that the principle of criminal responsibility for the crimes committed by the occupying powers throughout Europe should be propagated first and foremost among the Germans themselves and 'affect more than a few Germans as an inhibitor in their conduct with Poles'.[46] On 12–13 April 1942, the BBC's Polish outlet broadcast a programme titled 'German crimes in Poland'. In response to reports of increased reprisals against civilians in Poland, Mikołajczyk renewed pressure in April 1942 to have Frank's Trial approved for broadcasting in the BBC's German outlets. The propaganda instruments recommended by the Government's Delegate for Poland included constant condemnation of the Gestapo's crimes in foreign press and radio, 'combined with the most severe taking of the Germans to book after the war', and reiteration that the criminals' names and those of their superiors were being put on record, so that they could be 'adequately and severely punished after the war'.[47] Simultaneously, leaders of the Polish Underground State persistently demanded Allied reprisal bombings

---

44 Outline of Dr. Wagner's 'Criminals of War' conference (*Schemat konferencji prasowej dr Wagnera pt. „Criminals of War"*), AIPN GK 159.134, leaves 15–16.

45 Letter from Stanisław Mikołajczyk to the Ministry of Foreign Affairs, 24 January 1942, AIPN 159.1, leaf 583.

46 *Ibidem.*

47 Letter from Stanisław Mikołajczyk to the Minister of Foreign Affairs, 10 April 1942, AIPN GK159.1, leaf 581.

in retaliation for crimes committed on the civilian population. The idea was for the bombers to drop leaflets providing information about German crimes in Poland and anticipating the post-war punishment of those guilty.[48] Raczyński's entreaties in that regard were not successful, and the Foreign Office did not accede to his requests for retaliatory bombing.[49] In a letter to Mikołajczyk of 30 April 1942, he wrote about the lack of any prospects of change in the Foreign Office's position on the matter or of 'Polish requests being followed in the English propaganda concerning the Germans'. Raczyński recommended transferring the intensified information activities to American soil and establishing contacts with the broadcasters there through the Polish Information Centre in New York.[50]

The Polish authorities' intensified information and diplomatic campaign of June 1942 did lead to a heightening of interest among the British public in the situation in occupied Poland. Through the agency of Minister Mikołajczyk, the first fruits of the 'German Archive's' efforts – and especially information about the new wave of German terror along with most recent reports from the homeland, including the Bund's report of 11 May 1942 – reached the British media. The Minister of the Interior presented the materials on 9 July 1942 in the British Ministry of Information's press conference titled 'German Crimes in Poland'.

The first months of the 'German Archive's' activity concentrated on the processing of materials submitted thus far to the Ministry of the Interior by all departments of the Government-in-Exile and instilling order in the constantly arriving reports and witness accounts. A registration form was designed in the first half of 1942 by Jan Wagner and contained the following fields:

I. Personal information: 1. surname and name, 2. nationality, 3. date and place of birth; 4. title and function (specify time and territory when and where exercised);
II. general description of activity;
III. criminal activity: (a) date and place of imputed act; (b) detailed description of imputed act; (c) victims: name and surname, last address; (d) witnesses: name and surname, last address; (e) physical evidence; (f) place where evidence is kept; (g) source and date of information; (h) special remarks.[51]

---

48 Stola, *Nadzieja*, 363 and 369–370.

49 *Ibidem*, 367.

50 Letter from Edward Raczyński to the Ministry of the Interior, 30 April 1942, AIPN AIPN 159.1, leaf 576.

51 Ministry of the Interior 'German files' standard form, AIPN GK 159.1, leaf 497.

In February 1942, Jan Wagner estimated the size of the 'German Archive' at 2,000 names of 'representatives of administrative authorities, the police, the national-socialist party, the SS and the SA'.[52] These numbers also reflected the difficulties resulting from the lack of direct access to the crime scene, victims, and witnesses. For the majority of cases, the necessary evidence was available only in the occupied homeland. Evidence potentially sufficient to establish the guilt of individual perpetrators was limited to a little under 10% of the suspects, that is, about 150 names. By mid-April 1942, the files covered about 2,500 names,[53] which by spring 1943 increased to about 3,500.[54] According to Wagner's estimate at the time, the files were anticipated to include a total of 10,000 names to be identified through investigations conducted in occupied Poland. Wagner emphasized that the register maintained in the initial months on the basis of official journals from the General Government lacked personal information on members of the German administration in the annexed territories – the Warthegau, Upper Silesia, and Pomerania. Another gap in the records pertained to the judgments of German courts in Polish territories. As a result, Jan Wagner recommended that the Ministry of the Interior's outpost in Lisbon (Portugal was a neutral state) order a subscription of the official journals for the annexed territories and on that basis reconstruct the leadership structure of the German administration, including names of judges deciding cases involving Poles, applying discriminatory laws and committing judicial murders.[55] A 'questionnaire on the gathering of materials concerning war crimes' was sent to occupied Poland near the end of 1942.[56] Desirous to obtain the greatest possible volume of direct-witness accounts, Wagner proposed – at the beginning of 1943 – that the Polish government issue an order 'for all persons arriving from Polish territories under occupation or from German captivity to report to the German Office for the purpose of establishing any facts and names fit for the files and, if appropriate, recording depositions at the Min. of Justice with the validity of court documents'.[57]

Difficulties with completing the evidence arose not only from its fragmented and dispersed nature, involving the need to go through voluminous

52 Report from the inter-ministerial conference on German affairs, 22 January 1942, IPMS A. XII.1/88D pt. 1, leaf 22.

53 Ministry of the Interior Political Section note of 16 April 1942, AIPN GK 159.1, leaf 579.

54 Jan Wagner, Note concerning the files of German criminals, 4 February 1943, AIPN GK 159.1, leaf 412.

55 Note concerning the lack of materials for the German files, 15 June 1942, AIPN 159.1, leaf 554.

56 War Crimes Office, Note of 9 December 1943, AIPN GK 159.1, leaf 296.

57 Note concerning the files of German criminals, 4 February 1943, AIPN GK 159.1 leaf 412.

materials, but also from staff shortages. Until the transformation of the 'German Archive' into the War Crimes Office in autumn 1943, the cell's only staff member was its head. Wagner's illness, ultimately resulting in his resignation in summer 1943 and departure for Canada, further affected the unit's operations. Following Wagner's departure, the leadership of the 'German Archive' was taken over by the legal practitioner from Cracow, Dr. Jerzy Litawski. Following the creation of the UNWCC, the 'German Section' was transformed into the Polish War Crimes Office reporting to the Government-in-Exile.

3 The War-Crimes Office of the Polish Government-in-Exile

One month ahead of the UNWCC's inaugural conference, on 17 September 1943, the Polish MFA organized an inter-ministerial conference 'on the punishment of German criminals' to discuss the tasks placed before the Commission and the method of drafting of the charges expected to be submitted by the Polish government.[58] The intention was for the first stage of the Commission's works to focus on determining the types of crimes committed in the various countries, gathering the evidence and examining crimes of organized, systematic nature. It was agreed that Polish cases referred to the Commission would be prepared in line with the above guidelines. Materials on the gravest crimes and ones that were the best documented – from the early months of the war – would be coming first.[59] Detailed discussion was scheduled for the next meeting of the inter-ministerial committee, on 9 October 1943.

The agenda included: 1. Jerzy Litawski's report on the evidence stored in the 'German Archive'; determining what factual material Poland could submit to the UNWCC, and discussion of the method of preparation of materials for the Commission; 2. defining the Polish government's theses as to the scope of the Commission's works in line with Polish postulates relating to punishment for war crimes; 3. defining the Polish position to be taken in the Technical Committee, especially as to the type of jurisdiction and the organization of the

58 Note taken from the inter-ministerial conference held at the MFA on 17 September 1943 concerning the punishment of war criminals, AIPN GK 159.1, leaf 356. Participants included: from the Ministry of Foreign affairs: Professor Michał Potulicki, Władysław Adamkiewicz, and Roman Battaglia; from the Ministry of Justice: Tadeusz Cyprian, Stefan Glaser, and Wiktor Sukiennicki; from the Praesidium of the Council of Ministers: Ludwik M. Krajewski, Władysław Kulski of the Polish Embassy in London; Roman Piotrowski and W. Sokołowski from the Ministry of Preparatory Works.

59 Note taken by Jerzy Litawski, 7 October 1943, AIPN GK 159.1, leaves 349–350.

judiciary in whose purview the cases of war crimes would fall; and 4. the matter of extradition of suspects from neutral states.[60]

The basic problem concerned the gaps in the materials deposited in the 'German Archive' and taxonomy based on the suspects' personal information rather than the types and general descriptions of crimes.

A motion was tabled for the creation at the Ministry of Justice or at the Ministry of the Interior of a 'specialized and adequately, in quantitative terms, staffed cell (…) composed of jurists with judicial and prosecutorial qualifications, for the purpose of processing the materials in the shortest time practicable'.[61] Władysław Kulski noted that all materials at the disposal of the Ministry of the Interior's 'German Archive' and other ministries – Treasury, Commerce and Navigation and Preparatory Works – had to be analysed from the perspective of the UNWCC's tasks.[62] In October 1943, the 'German Archive' included approximately 4,000 suspect names with descriptions of positions held. The preparation of materials for the UNWCC on that basis called for a new analysis of the data, to supplement whatever was lacking. It was not clear whether all of the materials required further processing in line with the Commission's guidelines, including materials falling under the jurisdiction of domestic courts, or only the cases of the main criminals, expected to be judged by an international tribunal.

Given the approaching commencement of the UNWCC's works, the recommendation was to establish the Polish War Crimes Office as soon as possible. Letters concerning the creation of a unit tasked with working with the UNWCC were sent to the President of the Council of Ministers (prime minister) by Wacław Komarnicki and Stefan Glaser. Glaser recommended the establishment – either at one of the aforementioned Ministries or the Praesidium of the Council of Ministers – of an office of the Polish Delegate to the UNWCC, employing at least two 'legal practitioners having previously held the position of a criminal judge or prosecutor, for the proper processing of materials already held by our authorities and incoming in the future'.[63] Wacław Komarnicki supported the creation of such a cell within the Ministry of Justice, as this ministry was the competent body for war crimes. He mentioned the pro-

60 Note taken by Michał Potulicki, 6 October 1943, AIPN GK 159.1, leaf 352.

61 Note taken by Jerzy Litawski from the inter-ministerial conference on the punishment of war crimes, 9 October 1943, AIPN GK 159.1, leaf 347.

62 Minutes of the deliberations of the inter-ministerial Conference on the punishment of war crimes, AIPN 159.1, leaves 339–342.

63 Letter from Stefan Glaser to Stanisław Mikołajczyk, 15 October 1943, see AIPN GK 159.1, 346–347.

bative shortcomings of the materials being processed at the 'German Archives' and emphasized that the 'preparation of criminal materials for international and domestic tribunals for the judgment of war criminals' fell under the responsibility of the Minister of Justice serving also as Prosecutor General (often translated 'Attorney General').[64] The idea of creation of a new organizational unit had an opponent in the Minister of the Interior, Władysław Banaczyk (Mikołajczyk's successor in the position). Banaczyk instead recommended the expansion of the German Office, with increased staffing and reorganization in accordance with the UNWCC's guidelines. The interior minister emphasized that the incomplete nature of the evidence kept in the 'German Archive' was the consequence of operating in difficult conditions:

> on account of the working conditions of government cells in Poland and technical options for communicating with the homeland, the majority of the materials received are of rather situational nature and are out of necessity expressed in a more general way. (...) The technique for the examination and processing of materials for the Fact Finding Commission will have to diverge significantly from the rigid forms of investigation used in normal circumstances.[65]

On 1 November 1943, the government agreed to transform the 'German files' into a War Crimes Office under the Ministry of the Interior. The agreement involved the President of the Council of Ministers and the Ministers of Interior, Justice, and Foreign Affairs.[66] Jerzy Litawski was placed in charge, and his staff comprised prosecutor Kazimierz Epler as deputy head; criminal judge Edward Snop; and Aniela Battaglia as a secretary. The reasons for placing the Office under the Ministry of the Interior were of pragmatic nature. The Ministry's Social Section still constituted the Government's focal point for sourcing reports and accounts of German crimes committed in occupied Poland, which provided the primary source basis for the 'German Archive' maintained since autumn1941. Despite his scepticism, Komarnicki ultimately compromised in the view of the difficulties entailed by the hypothetical separation of the 'German Archive' from the 'aggregate of matters going through the Minis-

64 Letter from Wacław Komarnicki to Stanisław Mikołajczyk, 18 October 1943, AIPN GK 159.1, leaf 344.

65 Draft answer from Stanisław Mikołajczyk to letters from Minister Komarnicki and Stefan Glaser, AIPN GK 155.1, 335–336.

66 Ministry of the Interior, Note concerning the activities of the War Crimes Office, AIPN GK. 159.1, leaf 297.

try of the Interior'.[67] That, however, was not the end of the jurisdiction dispute between the Ministry of Justice and the Ministry of the Interior. Attempts at formal regulation of this aspect of the WCO's status only began in June 1945, after a year and a half of functioning within the Ministry of the Interior structure according to the organizational guidelines from autumn 1943.

The first meeting of the War Crimes Office took place on 4 November 1943 and was attended by Władysław Banaczyk, Stefan Glaser, Tadeusz Cyprian, as well as two members of WCO staff – Jerzy Litawski and Kazimierz Epler. Glaser gave a report of the UNWCC inaugural meeting of 20 October 1943, outlining its guidelines on evidence collection. The primary purpose of the materials sourced by the governments of the occupied states, according to the consensus, was to build lists of suspects for use after the war with extradition requests. The above applied to both the issuers and the executors of unlawful orders, as well as individuals responsible for the enactment of laws and regulations incompatible with international law in occupied territories, and individuals placed in charge of the administration of a given country. Three categories of war crimes were distinguished:

(1) causing the war;
(2) violation of international agreements and treaties by the hostilities;
(3) any crime 'committed by the enemy in the occupied territory in connection with war activities'.[68]

Stefan Glaser and Tadeusz Cyprian emphasized the need for the comprehensive processing of every single crime and for the use of as extensive an evidence basis as possible. The detailed requirements were for the case record to specify the type of crime, provide a description of the facts of the case, identify the date and place of commission of the crime, and the names of the perpetrators, victims and witnesses.[69] To that end, the recommendation was to use the UNWCC-approved list of war crimes designed in spring 1919 for the pur-

67 Letter from Minister of Justice Professor Wacław Komarnicki to Minister of the Interior Władysław Banaczyk concerning the draft decree on gathering and security the evidence of war crimes, 13 January 1944, AIPN GK 159, 1.

68 Note from the conference at the Ministry of the Interior concerning war crimes, 4 November 1943, AIPN 159.1, leaf 322.

69 With regard to witness identification in complaints forwarded to the UNWCC, in the latter's second meeting: 'Professor Glaser (Poland) suggested, and it was agreed, that where to give the name and address or other identification of a witness might endanger the witness or his family or persons connected with him, it would be sufficient to describe the witness as "Witness No,-" and register him under that number in the national files'. UNWCC, Notes of a second unofficial meeting held on 2 December, 1943, at 3 p.m. at the Royal Courts of Justice, London, 2.

poses of the peace conference in Versailles[70] and Hague Convention (IV) of 1907.

In the Notes on the activities of the War Crimes Office of 9 December 1943, Jerzy Litawski delineated the scope of the WCO's activities as follows:

- processing materials for submission to the International Commission;
- keeping files on German criminals;
- keeping regional files (lists of all German authorities in Poland according to the administrative division and staffing);
- interrogating persons arriving from Poland for evidentiary purposes and as supporting material for factual determinations concerning the specific crimes;
- matters of propaganda in the scope pertaining war crimes and WCO operations;
- participating in inter-ministerial conferences and liaising with relevant international bodies;
- studying and processing German criminal legislation introduced in the occupied territory of the Polish State, with a view to the needs of the International Commission.[71]

---

70 The list covered the following crimes: (1) murder and massacres – systematic terrorism; (2) putting hostages to death; (3) torture of civilians; (4) deliberate starvation of civilians; (5) rape; (6) abduction of girls and women for the purpose of enforced prostitution; (7) deportation of civilians; (8) internment of civilians under inhuman conditions; (9) forced labour of civilians in connection with the military operations of the enemy; (10) usurpation of sovereignty during military occupation; (11) compulsory enlistment of soldiers among the inhabitants of occupied territory; (12) attempts to denationalize the inhabitants of occupied territory; (13) pillage; (14) confiscation of property; (15) exaction of illegitimate or of exorbitant contributions and requisitions; (16) debasement of the currency and issue of spurious currency; (17) imposition of collective penalties; (18) wanton devastation and destruction of property; (19) deliberate bombardment of undefended places; (20) wanton destruction of religious, charitable, educational and historic buildings and monuments; (21) destruction of merchant ship and passenger vessels without warning and without provision for the safety of passengers and crew; (22) destruction of fishing boats and of relief ships; (23) deliberate bombardment of hospitals; (24) attack and destruction of hospital ships; (25) breach of other rules relating to the Red Cross; (26) use of deleterious and asphyxiating gases; (27) use of explosive or expanding bullets and other inhuman appliances; (28) directions to use no quarter; (29) ill-treatment of wounded and prisoners of war; (30) employment of prisoners of war on unauthorised works; (31) misuse of flags of truce; and (32) poisoning of wells. See UNWCC, Notes of a second unofficial meeting held on 2 December, 1943, at 3 p.m. at the Royal Courts of Justice, London, 2.

71 Note concerning the activities of the War Crimes Office, 9 December 1943, AIPN GK. 1, leaves 297–298.

It is noteworthy that the Ministry of the Interior's organizational charter, enacted on 28 December 1943, i.e. shortly after the establishment of the War Crimes Office, makes no mention of this unit.[72] Minister Zygmunt Berezowski, who had been in charge of the Ministry since November 1944, requested the Council of Ministers to approve a suitable amendment on 5 April 1945.[73] The stated objective of the modification was to 'streamline the ministry's internal work process and formalize the lawfully existing reality'.[74] The draft outlines a very broad scope of the WCO's activities: 'The War Crime Office is in charge of cases falling within the ambit of war crimes (investigations, securing of evidence)'. The Council of Ministers approved his request.[75]

Berezowski tabled further organizational motions relating to the War Crimes Office on 5 June 1945, in relation to exemption from the implementation of the Resolution of the Council of Ministers of 17 April 1945 concerning restrictions on budget spending.[76] The resolution prohibited specific-work contracts with state officials and employees and members of the military in active service. The Minister of the Interior requested an exemption for Social Section and WCO staff. In both cases, the desire was to maintain sufficient staffing levels in positions involved in the processing of information from the homeland.[77] The topicality gained in the international forum by the matter of war crimes, the preparations for the International Military Tribunal were a key factor in intensifying the War Crimes Office's activities and employment of: 'qualified individuals with expertise in the matter, who ha[d] already worked with the Office for a longer time and [we]re simultaneously employed in other offices of the state or other sections of the Ministry of the Interior and c[ould not] be reassigned from their current roles'. The most pressing objectives

72 Pursuant to the organizational charter from 28 December 1943, the Ministry was divided into six sections: General Section (*Dział Ogólny*), Social Section (*Dział Społeczny*), Nationality Section (*Dział Narodowościowy*) and Continental Works Section (*Dział Prac Kontynentalnych*) – Resolution of the Council of Ministers of 28 December 1943 concerning the organizational charter of the Ministry of the Interior for the duration of the hostilities. See PPRM, vol. VI, 361.

73 Motion by the Minister of the Interior to amend the Organizational Regulations of the Ministry of the Interior, 5 April 1945, IPMS PRM-K., 102/81a, leaves 3–6. *PPRM*, vol. VIII, 409.

74 *Ibidem*, 410.

75 Minutes of the meeting of the Council of Ministers, 5 April 1945, IPMS PRM-K., 102/81a, leaves 3–6. PPRM, vol. VIII, 400.

76 *Ibidem*.

77 Motion by the Minister of the Interior of 5 June 1945 concerning the admission of exceptions from the implementation of the Resolution of the Council of Ministers of 17 April 1945 concerning the limitation of budget spending, PPRM, vol. VIII, 549.

before the Office, according to Berezowski, were to prepare more UNWCC charges or supplement those already filed; to prepare complete sets of materials for the purposes of trials to be held before the international tribunal; and to compile targeted legal analyses.[78] Berezowski's motion was approved in respect of the Social Section of the Ministry of the Interior but rejected in respect of the War Crimes Office itself.

Discussion of the War Crimes Office's structure resumed in a 'consultative conference on war crimes' held by the Minister of Justice, Bronisław Kuśnierz, on 13 June 1945.[79,80] Kuśnierz pointed out the necessity of co-ordinating the works associated with preparations for a visit by Polish investigators to Germany, which involved the jurisdiction of investigative judges, their responsibilities, and the organizational logistics of the expedition. His priority was to define the current guiding lines of Polish government's policy on the prosecution of war crimes and to create a 'consultative cell' with responsibility for the implementation of that policy, comprising representatives of the Ministry of Justice, Ministry of Foreign Affairs and War Crimes Office. It was to be kept separate from the Committee of Ministers for War Crimes, also created in spring 1945.[81] Tadeusz Cyprian, Jerzy Litawski, Tadeusz Kisielewski, Józef Marlewski, and Włodzimierz Moderow, of the Ministry of Preparatory Works, were selected to serve on the consultative committee. The committee was intended to cooperate with the German Section of the Ministry of Information and Documentation, led by Tadeusz Katelbach.[82] The matter of cooperation between the War Crimes Office and the Ministry of Justice was once again

78 *Ibidem*, 550–551. *Ibidem*, 549.

79 Report on consultative conference on war crimes on 13 June 1945, AIPN, GK 159.2/leaves 192–199. Participants included: Bronisław Kuśnierz, Professor Eugeniusz Jarra, Dr. Tadeusz Cyprian, and Dr. Andrzej Nowotny of the Ministry of Justice; head of the German Section at the MFA, Dr. Józef Marlewski; head of the War Crimes Office, Dr. Jerzy Litawski; Józef Winiewicz of the Ministry of Preparatory Works; and representatives of the Ministry of Information and Documentation – S. Osiek and T. Grygier.

80 Invitation from Bronisław Kuśnierz to Jerzy Litawski to the conference on 11 June 1945, AIPN 159.2/227.

81 *Ibidem*, leaf 193. In the minutes, we can find information about the establishment of a War Crimes Committee in spring 1945: 'Minister Kuśnierz informs the assembled that a Committee of Ministers for War Crimes has been formed for decision-making in cases of greater import. Said committee comprises Ministers Pragier, Folkierski, and Kuśnierz, and a representative of the armed forces; it is chaired by the Prime Minister'. Additional information about the Committee's works could not be found to date.

82 The meetings were to be held once weekly, the first on 22 June 1945 – Report on consultative conference on war crimes on 13 June 1945, AIPN, GK 159.2, leaves 192–199.

discussed in the conference. Józef Marlewski, head of the MFA German Section, tabled a motion to integrate the War Crimes Office into the Ministry of Justice, emphasizing that, in the majority of governments, the national offices liaising with the UNWCC functioned under justice ministries.[83] The rationale supporting his motion was based on the need to accelerate the progress made on the WCO's proceedings, supplement the missing evidence on the existing Polish charges and draft new ones, distinguishing between the most severe crimes to be tried by international tribunals and lesser offences handled by domestic courts.[84]

Due to the great powers' withdrawal of diplomatic recognition from the Polish Government-in-Exile on 5 July 1945, the organizational changes to the War Crimes Office proposed in the June conference were never implemented. The proceedings of the newly created expert committees on war crimes – Committee of Ministers and Consultative Committee – soon came to a halt. After the creation of an Interim Treasury Committee for Polish Affairs, the Polish War Crimes Office was incorporated into the General Department of Treasury Committee Section C, which was headed by Dr. Adam Nowotny, and Jerzy Litawski remained at the helm of its War Crimes Division (*Wydział do Spraw Zbrodni Wojennych*) until 9 December 1945.[85] At the expiry of Litawski's term, he was succeeded by Kazimierz Epler.

3.1 *The Draft Decree of the President of the Republic of Poland on Gathering and Securing the Evidence of War Crimes*

Shortly after the creation of the War Crimes Office, works started on the narrowing down of the technical aspects of crime records. The large volume of materials assembled in the course of four years and supplemented with materials from interrogations held on an ongoing basis called for additional staff and clear procedures for securing evidence. The first solution, proposed in November 1943 by the Ministry of the Interior, was to amend the Decree of the President of the Republic of Poland on Gathering and Securing the Evidence in Cases of Common Crimes of 29 April 1940 (Dz.U.RP.9.1940.23), so that it would extend to war crimes. In the explanatory memorandum attached with the draft amendment, Minister Banaczyk emphasized that the main responsibilities of the WCO included gathering and securing the evidence of the occupying power's activities in Poland and especially the interrogation of wit-

83 *Ibidem.*
84 AIPN GK 159.2, leaf 194.
85 Letter from Jerzy Litawski, 12 December 1945, AIPN GK 159.2, leaf 72.

nesses. The Minister proposed granting those interrogations the status of judicial proceedings,[86] noting the probative value of the statements:

> Because such evidence – particularly interrogations – may be relevant in future court proceedings in Poland, it seems to be expedient for testimonies to be recorded in circumstances permitting recovery in circumstances foreseen by Article 340 CCP.[87] For one has to reckon that many of the persons interrogated here may not be there to be interrogated again in the future.[88]

Article 1(1) of the Decree of the President of the Republic of Poland on Gathering and Securing the Evidence in Cases of Common Crimes of 29 April 1940 (Dz.U.RP.9.1940.23) read: 'The Minister of Justice may authorize employees of the Ministry, as well as members of Investigative Commissions, to perform outside of the borders of the state any and all activities with a view to gathering, recording and securing the evidence in cases of common crimes'. Article 1(2) required any persons so authorized to hold judicial qualifications. Pursuant to Article 2, the proceedings had to comply with the provisions of the Code of Criminal Procedure of 19 March 1928 (Dz.U.RP.8.1939.44). Article 3 stipulated: 'Records of the activities done by virtue of Article 1 and 2 of this decree may be read out in a court trial on par with the depositions referred to in Article 340 CCP'. In line with Article 5, the Minister of Justice was empowered to 'confer on the records of activities done prior to the coming into force of the present decree the force set forth in Article 3, provided that such records shall have been executed by persons holding judicial qualifications'. The proposed amendment envisaged an express mention of war crimes in Article 1, 'so that the activities with a view to gathering, determining and securing the evidence cover both common crimes and war crimes'.[89] Moreover, the intention was to confer authority to conduct evidentiary activities, which had been reserved by the original wording of the Decree to the employees of the Ministry of Justice

---

86 Minister Banaczyk recommended that the depositions be used according to the prescript of Art. 338 of the Code of Criminal Procedure (CCP): 'Judicial depositions of defendants and witnesses taken in the pretrial investigation (Arts. 251–257) may also be read, provided that any such person has not attended on account of obstacles impossible or too difficult to be removed or, having attended, has either testified differently than in the prior proceedings or refused to testify'.

87 Art. 340 of the CCP of 19 March 1928 (Dz.U.RP.8.1939.44): 'Documents filed in the trial hearing, if relevant to the case, shall be exhibited by the court to the parties, put on the record and read out in whole or in part'.

88 AIPN, GK 159.1, leaf 320.

89 AIPN, GK 159.1, leaf 321.

or Investigative Commissions, also on one employee of the War Crimes Office. That intention, however, was abandoned in favour of drafting a separate legal instrument.

Professor Stefan Glaser prepared a Draft Decree on Gathering and Securing the Evidence of War Crimes near the end of November 1943, probably at Minister Banaczyk's request.[90] The draft forwarded to the Minister of the Interior on 26 November 1943 counted eight articles, and its redaction was modelled on the Decree of the President of the Republic of Poland of 29 April 1940.

> Article 1
> (1) The Minister of Justice may authorize employees of the state to perform outside of the borders of the state any and all activities with a view to gathering, recording and securing evidence in cases of war crimes, set out in the Criminal Code, additional statutes and Decree of the President of the Republic of Poland of 30 March 1943 on Criminal Responsibility for War Crimes /Dz.U.RP.3.1943.6/.
> (2) Persons authorized pursuant to this article must hold judicial qualifications.
>
> Article 2
> Persons authorized pursuant to Article 1 of the present decree shall apply to the extent of the activities set out in said Article the corresponding provisions of the Code of Criminal Procedure of 19 March 1928. /Dz.U.RP.8.1929.44/.
>
> Article 3
> The President of the Council of Ministers may authorize officials mentioned in Article 1 of the present decree to release the interrogated individuals from the duty to keep official secrets. Persons who during the applicability of the present decree remain in active military service or are employed by Polish state authorities may be released from the duty to keep official secrets by the officials mentioned in Article 1 of the present decree subject to the consent of the competent Minister at each time.
>
> Article 5
> The Minister of Justice may confer on the records of activities done prior to the coming into force of the present decree the force set forth in

90 AIPN, GK 159.1, leaf 306.

> Article 3, provided that such records shall have been executed by persons holding judicial qualifications.
>
> Article 6
> Files and evidence gathered or recorded pursuant to the present decree shall be kept by the Minister of the Interior.
>
> Article 7
> The implementation of the present decree shall be entrusted to the Ministers of the Interior, Justice and Foreign Affairs.
>
> Article 8
> The present decree shall come into force on the day of publication.[91]

The WCO's amendments to the draft dealt with Articles 1 and 6 and the division of responsibility for the implementation of the decree. Article 1 was to empower the Minister of the Interior to request the Minister of Justice for the authorization contemplated by that article and expanded the circle of persons to whom it could apply. As opposed to the analogous draft of April 1940, which was limited to the employees of the Ministry of Justice alone or those of the Investigative Commissions, the revised provision emphasized that the authorization could be conferred on 'employees of the state under other ministries to perform outside of the borders of the state any and all activities with a view to gathering, recording and securing evidence in cases of war crimes'.[92] The scope of the powers of the Office was defined in more detail compared to the original wording, by adding a section to Article 6:

> (1) The gathering and securing of materials and evidence in cases of war crimes shall belong to the War Crimes Office. The said Office shall be part of the Ministry of the Interior and shall co-operate with the Government Delegates to the competent international organs. (2) Files and evidence gathered or recorded pursuant to the present decree shall be kept by the Minister of the Interior.[93]

On 16 December 1943, Minister Banaczyk forwarded the amended Draft Decree on Gathering and Securing the Evidence of War Crimes to the Minister of

---

91 AIPN GK 159.1, leaves 307–308.

92 AIPN GK 159.1, leaf 309.

93 AIPN GK 159.1, leaf 309.

Justice for opinion. Wacław Komarnicki took a sceptical position on the draft and on the contemplated establishment of a government unit for cooperation with the UNWCC outside of the justice ministry, which would conflict with the principle of the separation of powers. Komarnicki believed the decree would effectively turn the War Crimes Office – a body under the Interior Ministry – into a judicial institution and 'place the judicial power in the competence of a different ministry'.[94] Komarnicki noted that the extraordinary statutory authorization for state officials who held judicial qualifications to perform certain judicial activities on the basis of the Code of Criminal Procedure was limited to two decrees – Decree on the Appointment of a Commission in Connection with the Outcome of the War Campaign in 1939 (Dz.U.RP.10.1940.27) and Decree of the President of the Republic of Poland on Gathering and Securing the Evidence in Cases of Common Crimes.[95] The latter had general applicability to all criminal offences committed after 1 September 1939, and the authorization conferred by it 'in the light of the impossibility of the creation of judicial bodies outside the limits of the Country' was only for the employees of the Ministry of Justice, not of other ministries.[96] In Komarnicki's opinion, the Decree of April 1940 applied to war crimes, as confirmed by the existing practice of witnesses being interrogated by employees of the Ministry of Justice at the request of the Ministry of the Interior on the basis of the provisions of that decree.[97]

Komarnicki proposed integrating officials into the Ministry of Justice. Alternatively, he suggested creating a special Investigative Commission to cooperate with the Ministry of the Interior – 'the persons authorized to secure evidence could be permanently present at the Ministry of the Interior and use the collected materials on site'.[98]

---

94 *Ibidem*, leaf 279.

95 *Ibidem*. In the case of the Decree on the Appointment of a Commission in Connection with the Outcome of the War Campaign in 1939, the Commission's activities were essentially limited to determining the political, administrative and military circumstances 'of which the whole contributed to the outcome of the war in 1939', whereas matters of criminal law were removed from the centre of its attention; due to the works taking place at the Ministry of National Defence, they were ultimately excluded from the purview of the Ministry of Justice.

96 AIPN GK 159.1, leaf 278.

97 In his letter, Wacław Komarnicki referred to Minister Banaczyk's request of 5 January 1943 for employees of the Ministry of Justice to interrogate witnesses in cases of war crimes pursuant to the provisions of the Decree of the President of the Republic of Poland on Gathering and Securing the Evidence in Cases of Common Crimes of 10 May 1940.

98 *Ibidem*.

Given the opposition from the Minister of Justice, the Decree of the President of the Republic of Poland on Gathering and Securing the Evidence in Cases of War Crimes was not enacted, and the employees of the War Crimes Office were not granted the authorization foreseen in Article 1 of the Decree of the President of the Republic of Poland on Gathering and Securing the Evidence of Common Crimes. The creation of an Investigative Commission of the Ministry of Justice for the Interrogation of Witnesses in Cases of War Crimes, proposed by Wacław Komarnicki, also fell through.

In line with the organizational charter of the War Crimes Office, the interrogations were conducted in accordance with the provisions of the Code of Criminal Procedure by employees of the Office with judicial qualifications – Judge Edward Snop and prosecutor Kazimierz Epler. From 1 March 1944 to the end of May 1945, the two lawyers carried out 756 interrogations, but due to the lack of authorization from the Minister of Justice, the depositions taken by them could not be treated as evidence within the meaning of Article 340 of the Code of Criminal Procedure. With the end of May 1945, Minister Berezowski made a new request to the Minister of Justice for both investigators to be granted the requisite authorizations with retroactive effect, so that the depositions already taken could be used in court.[99] Minister Kuśnierz granted the appropriate authorizations to WCO staff on 16 June 1945, simultaneously with recognizing the depositions taken by them to that date as valid judicial documents.[100]

3.2 *Polish War Crimes Office: Section for Crimes Committed against the Jewish Population*

In spring1944, a special section was created in the War Crimes Office with responsibility for the documentation of crimes committed against Jews – the 'Jewish section' under the leadership of Manfred Lachs. Its establishment was officially announced during the conference on crimes against the Jewish population held by the Ministry of the Interior at the request of Stefan Glaser and Ignacy Schwarzbart, on 15 June 1944.[101] Invitees included UNWCC Secretary

99 Letter from Zygmunt Berezowski to Bronisław Kuśnierz, 30 May 1945, AIPN GK 159.2/237.

100 Letter from Kuśnierz to Berezowski, 16 June 1945, AIPN GK 159.2/ 204–205. By order of 16 June 1945: 'In accordance with Art. 5 of the Decree of the President of the Republic of Poland of 29 April 1940 /Dz.U.R.P.9.23/, I confer the force envisaged by Art. 3 of the aforesaid decree on depositions taken in the time from 1 March 1944 to 16 June 1945 in the scope of the activities of the War Crimes Office in London for Deputy Regional Court Prosecutor Dr. Kazimierz Epler and Investigative Regional Court Judge (…) Edward Snop'.

101 See letter from Ignacy Schwarzbart to Jerzy Litawski, 12 June 1945, AIPN GK159.1, leaves 222–224; press note from the conference, leaf 233.

Hugh McKinnon Wood and representatives of Jewish organizations active in the United Kingdom: The Board of Deputies of British Jews (William Frankel and Dr Movhovitz), World Jewish Congress (A.L. Eastermann and Dr. Leon Zelmanowicz) Jewish Agency for Palestine (M. Rosette), Wiener Library (L.Bondy), Anglo-Jewish Association (S.D. Temkin), Council of Polish Jewry (R. Merkin), and Bund (E. Scherer).[102]

In the opening speech, Minister Banaczyk recalled the Polish government's efforts undertaken since the beginning of the war to inform the global public opinion about the crimes committed under the occupation and the great need for such efforts to be continued. 'The world already knows that, in the [occupied] territory of Poland, the most brutal acts of terror are undertaken towards the Polish population and especially the Jews. But it knows too little'.[103] The fact that the Nazi policy of extermination of the Jews was being pursued in Polish territories placed a special moral obligation on Polish authorities to prosecute the perpetrators and bring them to judgement. Banaczyk offered assurances that the Polish government was making every effort – also in the UNWCC forum – for those guilty of crimes committed in Poland against the Jewish population to be tried and punished.

> The German crimes against the Jews are calling for strict punishment of the guilty. No one can give back human life (...) but let the punishment that is to befall the criminals constitute a historic document of German bestiality and be a warning to future generations.[104]

The purpose of the conference was to publicize the efforts undertaken by the Polish government to date on behalf of bringing war criminals to justice, including perpetrators of crimes committed against Polish and European Jews, and to establish an evidentiary cooperation among the participants.[105] Jerzy Litawski outlined the Polish War Crimes Office's activities, the evidentiary material assembled by it to date, charge files forwarded thus far by the Polish government to the UNWCC, and the proceedings of the special section on crimes committed against the Jewish population.

Stefan Glaser and Manfred Lachs covered the legal aspects of the punishment of war crimes. Recalling the principles of jurisdiction adopted in the

---

102 *Ibidem*, leaf 227.

103 Minister Władysław Banaczyk's speech in the War Crimes Office conference on 15 June 1944, AIPN GK 159.1, leaf 220.

104 *Ibidem*.

105 *Ibidem*, leaf 221.

Moscow Declaration, S. Glaser discussed the principles of Polish criminal law that would be applicable to cases of crimes against the Jews. He attached special importance to the consequences arising from Articles 3 and 5 of the Polish Criminal Code, linking the jurisdiction of Polish courts not solely to the place of commission of the crime ('in the territory of the Polish State' – Article 3(1) CC) but also to acts committed by foreign nationals outside of the country's borders against the 'welfare of interests of the Polish state or of a Polish citizen or Polish legal person' (Article 5 CC).[106] Glaser stressed the obligation – of not only moral but also legal nature – incumbent on the Polish government to hold trials for 'German criminals [having] committed crimes against the Jewish nationals of Poland and other states in Poland and against Polish Jews abroad'.[107] He emphasized that, notwithstanding the lack of precise definitions in international law, atrocities and mass executions committed on the Jewish population '[were] and [had to] be treated as war crimes'. The principal problem facing Polish authorities in preparing charges for the UNWCC was the difficulty contacting the homeland and lack of ability to gather full documentation from the scene of the crime (*prima facie* evidence). The active engagement of the invited representatives of Jewish organizations with the documentation works improved the prospects of expedited preparation of charges for the UNWCC, required to specify the names of the perpetrators and provide descriptions of their acts, witness testimonies, and related documentation. It was desirable to collect all sorts of materials from German and foreign press, books, German texts, anti-Semitic regulations, as well as private correspondence and testimony from whatever witnesses had been able to escape the occupied territories.

As Manfred Lachs underscored, Polish authorities had plans to draft an indictment containing the analysis of all stages of German policy of extermination of the Jews in Poland.[108] The stages were expected to encompass economic violence and expropriations begun in 1939, discriminatory legislation against the Jews, establishment of ghettoes, food rationing leading to the extermination of thousands of Polish Jews by starvation, the establishment of concentration camps, and mass murders in death camps. The goal pursued by the Polish government was to collect as much evidence as was possible and build 'the strongest indictment [possible]' covering also the first months of the

106 Stefan Glaser's speech in the War Crimes Office conference on 15 June 1944, AIPN GK159.1, leaf 206.

107 *Ibidem.*

108 Manfred Lachs, Draft speech for a conference on war crimes at the Ministry of the Interior on 15 June 1944, AIPN 159/1, leaves 209–211, here: leaf 210.

war, a period of which the memory may have faded due to the passage of time or later traumatic events.

The need to act with alacrity and be prepared for trials following immediately after the end of the war – so as to mitigate the risk of the defendants' absconding and of the destruction of the evidence of their crimes, such as had been the case in the aftermath of the First World War– required cooperation and the prompt processing of any information becoming available. Apart from making an appeal for participation in the Polish government's evidence-gathering efforts, Manfred Lachs noted the importance of war-crimes policy in the context of post-war international relations and of the legal frameworks for the anticipated trials, including the interpretation of the principle of *nullum crimen sine lege*. In his view, punishing perpetrators of the crimes would become the basis for rebuilding Europe after the war on the foundation of justice, breaking with the remnants of a 'shameful and criminal past'. He argued that only the adoption of principles from the Declaration of St. James's Palace – later affirmed in the Moscow Declaration – and the prosecution of war criminals in the occupied territories, including crimes not expressly defined in criminal statutes applicable before 1 September 1939, in formal trials, could ensure accountability and restore justice. Lachs underlined that the punishment of the guilty hinged on the engagement of politicians and legal experts alongside each other, in the form of advocacy for the principle of personal responsibility of perpetrators of war crimes, as well as involvement in the gathering of documentation and processing of the charge files being prepared on the suspects.[109]

The initiative advanced by the Polish authorities met a favourable reception from the participants in the conference, who were in agreement as to the necessity of cooperating closely in order to build documentation on crimes committed against the Jewish population. Ignacy Schwarzbart recommended that the Polish authorities establish a special cell under the Government Delegation for Poland to supervise the gathering of materials on crimes committed against the Jews and cooperate in that regard with the Jewish organizations in occupied Poland, the Bund, and the Jewish National Committee. Schwarzbart stressed that the Polish government, similarly to other governments of occupied states, had significantly better prospects of access to source materials and witnesses than the options available to private Jewish organizations abroad. A similar motion was tabled by the representative of the Council of Polish Jewry, who proposed that a delegate of the Polish government be dispatched to the occupied homeland on a mission of collecting evidence of crimes committed

109 *Ibidem*, leaves 210–211.

against the Jewish population.[110] Emanuel Scherer appealed for the immediate use of retorsions against the German Reich to save the Jewish population in the occupied territories. He also advocated for publishing the lists of criminals, with a view to the deterrence of any more massacres. As for the submission of indictments to the United Nations War Crimes Commission, two motions surfaced in the Polish ministerial conference – one to include anti-Semitic crimes committed in the German Reich before the outbreak of the war and another, from Leon Zelmanowicz of the World Jewish Congress, for the cases of systemic crimes committed against Jews to be judged by an international tribunal rather than by domestic courts.[111] Zelmanowicz, moreover, sponsored the request of the World Jewish Congress for Jewish organizations ('Jewish bodies') to be authorized to file charges with the UNWCC in cases of crimes having an anti-Semitic context.[112]

It cannot be unequivocally ascertained to what extent the cooperation between Polish authorities and Jewish organizations active in the United Kingdom and Unites States with regard to securing documentation on crimes committed against Jews was successful. In summer 1944, Manfred Lachs established correspondence with UK Jewish organizations on the matter of providing Polish authorities with materials needed for charges,[113] and in October Jerzy Litawski approached Polish Jewish organizations in New York and Tel Aviv with a similar request.[114] In his letter, the WCO head requested access to depositions of Jewish refugees from Poland for the purposes of charges being drafted for the UNWCC. The autumn of 1944 brought invigoration to such contacts in connection with the interrogations conducted by the War Crimes Office. On 13 November, one was held for A. P. Michaelis, a former executive of the Reich Representation of German Jews (*Reichsvertretung der Juden in Deutschland*), serving as a deputy president of the Association of Jewish Refugees in Great Britain, revealing information about members of the Gestapo responsible for the persecutions of the Jews, for the organization of concentration camps, and for 'matters relating to the Gestapo's pre-war action in Polish

110 Minutes of a Conference concerning crimes committed by the Germans upon the Jewish population in Poland, AIPN 159.1, leaf 196.

111 *Ibidem.*

112 'War Crimes against Polish Jews'. *Jewish Telegraph Agency Bulletin*, 18 June 1944, 2, AIPN 159.2/203.

113 Note from Manfred Lachs to Jerzy Litawski, 24 August 1945, AIPN GK 159.2, leaf 112.

114 *Cf.* Letter from Litawski to the Representation of the Polish Jewry in New York, 6 October 1944 and Letter from Litawski to the Representation of the Polish Jewry in Tel Aviv, of 6 October 1944, AIPN GK 159.1, leaves 75–76.

territory'.[115] Attending the interrogation were Dr. Norbert Lubasz and Alfred Goldstein as reporting clerks, as well as Jerzy Litawski and Manfred Lachs. On Michaelis's instruction, a witness statement on crimes against Jews was also given to the Polish War Crimes Office by another member of his organization, H. Reichemann. On 29 November 1944, Lachs and Litawski met with the representative of The Board of Deputies of British Jews, Dr. Movshovitz, who was appreciative of the Office's progress and promised to share whatever materials on anti-Semitic crimes he had in his possession.[116] The materials assembled by the section for crimes committed against the Jewish population served the Polish government as the basis for the drafting of numerous charges submitted to the UNWCC. Among others, they related to the Auschwitz and Treblinka camps; the extermination of the Jews in camps in Belzec, Majdanek, Sobibór, Kosów Polaski, and Kulmhof; the crimes of the Wehrmacht against the Jewish population during the September Campaign (1939); and the situation of the Jewish population under German occupation, as well as the discriminatory special legislation.[117]

3.3 *The Activities of Polish War Crimes Office Delegation in Scotland*

An important source of information for the staff of the Polish War Crimes Office was eyewitness testimonies – a significant group of Polish witnesses, soldiers previously forcibly conscripted into the Wehrmacht (over 225,000 Polish pre-war citizens had been forced to join the German military service under the provisions of the *Deutsche Volksliste*), who were kept in Allied prisoner-of-war camps after the invasion of Normandy in summer 1944.

One of the WCO's initiatives was to interrogate those Polish military personnel formerly employed by the Wehrmacht who had been held in Scottish prisoner of war camps since autumn 1944 (at the beginning of December 1944, the transit camps in Scotland held approximately 30,000 soldiers).[118] To support these interrogations, the Ministry of the Interior, working with the Ministry of National Defence, established a War Crimes Office Delegation in Scot-

115 Note: Cooperation of the Jewish Section of the War Crimes Office with Jewish Organizations, 3 January 1944, AIPN GK 159.2, leaf 353.

116 Note: Cooperation of the Jewish Section of the War Crimes Office with Jewish Organizations. Conversation with Dr. Movshovitz, AIPN GK 159.2/ leaf 355.

117 UNWCC, *Polish Charges against German War Criminals,* RN 123/PG/21, RN 304/P/G/30, RN 473/P/G/34, RN 591/P/G/35, RN 785/P/G/37. Also see the table on pp. 306–321. Letter from Jerzy Litawski to Lord Wright, 29 April 1944, AIPN GK 159.125, leaf 218.

118 This is the number of Polish prisoners-of-war Jerzy Litawski stated in his report to General de Baer on the works of the delegation in Scotland; cf. letter from Litawski to General Marcel de Baer, of 1 December 1944, AIPN GK 159.125, leaf 146.

land.[119] Authorizations to interrogate at the Field Outpost for Prisoners of War of the Polish Armed Forces Units Command in the United Kingdom were granted by the Minister of National Defence, Marian Kukiel, on 12 October 1944, for Jerzy Litawski, Kazimierz Epler, and Edward Snop. The organizational aspects of the work of the delegates were handled by the Outpost Office of the Defence Intelligence Section of Ministry of National Defence in Edinburgh, by Major Gorgolewski, the head of the MoND Defence Intelligence[120] Kazimierz Epler had been delegated by Litawski to carry out the first interrogations.[121] On 6 October 1944, Jerzy Litawski sent to the Head of Defence Intelligence Section 300 copies of the standard form for interrogations in cases of war crimes, requesting the military authorities to identify the prisoners of wars having the relevant information. Litawski noted that the evidence base being thus built was intended to provide the basis for charge files to be submitted by the Polish national office to the UNWCC and for updates to the lists of war criminals whose extradition would be requested by Polish authorities after the war. He stressed the importance of whatever information was known to the formers prisoners of war:

> To the works of the War Crimes Office, the testimonies of persons who in September 1939 and later years were staying in Poland, and therefore people who personally witnessed the conduct of Germans in our Country, are invaluable. Persons who could describe specific facts in practicable detail, specify the names of those Germans who have committed some criminal act, give the names of Polish victims, as well as the names of witnesses, will constitute an important contribution to the Polish government's efforts on the international stage. Owing to the victorious advance of the Allied armies through Italy and France, the fortunate coincidence allowed thousands of Poles who had been inducted into the German armed forces to unite with the compatriots in the territory of the United Kingdom. In this connection, there has arisen an exceptional opportunity for obtaining from them the information aforesaid.[122]

Upon arriving in the United Kingdom, prisoners-of-war from the German military were placed in interim camps, where they were segregated by nationality

119 The Minister of the Interior approved the establishment of an off-campus agency by WCO in Scotland on 23 September 1944. Authorization to interrogate AIPN 159.1, leaf 62.
120 AIPN GK 159.1/ leaf 71. The first interrogations were scheduled for 23 October 1944.
121 Kazimierz Epler, Report on official trip to Scotland, AIPN 159.1. leaves 33–37.
122 Guidance on Screening Interrogation Form, 6 October 1945, AIPN GK, 159.1, leaf. 73.

and assigned to transit camps. In transit camps for Polish nationals (initially Johnstone, Stewarten, Auchinraith, and Woodhouselee), they were interrogated by the commissioned and non-commissioned officers of the field outpost for prisoner-of-war affairs, with a specially designed questionnaire.[123] The second stage of selection in transit camps included the examination of the questionnaires by the staff of the Defence Intelligence outpost. Every prisoner of war having completed both stages was obliged to sign a declaration of voluntary accession to the Polish Armed Forces. Afterward, they were transferred to distribution camps exclusively for former officers of Polish Armed Forces in Polkemmet and Auchtertool. Following medical and consular screenings, they were incorporated into the Polish military.[124] For WCO purposes, the prisoners-of-war were interrogated by commissioned officers of the intelligence service stationed at the distribution camps, from where the 'screening interrogation questionnaires' were forwarded to the WCO delegates at Polkemmet and Auchtertool camps. There, judges Kazimierz Epler and Edward Snop took individual depositions with the force of a judicial transcript.

The first interrogations of Polish soldiers took place towards the end of October 1944 at the distribution camp in Auchtertool, and the last one in May 1945 at Polkemmet. The information sourced from the interrogations concerned the course of the September Campaign, conditions of living under German occupation, extermination of the civilian population, concentration camps and prisoner-of-war camps. Regarding the camps, those were especially Sachsenhausen, Dachau, Mauthausen, Ravensbrück, and Gusen, and the information included camp layouts, lists of prisoners and staff,

123 The 'Questionnaire for the interrogation of Poles – prisoners of war' designed by the Defence Intelligence at the Headquarters of the Commander-in-Chief contained the following items: personal details of the interrogated person; duration of German captivity; circumstances of entering the German armed forces; voluntary or forced accession to the Deutsche Volksliste; 'what manifestations of German propaganda he encountered'; 'During German captivity (…) was he enlisted for co-operation with German authorities, what tasks, where, when and from whom was he given'; 'information known about concentration camps'; names of Poles, former German servicemen, in British or American prisoner-of-war camps not having reported for service in Polish Armed Forces; circumstances of capture; 'Reasons for joining Polish Armed Forces'; requests concerning service in Polish Armed Forces. AIPN GK. 159.1, leaves 32–33.

124 Kazimierz Epler's report on official journey to Scotland, 16–18 October 1944, AIPN GK 159.1, leaves 33–37. Persons refusing to sign a declaration of accession to Polish Armed Forces and prisoners of war subjected to 'reservations and objection from an officer of the Defence Intelligence' were returned to general prisoner-of-war camps. According to the recent estimates, approximately 89,000 Polish soldiers forcibly drafted into the Wehrmacht were recruited into the Polish army in 1944 and 1945, which accounted for 36% of the Polish Army's personnel.

description of the conditions of camp life, and facts concerning the persecution and extermination of prisoners. Litawski's office designed a special interrogation questionnaire. After translation into English, the questionnaire itself and the very idea of interrogating prisoners-of-war about war crimes were used by the UNWCC as a model for the interrogations of German prisoners.[125] The 'screening interrogation questionnaire' was distributed to intelligence officers, who used it to interrogate persons having desirable information.[126]

In the original Polish questionnaire and in the first draft proposal at the UNWCC, the interrogating officer also had to evaluate the information received: 'I assess the information available to the interrogated person with regard to the above questions to be: extensive/satisfactory/scarce,'[127] followed by place for date and signatures of the interrogated person and reporting clerk.

The final English-language text of the questionnaire adopted by the UNWCC on 17 January 1945,[128] following a proposal[129] and amended proposal,[130] read as follows:

1) Have you been stationed in an occupied country, where and when?
2) Have you been a member of the police (state unit, etc. ... with particular reference in the case of Germans, to the Gestapo, the S.S. and the S.A.)?

---

125 Letter from Dr. Jerzy Litawski to the head of the German Section at the MFA, Józef Marlewski, 11 June 1945, IPMS, A11E/124, leaf 340. Jerzy Litawski notified the chair of the UNWCC's Committee I – General Marcel de Baer – of the establishment of the WCO Delegation in Scotland on 16 October 1944 and, on 1 December 1944, forwarded to him a report on the works with model 'screening interrogation questionnaire' in English translation attached. AIPN GK 159.125,145–146 and 170. The UNWCC announced its recommendation to all members concerning the interrogations of prisoners of war during the meeting on 17 January 1945. See UNWCC. Interrogation of Enemy Prisoners of War, AIPN GK 159.2, leaves 317–318.

126 Ibidem.

127 Corresponding to the formula used under the Second Questionnaire in 'Opinion of the interrogating officer as to the extent and quality of information which the interrogated person can give' in Interrogation of Enemy Prisoners of War. Draft Proposal by the Chairman of Committee I, 6 December 1944, C.65(2), UNWCC Archive, Reel 34, 281.

128 UNWCC, Interrogation of Enemy Prisoners of War. Recommendation adopted by the Commission on 17th January, 1945, 18 January 1945, C.65(2), UNWCC Archive, Reel 34, pp. 284–285.

129 UNWCC, Interrogation of Enemy Prisoners of War. Draft Proposal by the Chairman of Committee I, 3 January 1944, C.65(2), UNWCC Archive, Reel 34, 280–281.

130 UNWCC, Interrogation of Enemy Prisoners of War. Amended Proposal by the Chairman of Committee I, 6 December 1945, C.65(2), UNWCC Archive, Reel 34, 282–283.

3) Have you been employed in the civil or military administration of an occupied country (state place and time)?
4) Have you belonged to the personnel of a prisoner of a camp for prisoners of war, of a concentration camp, of a forced labour camp, and the like (for Germans add the Todt organization)?
5) Have you any knowledge – either from your own observation or from other persons' accounts – of facts concerning execution or ill-treatment of prisoners of war during the 1939 campaign, or thereafter in the war prisoners' camps?
6) Have you an exact knowledge – either from your own observation or from other persons' accounts – of any offences committed against the civil[ian] population of occupied countries:
   (a) deportation, mass-arrests, street round-ups?
   (b) execution of hostages?
   (c) torturing in prisons?
   (d) mass-shooting of inhabitants of villages – setting on fire of houses or[?] settlements?
   (e) rape of women and coercion to prostitution?
   (f) attempts to demoralise and inducing of children and youth to drunkenness?
   (g) robbery of private or public property – destruction of buildings, museums, libraries, monuments?
   (h) reprisals following the non-delivery of contingents of corn and cattle?
7) Can you state any names of Germans holding an office in Gestapo, S.S., Police, civil servants, except Governors and Gauleiters?

Opinion of the interrogating officer as to the extent and quality of the information which the interrogated person can give:

Approximately 600 interrogations of Poles forcibly conscripted into the German armed forces were held in the period from October 1944 to January 1945, and by the end of May 1945, more than 700 depositions were recorded.[131] Officials used the collected materials to update the lists of war criminals in charges prepared for the UNWCC – such as Polish charge no. 39 concerning the Oranienburg-Sachsenhausen camp, filed on 16 May 1945, and charge no. 41, of 17 July 1945, concerning crimes committed in the camps at Mauthausen and Gusen.[132]

131 Many of the depositions have survived. See AIPN GK 159.209 and AIPN GK 159.217.
132 UNWCC, Polish Charges against German criminals, RN 1038/P/G/40.

The depositions taken by the WCO's delegation in Scotland and the data processed on their basis were also shared in November 1945 and January 1946 with the US Armed Forces for the purposes of the trials of Mauthausen-Gusen and Dachau camp staff.[133] The matter of sharing the WCO's 'evidence for the criminal trial against perpetrators of crimes committed in the concentration camp in Dachau' was raised on 24 October 1945 by Major Teofil Krzyżaniak at the instruction of American military authorities.[134] The American authorities received depositions of Polish officers, including Rudolf Osiecki, Jan Wyrob, Franciszek Joniec, Michał Białas, and Lech Moniński. These were collected by Kazimierz Epler and Edward Snop. Additional materials from the WCO, including lists of Poles shot at Dachau in September 1940 and camp staff, were also provided.[135] American military prosecutors requested materials on crimes committed at the camps in Mauthausen and Flossenburg through Major Wojciech Szułdrzyński in December 1945.[136] The materials shared by the WCO included copies of depositions of Eryk Słonina, recorded on 19 February 1945 at the military camp in Polkemmet; depositions of Andrzej Wantuła of 20 April 1945 at the camp in Polkemmet and of Józef Burek, who testified on 25 October 1944 at the distribution camp in Auchtertool,[137] as well as the deposition of Franz Ziereis, commandant of Mauthausen camp, of 23 and 24 May 1945, recorded by the head physician of the prisoner-of-war hospital, Dr. Antoni Gościński.[138]

---

133 Trials of Dachau camp staff and Mauthausen-Gusen camp staff before the American Military Tribunal in Dachau, 15 November – 13 December 1945, on 6–21 August 1947, Joshua M. Greene, *Justice at Dachau – The Trials of an American Prosecutor* (Broadway: 2003), Tomaz Jardim, *The Mauthausen Trial: American Military Justice in Germany* Cambridge, (Massachusetts : Harvard University Press 2012).

134 Letter from Major Teofil Krzyżaniak to Adam Nowotny, 24 October 1945, and letter from C.B. Mickelwait of the Deputy Theater Judge Advocate's Office (War Crimes Branch) in the matter of sharing the evidentiary material concerning the Dachau concentration camp, 19 October 1945, AIPN GK 159.2/ leaves 95–96.

135 Kazimierz Epler's letter of 13 November 1945 with appendices AIPN GK 159.2/leaves 94–108. Depositions of witnesses of crimes committed at Dachau camp, see: AIPN GK 159/63.

136 Letter from C.B. Mickelwait of the Deputy Theater Judge Advocate's Office (War Crimes Branch) in the matter of sharing the evidentiary material concerning the concentration camps of Mauthausen and Flossenburg, AIPN GK 159.2, leaf 24.

137 Letter from Adam Nowotny to the commander of the Polish liaison officers for war crimes attached to the US Army, Major W. Szułdrzyński, AIPN GK 159.2/ leaf 22. Partial deposition of Eryk Słonina, recorded on 19 February 1945 at the prisoner-of-war camp in Polkemmet, AIPN GK 159.2, leaves 25–30.

138 Copy of the Deposition of the Lagerkommandant of KL Mauthausen, Franz Ziereis, 24 May 1945, AIPN GK 159.2, leaves 35–46.

3.4 *The Establishment of Groups of Liaison Officers for War Crimes at the* SHAEF

Successful interrogations of former prisoners of war at Polish military camps prompted the formation of specialized investigator groups under the WCO. Their aim was to interrogate witnesses and gather evidence in Reich territory liberated by the Allies. In early April 1945, Jerzy Litawski drafted a request concerning the establishment of groups of liaison officers for war crimes as part of the detachment of Polish Liaison Officers for Repatriation at the Supreme Headquarters of the Allied Expedition Force (SHAEF).[139] The Detachment of Polish Liaison Officers for Repatriation at the SHAEF was created on 7 September 1944. According to Litawski, there was a need for a special group of liaison officers either having judicial or prosecutorial qualifications or licensed to practice law, with further training in UNWCC Guidelines. They would be exempt from other SHAEF liaison duties. Unlike repatriation officers, the legal liaisons would be subordinated jurisdictionally not to the Minister of National Defence but to the Minister of the Interior, who would also nominate candidates for vacancies.

Their duties included reaching out to Polish hubs such as transit camps holding civilians or prisoners of war; carrying out informational interviews and taking depositions in compliance with court procedure; securing evidence of crimes involving:

> (a) the conduct of Germans in Poland before their resettlement to the Reich heartlands – for the purpose of identifying specific crimes; names of German perpetrators, as well as names of victims and witnesses;
>
> (b) treatment of Poles forcibly removed from Poland and placement in German prisoner-of-war camps, concentration camps or labour camps or Todt organization (...) – for the purpose of identifying the system and method of extermination, collective and individual responsibility for the persecution, deportations or internments of the civilian population in inhumane conditions, unlawful expropriation, and pillaging, as well as the forced labour of Polish civilians, particularly workers, in support of the German war machine.[140]

---

139 Motion concerning the establishment of a group of liaison officers at the SHAEF for war crimes, 3 April 1945, AIPN GK 159.2, leaves 285–286.

140 Motion concerning the establishment of a group of liaison officers at the SHAEF for war crimes, of 3 April 1945, AIPN GK 159.2, leaves 285–286.

The groups of liaison officers for war crimes were created near the end of May 1945, following General Eisenhower's order of 9 May 1945 for Polish, Greek, Yugoslavian, and Czechoslovak liaison officers to cooperate in collecting evidence with UK and US Armed Forces.[141] While the groups of liaison officers for war crimes were organizationally subordinated to the Ministry of National Defence, their tasks were to be carried out in consultation and cooperation with the War Crimes Office. On 26 May 1945, Minister Bronisław Kuśnierz granted investigative authorizations to the delegated judges in accordance with Article 1 of the Decree of the President of the Republic of Poland on Gathering and Securing the Evidence in Cases of Common Crimes.[142] In the British occupation zone, a group of liaison officers was established under the leadership of Judge Major Tadeusz Kaczorowski, attached to the 21st British Army of the Rhine. In the American zone, the corresponding group was led by Judge Major Wojciech Szułdrzyński of the Counter-Intelligence Service and Judge Major Teofil Krzyżaniak, both attached to the 12th American Army. Interrogations followed the UNWCC's list of war crimes and used a standardized form created by WCO staff. The latter contained topics and sets of questions to be covered by the interrogation.[143] Those were as follows:

1. Duration and cause of placement in a concentration camp.
2. Personal information (name of the organization, position) of the person responsible for the camp placement.
3. What was the number of prisoners at the time the witness arrived at the camp?
4. Did that number change?.
5. Whether and what transports came to the camp?
6. Age group of concentration-camp inmates; [their] gender and nationality.
7. What was the procedure for handling new arrivals (registration numbers, mugshots, issue of clothing, matter of money and valuables in possession)?
8. What did the daily schedule at the concentration camp look like?
9. Who held authority at the camp?; names of the Lagerführer, Lagerkommandant, Blockführers, and Arbeitsführers, with details enabling identification.
10. What did the administration system at the camp look like?
11. What works were the prisoners forced to do?

141 AIPN 159.125/ leaf 48, Ryszka, *U progu Norymbergi*, 183–184.

142 Authorization of 26 May 1945, AIPN GK 160.3/ no pagination.

143 War Crimes Office deposition transcript, AIPN GK 160.3/ leaves 16–17.

12. General treatment of prisoners at the camp and at work; treatment of the Jews.
13. Punishment system for the prisoners.
14. What punishments were used at the camp and for what infractions? (individual punishment or collective: flogging, pole, bunker, punishment detail – *Strafkompanie*)
15. Who decided the penalty and who enforced it?
16. System of abuse at the camp.
17. How frequent were fatalities resulting from: (a) penalties; (b) malnutrition; (c) overwork; (d) gas chambers?
18. Whether suicides occurred and for what reasons?
19. Manner of dealing with the bodies of the deceased (crematory, interment, etc.).
20. Whether and in what forms did medical, spiritual or other assistance exist?
21. Was it possible to take part in religious practices?
22. What examples of special atrocities is the witness aware of (experiments, etc.)?
23. Composition of camp guards (organization, composition with regard to nationality).
24. Were there any instances of release from camps and in what circumstances did that happen?

The liaison-officer groups for war crimes conducted investigations in American and British occupation zones until early 1946, when the Polish Military Mission for the Investigation of War Crimes in Europe was created under the Polish Military Mission in Germany in Wiesbaden. In the American zone, outposts of the Polish Military Mission for the Investigation of War Crimes were located at Dachau and Heidelberg-Ludwigsburg, and in the British Zone at Bad Oeynhausen, Lübeck, Braunschweig, and Paderborn. In April 1946, the Polish Military Mission for the Investigation of War Crimes received the documentation of more than 800 investigations conducted in the British zone by the group led by Major Tadeusz Kaczorowski, and approximately 270 from the groups of Wojciech Szułdrzyński and Teofil Krzyżaniak in the American zone.[144]

144 Kobierska-Motas, *Ekstradycja*, 90.

4 Investigative Commissions of the Ministry of Justice

Investigative Commissions of the Ministry of Justice were created as foreign agencies of the Ministry of Justice in areas having significant Polish communities, pursuant to Article 1 of the Decree of the President of the Republic of Poland on Gathering and Securing the Evidence in Cases of Common Crimes of 29 April 1940, which read:

> The Minister of Justice may authorize employees of the Ministry, as well as members of Investigative Commissions, to perform outside of the borders of the state any and all activities with a view to gathering, determining and securing evidence in cases of common crimes.[145]

The Investigative Commissions of the Ministry of Justice in the Middle East – Istanbul and Jerusalem – began their operations in November and December 1940, following the evacuation of Polish authorities from Romania. They continued the work of the Investigative Commission established in February 1940 in Bucharest,[146] of which the members were Aleksander Robinson, Zygmunt Blenau, Jan Szułdrzyński, and Karol Aleksandrowicz as chairman.[147] After the departure of Aleksandrowicz from Istanbul to London, the Commission in Istanbul was led by Zygmunt Blenau, and the one in Jerusalem by Aleksander Robinson. Through its interrogations of Poles in Palestine, the Commission gathered eyewitness accounts of life in occupied Poland and crimes by the occupying power. Accordingly, in April 1942, Aleksander Robinson petitioned Stanisław Mikołajczyk 'in consultation with Mr Minister of Justice of the Republic of Poland to give the Investigative Commission of the Ministry of Justice in Jerusalem the mandate to keep a register of German crimes [committed] in Polish territory'.[148] Pursuant to Mikołajczyk's instructions given on 30 June 1942, the Investigative Commission was to conduct its recording works with regard to war crimes in consultation with the Polish Consulate in Jerusalem.[149]

---

145 Decree of the President of the Republic of Poland on Gathering and Securing the Evidence in Cases of Common Crimes, Dz.U. R.P. 9.1940.23, art. 1.

146 Report of the visitation and general inspection of the Investigative Commission in Jerusalem reporting to the Minister of Justice carried out on orders from the Minister of State Plenipotentiary of the Government of the Republic of Poland, Professor Stanisław Kot, by Dr. Wiktor Sukiennicki, from 23 December 1942 to 6 February 1943, IPMS Kol. 214.15, leaf 297.

147 AIPN GK 159.1, leaf 592.

148 Letter from Aleksander Robinson to the Ministry of the Interior, 27 April 1942. AIPN GK 159.1, leaf 528.

149 AIPN GK 159.1, leaf 550.

The staff of the Investigative Commission in Tehran (moved to Beirut close to the end of the war) also interrogated Poles deported to the USSR, including former embassy delegates.[150] The investigative works of the Ministry of Justice in Africa were entrusted to the Investigative Commission in Nairobi.[151]

Foreign delegations of the Ministry of Justice for the investigation of crimes committed by the occupying powers also operated in New York, Paris, and Stockholm. In January 1943, the Minister of the Interior approached Polish authorities in the United States for nominations of suitably qualified persons to source informational and evidentiary material on crimes committed by the occupying powers in Poland from direct witnesses or victims in America.[152] Efforts to obtain the approval for the establishment of a Commission and the necessary funding for its operations were initiated by Wacław Komarnicki in spring 1943. In April, he asked the Polish Ambassador in Washington, D.C., Jan Ciechanowski, to name a candidate for the position of chairman of the Commission,[153] which ultimately went to Dr. Włodzimierz Sokalski, a justice of the Criminal Chamber of Polish Supreme Court, where he had served as chairman of the Opining Committee. Justice Sokalski participated in the 3rd International Conference on the Unification of Criminal Law in 1936, alongside Emil Stanisław Rappaport and Raphael Lemkin..[154] Sokalski was officially appointed to head the New York Commission in early June 1943.[155] Due to the lack of approval from the US Department of State for diplomatic visas for Polish citizens or for the expansion of 'any Polish diplomatic posts whatsoever',[156] Minister Komarnicki's plan could not be brought to fruition. After a year of preparation, the Investigative Commission of the Ministry of Justice in New York fell through.

150 IPMS, A.20.4a, 154–160.

151 Letter from Adam Nowotny, Head of Section VI (for the liquidation of the outposts of the Ministry of Justice) of the Interim Treasury Committee for Polish Affairs, November 1945, AIPN GK 160.3, leaf 17.

152 Letter from the Minister of the Interior to the Minister of Justice, 5 January 1943, IPMS A.20.4a/ 179/ no pagination.

153 The list of candidates nominated by the Polish Embassy comprised: Dr. Włodzimierz Sokalski, Justice of the Supreme Court; Artur Miller, Supreme Court Prosecutor; and the following municipal judges: Oskar Schenker, Karol Czałczyński, and Józef Gidyński. *Cf.* Wacław Komarnicki's report concerning the creation of an Investigative Commission in the USA, IPMS A.20.4a/179.

154 Szawłowski, 'R. Lemkin. Warszawski adwokat', 298.

155 Wacław Komarnicki's report concerning the creation of an Investigative Commission in the USA, IPMS A.20.4a/179.

156 Adam Romer's letter to Wacław Komarnicki, 23 March 1944, IPMS A.20.4a, 179.

The autumn of 1944 saw the beginning of efforts to have an Investigative Commission established in France under the leadership of the Head of the Criminal-Judicial Section at the Ministry of Justice in the Government-in-Exile, prosecutor Jerzy Jaczynowski. France was the temporary abode of the second largest number of refugees from Poland after the United States of America, totalling about half a million people according to estimates calculated by the Ministry of Justice during the same season. After the Vichy government was formed and Polish diplomatic missions in France were dissolved in summer 1940, Polish nationals were left without legal protection. The need to handle the various aspects of issuing replacement documents relating to their civil status and the administration of justice in France specified in the Decree of the President of the Republic of Poland on Gathering and Securing the Evidence in Cases of Common Crimes provided Minister Komarnicki with an important argument for obtaining a diplomatic visa for Jaczynowski and for expediting the latter's departure for France.[157]

Accountability for crimes committed under Nazi rule was a significant matter for the Polish diaspora in France, which demanded the punishment not only of the Nazi perpetrators but also of Poles collaborating with the Vichy-government. A letter from the Polish Embassy in Paris to the Ministry of Justice, dated 10 October 1944, addressed this problem and the need for a response from the Polish justice system concerning persons 'who had collaborated with the occupation authorities in France (…)' and 'for them to be taken to account for acts and deeds contrary to the interests of the Polish State'.[158] The recommendation was to have special proceedings in such cases conducted by heads of consular offices in cooperation with Polish non-government organizations, for which the Minister of Justice categorically refused his approval.[159] Komarnicki emphasized that the investigation of crimes committed by Polish nationals against the interests of the Polish State in the territory of France had to be entrusted to an Investigative Commission of the Ministry of Justice, and any trials need to wait until after the end of the war and could proceed 'only on the basis of the Polish Criminal Code and before Polish courts'. Pending the commencement of the UNWCC's activities, tasks in relation to securing evidence already gathered, or still being gathered, on the occupation authorities' Polish

157 *Cf.* Wacław Komarnicki's letters to the Ministry of Foreign Affairs, 28 September, 11 October, and 2 November 1944, IPMS A.20.4a/170.

158 Answer from Secretary General Eugeniusz Jarra of the Ministry of Justice, of 7 November 1944, to a letter from the Polish Embassy in Paris of 10 October 1944, IPMS A.20.4a/170.

159 *Ibidem.*

collaborators were entrusted to Polish outposts reporting to the embassy in France.[160]

Jerzy Jaczynowski began his work in France in November 1944 as a delegate of the Minister of Justice. His responsibilities, assigned by Wacław Komarnicki (who would resign thereafter with the rest of Stanisław Mikołajczyk's cabinet on 24 November 1944) included: performing investigative activities specified in the Decree of the President of the Republic of Poland of 20 April 1939; drafting a report on criminal activity among Polish expatriates in France accounting for the specific circumstances of that group (Polish nationals permanently residing in France; refugees arriving after 1 September 1939; and Polish labourers or prisoners brought in by German occupation authorities), and especially crimes committed against the interests of the Polish State; determining the future scope of works and staffing needs of the Commission; issuing replacement documents pertaining to civil status for Polish nationals in France; and examining the situation of the lawyers present in the territory with a view to 'options for organizing assistance for them and (…) putting them to use in the scope of their profession and delegating tasks to them'.[161]

Jerzy Jaczynowski dispatched his first report on the situation of the Polish diaspora in France on 15 December 1944. Therein, he emphasized the distinct social need for a response from the Polish justice system to persons denounced for collaboration.[162] On the basis of Jaczynowski's write-up and the recommendations of Polish Embassy in Paris, Minister Bronisław Kuśnierz – in office from 29 November 1944 – supported establishing an Investigative Commission in France as soon as possible, along with a special institution responsible for the urgent examination of particularly manifest cases of Nazi collaborators and for the 'rehabilitation of those Polish citizens who [we]re appealing to Polish authorities with a plea to investigate the merit of allegations of collaboration with the enemy offered against them'.[163] Such cases were to be entrusted to specially created 'citizens' courts of honour' (an institution not previously regulated by Polish legislation, which is why Minister Kuśnierz

160 *Ibidem.*

161 Instruction for the Delegate of the Ministry of Justice in France, IPMS A.20.4a/170.

162 Remarks and conclusions illuminating the problem of the Polish diaspora in France from the position of the Ministry of Justice, IPMS A.20.4a/170. Demands for reaction from the Polish government and for cooperation with French authorities in the interest of 'freeing our society of suspected elements and so they see to the punishment of the traitors, irrespective of whatever they may be doing today or under whose protection they may have found refuge' were voiced in Polish émigré press in France. See *Wolna Polska*, 12 (1944).

163 Remarks and conclusions…, IPMS A.20.4a/170.

advocated for the enactment of suitable legal provisions). In spite of the determination shown by the Polish government, the establishment of the aforementioned institutions proved to be impossible. The Delegate of the Ministry of Justice in France continued the investigation and registration of cases of Polish nationals suspected of crimes against the interests and security of the Polish state until the abolition of the office in December 1945.

Moreover, Jaczynowski constantly exerted himself, together with the board of the Polish Red Cross and with the Polish Military Mission, on behalf of Poles released from concentration camps and labour camps. As part of his assistance to Polish former prisoners, he liaised with the SHAEF to locate Polish lawyers and provide them with material support; he looked into options for employing Polish lawyers released from the camps as administrative officials or liaison officers. In many instances, Jaczynowski's intermediation was successful.[164]

The activities of the Investigative Commissions of the Ministry of Justice essentially focused on interrogating Polish citizens, conducting investigations and providing co-ordination for matters relating to the administration of justice outside of Polish territory, also with regard to investigations into war crimes. An exception from this model was the idea of creating a special investigative commission in May 1945 for the war crimes committed by the head of the General Government of the occupied Polish territories, Hans Frank. Bronisław Kuśnierz's motion to that effect was approved by the Council of Ministers. By resolution of 11 May 1945, the Minister of Foreign Affairs was tasked with:

> undertaking the appropriate steps towards the governments of the United Kingdom and of the United States with a view to remanding Dr. Hans Frank (...) to the judicial authorities of the Republic of Poland for the purpose of his being interrogated as a suspect in criminal offences committed against the Polish State and its citizens and handing over to the same authorities the evidence of crimes and any property of the Polish Nation and State found in his possession.[165]

The Council of Ministers instructed the Minister of Justice to establish an investigative commission with jurisdiction to interrogate Hans Frank and

164 Report from the Delegate of the Minister of Justice in France, 2 May 1945, IPMS A.20.4a/170.

165 Motion by the Minister of Justice for the [meeting of the] Council of Ministers on 11 May 1945, IPMS, PRM-K. 103/17B, leaf 21, PPRM vol. VIII, 481.

investigate the crimes committed by him.[166] The rationale attached with the decision stated:

> Dr. Frank [is] one of the main war criminals whose activities have chiefly affected Poland. The Government of the Republic of Poland has the right and duty to address to the Allied Governments a request for (…) Dr. Frank to be remanded to the judicial authorities of the Republic of Poland. The Minister of Justice as the Prosecutor General of the Republic of Poland has the jurisdiction to conduct the investigation and secure the evidence in this matter.[167]

As the Polish authorities failed to obtain the approval for the interrogation of Hans Frank, the special investigative commission intended for that purpose was not created.

Also in May 1945, an Investigative Commission of the Ministry of Justice was established in Sweden for 'gathering, recording and securing, pursuant to the Decree of the President of the Republic of Poland, of 29 April 1940, the evidence of war crimes committed by Germans against the Polish State and Nation'.[168] Its main task was to interrogate Polish women – former prisoners of German concentration, POW, and labour camps – who were in Sweden following the rescue mission led by the Swedish Red Cross and Danish authorities in spring 1945, known as the 'White Buses' operation.[169] Initiated by Count Folke Bernadotte, its objective was to evacuate Scandinavian nationals from German labour camps and concentration camps. From April 1945 onward, the rescue efforts were extended to foreign nationals as well. Approximately 21,000 former prisoners of various nationalities – including 7,000 Polish citizens… – were taken from the territory of the German Reich to Sweden.[170] By July 1945, another 10,000 were expected, including 8,000 Polish nationals.[171] A large group among those were the former female prisoners of Ravensbrück. As

166 *Ibidem.*

167 Minutes of the meeting of the Council of Ministers, 11 May 1945, PPRM, vol. VIII, leaves 485–486.

168 Minutes of the meeting of the Council of Ministers, 25 May 1945, PPRM, vol. VIII, 512.

169 Sune Person, *Escape from the Third Reich : Folke Bernadotte and the white buses* (Barnsley : Frontline Books 2019).

170 Izabela A. Dahl "'… this is material arousing interest in common history; …" Zygmunt Lakocinski and Polish Survivors' Protocols'. *Kwartalnik Historii Żydów*, September 2007, 320; Zygmunt Łakociński, *'Folke Bernadotte* i akcja Szwedzkiego Czerwonego Krzyża'. *Przegląd Lekarski* (1968), 145–152.

171 Letter from Henryk Zajączkowski to the Minister of Justice, 2 July 1945, AIPN GK 160/3, leaf 62.

emphasized by Bronisław Kuśnierz in his rationale for the establishment of the Investigative Commission:

> these women, abiding in Poland under the German occupation, and subsequently in Germany, were witnesses to German crimes, and besides that, many of them were victims of those crimes. As eyewitnesses, they will by their testimony import new facts or illuminate such as are already known but only vaguely so. That will permit both the factual and the legal classification of the war crimes.[172]

Speaking in favour of the establishment of an Investigative Commission in Stockholm – the Minister of Justice argued – was also the fact that SHAEF liaison officers could not perform documentation tasks or otherwise operate in the territories of neutral states. In the opinion of Kuśnierz, the only legal way to secure such evidence of German crimes as could be found in Sweden was through the procedure foreseen by the Decree of the President of the Republic of Poland on Gathering and Securing the Evidence in Cases of Common Crimes.[173] On 25 May 1945, the Council of Ministers decided to create the Investigative Commission of the Ministry of Justice in Stockholm.[174]

The Commission's work began on 1 June 1945. Two Polish lawyers who had lived in Stockholm since the outbreak of the war were employed – Regional Court Judge Jan Reykowski and Deputy Prosecutor of the Regional Court in Vilnius Henryk Zajączkowski, the latter as chair. Both received their appointments on 30 May 1945.[175] The administrative activities were carried out from the headquarters of the Polish legation in Stockholm, and the interrogations themselves in transit camps in the vicinities of Malmö, Stockholm, and Gothenburg, where Poles liberated from the camps were also employed as reporting clerks.[176] The specified duration of the Commission's appointment was two months, and in that time it was expected to interrogate prescreened witnesses out of over 6,000 former Polish female prisoners then in Sweden. In

---

172 Reasons for the motion for the [meeting of the] Council of Ministers of 25 May 1945, IPMS, PRM-K. 103/17E, leaves 58–59, PPRM, vol. VIII, 520.

173 *Ibidem.*

174 PPRM, vol. VIII, 521.

175 Jan Reykowski and Henryk Zajączkowski's date of appointment to the Commission was 30 May 1945. *Cf.* AIPN GK 160.3/leaves 26–27.

176 Henryk Zajączkowski's letter to the Minister of Justice, 2 July 1945, AIPN GK 160, leaf 62. Two such reporters were Janina Koźlikowska and Helena Miklaszewska, see: Depositions taken by the Investigative Commission in Stockholm, IPN GK 159/219, leaves 34–54.

reality, the operation lasted until the end of 1945[177] due to the increasing number of internees and the difficult conditions under which the investigations were conducted – residence in transit camps and ongoing medical treatments, as well as the physical and mental health of the former prisoners and their sometimes limited ability to testify. Henryk Zajączkowski rendered the following account of the situation in early July 1945:

> Despite working all day long, we are unable to interrogate more than two persons [a day]. They are both victims and eyewitnesses. The enormity of those people's experience has caused a certain numbing of the memory and requires significant focus on their part in the giving of testimony. Recalling the years lived at the camps evokes a state of trepidation, weeping; a series of tragic memories often leads them to go off-topic. All this affects the speed of the recording of the transcript.
>
> New transports (…) are already arriving. In terms of health, the condition of the people is significantly worse than that of those having arrived at the end of April and in May of the present year. The majority cannot move by their own effort [i.e. have reduced mobility]. Due to infectious diseases (tuberculosis, spotted typhus, paratyphoid, dysentery, diphtheria), contact with the arrivals is immensely difficult.[178]

While collecting and processing evidence, the Investigative Commission cooperated with the Polish legation in Stockholm and, through its mediation, also

177 The Investigative Commission of the Ministry of Justice in Stockholm was the longest-operating of all foreign agencies of that ministry. In November 1945, with all the other Investigative Commissions being in liquidation, the Commission in Stockholm was still operating. In a report from November 1945, the head of Section VI of the Treasury Committee for Polish Affairs responsible for the liquidation of the agencies of the Ministry of Justice, Adam Nowotny, requested a deferral until early 1946 in order to interrogate the large number of former prisoners and secure the evidence.: 'Section VI provides the Commission with explanations and guidelines and receives from it the transcripts of evidence secured by the Commission, which [the Section], after inspection, forwards to the War Crimes Office. As the Commission, on account of the large number of those interned, has been unable to gather all the evidence found there, Section VI has petitioned Mr. Chief Representative of the Treasury Committee for Polish Affairs for an extension of the activities of the Commission for a further two months'. AIPN GK 160.4, leaf 17.

178 Letter from Henryk Zajączkowski to the Minister of Justice, of 2 July 1945, AIPN GK 160.3, leaves 62–63.

with the diplomatic missions of other states,[179] as well as the Delegate of the Ministry of the Interior in Sweden, Stanisław Kocan.[180] There were plans to establish a cooperation with the Polish Source Institute (*Polski Instytut Źródłowy*, PIŹ) in Lund. The Institute was a private initiative by Polish scholars residing in Sweden undertaken at the beginning of 1940 to source information about the victims of the war and the situation in occupied Poland. Its associates had been assisting Polish refuges in Denmark and Sweden in spring1945 already before the establishment of the Investigative Commission in Stockholm.[181]

5 The Polish Source Institute in Lund

A prominent place among Polish institutions abroad involved in the documentation of the crimes committed in occupied Poland belonged to the Polish Source Institute (*Polski Instytut Źródłowy*) in Lund.

The origins of the Source Institute, officially inaugurated in Lund in 1945, go back to 1939 and 1940, which is when Polish diplomatic missions worldwide launched a campaign of information and documentation on the German and Soviet invasions of Poland.[182] As soon as 17 September 1939, the Polish Legation in Stockholm requested the teachers of the Polish language who were in the employ of Swedish universities for assistance with the flow of information

---

179 For example, in June 1945, the British Embassy in Sweden delivered to Polish authorities a list of Polish women on whom medical experiments had been performed at the camp in Ravensbrück, specifying victims murdered after the procedures and those having died in the aftermath. *Cf.* AIPN GK 160/3, leaves 53–55.

180 At the beginning of June 1945, Stanisław Kocan, Acting Delegate of the Ministry of the Interior in Sweden, inquired with Kazimierz Epler about transports of former prisoners of concentration camps to Sweden and about the possibility of having them interrogated for the purposes of the War Crimes Office. In the light of the commencement of the operations of the Investigative Committee, the Ministry of the Interior decided: 'there is no need for the delegate of this Ministry (…) to occupy himself with the examination of persons or processing of materials of probative value to the War Crimes Office; it would be expedient for Mr Kocan to consult with Messrs Zając̨zkowski and Rajkowski on the matter and forward to them such documents as he may already have in his possession' – Letter from Karol Epler to the Head of the Ministry of the Interior Social Section, of 21 June 1945, AIPN 159.2, leaves 200, 202 and 203.

181 Dahl, '… this is material'; Łakociński, '*Folke Bernadotte*'; Paul Rudny, *Polski Instytut Źródłowy w Lund* (PIZ) *The Polish Research Institute in Lund. A Presentation of the Archives*, Lund University website, available at http://www3.ub.lu.se/ravensbruck/piz-eng-presentation.pdf (accessed 30 January 2025).

182 Eugeniusz S. Kruszewski, *Polski Instytut Źródłowy w Lund (1939–1972). Zarys historii i dorobek* (London-Copenhagen: Polish University Abroad, Polish Scandinavian Institute 2001), 16–21.

from occupied Poland. In January 1940, a convention of Polish language instructors and culture teachers working in Sweden was held in Stockholm. Those in attendance included Zygmunt Łakociński of Lund University, who had worked as a press correspondent of the Polish Consulate in Malmö before the war, Józef Trypućko of Uppsala, and Zbigniew Folejewski of Stockholm. Documentation and archive works began on Polish affairs, Polish-British relations, Polish–German relations, and whatever information was available about the situation in occupied Poland. The information was obtained from Swedish, German, and British press, propaganda publications, books, and statements from refugees fleeing Poland from January 1940 onward. The archive would store publications and documentation, process materials, and write reports for Polish diplomatic outposts in the country. It was subdivided into five sections: (1) war library; (2) war archive; (3) war bibliography; (4) records of cultural damage; (5) Polish–German relations.[183] In March 1944, the archive was transformed into a Polish Source Institute, which, however, continued to operate as a private initiative financed by its associates.[184] The arduous task of interviewing hundreds of witnesses out of the Ibidem. evacuated to Sweden in spring 1945 by the 'White Buses' called for a reorganization, as well as institutional and financial assistance.[185]

On 17 May 1945, Zygmunt Łakociński addressed the Polish authorities in London with the idea of establishing the Polish Source Institute in Sweden, outlining the work done by his team to that date.[186] Interviews with the Poles arriving in Sweden, he emphasized, created a unique opportunity to verify the documentation built thus far on German crimes, supplement it with witness accounts and determine new facts. He drew attention to the necessity of securing documents and other physical evidence, as well as interviews with former prisoners to be conducted quickly by qualified professionals, both because of the health condition of the interviewees and their 'unblurred' memory of their wartime experiences.[187] As he noted:

183 Ibidem.

184 AIPN GK 159.235, leaf 2.

185 Scans of interview transcripts recorded by the employees of the Polish Source Institute in Lund (the Voices from Ravensbrück Archive) are available from the Lund University Library website at https://www.ub.lu.se/en/voices-from-ravensbruck (accessed 30 January 2024). See also Zbigniew Stanuch (ed.), *Golgota kobiet: relacje więźniarek Ravensbrück i innych obozów koncentracyjnych ze zbiorów Polskiego Instytutu Źródłowego w Lund* (Szczecin, Warszawa: IPN 2018).

186 *Ibidem.*

187 AIPN GK 159.2, leaf 225.

> The immensely important field of war crimes can at this time be studied and documented with the aid of a multitude of witnesses numbering in the thousands – victims, individuals who often brought documents of great historical value relating to the camps, prisons, torture and death not only of Poles but also other nationalities.[188]

The Institute's documentation efforts included a source archive, developed since autumn 1939, covering the background, course, and outcomes of the war. In spring 1945, it also established 'documentation commissions' following the arrival of the first Polish transports to Sweden.[189] Five such commissions operated in Lund and one in Landskrona; each had a staff of four to six people. In the hinterlands, where recuperation camps for Poles were arranged – localities such as Nörrköping, Jönkoping, Doverstorp, Tranäs, Rosöga, Avesta, Vissingö, Muisjö, Trelleborg, Krisjanstad, and Öreryg – testimonies and documentation were collected by rapporteurs from the documentation committees.

Łakociński's intention was for the Institute to be subdivided into specialized sections comprising historians, physicians, and jurists and to create study teams dealing with specific types of crimes and categories of victims. His estimate put the number of employees at approximately 50.[190] The evidence collected by the Institute's staff was divided into the following categories: 1. sources, including lists of prisoners, orders of camp authorities and all camp documents brought by the prisoners to Sweden, which were to be 'copied, annotated and processed on-site';[191] 2. depositions (interrogation transcripts) concerning the events of which the former prisoners were witnesses or victims or of which they had second-hand knowledge; 3. inventory of losses; 4. stages of transports; 5. camp poetry and songs, the compilation of a 'camp dictionary'; and 7. the prisoner's dress, clothing patches, utensils, and souvenirs of camp life, which would be donated as exhibits to Polish museums after the war.[192]

Although the Polish authorities in London expressed interest in incorporating the Polish Source Institute into the government's war-crimes documentation efforts, as well as the Institute's cooperation with the Investigative Commission of the Ministry of Justice in Stockholm, the Government-in-Exile ultimately abandoned plans to establish the Polish Source Institute due

---

188 *Ibidem.*

189 Copy of an aide-mémoire by Zygmunt Łakociński concerning the Polish Source Institute in Lund, 17 May 1945, AIPN GK 159.2, leaf 225.

190 AIPN 159.2, chart 226.

191 AIPN 159.235, chart 2.

192 *Ibidem.* See also Kruszewski, *Polski Instytut*, 24.

to mounting international pressures.[193] A motion for government funding for the Institute was tabled by the Minister of Foreign Affairs, Tadeusz Gwiazdowski, on 14 June 1945, thus almost on the eve of the loss of diplomatic recognition.[194]

In spring 1945, Łakociński began talks with the leadership of the Swedish Institute of International Affairs to establish and fund the Polish Source Institute. Through the agency of the Swedish Institute's then-leader, Sven Dahl, Swedish authorities approved the creation of a team of Polish researchers under the leadership of a Lund University historian, Professor Sture Bolin. Officially, the Study Team in Lund began to operate on 22 October 1945. Łakociński invited the cooperation of former Polish prisoners who were in Sweden at the time and had the benefit of higher education and qualifications relevant to the expected tasks.[195]

Within a year into the Study Team's operation (which the Swedish authorities decided to discontinue with the end of September 1946), the team conducted 514 interviews with former prisoners of German concentration and labour camps and collected documents, journals, and various camp artefacts. On that basis, it was possible to reconstruct prisoners lists, personal information of the staff members, as well as camp and sub-camp topographies, such as plans of Auschwitz-Birkenau, Bergen-Belsen, Bendorf, Gross Rosen, Hanover, Majdanek, Malchow, Pustków (the *SS-Truppenübungsplatz Heidelager*), Radom, Ravensbrück, and Sachsenhausen.[196] In autumn 1946, Keith Mint, the British forensic pathologist in charge of the British Army's War Crimes Group studying the war crimes and medical experiments at Ravensbrück had the opportunity to acquaint himself with the work products of the Lund Study Team. As a result, the materials put together by Polish researchers could be used in the British trial of Ravensbrück staff held in Hamburg. Helena Dziedzicka, a former prisoner and member of the Team, testified during the trial.[197]

---

193 AIPN GK 159.2/ leaf 224, AIPN GK 159.2, leaf 200.

194 Tadeusz Gwiazdowski's motion for government financing for the PIŹ, 14 June 1945, AIPN GK 159.2, leaf 224.

195 The Team's associates included Helena Dziedzicka, Krystyna Karier, Bożysław Kurowski, Helena Miklaszewska, Luba Melchior, Józef Nowaczyk, Ludwika Broel-Plater, Irena Jaworowicz, and Halina Strzelecka. A detailed description of the selection process is provided by Kruszewski, *Polski Instytut*, 34–41. See *ibidem*, 134–138; Dahl, '... this is material', 326.

196 Kruszewski, *Polski Instytut*, 52–54.

197 Dahl, '... this is material', 327.

CHAPTER 5

Legislative Works and Their Reception in Legal Circles

The Polish Government-in-Exile's policymaking on justice for crimes committed in occupied Poland culminated with the drafting of the Decree of the President of the Republic of Poland on Criminal Responsibility for War Crimes. Work on the decree began at the Ministry of Justice in spring 1942, and it was promulgated in the Journal of Laws on 31 March 1943. That was half a year before the establishment of the United Nations War Crimes Commission, and the conceptual discussions on the decree followed by the travaux preceded the Western Powers' decisions on the organization of a justice system for crimes committed in occupied territories. The Decree of 30 March 1943 was the first domestic enactment of an Allied power during the Second World War laying down the rules of individual responsibility for violations of international law, as well as the basics of substantive law, with a view to criminal trials before domestic courts after the war.

As a legislative enactment, the Decree of the President of the Republic of Poland on Criminal Responsibility for War Crimes functioned as both a tool and a symbol of the implementation of Polish war-crimes policy. That doctrine was predicated on the assumption of holding violators of international law personally accountable by putting them on trial. Under the Polish concept, an effective justice system for war crimes would require a division of jurisdiction between domestic and international courts; guarantees of extradition from neutral states, and adaptation of substantive law to the needs of anticipated criminal trials.

What makes the works on the text of the decree stand out is not only their early timing and extensive preparations for the prosecution of war criminals but also the participation of experts from different fields in government discussions, with leading academic jurists of the inter-war period among them, such as Wacław Komarnicki, Stefan Glaser, Bohdan Winiarski, and Wiktor Sukiennicki. Their scholarly and practical experience from before the war had a significant influence on the shape taken by the Polish Government-in-Exile's war-crimes policy, including the principles espoused by the Decree of the President of the Republic of Poland on Criminal Responsibility for War Crimes.

The debates on the Polish draft saw numerous references to inter-war initiatives to regulate individual responsibility for violations of international law.

The topics discussed included the lack of sanctions in international law and lack of effective extradition law, the question of state sovereignty and limits of state immunity under the act-of-state theory, including jurisdictional immunity,[1] as well as the interpretation of the principle of *lex retro non agit* and the possible scope of domestic and international jurisdiction for international crimes. The focal point of the Polish debate was the theory of culpability and the grounds of the attribution of guilt for offences against international law. This included the principle of responsibility of both issuers and executors of unlawful orders, as well as circumstances excluding or mitigating culpability, such as acting on orders from superior authority (*respondeat superior*) or in life-threatening situations (necessity). Furthermore, the analyses underscored the unprecedented scale of persecution of civilians in occupied territories, and subjection of the entire administrative and military apparatus to the Nazi policy of extermination. Attention was drawn to new types of crimes – such as concentration camps, mass executions, forced resettlement, forced labour under inhuman, starvation-level conditions, or forced insemination – as well as the purpose of the systemic violence aimed at the persecution and extermination of entire groups, discrimination on racial and ethnic grounds, and the destruction of cultural legacy, and social fabric. The arguments and expert studies cited during those debates were of considerable significance not only to the subsequent work on the Decree of the President of the Republic of Poland on Criminal Responsibility for War Crimes but also to the wartime discussion of new definitions of the crimes of international law – 'crimes against humanity' – and their special form that was the crime of genocide, defined by Raphael Lemkin in 1944.

1 The Law vis-à-vis 'Statutory Lawlessness'

Underpinning the works leading up to the Decree of the President of the Republic of Poland on Criminal Responsibility for War Crimes, along with the international efforts undertaken by Polish legal minds to muster support for the idea putting war criminals on trial, was the desire to establish an effect-

1 Hersch Lauterpacht, 'The Problem of Jurisdictional Immunities of Foreign States'. *British Yearbook for International Law* 1951. Even to this day, the limits of a state's jurisdictional immunity are subject to divergent interpretations in international-law scholarship. See Marcin Kałduński, 'Immunitet państwa w prawie międzynarodowym w kontekście zbrodni wojennych i zbrodni przeciwko ludzkości'. *Zeszyty Prawnicze Biura Analiz Sejmowych Kancelarii Sejmu* 58 (2018), 67–95.

ive justice system founded upon legal bases derived from domestic legislation and from the principles of international law.

The hope was that the normative definition of such legal bases for the post-war criminal trials would embody the principles of rule of law and legal certainty. The accountability model designed by Polish lawyers for crimes committed by the occupying powers was predicated on the channels of criminal justice, as opposed to revenge killings, summary executions, or political retribution. Nevertheless, legislative drafts purporting to establish the terms of responsibility for crimes committed before the coming into force were met with accusations of contravening the principles of legality and *lex retro non agit*.[2] As a result, legitimacy for the principle of holding Nazi criminals personally liable was sought in international custom and in the axiological sources of the law of nations, as well as principles of justice and equity, viewed as basic and universal principles of law.

The debate focused on the relationship between positive law and legal positivism – recognizing the constitution, statutes, and other positive legislation as the sole sources of law – on the one hand, and doctrines of morality or law of nature – presupposing the existence of a superior normative order and objective values constituting a source of law, independent from and superior to positive law – on the other hand.[3] It was noted that the absence of sanctions for violations of laws and customs of warfare did not necessarily have to imply a lack of binding legal force. Cited in support of the legitimacy of the principle of individual responsibility for violations of international law were Articles 227–230 of the Treaty of Versailles, as well as customary international law, principles of justice and equity, and the axiological sources of the law of nations, expounded *inter alia* by the Martens Clause.[4] The rationales offered by Polish jurists and in government publications placed key importance on principles of justice and equity. The legal bases for the punishment of war criminals were traced both to international treaty law (Hague Conventions and Treaty of Versailles) and to the higher legal order (morality and law of nature). According to that path's reasoning, bringing the criminals to account and exacting compensation for their victims meant giving effect to the endur-

2 *Cf.* Douglas, 'Was damals', 49–50.

3 For more on this topic, see: Zygmunt Ziembiński, *O pojmowaniu pozytywizmu oraz prawa naturalnego* (Poznań: Ośrodek Wydawnictw Naukowych 1993); Maria Zmierczak (ed.), *Prawo natury w doktrynach polityczno-prawnych Europy* (Poznań: Wydawnictwo Naukowe UAM 2006).

4 Polish Ministry of Information, *The German Invasion of Poland: Polish Black Book containing Documents, authenticated reports and photographs. Preface by His Grace the Archbishop of York* (London, Melbourne: Hutchinson & Co. Ltd. 1940), 14.

ing universal principles of the law of nations and to the ideal of justice lying at the very source of positive law.

Without the benefit of a normative definition in sources of law existing at the time, the search for a basis of criminal responsibility for violations of international law and organized mass-scale violence against the civilian population of occupied territories touched closely on the question of the criteria of a just law. The search explored the value system of criminal and international law from the perspective of preparation for post-war trials of those guilty of mass-scale crimes committed throughout occupied Europe, where refraining from prosecution because of the lack of positive legal norms regulating the terms of individual responsibility would have been offensive to the sense of justice. It also stressed the need to reveal the systemic nature of Nazi criminality, grounded in the positive law of the German Reich.[5]

In their analyses of the German legal system – highlighting the issue of judicial crimes and discriminatory nature of the legislation enacted by the occupation authorities – Polish lawyers challenged the positivist approach and the separation of law and morality. They problematized the binding force of an unjust positive law, while asking about the criteria of a just law, embodying the idea of justice and transcending the formal limits of positivist legal doctrine. Theirs was a quest for solutions to the conflict, defined in 1945 by Gustav Radbruch as the contraposition of 'statutory lawlessness and supra-statutory law' (*gesetzliches Unrecht und übergesetzliches Recht*).[6] Radbruch's key arguments and the elements of his formula are outlined by himself in an article titled *Gesetzliches Unrecht und übergesetzliches Recht*:

> The conflict between justice and the security offered by legal certainty could be decided in such a way that positive law, guaranteed by legisla-

5 Ryszka, *Państwo stanu wyjątkowego*, Karol Jońca, 'Dylematy prawa natury Trzeciej Rzeszy'. *Studia nad Faszyzmem i Zbrodniami Hitlerowskimi* 17 (1994), 5–22. Manfred Walther, 'Hat der juristische Positivismus die deutschen Juristen wehrlos gemacht?', in Redaktion Kritische Justiz (Hg.), *Die juristische Aufarbeitung des Unrechts-Staats* (Baden-Baden 1998), 299–322.

6 The German legal philosopher's theory that 'manifestly unjust' statutes lack the binding force or nature of an act of law is a theoretico-legal construct distilled from several of his writings. The most important elements of the Radbruch formula are laid out in an article published as *Gesetzliches Unrecht und übergesetzliches Recht* in autumn 1946. Spearheading the critical debate on the extreme legal formalism and positivist legal interpretation that had become one of the instruments of Nazi criminality, Radbruch developed one of the most influential concepts in legal philosophy of the twentieth century. See: Gustav Radbruch, 'Gesetzliches Unrecht und übergesetzliches Recht'. *SJZ* 1 (1946), 1–8; Arthur Kaufmann, *Gustav Radbruch. Rechtsdenker, Philosoph, Sozialdemokrat* (München: Piper Verlag 1987); Frank Saliger, *Radbruchsche Formel und Rechtsstaat* (Heidelberg 1995); Herbert Lionel Adolphus Hart, 'Positivism and the Separation of Law and Morals'. *Harvard Law Review* 71 (1978), 593–629.

> tion and authority, would preserve its primacy even in the fact of inutility and injustice of its content – except for a statute so 'unbearably unjust' that justice itself must ultimately prevail over the 'unjust legislation'. It is not possible to draw a sharper distinction between cases of statutory lawlessness and those laws that are binding despite the injustice of their contents. A clear line, nevertheless, can be drawn where no one is aspiring to justice and the legislation deliberately ignores the equality that is the kernel of justice, at which point a statute is not merely an 'unjust law' but loses altogether the status and nature of law.[7]

Polish concepts originating from the Second World War era searched for an answer to the question of what constitutes a just law, among the axiological sources of the law of nations, the principles of justice and equity, and teleological interpretation of law. One can view this universalistic approach as part of the 'second renaissance of natural law' characteristic of the Second World War era – an element of accounting with a conflicted legal past, 'overcoming the distortions of legal practice and corruption of legal science in the bygone period', as well as laying the bases for a just legal order and 'determination of the criteria of equitable law'.[8] In the course of conceptual works on the principles of accountability for Nazi crimes, Polish jurists emphasized that under the Nazi system, the law had become an instrument of persecution wielded for purposes opposed to the principle of justice and to the protective and guaranteeing functions of law.

The colonial dimension of Nazi law in occupied Poland stemmed from the ideology of *Blut und Boden*, but its discriminatory nature and its departure from legalist principles, including the retroactive application of law, the absence of a legal hierarchy, and the lack of a uniform legislative process, were a continuation of the criminal law reforms carried out after Hitler's rise to power.[9] In accordance with the *Führerprinzip*, introduced by Adolf Hitler in 1933, the source of law in Nazi Germany was the will of the Führer, and the

---

7 See: Gustav Radbruch, Statutory Lawlessness and Supra-Statutory Law (1946), transl. by Bonnie Litschewski-Paulson and Stanley L. Paulson, 1 (26) Oxford Journal of Legal Studies 2006, 1–11. The Polish translation used by the author of this book is Gustav Radbruch, *Ustawowe bezprawie i ponadustawowe prawo*, in Gustav Radbruch, *Filozofia prawa*, translated by Ewa Nowak (Warszawa: Wydawnictwo Naukowe PWN 2009), 250.

8 Kazimierz Opałek, *Studia z teorii i filozofii prawa* (Kraków 1997) 17, cited after Jerzy Zajadło, *Formuła Radbrucha: filozofia prawa na granicy pozytywizmu prawniczego i prawa natury* (Gdańsk: Arche 2001), 77

9 Maximilian Becker, *Mitstreiter im Volkstumskampf, Deutsche Justiz in den eingegliederten Ostgebieten 1939–1945* (München: De Gruyter. Oldenburg 2014), 42–45.

purpose was to protect the German national community (*Volksgemeinschaft*).[10] The belief in German racial superiority over other nations and ethnicities, and of the priority of a "Germanic sense of law" and the "morality of the peoples' community" justified reforms of state institutions and all branches of the law, in opposition to the established legal principles and liberal–democratic concepts. The 1935 Nazi criminal law reform abandoned the *lex retro non agit* principle and included amendments to §2 of the 1871 Penal Code (StGB), introducing new principles of criminal responsibility that enabled sentencing by analogy, in cases of crimes not regulated by statutory law, if the act in question violated the "healthy sensibility of the people" (*gesundes Volksempfinden*) or the idea of law (*Rechtsgedenken*) expressed in the law.[11] In addition, new instances of criminal jurisdiction competent to rule in cases of political offences and apply an extraordinary procedure were introduced – the special courts (*Sondergerichte*, 1933) and a higher instance, the Peoples' Court (*Volksgerichtshof*, 1934).[12] A glaring example of the embodiment of the racist ideology in the German criminal justice system were the Nuremberg Laws of 15 September 1935 – the Reich Citizenship Law and the Law for the Protection of German Blood and German Honour, introducing criminal liability for marriage and extramarital sexual relations between Jews and Germans (*Deutschblutigen*) and the crime of 'dishonouring the race' (*Rassenschande*). Shortly thereafter, Romani and Black individuals were also subjected to these discriminatory regulations, which became tools for exclusion from social, economic and political life, racial persecution, and of enforcing the Nazi eugenic policy in the Third Reich.[13] In autumn 1941, the Nuremberg Laws were extended to the western Polish territories, illegally incorporated into the Reich,[14] with the exception of the Poznań region,

---

10 Kai Ambos, *National Socialist Criminal Law. Continuity and Radicalization* (Nomos: Baden-Baden 2019), 36–71.

11 The Amendment on the criminal code of 28 June 1935, 'Amendment on criminal procedure' of 28 June 1935 (*Gesetz zur Änderung von Vorschriften des Strafverfahrens und des Gerichtsverfassungsgesetzes vom 28 Juni 1935*, RGBl. I, p. 844), Martin Loehning, 'Germany: The Reichsgericht 1933–1945.', in: D. Venema (ed.), *Supreme Courts Under Nazi Occupation* (Amsterdam University Press 2022), 65–68.

12 Special courts in the Reich were created based on the *Government's order on establishing Special Courts'* of 21 March 1933 (Verordnung der Reichsregierung über die Bildung von Sondergerichten RGBl.I, p. 136), Loehning, 'Germany', 63–65.

13 Reich Citizenship Law and the Law for the Protection of German Blood and German Honour of 15 September 1935 (Reichsbürgergesetz Gesetz zum Schutze des deutschen Blutes und der deutschen Ehre vom 15. September 1935, RGBl. I, S. 1146–1147).

14 Verordnung über die Einführung der Nürnberger Rassengesetze in den eingegliederten Ostgebieten. Vom 31. Mai 1941 – RGBl. I, Jg. 1941.

known as the *Reichssgau Wartheland*. The Nuremberg Laws were in force there already in autumn 1940 by the decision of the head of regional administration, Arthur Greiser, who stood out for inventing and enforcing extremely brutal and radical methods of Germanisation and persecution of Poles and Jews under his jurisdiction.[15] Repressive orders and regulations defining the legal status of Jewish and Polish civilians were introduced in both systems of occupation – in the Polish annexed territories and in the General Government. These special laws concerned the compulsory labour, restrictions in civil law (in particular, family and marriage law), ghettoization, identification marks, a system of residence and work permits, economic burdens, and limitations (food contingents, rationing).[16] On 8 March 1940, the Reich Security Main Office promulgated the so-called 'Polish Decrees' (*Polen-Erlasse*), which introduced discriminatory regulations for the Polish forced labourers, including a mandate on special identification marks (badges bearing the letter "P").

Another form of special criminal legislation imposed by the Third Reich on Polish civilians, both during the military occupation and under the German administration of occupied territories, were the laws and orders supporting the German war effort and protecting the *Volksgemeinschaft* from political and national enemies, which were promulgated even before the outbreak of the war and in its first months. As examples of these laws defining new types of offences, introducing harsh sanctions and imprecise norms, may be mentioned the Special Wartime Military Decree of 17 August 1938 (*Kriegssonderstrafrechtsverordnung*)[17] and the Decree against Public Enemies (*Volksschädlingsverordnung*) of 5 September 1939, aggravating sanctions for common crimes 'endangering the community' and imposing the death penalty, if required, by 'sound popular judgment [*gesundes Volksempfinden*]' or, if needed, to 'especially repudiate the criminal act'. Another example provides the Decree of 5 December 1939 against violent criminals (*Verordnung gegen Gewaltverbrecher*), the provisions of which applied retroactively from 1 September 1939, and in certain cases, also to the offences com-

---

15 Catherine Epstein, *Model Nazi: Arthur Greiser and the Occupation of Western Poland* (Oxford: OUP 2010).

16 Stanisław Salomonowicz, 'The Legal Status of Poles under German Occupation (1939–1945). Some Remarks on the Need for Research.' *Krakowskie Studia z Historii Państwa i Prawa* 10 (2017), 101, Becker, *Mitstreiter*, 21–35.

17 Special Wartime Military Decree of 17 August 1938 (Kriegssonderstafrechtsverordnung vom 17 August 1938, Reichsgesetzblatt 1939 I, 1455. On the application of this legslation by the Wehrmacht court-martial against 28 defendants oft he Polish Post Office in Danzig in September 1939 (all sentenced to death and executed), see Dieter Schenk, *Die Post von Danzig. Geschichte eines deutschen Justizmords* (Reinbek bei Hamburg 1995).

mitted before the outbreak of war. During the military occupation, the provisions of German penal law were applied against Polish citizens by the special courts (*Sondergerichte*) established on 5 September 1939, military field courts, military summary courts (*Standgerichte*) subordinated directly to the commanders of the respective army units, and police summary courts. The latter judicial body was established by the Decree on the Possession of Weapons of 12 September 1939, banning the Polish population from possessing firearms, ammunition and explosives, and from attacking the German armed forces on penalty of death.[18]

In the General Government, the police summary courts were upheld (although outside of the judicial bodies subordinated to the Department of Justice of the General Government), their jurisdiction was extended by Hans Frank's decrees of 31 October 1939, introducing death penalty for „acts of violence" and of 2nd October 1943, which imposed the capital punishment for attacks on the „German Reconstruction Plan".[19] With broadly defined powers, no procedural or evidentiary rules, and no oversight by higher courts, the police summary courts were means of every day terror used as instruments of extermination, targeting civilians and political opponents.[20] Despite – or perhaps precisely because of – their extraordinary operation mode and the lack of formal rules of procedure, the jurisdiction of *Standgerichte* was considered by the administration of GG as superior to the Special Courts (*Sondergerichte*), which were created in November 1939 with the authority to try Polish citizens under the provisions of the German Penal law, special criminal legislation of the Third Reich, and acts issued by General Governor and his subordinates.[21] The discriminatory nature of the Nazi judiciary in occupied Poland was also mirrored in the organization of common courts in General Government that functioned in dualistic, independent systems of Polish and German courts. The latter had authority over all – criminal and civil cases – involving German nationals or legal persons. The Polish courts, whose structure and authority were significantly reduced in relation to the judiciary of the Second Republic,

---

18 Decree on the Possession of Weapons of 12 September 1939 Verordung über Waffenbesitz – 12 September 1939, Pospieszalski, *Documenta occupationis* v. VI 45, 47, VOBL. Polen, 8–9, 32.

19 Governor-General's Decree on the Suppression of Acts of Violence of 31 October 1939, VBLGG 1939, 9 Regulation for the combatting of attacks on the German work of reconstruction of 2 October 1943, VBLGG, 535.

20 Polish Information Centre, *German Organisation of Courts in General Government of Poland,* New York 1941; Pospieszalski, *Documenta* v. VI, 145.

21 For more on that topic see: Diemut Majer *'Non-Germans' Under the Third Reich: The Nazi Judicial and Administrative System in Germany and Occupied Eastern Europe, with Special Regard to Occupied Poland, 1939–1945* (Washington D.C: Texas Tech University Press 2014).

adjudicated in civil cases involving 'non-Germans' (e.g. Poles, Ukrainians), while in the criminal matters, a German prosecutor had the authority to refer a given case to the Polish or German court or to the *Sondergericht*.[22] As rightly pointed out in a report published by the Polish Government-in-exile in 1941, the German organisation of courts in the General Government served two purposes: 'legitimization of terror and guarantee of privileges for Germans (...) and their interests by using special legal means'.[23] The situation of Poles in the territories incorporated into the Reich was entirely different, where by the decree of 8 October 1939, Polish courts were demolished and the material and procedural criminal law of the Third Reich was introduced.[24] Jewish and Polish people in the incorporated territories were subjected to special criminal legislation, serving the goals of Reich's policy of Germanization, forced labour exploitation, and physical extermination. These objectives were achieved through special criminal legislation, particularly the *Decree of 4 December 1941 on criminal law for Poles and Jews,* which was used as a tool of severe criminal repression of Polish and Jewish civilians in the Third Reich and in the annexed territories.[25]

Demonstrating the contradiction between the German legal system, particularly its criminal law, and the principles of justice was an essential element of Polish Government-in-Exile's definition of Nazi violence as a systemic attack on the fundamental values of European legal culture.[26] Emphasis was placed on the threat posed by it not only to the population of the occupied territories (as direct victims of the extermination policy) but to humanity as a whole and to the values of Western culture. In autumn 1941, Stefan Glaser referred to the German Reich's system of terror in occupied Europe as a war against the legal order and against 'all traditional concepts of law'.[27] Publications and speeches dealing with Nazi crimes in Poland and the rest of Europe

---

22 Konrad Graczyk, Hubert Mielnik, 'Special Courts (Sondergerichte) in the General Government (1939–1945)', *The Legal History Review* 91 (2023), 271–308.

23 Polish Information Centre, *German Organisation of Courts in General Government of Poland,* New York 1941.

24 Becker, *Mitstreiter,* 47–62, 165–204.

25 Decree of 4 December 1941 on criminal law for Poles and Jews of 4 December 1941 (*Verordnung über die Strafrechtspflege gegen Polen und Juden in den eingegliederten Ostgebieten* vom 4. Dezember 1941, RGBl. 1941 I, 759); Pospieszalski, v. V, 411–413.

26 *The German Occupation of Poland*; Stefan Glaser, *'Nullum Crimen Sine Lege'. Journal of Comparative Legislation and International Law* 24 (1942), 29–37; Henry Slesser (foreword), *Justice Outlawed: administration of law in German-occupied territories* (London: Liberty Publications 1943).

27 Stefan Glaser's speech during the inauguration meeting of the Cambridge Commission on Penal Reconstruction and Development on 14 November 1941.

often addressed the antinomy between the 'sense of justice of civilized nations' and the perversity of Nazi law; the legal foundations of Western civilization and the German 'barbarity'. A protest note titled 'The German Occupation of Poland' summed up the organized and systemic nature of the Nazi crimes legitimized by the legal system of the Third Reich as follows in:

> (1) there is no single principle of the law of nations, nor a single provision of positive international law, which has not been trampled underfoot by the occupant;
> (2) The German Reich, as in 1914–1918 continues to regard its own international obligations as 'scraps of paper';
> (3) Germany persists in the belief that Right is the product of Might alone and scorns the essential principles of Justice and Equity. And these are facts which the civilized world will have to remember in years to come.[28]

The purpose of the arguments was to demonstrate the criminal nature, illegality, and 'lawlessness' of Nazi legislation as a tool for the implementation of a policy of persecution. The goal was also to reinforce the sense of community among the Allied states, which – according to the Polish concept – in preparing the trials of war criminals were taking a stand in defence of the basic principles of Western culture. Calls for war criminals to be tried under domestic and international law were presented as the giving of effect to the principles of justice and rule of law, in contradistinction to the anomie and anarchy of Nazi rule. Punishment for mass-scale crimes was believed to be an indispensable element of post-war reconstruction and an instrument by which to rebuild the citizens' confidence in the state and law and restore the equilibrium in international relations. With a focus on crimes against civilians and their persecution on racial and ethnic grounds, on the principles of humanity, Polish lawyers appealed to the shared values of the Western world as to the 'guardian of justice'.[29]

To reinforce the sense of community of values among the Allied states, Polish authorities invoked the provisions of the Atlantic Charter of 14 August 1941 and the 'ideal of justice' expressed in it.[30] In their interpretation, the fruition of that ideal would guarantee the sovereignty and freedom of the states and punishment for those guilty of waging a war of aggression and crimes committed during it. Such an understanding of the 'ideal of justice' was propagated – in

---

28 *The German Occupation of Poland*, 35.

29 Von Lingen, *Legal flows*.

30 The Atlantic Charter of 14 August 1941 https://avalon.law.yale.edu/wwii/atlantic.asp.

the works of his ministry, in publications and numerous speeches and other addresses – by the Minister of Justice in the Polish Government-in-Exile, Wacław Komarnicki. In his speech titled *O sprawiedliwość dla Polski* ('For justice for Poland'), Komarnicki expressed his belief in the triumph of justice 'in relations among states and in the internal life of states'; he demanded punishment for the German crimes that were 'contrary to divine and human law, trampling upon all moral principles and prescripts of international law'.[31] Both of the above emphasize the overarching importance of the principle of justice and the strong correlation between guarantees of punishment for criminals and the universal demand for peaceful organization of international relations after the war:

> As we speak of a philosophy of four years of war, as lawyers, defenders of law and justice, we can pose to ourselves the question: what does the population of our countries, which is being tormented with bestial brutality by a common enemy, demand?.
>
> We can answer in one word: we demand justice. The conduct of the present war would be of no use, were justice not to prevail thereafter. Justice should secure for us peace, welfare [and] safety. Justice should make humanity better and give [it] a future sheltered from the bloody atrocities of which our martyred nations fall victims today. (...) I demand justice for my Country, for a people (...) whom the enemy is maltreating with cold sophistication and attempting to exterminate. For having been the first to resist the invaders, the Polish nation is now suffering its 'punishment'. The enemy is taking his revenge, for with our resistance, we have denied German hegemony over the world. (...).
>
> It is, therefore, an unthinkable supposition that justice be denied to Poland out of all countries, a country having suffered for the Allied cause and the freedom of the world doubtless the greatest sacrifices. (...) Denial of justice to Poland would be unworthy of the [world] order for which we are fighting (...). Justice is not 'zones of influence' – anti-democratic in their principle; justice is not a strategic border of sorts, but it is the banner of the United Nations, the Decalogue of the Atlantic Charter.[32]

---

31 Wacław Komarnicki's speech titled 'O sprawiedliwość i panowanie prawa' ('For justice and the rule of law'), IPMS Kol. 38/7.

32 Wacław Komarnicki's speech *O sprawiedliwość dla Polski* ('For justice for Poland'), given on 27 September 1943 during an Allied lawyers' conference titled *La Leçon de quatre années de guerre*. IPMS Kol. 38/7.

If Poland's self-sacrifice in 1939 (…) is not to go to waste, there must emerge in the aftermath of this war, a new world – better and more just. This is the purpose of the principles enshrined in the Atlantic Charter. (…).

2 The Ministry of Justice: The Concepts of Wacław Komarnicki

A prominent place among the bodies responsible for the making and implementation of Polish Government's war-crimes policy belongs to the Ministry of Justice.[33] Whereas in the initial two years of the war, the main hubs in the government's policymaking on war crimes were the Ministry of Foreign Affairs and the Ministry of the Interior, the situation changed after Wacław Komarnicki took the lead of the Ministry of Justice in January 1942. The Ministry soon became involved in the work and took in in new directions. Under the influence of Komarnicki, the legal aspects of exacting justice for war crimes and eliminating the consequences of the occupation found their way to the front and centre of Sikorski cabinet's legislative effort.

The debates on the text of the Decree of the President of the Republic of Poland on Criminal Responsibility for War Crimes were an element of an extensive legislative programme for the post-war period that Kormanicki pursued, practically from the beginning of his time in office. The reorganization of the justice ministry and creation of a Legislative Works Commission (*Komisja Prac Ustawodawczych*, KPU) according to the design of Komarnicki's predecessor, Hermann Lieberman, was a conducive factor in this development. The Commission was an expert body responsible for preparing and evaluating drafts and theses needed for a 'constitutional reform for the post-war Polish state'.[34] The Commission began to operate in March 1942. Its members included 'eminent legal scholars and practitioners', whose task was to pass their opinions on legislative drafts referred to them by the Minister of Justice, who served as the Commission's president, with the Head of Legislative Section as his deputy. The Secretary was appointed by the Minister, and the members of the Commission chose rapporteurs from among themselves for such matters as were referred to it. The Legislative Works Commission incorporated six sections: (I) Political Law (chaired by Tadeusz Brzeski); (II) Organization of the Judiciary (chaired by Stanisław Szurlej); (III): Civil Law and Procedure

---

33 The internal organization of the Ministry of Justice is described in Chapter 2 of this book.

34 Wacław Komarnicki's address in the meeting of the Budget Committee of the National Council of the Republic of Poland on 27 March 1942, AAN 2/133/0/6/90, leaves 170–173. See also Jankiewicz, *W poszukiwaniu*, 74–76.

(chaired by Zygmunt Nagórski); (IV) Commercial and Maritime Law (chaired by Bronisław Hełczyński); (V) Criminal Law and Procedure and Prisons (chaired by Stefan Glaser); and (VI) Legislative Technique (chaired by Ludwik Krajewski).

The activities of the Legislative Works Commission were closely linked to the implementation of the government policy laid out in the declaration of 24 February 1942 (so-called February Declaration). Stanisław Grabski – an economist and professor of Jagiellonian University, as well as parliamentary deputy in 1919–1927 and intermittently Minister of Religious Affairs and Public Education – was a co-drafter with Komarnicki. The February Declaration defined the Polish goals for the war and peace and the terms of reconstruction of the country's political system after the war, with the proviso that the exiles would hand over the legislative power to a democratically elected parliament. The Declaration fleshed out the political and constitutional goals announced in Prime Minister Sikorski's speech of 6 October 1939, following the creation of his cabinet, and in his Address of 18 December 1939. Sikorski insisted that 'the sole goal of the Government of National Unity w[ould] be to rebuild a great and well-ruled Poland, (…) equally just to all her citizens'.[35] The February declaration promised:

> Poland will be a democratic, republican state, adhering strictly to the principle of rule of law, accountable before a fair national deputation fully representing the will of the whole society, and elected by universal, equal and direct suffrage in a secret ballot. The Polish Nation distances itself absolutely from any undemocratic, totalitarian systems of governance, and from any form of dictatorship.[36]

As emphasized by Komarnicki, the overarching principle of the political programme of the Government-in-Exile was the principle of justice, understood to mean 'social and ethnic justice' guaranteeing social and economic rights, individual freedom and rights of ethnic and religious minorities, as well as 'justice in the sense of rule of law (…)'.[37] In the sphere of internal politics, that would be achieved through the restoration of Polish parliamentarianism, democracy, rule of law and respect for individual rights, stronger self-governments and a

35 Minutes of the meeting of the Council of Ministers, 6 October 1939, PPRM, vol. 1, 4–5.

36 Declaration of the Government of National Unity, 24 February 1942, Dz.U. RP 1943 nr 8, poz. 40.

37 Wacław Komarnicki, 'O sprawiedliwość i panowanie prawa' ('For justice and rule of law'), IPMS Kol. 38/7.

clean break with the authoritarian policies of the *Sanacja* regime. The principle of justice, being the highest principle applicable to international relations and the foundation of democratic legal systems, was of the focal point of Komarnicki's ministry's work on war-crimes policy and post-war political reconstruction. In his view, the satisfaction of wrongs suffered under the occupation and punishment of those guilty would guarantee the rule of law and re-establishment of public confidence in the state institutions. In the sphere of domestic policy, the same would be achieved by protecting individual rights and safeguarding an independent judiciary. Accordingly, Komarnicki initiated not only work on Poland's post-war judicial system, pursued by the Legislative Works Commission, but also training programmes for legal professionals and future judges, as well as topic-specific studies. Significantly, he outlined his concept of state and law – based on the principles of legality, rule of law and social solidarity – during the inauguration of a Polish programme in legal and administrative studies at the University of St. Andrews, Scotland, on 23 March 1942.[38]

Komarnicki and Grabski's decalogue of programmatic principles espoused by the Polish Government-in-Exile and expressed in the February Declaration, leaned strongly on Wacław Komarnicki's ideas of state and law dating from the *interbellum* period. Following in 1918, Komarnicki served re-emerged Poland as an expert in constitutional law (from January 1920 onward in charge of the Department of State Law and Science at Stephen Báthory University in Vilnius) and civil servant, participating in the development of the principles of Polish constitutionalism and parliamentarianism. He participated in the drafting of the so-called Small Constitution (*Mała Konstytucja*) of 1919, sat in the Constitutional Committee (*Komisja Konstytucyjna*) of the Legislative Sejm (*Sejm Ustawodawczy*), and became the author of respected classics in state law, such as *Polskie prawo polityczne. Geneza i system* ('Polish political law. History and system') (1922), *O praworządność i zdrowy ustrój państwowy* ('For rule of law and a healthy state system') (1928) or *Ustrój Państwowy Polski współczesnej. Geneza i system* ('The state organization of modern Poland. History and system') (1937). He was an opponent and critic of the constitutional changes and reforms of all branches of law embarked upon by members of Marshal Piłsudski's *Sanacja* camp. After the May Coup of 1926 against the cabinet of Wincenty Witos,[39] the August Amendments to the March Constitution

38 Wacław Komarnicki, 'Rola prawnika w wyzwolonej Polsce' ('The lawyer's role in liberated Poland'), speech, IPMS, Kol. 37/7. On this topic, see also: Jankiewicz, *W poszukiwaniu*, 66–71.

39 Wacław Komarnicki, *O praworządność i zdrowy ustrój państwowy: aktualne zagadnienia konstytucyjne z okresu maj 1926-marzec 1928 r.* (Vilnius: Dom Książki Polskiej 1928).

strengthened the President's position at the expense of the legislature and judiciary. This ultimately resulted in a new constitution – the so-called April Constitution of 23 April 1935, leading to authoritarian rule in Poland.[40]

In his criticism of the centralization of power under the *Sanacja* regime, Komarnicki would reiterate: 'the first cardinal condition for securing the healthy governance of the state is the complete and successful assurance of the rule of law'.[41] He was the author of numerous commentaries on the constitutional reforms implemented in the aftermath of the May Coup, as well as the drafter of a constitutional amendment sponsored by the National Party.[42] In a way, his withdrawal from public life in 1935 marked a protest against the totalitarian tendencies of those holding the reins of power in Poland. On the one hand, that meant the ruling camp's new April Constitution, and on the other hand, the ideological division in the National Party and radicalization of its leaders, 'with their eyes fixed on totalitarian models',[43] as a result of which he resigned his membership. Near the end of the 30s, Komarnicki became close to the Front Morges alliance of centrist parties gathered around Władysław Sikorski and Ignacy Jan Paderewski, in opposition to the *Sanacja* regime, whose members established the Polish Government-in-Exile in autumn 1939.

2.1 *Legislation for the Transitional Period*

The justice ministry's legislative drafts touched upon a broad spectrum of legal issues relating to the elimination of the occupation system from Polish territories. Moreover, the ministry – through its Investigative Commissions – investigated war crimes and kept in its Criminal-Judicial Section, a register of legislation enacted by the occupation authorities. It also commissioned persons linked to Polish lawyers' associations worldwide to conduct thematic

---

40 Joseph Rotshild, *Piłsudski's coup d'état* (New York, London: Columbia University Press 1966); Joshua Zimmerman, *Jozef Pilsudski. Founding Father of Modern Poland* (Cambridge: Harvard University Press 2022), 380–431; Wawrzyniec Kowalski, 'From May to Bereza: A Legal Nihilism in the Political and Legal Practice of the Sanation Camp 1926–1935'. *Studia Iuridica Lublinensia* XXIX (2020), 133–145.

41 *Ibidem.*

42 Wacław Komarnicki, *O zmianie konstytucji polskiej* ('On the amendment of the Polish Constitution') (Wilno: Józef Zawadzki 1927); Wacław Komarnicki, *O konstytucję narodową. Stanowisko Stronnictwa Narodowego w sprawie rewizji konstytucji oraz tekst projektu rewizji złożonego przez Klub Narodowy w Komisji Konstytucyjnej Sejmu* ('For a national constitution. The National Party's position on the amendment of the Constitution and the text of the draft amendment submitted by the National Club to the Sejm's Constitutional Committee') (Warszawa 1930).

43 Wacław Komarnicki, 'Wśród dwóch światów' ('Amid two worlds'), typescript of Komarnicki's memoirs, cited after Jankiewicz, *W poszukiwaniu*, 15.

studies and write expert reports, and initiated a debate on topics relating to war-crimes policy.[44]

Works connected with the preparation of legislative instruments for after the anticipated liberation of Polish territories were handled by the Legislative Works Commission. Komarnicki's priority projects included drafts of statutes dealing with the principles of criminal responsibility for crimes committed by the occupying powers, the restoration of the justice system after throwing off the German occupation, the organization of the central authorities of post-war Poland, and an election code for the first elections. The ministry also developed transitional provisions in criminal, civil, and administrative law for Polish territories under German and Soviet occupation, with a view to protecting the legal interests of the inhabitants and to the future implementation of Polish law.[45] There was a detailed discussion going on about the problems of the future transfer of property rights, restitution of public and private property, as well as validity of the occupying powers' legislation and judgments issued by their courts.

To regulate the state of affairs in occupied Polish territories, already on 30 November 1939, the President issued a Decree on the Nullity of the Legal Acts of the Occupying Powers, which was promulgated in the Journal of Laws. Notwithstanding the question of legality of the functioning of the occupation authorities, the legal effects and factual consequences of their activities throughout the several years of the occupation affected the legal situation of the inhabitants of the affected territories. In spring 1942, the Legislative Works Commission – in tandem with the Ministry of the Treasury – began efforts to regulate legal and economic affairs in Poland affected by the occupation. January 1943 saw the creation, within the LWC, of Subcommittee VIII, to keep records of laws and regulations enacted by the occupying powers, and deal with their annulment. On the initiative of Ludwik Krajewski, Subcommittee X for the amendment of the Decree of the President of the Republic of 30 November 1939 on the Nullity of the Legal Acts of the Occupying Powers began to operate in February of the same year.[46]

After Komarnicki took over as Minister of Justice, the reform of the system of the judiciary and preparation of legal cadres became the ministry's central interest. Section II for the Organization of Common Courts commenced its

44 Wacław Komarnicki's address in the meeting of the Budget Committee of the National Council of the Republic of Poland on 27 March 1942, AAN 2/133/0/6/90, leaves 170–173. See also Jankiewicz, 'W poszukiwaniu', 74–76.

45 *Ibidem.*

46 Jankiewicz, *W poszukiwaniu*, 111–114. IPMS Kol. 403/10.

work under Stanisław Szurlej, already in spring 1942, resulting in a Decree on the Amendment of Certain Provisions on the Organization of Common Courts, signed by President Władysław Raczkiewicz on 21 October 1944.[47]

Simultaneously, the justice ministry launched training programmes for Polish lawyers in exile, whose task after the war would be to develop Polish law and 'raise its profile in Polish community life'.[48] On 22 March 1942, a Law and Administration Study was inaugurated at St. Andrews University under the auspices of The Polish Lawyers' Association in the United Kingdom. In 1943, judge traineeships were opened at the Ministry of Justice, and March 1944 saw the establishment of a Polish Faculty of Law at the University of Oxford. This faculty continued the tradition of organizing Polish academic life in exile and aimed to train legal professionals and administrative staff for the post-war period. Among the lecturers were Stefan Glaser, Stanisław Celichowski, Wacław Komarnicki, Stanisław Grabski, Bronisław Hełczyński, Eugeniusz Jarra, Marian Jedlicki, Zygmunt Nagórski, Wiktor Sukiennicki, and Bohdan Winiarski.[49]

The core tenet in plans of reconstruction of the Polish state in a spirit of justice and democracy was a categorical distance 'from any undemocratic, totalitarian forms of governance and any form of dictatorship'. Especially during the first months of the war, General Sikorski's cabinet accordingly pressed the matter of political and criminal responsibility of the leaders of the Second Polish Republic and Polish Armed Forces, who were blamed for the failure of the Defensive War and Poland's defeat in September 1939. This internal-affairs dimension of transitional justice, as perceived by General Sikorski's cabinet, is particularly interesting in the context of the anticipated reckoning for the crimes committed by the occupying powers against the Polish population. Some of the institutions and legal mechanisms created for the purposes of exacting political justice and holding the leaders of the *Sanacja* regime accountable found significantly greater practical applicability to the question of

---

47 'O poziom sądownictwa polskiego'. *Dz.P.Dz.Ż.* (*Dziennik Polski i Dziennik Żołnierza* – 'The Polish Journal and the Soldier's Journal') 231 (29 September 1944); 'Na zasadach demokracji i prawa. O reformie ustroju sądów powszechnych. Przemówienie radiowe min. Komarnickiego'. *Dz.P.Dz.Ż.* 269 (13 November 1944).

48 Komarnicki, *Rola prawnika*, IPMS Kol. 37/7.

49 Decree of the President of the Republic of Poland of 14 April 1944 on the Polish Faculty of Law at the University of Oxford, Dz.U.1944.5.11. See also: Janusz W. Cywiński, Tadeusz S. Rojewski, Wiesław Toporowski (eds.), *Monografia Polskiego Wydziału Prawa 1944–1947* (London: Polska Fundacja Kulturalna 1997); Janusz Mierzwa, 'Działalność Polskiego Wydziału Prawa w Oksfordzie oraz organizacji zrzeszających polskich prawników na terenie Zjednoczonego Królestwa w latach 1940–1947'. *Niepodległość i Pamięć* 63 (2018), 77–94.

war crimes committed in occupied Poland. For example, it will be worth mentioning the Decree of the President of the Republic of Poland on Gathering and Securing the Evidence in Cases of Common Crimes, of March 1940, of which the provisions were also applicable to securing the evidence of war crimes. Another example is the Investigative Commissions of the Ministry of Justice, which was established on the basis of the same decree. Whereas the beginning of their operation was linked to the investigations of 'Commission for the Investigation of Causes of the Defeat in the September Campaign', chaired by General Józef Haller, the main purpose for which new Investigative Commissions was created from 1942 onward was to gather documentation on the occupying powers' crimes and information about the victims. The chartered objectives of Section V for Criminal Law and Procedure and Prisons – in which the Decree of the President of the Republic of Poland on Criminal Responsibility for War Crimes originated – included revision of the Criminal Code and Code of Criminal Procedure, together with the elimination of 'defective amendments', introduced 'during a period of dominance of authoritarian tendencies in state life'.[50] In both cases – the accountability of *Sanacja* regime, and justice for crimes committed by the German Reich in occupied Poland (and, in a more distant perspective, also by the USSR) – the path to rebuilding the citizens' confidence in state institutions was thought to lead through both systemic reforms and satisfaction of society's sense of justice, including compensation for the victims. Securing justice and compensation for victims of war crimes became a top priority.

3 Works on the Text of the Decree of the President of the Republic of Poland on Criminal Responsibility for War Crimes

The tasks of the Ministry of Justice with regard to the drafting of criminal provisions regulating the liability for crimes committed in occupied Poland were entrusted to the Legislative Works Commission's Section V for Criminal Procedure and Prisons. In addition to Professor Stefan Glaser as chair, Section V's members were Tadeusz Cyprian, Stanisław Celichowski, Roman Piotrowski, Wiktor Sukiennicki, Mieczysław Szerer, and Stanisław Szurlej.[51] During the period from April 1942 to June 1944, Section V held seventeen meetings, out of which nine in the first three months, of which five were spent exclusively on the drafting of the presidential decree on responsibility for war crimes.

50 Jankiewicz, *W poszukiwaniu*, 75.
51 AAN 2/133/0/6/ 44, leaf 3.

The tasks of Section V for Criminal Law and Procedure and Prisons were defined at the turn of March and April 1942.[52] They included: revision of the legislative drafts of the Codification Commission of the Republic of Poland, especially amendments of the Criminal Code and Code of Criminal Procedure under the *Sanacja* regime, 'for the purpose of their purification of subsequent defective amendments' and revision of 'special supplementary criminal statutes',[53] as well as 'gathering of materials relating to the prison system useful to future legislative works in that respect'.[54] The remainder of Section V's responsibilities was directly linked to the accountability for the occupiers' crimes and preparations for criminal trials, including: 'such draft statutes as may be expedient in consideration of new circumstances caused by wartime events and not foreseen by the lawmakers in existing statutes, e.g. through the creation of new, [t]heretofore unknown essences of a criminal offence (...) taking into account new forms of activity harmful to the interests of the state or of individuals'.[55] In the summary of the first two sessions of the Inter-Ministerial Conference on criminal liability for war crimes on 27 April 1942, it was resolved that 'topics raised in the meetings of the inter-ministerial conference for war crimes' were to be referred to the LWC Section V 'for further processing'.[56]

The instruction detailing the scope of works of LWC Section V referenced the stipulations of the Declaration of St. James's Palace, not only as a matter of direction but also in order to underscore their necessity and significance owed to the international context. The conference of governments of occupied states organized by Polish Ministry of Foreign Affairs in November 1941 was perceived, on the one hand, as an important argument in favour of expediting the works on substantive and procedural legislation to regulate criminal responsibility for the occupiers' crimes, and on the other hand a source of legitimacy. The LWC Section V's responsibilities also included the continued collaboration of Polish lawyers with international organizations in the form of 'taking a position on the initiative, requests and drafts put forward by international organizations, above all by the International Commission for Penal Reconstruction and Development at Cambridge'.[57]

The legislative works on the Decree of the President of the Republic of Poland on Criminal Responsibility for War Crimes of 30 March 1943 can be div-

52 Remarks concerning the scope of operation and works of the Legislative Works Commission Criminal Law Section, AAN, 2/133/0/6/44, leaf 408.

53 *Ibidem*, AAN, 2/133/0/6/44, leaves 60–118.

54 AAN, 2/133/0/6/ 44, leaf 3.

55 *Ibidem*.

56 AAN 2/133/0/6/ 69, leaf 18.

57 Remarks, AAN 2/133/0/6/44, leaf 408.

ided into four stages: 1/ deliberations of the Inter-Ministerial Conferences on the: 'matter of the responsibility of Germans for criminal offences committed in occupied territories'; 2/ drafting and discussion of the contents in meetings of LWC Section V for Criminal Law and Procedure and Prisons, as well as plenary meetings of the LWC in May and June 1942; 3/ debates on the text of the decree during meetings of the Council of Ministers in the period from June to October 1942; 4/ deliberations on the text of the decree in the Legal–Political Committee of the National Council of the Republic of Poland on 7 December 1942 and 5 January 1943 and the final edits and promulgation in March 1943.

3.1 *Inter-ministerial Conferences on the 'Responsibility of Germans for Criminal Offences Committed in Occupied Territories'*

The Inter-Ministerial Conferences organized by Komarnicki to deal with the 'matter of the responsibility of the Germans for criminal offences committed in occupied territories' met on 27 and 30 April 1942.[58] Their purpose was to agree on a set of basic tenets of Poland's war-crimes policy[59] and intensify the cooperation among the Ministries concerned – Justice, Internal Affairs and Foreign Affairs. In Komarnicki's opinion, the ministries ought to 'represent Poland's position uniformly in the international sphere'.[60] Those attending the meetings included Wacław Komarnicki, presiding; Eugeniusz Jarra as head of the Legislative Section; Ludwik Krajewski, councillor of the Praesidium of the Council of Ministers; Witold Czerwiński and Bernard Ziffer as representatives of the Ministry of Information and Documentation; Józef Wagner, head of the 'German files' at the Ministry of the Interior; Władysław Kulski and Michał Potulicki of the Ministry of Foreign Affairs; Roman Piotrowski of the Bureau of Political Works, and members of the Legislative Works Commission: Tadeusz Cyprian, Zygmunt Nagórski, Stanisław Szurlej, as well as Professors Stefan Glaser and Bohdan Winiarski, Polish representatives to the Cambridge Commission and International London Assembly.

Stefan Glaser was the first to speak, pointing out the two principal needs – to organize an effective justice system and to prepare suitable provisions of substantive law. In his opinion, the Polish Government-in-Exile's taking of a clear stance on both matters would strengthen the international position of Poland and provide an opportunity to 'alleviate the fates of the citizens of the

58 Minutes of the meeting of the 1st Inter-Ministerial Conference, 27 April 1942: AAN 2/133/0/6/69; see also: Jankiewicz, *W poszukiwaniu*, 124–128.

59 *Ibidem.*

60 Minutes of the meeting of the 1st Inter-Ministerial Conference, 27 April 1942, leaf 1.

Republic' and stop the extermination of civilians, given the deterrent effect of such type of legislation.

He moved on to the topic of the scope of jurisdiction of domestic and international courts' competence to judge war criminals, noting the lack of a tried and true model of international jurisdiction and the limitations on the agency of domestic bodies with regard to extradition. In his view, the advantages of international justice included greater impartiality and objectivity, as well as facilitated extradition procedures, especially for criminals absconding to neutral states. Favouring the domestic jurisdiction were pragmatic considerations – the availability of existing law-enforcement and judicial bodies, guaranteeing that the criminal proceedings would in fact proceed. Glaser supported the domestic model, stressing the dependence of the success of the trials on the effectiveness of the extradition procedure. He advocated 'for the Allied powers to adopt the decision that [persons] committing crimes in the territories of the occupied states would not be treated as political criminals, and would be handed over at the request of the appropriate authorities'.[61]

Another difficulty in legislating on the accountability of war criminals consisted in the lack of provisions in either domestic or international law, penalizing all of the offences committed by the occupying powers. Whether the courts were to apply domestic or international law, both – according to Glaser – needed to be supplemented with norms covering factual hypotheses not addressed to date. There was a risk of conflict with the principle of legality, with its consequent principle of non-retroactivity: 'A statute presently enacted in connection with the crimes committed by the Germans, providing for new forms of criminal offences – would be unable to capture the criminals, as it would not have retroactive force'.[62] Glaser was a firm adherent of upholding *lex retro non agit* and *nullum crimen sine lege*. In his article published in early 1942, he outlined the historical development of the latter principle as a foundation of criminal law and 'a guarantee of civic liberty against the omnipotence and despotism of the State and of the judge'.[63] He was critical of tendencies shown by the legislation of the criminal statutes of totalitarian states – the Criminal Code of the USSR of 1927, and especially of the reforms of criminal law enacted in the Third Reich following Hitler's accession to power in 1933, eliminating the prohibitions on retroactivity and analogy. Simultaneously, during works on substantive provisions regulating the principles of responsibility for war crimes and crimes committed by members of the occupation

61 AAN 2/133/0/6/69, leaf 3.

62 AAN, 2/133/0/6/ 69, leaf 2.

63 Glaser, '*Nullum*', 30.

forces against the civilian population, Glaser reflected on the actual significance and expediency of the prohibition against retroactivity. He focused on the question of the protective functions of law and of the values to which it extended its absolute protection. He was unequivocal that 'the liability of [war] criminals must be as effective and realistic as possible, and with it the administration of justice'. It is to pragmatic considerations that he gave priority, problematizing the absolute force of *lex retro non agit*. He argued: 'if one could push the "violability" [of *lex retro non agit*] through, solving the problem of extradition would be simpler and more effective'.[64]

Michał Potulicki, legal advisor to the MFA and one of the drafters of the Declaration of St. James's Palace, outlined three variants of a legal framework for the punishment of war crimes: (1) reference to the provisions of the Hague Convention of 1907, as well as international custom (the *lex lata internationalis*); (2) drafting an 'international criminal code' as a compilation of the provisions of the Hague Convention and domestic statutes, taking into account the 'principles of ethics and international morality' and 'characterization of criminal activities having taken place in the present war'[65] (the *lex ferenda internationalis*); or (3) application of the provisions of the domestic law of the state in whose territory the crime was committed.

According to Potulicki himself, the first-mentioned solution was not recommended due to the generality of international customary law, vagueness of the definitions of criminal offences in the Hague Convention of 1907 on the laws and customs of warfare, and lack of sanctions stipulated for violations. The provisions of the Convention were of key importance to determining 'whether a given act is or is not justified by the state of war' but could not guarantee 'effectively and with the necessary uniformity of adjudication judging such cases as may there be to judge'.[66]

Adopting the second solution and defining the contents of suitable provisions for the judgment of war criminals *de lege ferenda internationali* would have been of momentous procedural importance. It would have enabled precise definition of crimes and penalties, resulting in the harmonization of the jurisprudence as to the *mens* and *actus* and the sentencing rules. The creation of a new act of international criminal law with retroactive applicability would have been incompatible with the principle of *lex retro non agit*, the violations

---

64 Minutes of the meeting of the Inter-Ministerial Conference, 30 April 1942, 2, AAN 2/133/0/6/69, leaf 17.

65 Michał Potulicki's speech during the Inter-Ministerial Conference on 27 April 1942, AAN, 2/133/0/6/69, leaf 21.

66 *Ibidem*.

of which by the occupation authorities – precisely in the field of criminal law[67] – were among the main arguments for the criminality of German occupation. 'We can hardly take as [our own] starting point that which we criticize in the enemy', concluded the diplomat. Practical considerations – linked to the legislative technique used in international law, the large number of stakeholders and domestic criminal statutes for inclusion in an 'international code' – also presented a factual obstacle to the proposed method. Concurring with Potulicki on that point was Professor Bohdan Winiarski, who viewed the idea of a compilation of criminal statutes as inexpedient 'due to difficulties of technical nature and lack of time'.[68] The time-consuming nature of international lawmaking, the multitude of stakeholders involved in the process, and the specific characteristics of the law of nations, all would have compounded the difficulty of drafting, in a short time frame, tight and precise provisions laying out the penal sanctions and rules of jurisdiction. Finding a sure and effective solution to the problem was a priority, according to him. The protraction of the international lawmaking is something Winiarski noted in numerous publications, such as *Bezpieczeństwo, arbitraż, rozbrojenie* ('Security, arbitration, disarmament'), where he asserted:

> The development of the law of nations – and without it, one could scarcely imagine the development of an international judiciary – is guaranteed by the free and naturally slow process of its formation, depending on the equally slowly developing legal sense of nations in proportion to the alignment of their true needs and interests.[69]

Of a like mind was the Vice-President of the Supreme Audit Office, Zygmunt Nagórski, arguing: 'the acceptance of a thesis concerning the creation of international criminal law is possible only in a time of peace, not in the current state of war, because to create such is fraught with special difficulties of political and scholarly nature and requires the dedication of a special length of time'.[70] Rather than creating new provisions to encapsulate all existing sets of facts, Nagórski recommended increasing the sentencing limits prescribed by the Criminal Code of 1932.

---

67 Andrzej Wrzyszcz, *Okupacyjne sądownictwo niemieckie w Generalnym Gubernatorstwie. 1939–1945. Organizacja i funkcjonowanie* (Lublin: Wydawnictwo UMCS 2008), 44 f.

68 Minutes of the meeting of the Inter-Ministerial Conference, 30 April 1942, 5, AAN 2/133/0/6/69, leaf 16.

69 Bohdan Winiarski, *Bezpieczeństwo, arbitraż, rozbrojenie* (Poznań: 1928), 207–208.

70 Minutes of the meeting of the Inter-Ministerial Conference, 27 April 1942, AAN 2/133/0/6/69, leaf 8.

The third of Potulicki's proposals – use of the existing criminal provisions of the state in whose territory the crimes had been committed, supplemented with 'existing instruments of international law' from the Treaty of Versailles and Hague Convention – was hailed by the members of the April conference as the most fitting solution for the 'implementation of the January Declaration' (Declaration of St. James's Palace). The application of the law of the place of commission of the crime, whatever the defendant's nationality, offered – in Potulicki's view – a solid legal basis in existing criminal provisions and guaranteed that *lex retro non agit* would be kept inviolate.

Resorting to domestic provisions would largely mean avoiding two bars to the criminal responsibility of war criminals – (i) the defence of *respondeat superior* (the defence of acting on orders) and (ii) the construct of liability of aiders and abettors (engaging the issue of accessory liability). As for the former, the Polish Criminal Code of 1932 left a sufficient avenue for the limitation of the applicability of the defence by permitting the examination of the circumstances of a crime committed upon the orders of a superior authority, so as to verify the existence of defences such as absolute force (*vis absoluta*, Article 19 of the Criminal Code), legitimate defence ('necessary defence') (Article 21 CC) or dire necessity ('state of higher necessity') (Article 22 CC). 'An exception in favour of the defendant may arise when, and only when, having examined what authority issued and what type of order, as well as the manner and circumstances of the execution of the act, the judge becomes persuaded that the author [of the crime] was unable to oppose the received order'.[71] Also, Articles 26–29 of the Criminal Code defining the terms of criminal responsibility for instigation and aiding and abetting, especially Article 28 establishing the principle of individualization of culpability,[72] provided – according to Potulicki – sufficient legal grounds for bringing charges against persons complicit in the crime. It will be expedient to quote from a commentary on Article 28 CC by Professor Juliusz Makarewicz:

> Article 28 contains the most essential part of the legal construct concerning the aider and abettor. (…) [They] are individualities answering within the limits of [each] their own intent. [They] are responsible even when the individual who was to be the perpetrator is not responsible due to not having undertaken any activity.[73]

---

71 *Ibidem.*

72 Art. 28 CC: 'The aider and abettor shall be criminally liable within the limits of their intent, irrespective of the liability of the one having accomplished, or having been anticipated to accomplish, the act' (Dz.U.571 and 572).

73 Juliusz Makarewicz, *Kodeks karny z komentarzem, wydanie piąte* ('Criminal Code with commentary. Fifth edition'), (Lwów: ZNiO 1938), 137.

Dr. Ludwik Krajewski – editor of the Journal of Laws (Dz.U.) and of the Official Journal (Dz.Urz.) of the Ministry of Justice under the Second Polish Republic, councillor of the Praesidium of the Council of Ministers and Head of LWC Section VI – took a different view of the provisions of Polish Criminal Code in this area. He stressed that the use of domestic provisions would curb the effectiveness of the prosecutions due to its failure to cover the majority of the crimes. He emphasized the problems coming to the fore in the later stages of the works on the decree. The first of those was the systemic nature of the German crimes and the resulting difficulties with the identification of the one or more perpetrators of a given crime for the purposes of the attribution of culpability, as well as the fact that the new legal system introduced in Polish territories by the Third Reich legitimized the majority of the criminal actions undertaken by the German administrative, military, and judicial authorities.[74] Moreover, the defences allowed by the Polish Criminal Code opened – according to him – the path to the avoidance of responsibility by a great number of those accused of crimes, such as inferior officials obliged to carry out the orders of their superiors, as well as persons acting 'under compulsion and in defence of their own life'.[75]

In turn, according to Professor Roman Piotrowski, the problem of *respondeat superior* was unequivocally answered by Article 9 of the Military Criminal Code. Under that provision, the perpetrator was criminally liable if aware, while committing an act resulting from the execution of a command received in matters pertain to the service, that 'the command pertained to an act constituting a felony or misdemeanour'.[76] In Piotrowski's opinion, both international provisions – those of the Hague Convention and of Treaty of Versailles – as well as Polish Criminal Code and Military Criminal Code sufficiently defined the substantive basis and procedure for criminal proceedings in cases of crimes committed by a member of foreign armed forces or civilian administration. Piotrowski argued that Article 3 of the Hague Convention contained a precise definition of the 'unlawfulness of the operation of a foreign army in occupied territories' and violations of the Convention by members of hostile armed forces should fall within the jurisdiction of domestic courts. Articles 227 and

74 Minutes of the meeting of the Inter-Ministerial Conference, 30 April 1942, 2, AAN 2/133/0/6/69, leaf 17. In the 30s of the twentieth century, Krajewski published several studies of the political and legal system of the German Reich and the legal doctrines of Nazism. Concerning this topic, see: Maciejewski, 'Polscy uczeni', 104–108, and the literature cited therein.

75 AAN 2/133/0/6/69, leaf 17.

76 Regulation of the President of the Republic of Poland of 21 October 1932 – Military Criminal Code, Dz.U.765.91.

228 of the Treaty of Versailles stipulated the jurisdiction of domestic courts to hear cases of an 'act against the laws and customs of war' in the territory of another state and 'mixed tribunals' in cases of defendants having acted in the territories of several states, as well as the obligation to extradite defendants.[77] Those should be applied to crimes committed during the Second World War. The scope of applicability of Polish Criminal Code provided a solid basis for the prosecution of criminals lacking Polish nationality or having acted in the territory of another state. Pursuant to Article 3(1) CC, the Code covered all who had 'committed a criminal offence in the territory of the Polish State or in a Polish vessel or aircraft'. Article 5 expanded the territorial application of the Code:

The Polish criminal statute shall apply to foreigners having committed abroad a criminal offence directly against the welfare or interests of the Polish State, of a Polish national, or Polish legal person. 'Recognition (...) of the act as a criminal offence by the statute applicable at the place of commission' was required for prosecution (Article 6).

In accordance with Article 8 CC, irrespective of the provisions in force where the act was committed and the perpetrator's nationality, the Polish Criminal Code was applicable to persons having committed abroad:

(a) a criminal offence against the internal or external security of the Polish state;
(b) a criminal offence against the authorities or officials of the Polish state;
(c) false testimony before an authority of the Polish state.[78]

The 'criminal offences against the internal or external security of the Polish state' mentioned in the general part of the Criminal Code were not given statutory definitions in the detailed part of the Code. This group of crimes included felonies of state (Chapter XVII), offences against the interests of the state and international relations (Chapter XVIII), as well as high treason and betrayal of military secret, as specified by the Regulation of the President of the Republic of Poland of 24 October 1934 on Certain Criminal Offences Against the Security of the State.[79] Among the aforementioned criminal offences committed by the German occupying forces and addressed by Polish Criminal Code, Tadeusz Cyprian included some of the crimes against the public order defined in Chapter XXV – 'public revilement or derision of the Polish State or Nation' (Article 152 of the Criminal Code), 'revilement of national symbols' (Article 153 CC), and

77 Arts. 227–229 of the Treaty of Versailles (Treaty of Peace between the Allied and Associated Powers and Germany, signed at Versailles, 28 June 28, [1919] UKTS 4 (Cmd. 153); [1920] ATS 1).

78 *Cf.* Art. 6 and 8 of the Criminal Code of 1932.

79 Regulation of the President of the Republic of Poland of 24 October 1934 on Certain Criminal Offences Against the Security of the State, Dz.U.1934.94.851.

'calling publicly for the commission of a criminal offence' (Article 154 CC). Cyprian noted the deficiencies of the domestic legislation failing to define in a precise manner, the *actus reus* of all of the crimes committed under the occupation but believed that 'other sets of facts m[ight] the subsumed under the liability arising from one of the aforementioned articles'. He regarded the use of domestic provisions as the most surefire solution in the absence of precise provisions of international law. 'This is about creating a system effective in practice and not about the purity of legal constructs'.[80] At the same time, he recalled that the very idea of prosecution of war criminals, even on the basis of existing domestic legislation, had not yet won the full support of British and American governments, perceived by him as being 'very sensitive on the point of the term "retribution"'.[81]

The matter was also brought up by Władysław Kulski (legal advisor to the MFA), who noted the need to continue with the informational campaigns about the crimes in Poland and to persuade all of the Allied powers of the merit of holding the perpetrators criminally responsible.[82] In his opinion, the conferences should focus on three points: the incorporation of a penal clause concerning criminals already in the ceasefire; analysis of the scope of jurisdiction of domestic courts; and development of an extradition concept guaranteeing the delivery of perpetrators from the Reich, as well as Allied and neutral states. Concerning the anticipated rules of extradition, Stanisław Szurlej – the man in charge of Polish military justice and president of the Polish Lawyers' Association in the United Kingdom – recommended focusing on guarantees of delivery of defendants, upon the demand of an Allied state, and on 'compliance with *ex delicto* obligations'. The latter connoted the recognition of the 'civil-law effects caused by the enemy's criminal activities' and 'securing the compliance with these terms by the occupation of the country pending compensation of the wrongs'.[83]

Participants of the inter-ministerial conference of April favoured the use of domestic provisions in cases of war crimes. Despite the consensus that doing so would avoid a clash with the prohibition against retroactivity, Stefan Glaser was in no way alone in his view that 'if one could push the "violability" [of *lex retro non agit*] through, solving the problem of extradition would be simpler and more effective'.[84] It remains an open question whether the fact sets dealt

80 Minutes of the meeting of the Inter-Ministerial Conference, 30 April 1942, 2, AAN 2/133/0/6/69, leaf 12.

81 *Ibidem.*

82 *Ibidem*, leaf 16.

83 *Ibidem*, leaf 17.

84 *Ibidem.*

with and sanctions provided by Polish Criminal Code were sufficient for the effective penalization of war criminals, as does the merit of hypothetical supplementation with a special statute to narrow down the rules for the individual responsibility of offenders against the laws and customs of war.

Differences in the outlook on this problem surfaced both in the discussions and in the final conclusions of the conference. Professor Eugeniusz Jarra, chairing, concluded that topics of war-crimes policy should continue to be debated in the inter-ministerial conference and addressed in a more detailed manner by Section V of the LWC. He insisted: 'the Ministry of Justice concurs with the view favouring the applicability of own courts and domestic codes to the generality of the crimes, and for the main criminals an Inter-Allied Tribunal'. The matter of the provisions to be applied in the proceedings was to be examined in the forum of LWC Section V. At the motion of the representatives of the MFA, the summation of the inter-ministerial conference concluded that the principle of *lex retro non agit* should be upheld and 'principles of domestic legislation in conjunction with international law' applied to war-crime cases.[85]

3.2 *Debate on the Text of the Decree in Section V for Criminal Procedure and Prisons and in the Plenary Meetings of the Legislative Works Commission*

The next step involved a specific legislative proposal – the Decree on Punishment for Certain Crimes Committed in a Time of War, drafted by Stefan Glaser and Wacław Komarnicki. The document was first debated in a meeting of the LWC Section V on 15 May 1942.

Article 1 provided:

> whoever, contrary to the principles of international law, acts, in Poland or abroad, to the detriment (*na szkodę*) of the public interest (*interesu publicznego*) of the Polish State, of a Polish legal person or of the private interest of a Polish national shall be liable to the penalty of imprisonment.

Aggravation to life imprisonment or the capital penalty was provided for cases resulting in death, a physical or mental issue, loss of freedom for a period of one month, displacement, or resettlement of a Polish national (Article 2) or 'public danger to human life and health in Poland' (Article 3).[86]

---

85 *Ibidem.*

86 Decree on Punishment for Certain Crimes Committed in a Time of War. AAN 2/133/0/6/44, leaf 11.

In line with Article 4 of the draft, imprisonment for life was to be available in cases of compelling a Polish national – in a manner contrary to 'principles of international law' – to: 'join foreign armed forces or work for the enemy'.

Article 5 criminalized judicial abuses by the Nazi regime, including adjudication based on domestic regulations violating international law (issued by occupation authorities in violation of Article 45 of the Hague Convention): 'Whoever, in Poland or abroad, issues a judgement with regard to a Polish national on the basis of legal provisions enacted contrary to the provisions of international law shall be liable to imprisonment'. Article 6 stipulated the criminal responsibility of judges for the homicide of defendants sentenced to death penalty, thus confronting the problem of judicial crimes and liability of judges for the application of the German Reich's criminal law in a manner contrary to the purpose of the administration of justice.[87] In accordance with Article 6, where the judgment mentioned in Article 5 resulted in the outcomes listed in Articles 2 and 3, the penalty was escalated to life imprisonment or death.

Articles 7 and 8 concerned the individualization of culpability and marked an attempt to solve the interpretative problem with the defences recognized by the Criminal Code of 1932. The general clause in Article 7 stipulated: 'provisions of the general part of the Criminal Code shall apply to acts covered by this decree unless the present provisions mandate otherwise'. In line with Article 8, sanctions applied 'both [to] the one giving the order to commit an act set out in this decree and the one executing such order'. Article 9 regulated procedural issues: 'cases of criminal offences covered by this decree shall belong to the jurisdiction of Courts of Appeals adjudicating in the first instance'. Details such as competent venue by reason of place or matter or appellate proceedings were not narrowed down. Article 10 defined the temporal applicability of the provisions '(…) to acts committed after 31 August 1939'. The implementation of the provisions of the decree was entrusted jointly to the Minister of Justice and the Minister of the Interior.

Referring the draft to debate in the LWC Section V, Glaser emphasized the firmness of his own adherence to the principle of *nullum crimen sine lege* and *lex retro non agit*, which he viewed as fundamental guarantees of security of the citizens from abuse of authority and manipulation of justice. The exceptionality of the situation in which Polish society found itself in an occupied

87 Gustav Radbruch, 'Gesetzliches Unrecht'. For more on this topic see: Karol M. Pospieszalski (ed.), *Nazi occupation "law" in Poland, Selected Documents*, Part I: The incorporated territories; Part II: The Government General (Poznań: Instytut Zachodni 2019); Gerhard Werle, *Justiz-Strafrecht und polizeiliche Verbrechensbekämpfung im Dritten Reich* (Berlin: DeGruyter 1989).

country – bereft of the protection of international and national law – did, however, in his opinion, justify an exceptional dispensation from this principle.[88]

An important argument cited by Stefan Glaser was the 'politico-propagandistic' resonance of the promulgation of the decree and the belief in its deterrent effect. He saw a realistic 'possibility of alleviating the fates of the compatriots' under German occupation: 'if the decree, published in the Homeland, deters at least some Germans from committing further crimes, such a decree will fulfil its task and is justified'. Neither was he afraid of the response of international legal circles to the Polish authorities' enactment of a special criminal statute. He offered the following conclusion: 'departure from the principle of *lex retro non agit*, generally accepted in law, will not be met by the English opinion with any special indignation or resistance, given that abundant English legal literature not infrequently regards as crimes unlawful acts not covered by any statutes'.[89]

Professor Roman Piotrowski took a different view of the decree, being critical of the 'undermining of the perennial legal principle' of *lex retro non agit*. He feared the 'international resonance of the adoption of the act without a prior understanding with the competent English factors (...) because this decree ha[d] the nature of a political act and failure to consult opinions c [ould] cause an unpleasant complication in relations with the Allies',[90] and even difficulties with the implementation of the extradition procedure in the future. Stefan Glaser and Stanisław Szurlej did not view the Polish side as having a duty to consult with the Allies. The Chief Prosecutor of the Polish Armed Forces believed that it was: 'fitting to dispatch to the English Government a formulation of the motives supporting the enactment of the decree' but opposed the idea of seeking the British authorities' approval for the promulgation.[91] 'Because the decree would only be applicable in the territory of the Polish state', Glaser argued: 'Polish authorities should not be constrained by Allied policy'. In the opinion of Piotrowski, the matters of the responsibility of the person carrying out an unlawful order and of dire necessity required more precise delimitation because the proposed wording of Article 8 did not abolish necessity, leaving that classic line of defence on the table.

---

88 *Cf.* Glaser, '*Nullum*'.

89 Minutes of the meeting of the Section for Criminal Law and Procedure and Prisons, 15 May 1942, AAN 2/133/0/6/44, leaf 6.

90 *Ibidem.*

91 *Ibidem*, leaf 7.

Stanisław Szurlej submitted some reservations concerning the linguistic and editorial aspects of the decree, noting the lack of terminological harmonization of Articles 1, 4, and 5. Articles 1 and 4 employed the term 'principles of international law' ('... whoever, contrary to the principles of international law ...'), and Article 5 the term 'provisions of international law' ('... a judgement with regard to a Polish national on the basis of legal provisions issued contrary to the provisions of international law ...'). Szurlej recommended the use of the term 'principle' in all of the articles due to its broader meaning and applicability.[92] On that, Jarra supported him, recalling: 'the term "principle" as used in the decree, corresponds the most completely to the terminology of international law, which in international acts, e.g. the Treaty of Versailles, even invokes the principles of the law of nature'. The proposal of harmonization of the terms used for references to international law was approved. Nevertheless, the text of the decree passed in the meeting of Section V on 15 May 1942 used neither the term 'principles of international law' nor 'provisions of international law' but instead 'norms of international law' across all three articles (1, 4 and 5).

The problem of the interpretation of the articles of the decree containing references to norms of international law and their application by domestic courts was taken up in a meeting of LWC Section VI for Legislative Technique on 27 May 1942, convened for the purpose of editing the draft to bring it in line with the principles of legislative technique.[93] Supreme Court Justice Dr. Ignacy Baliński saw its redaction as being too vague, anticipating problems with the interpretation of the term 'norms of international law' and doubts from the bench as to which law should be considered when looking into individual sets of facts.[94] Professors Winiarski and Hełczyński believed that the terms 'domestic law' and 'international law' were 'completely clear and c[ould] not be placed in doubt'. Bohdan Winiarski suggested arriving at more precision by adding the phrase: 'contrary to the norms of customary and contractual international law'. His was a voice expounding the concept of sources of the law of nations followed by the authors of the Polish doctrine of criminal responsibility for war crimes, recognizing written and unwritten sources, including custom.[95] Ultimately, the wording of the relevant articles was left unchanged. During the same meeting, Section VI for Legislative Technique added two art-

92 *Ibidem.*

93 Minutes of the meeting of Section VI of Legislative Technique, 28 May 1942, AAN 2/133/0/6/45, leaf 1.

94 *Ibidem.*

95 Manfred Lachs, 'The unwritten laws of warfare', reprint from *Tulane Law Review* (XX) 1945, 120–128.

icles to the original text – Article 10, which took care of statutes of limitations by mandating: 'the course of statutes of limitations set forth by Article 86 of the Criminal Code shall commence upon the resumption of the activities of the Supreme Court' and Article 13 of the implementing provisions: 'This decree shall take effect on the day of promulgation'. Article 9 – containing procedural provisions – was supplemented with three additional paragraphs, including one regulating the rules for a cassatory appeal against the judgment of a court of appeals given at the first instance.[96] The draft adopted by the LWC Section for Legislative Technique was referred to debate in a special plenary meeting of the LWC on 29 May and 3 June 1942.[97]

3.3 *Debate on the Decree in the Plenary Meeting of the Legislative Works Commission on 29 May and 3 June 1942*

The plenary of the Legislative Works Commission on 29 May and 3 June 1942 gathered the following participants: Wacław Komarnicki, Eugeniusz Jarra, Karol Aleksandrowicz, Ignacy Baliński, Tadeusz Brzeski, Tadeusz Cyprian, Władysław Czapiński (Head of the Legislative Section), Stefan Glaser, Bronisław Hełczyński, Marian Jedlicki, Ludwik Krajewski, Roman Kuratowski, Konstanty Makomski, Włodzimierz Moderow, Roman Piotrowski, Piotr Siekanowicz (presiding), Mieczysław Szerer, Stanisław Szurlej, Bohdan Winiarski, and Karol Poznański.[98]

The debate on the draft Decree on Punishment for Certain Crimes Committed in a Time of War in the LWC plenary concentrated on three core problems: whether the instrument should be enacted in the form of a presidential decree; the international political resonance of the works underway, and remarks pertaining to the merits of the individuals provisions of the draft. Some of the members spoke against the drafting of a domestic legal instrument to lay down the rules for post-war trials of war criminals before consult-

96 *Ibidem*, leaf 3. Art. 9 was given the following wording:
'(1) Cases of criminal offences covered by this decree shall belong to the jurisdiction of Courts of Appeals adjudicating at the first instance.
(2) The Court of Appeals shall rule in a panel of 3 justices according to the provisions on the procedure before a Regional Court.
(3) Against the judgment of the Court of Appeals, the parties may bring an appeal-in-cassation to the Supreme Court.
(4) An appeal against an judgment imposing death penalty shall be heard by the Supreme Court no late than one month following the arrival of the files of the case in the said court'.

97 Minutes of the plenary meeting of the Legislative Works Commission, 29 May; 2, 3 and 8 June 1942, AAN 2/133/0/6/29, leaves 8–19.

98 *Ibidem*, leaf 1.

ing with the Western Allies on the matter. Stanisław Szurlej emphasized the risk that the promulgation of the decree could have the effect of weakening the informational campaign led by the Ministry of Foreign Affairs and Ministry of Information and Documentation by giving the impression 'that all h[ad] already been done in the field of propagating the idea of punishment for the Germans, whereas in [that] field more [wa]s to be done and w[ould] have a greater effect than the statute'.[99] In his opinion, the lack of Allied support for Poland's firm stance posed a threat to Poland's position in the international arena: 'The Allies will not adhere to us for various reasons, which will cause the impression that we alone are thirsting for revenge and a bloody one at that. For the statute mostly introduces death penalty'.[100] Szurlej's fears were shared by Tadeusz Cyprian, who argued: 'in the event of any complications of diplomatic nature, the promulgation of the decree should be deferred to post-war times'. At the same time, he emphasized that the most important argument in favour of enacting the decree was the insufficiency of the provisions of Polish Criminal Code in respect of facts and sanctions. He admitted 'that the decree ma[de] a breach in the principles of *nullum crimen sine lege*', with the caveat that 'with regard to the Germans, who ha[d] placed themselves outside of the law, one [wa]s not to be constrained by [that]'.[101]

Bohdan Winiarski and Marian Jedlicki also noted the international context of the works underway. On behalf of the LWC, they lodged two motions laying out the Polish stance on the problem of penal repression against war criminals. Winiarski came forward with the proposal of presenting 'in the Council of Ministers a motion to undertake, with regard to those Allied states who territories have not been occupied (...), an action intended to bring about the ordering already now of a retributive treatment of such subjects of enemy states as remain[ed] in their power'. In turn, Professor Jedlicki moved for the Council of Ministers to undertake 'an initiative for all Allied states to enact statutes, alternatively decrees, announcing repressions for crimes committed by the German occupants in violation of the provisions of international law'.[102] The motion was submitted to the Council of Ministers on 23 June 1942.

The first motion dealing with the substance of the decree was tabled by Ignacy Baliński. It dealt with an issue already raised by Stanisław Szurlej, namely for the inclusion of the principle of *ex delicto* liability in damages in the draft. The goal would be, as pointed out by Justice Baliński, to enact provi-

99 *Ibidem*, leaf. 11.
100 *Ibidem*.
101 *Ibidem*, leaf 9.
102 *Ibidem*.

sions 'giving the persons harmed by the acts set out in Articles 1–6, alternatively their heirs, a basis to bring civil action against [their] wrongdoers for the compensation of tangible damages'.[103]

The next point in the debate concerned the wording of Article 1 of the draft, which provided:

> This decree shall apply to the members of the enemy armed forces, occupation officials, civilian citizens of the German Reich and its allies, as well as such Polish nationals as may have breached the duty of allegiance to the Republic of Poland by collaboration with the enemy, and shall encompass acts committed following 31 August 1939 until the end of the war, irrespective of the place of commission of the act.

Karol Aleksandrowicz noted: 'In its current styling, as referred not only to the occupiers (German authorities) but also Polish nationals, it can be used against the latter, which is not and cannot be the intention of the sponsor of the bill'. Aleksandrowicz pointed out that thousands of Polish nationals had been employed by German administration, police, or judiciary, carrying out the orders of occupation authorities; he emphasized that, for those, the general provisions of Polish Criminal Code ought to be used.[104] The modification of the language of Article 1 with regard to the criminal responsibility of collaborationists was introduced in the next meeting of LWC Section V, on 22 and 23 June. The Section decided to leave those who 'may have breached the duty of allegiance to the Republic of Poland by collaboration with the enemy' out of the facts of Article 1.[105] As emphasized by Wacław Komarnicki: 'the decree [wa]s a political act, venturing into the sphere of norms of international law' and: 'Polish nationals collaborating with the enemy w[ould] be held responsible on the basis of the provisions of substantive criminal law [already] in force'.[106] Therewith, Komarnicki highlighted the disjuncture between the terminological scopes of war crimes and collaboration, as well as the necessity of separate regulation of the terms of responsibility in the two cases.

The redaction of Article 1 of the draft decree and the delineation of its personal scope of applicability was a muddy ground because of the anticipation of a negative Soviet response to the enactment of Polish legislation,

---

103 *Ibidem.*

104 *Ibidem*, leaf 10.

105 Minutes of the meeting of LWC Section V, 22 and 23 June 1942, AAN 2/133/0/6/44, leaf 27.

106 Attachment 2 to the minutes of the meeting of LWC Section, 22 and 23 June 1942, AAN/133/0/44, leaf 24.

potentially applicable to crimes committed in Poland's territories occupied by the USSR. The probability of open censure from Moscow was, however, assessed to be low, because of contradicting the Soviets' own claim that 'in the occupied territories, no atrocities or acts incompatible with international law [had been committed]'.[107] It was appreciated, however, that even the mere suspicion of an intention to prosecute Soviet crimes would make the prospect of international acceptance for the new legislation look bleak. In the meeting of the Council of Ministers on 2 July 1942, Sikorski cut the debate short by directing that 'the decree, in [its] final revision, must have an anti-German tone'.[108]

Further remarks submitted in the LWC plenary on the break of May and June 1942 concerned conflicts between the provisions of the Decree on Punishment for Certain Crimes Committed in a Time of War and those of the Decree of the President of the Republic of Poland on Summary Courts, of 19 March 1928.[109] There was also a proposal to include 'criminal responsibility of the occupying powers for the destruction of Polish cultural property'[110] and additional penalties of confiscation of property and forfeiture of inheritance capacity, and finally some edits and supplementations affecting specific parts of the draft.

The first of the above issues was raised by Władysław Czapiński, who pointed out the introduction of martial law and summary justice in Poland on 1 September 1939,[111] with the result of hard labour being escalated to death penalty by operation of the law.[112] His concern was 'that, in a certain measure, the application of the provisions of the contemplated decree could alleviate both the procedure and the sanctions imposed by the provisions on summary justice'.[113] Article 9 of the draft, stipulating the jurisdiction of common courts (Courts of Appeals as the first instance) received an additional section provid-

107 Minutes, AAN 2/133/0/29/69, leaf 10.

108 PPRM vol. IV, 352–353.

109 Dz.U.1928.33.315.

110 AAN 2/133/0/29, leaf 12.

111 Order of the President of the Republic of Poland of 1 September 1939 concerning martial law, Dz.U.1939.86.544. Regulation of the Council of Ministers of 1 September 1939 concerning the introduction of summary proceedings before common courts in cases of certain crimes, Dz.U.1939.87.554.

112 Decree of the President of the Republic of Poland on Summary Justice, Dz.U.1928.33.315, art. 32: 'If the court unanimously finds the defendant guilty, then, for a criminal offence liable in ordinary proceedings at least to the penalty of hard labour, death penalty shall be imposed in summary proceedings' (Dz.U.1928.33.315).

113 Minutes of the plenary meeting of the Legislative Works Commission, 29 May; 2, 3 and 8 June 1942, AAN 2/133/0/29, leaf 13.

ing: 'cases under this decree may proceed *in absentia* if the perpetrator's appearance before the court cannot be secured'. The question of the procedural track for trials of war criminals – summary justice, courts martial or common courts – was the topic of lively debate until the very last stage of works on the decree.

During the deliberations of 3 June 1942, members of the LWC accepted by unanimous vote Justice Ignacy Baliński's proposal to add the offence of destruction of cultural property or devastation of public or private cultural property.[114] The new wording of Article 6 provided: 'Whoever, contrary to norms of international law, destroys Polish cultural property, shall be liable to imprisonment for life or death penalty'.[115] Modifications were also made to the language of articles 4, 5, and 7. Article 4 saw the expansion of the range of penalties available for the forcible induction of a Polish national in enemy armed force or forced labour, to be from life imprisonment to death. Article 5 provided:

> (1) Whoever, in Poland or abroad, adjudicating on behalf of the occupation authorities on the basis of legal provisions enacted contrary to provisions of international law, does a wrong to a Polish national shall be liable to imprisonment.
> (2) If such judgment has caused one of the consequences mentioned in Article 2 or 3, the perpetrator shall be liable to life imprisonment or death penalty.[116]

Article 7 of the draft, moreover, established the additional penalties of confiscation of property and forfeiture of inheritance capacity. By a majority of the vote, Articles 10 to 13 passed unchanged.

The tone is vividly captured in Tadeusz Cyprian and Minister Komarnicki's remarks following the vote on 2 June 1942. Cyprian insisted:

> In voting for the statute, I emphasize that until such time as it can be given effect, it is merely a political act and must be regarded as such. Moreover, due to the undermining of base legal concepts, it is a very dangerous topic, as it can shake the confidence of Western societies in our sense of rule of law.[117]

---

114 Ibidem, leaf 12.
115 Ibidem, leaf 10.
116 *Ibidem.*
117 *Ibidem*, leaf 14.

Tadeusz Cyprian was convinced of the necessity of consulting Allied opinion before promulgating the statute and 'sounding their opinion on the subject both in the political and the legal angle'. In the event of a negative response to the Polish draft, the text should be kept in secret.[118] The Minister of Justice, Wacław Komarnicki, responded to the remarks, conscious of reservations as to the contemplated retroactivity: 'The cynical trampling by the Germans of all legal and moral principles' justified, in his opinion, the use of an extraordinary measure such as the statute in the works. In Komarnicki's view, the enactment of the decree would be 'met with the best reception in the Homeland and give it moral support; on the other hand, it could have a degree of inhibitory influence on the German tormentors'. Furthermore, he concluded that 'Poland's exceptional situation' would be 'particularly emphasized by the enactment of [the] decree'.[119]

3.4 *Special Meeting of Section V of the Legislative Works Commission*

On 22 and 23 June, special meetings of LWC Section V for Criminal Law and Procedure and Prisons took place, debating further amendments to the text of the Decree of the President of the Republic of Poland on Punishment for Certain Crimes Committed in a Time of War.[120] The facts of Article 1 were revised by removing the section on Polish nationals and expanding the liability of instigators, aiders, and abettors. Article 1 took the following wording: 'This decree shall apply to the members of the enemy armed forces, occupation officials, civilian citizens of the German Reich and its allies, as well as their instigators and aiders and abettors, and shall encompass acts committed following 31 August 1939 until the end of the war, irrespective of the place of commission of the act'.[121] A new title was adopted for the decree: 'Decree of the President of the Republic of Poland on Punishment for War Crimes' ('concerning the liability for War Crimes' in a contemporary translation). Article 9, establishing the jurisdiction of common criminal courts, was removed; instead, 'war courts' (*sądy wojenne*, a different institution from regular courts martial – *sądy wojskowe* – 'military courts') were made the competent venue, which corresponded – according to Wacław Komarnicki – 'with international law and the existing practice of the states' and provided a guarantee of swift justice to the criminals.[122] The new wording of Article 10 was 'cases of criminal

118 *Ibidem.*

119 *Ibidem*, leaf 16.

120 Minutes of the meeting of the LWC Section, 22 and 23 June 1942, AAN 2/133/0/6/44, leaves 23–29.

121 *Ibidem*, leaf 25.

122 *Ibidem.*

offences covered by this decree shall be in the jurisdiction of the war courts'. Accordingly, Article 11 providing for statutes of limitations to begin their course with the resumption of the works of the Supreme Court was deleted, and, in Article 12, the implementation of the decree was entrusted to the Minister of Justice and to the Minister of the Interior. Article 13 remained unchanged.

Komarnicki forwarded the text of the draft decree adopted on 23 June by the LWC, in the company of an explanatory memorandum to the other ministers of the Government-in-Exile.[123] The Director of the Praesidium Bureau, Adam Romer, responded on behalf of the Praesidium the next day.[124] The Praesidium was critical of modifications to the procedural track in Article 10 and preferred for the jurisdiction of common courts to be maintained, noting the existence of a conflict between the provisions of the Law on the System of Courts Martial and the policy on the prosecution and punishment of war criminals. As emphasized by Romer, prosecutions of war criminals could only begin after the cessation of hostilities, whereas by virtue of Article 8(2) of the Law on the System of Courts Martial,[125] war courts were the competent venue 'in the army and navy in wartime'. Other objections related to the final and unappealable status of the judgments of war courts imposing death penalty, which was the upper sentencing limit in the majority of the provisions of the draft presidential decree. In line with Article 424 of the Code of Military Criminal Procedure[126] (CMCP), a capital sentence from a war court would become final and unappealable, on approval by the Commander-in-Chief, or, in the case of a 'fortress area or fortified district, enclosed by the enemy', by its top commander. Due to there not being a Commander-in-Chief in peacetime, a death sentence handed down after the war could never become final and unappealable. More difficulties were entailed by Article 410 CMCP, whereby 'in proceedings before war courts, the procedural powers of the military regional prosecutor' belonged to the 'judicial-criminal superior' (*zwierzchnik sądowo-karny*). The latter would make the decision whether the indictment was to proceed to a war court (Article 414 CMCP), thus serving as a sort of convening authority. The judicial–criminal superior for cases in the jurisdiction of war courts was the unit commander or the area commander. Romer noted: 'It is a doubtful matter whether such type of public prosecutor will have sufficient qualifica-

123 IPMS, Stanisław Stroński Collection, 180/3, no pagination.

124 Adam Romer's letter to Wacław Komarnicki, 24 June 1942; AAN 2/133/0/6/44, leaves 22–23.

125 Decree of the President of the Republic of Poland of 29 September 1936 – Law on the System of Courts Martial, Dz.U.1936.76.536.

126 Dz.U.1936.76.537.

tions to decide whether the act being the object of the proceedings is contrary to the norms of international law'.[127]

A special plenary of the LWC, held on 29 and 30 June 1942, was dedicated to the remarks submitted by the Praesidium of the Council of Ministers and selection of the procedural track for war-crime cases. Participants included: Wacław Komarnicki, Eugeniusz Jarra, Stefan Glaser, Roman Piotrowski, Stanisław Szurlej, Mieczysław Szerer, Ludwik Krajewski, and Tadeusz Cyprian. The changes recommended by Romer were supported by Ludwik Krajewski, who advocated for the jurisdiction of common courts and 'if that were not possible, [then] summary courts'. Tadeusz Cyprian and Roman Piotrowski supported him and proposed the following wording for Article 10: 'Cases of crimes covered by this decree shall be within the jurisdiction of common courts adjudicating in summary proceedings'. Stanisław Szurlej firmly opposed the introduction of summary proceedings, recommending that Article 10 provide for the jurisdiction of courts martial adjudicating on the war track.[128] In a joint vote of LWC members on both proposals, the new wording of Article recommended by Stanisław Szurlej was approved,[129] and the reservations submitted by the Praesidium of the Council of Ministers were thus rejected.

The second point on the agenda was Article 1 of the draft decree. Tadeusz Cyprian advocated for the retention of the original wording: Whoever, contrary to the norms of international law, commits, in Poland or abroad, an act to the detriment of the Polish State, a Polish legal person or Polish national shall be liable to the penalty of imprisonment. Roman Piotrowski and Stanisław Szurlej opted for the elimination of the principle of liability of instigators, aiders, and abettors. On 30 January 1942, the Legislative Works Commission accepted Cyprian's wording of Article 1 of the decree, but because of the discussions concerning the scope of the facts, the vote was removed from the agenda of the next meeting of the Council of Ministers.

3.5 Lex retro non agit? *Debate on the Text of the Decree in the Plenary Meetings of the Council of Ministers – July–October 1942*

Minister Komarnicki gave the first presentation of the draft Decree of the President of the Republic of Poland on Punishment for War Crimes in the plenary of the Council of Ministers on 2 July 1942. The interpretative difficulty posed by the several-times-amended Article 1 of the draft was noted by Pro-

127 Letter from Adam Romer to Wacław Komarnicki, 24 June 1942, AAN 2/133/0/6/44, leaves 22–23.

128 AAN 2/133/0/6/44, leaf 35.

129 AAN 2/133/0/6/44, leaves 36–37.

fessor Stanisław Stroński. According to the professor, the original wording had 'an exclusively anti-German edge, whereas the last one, through the omission of Article 1, ha[d] an edge turned against all occupying powers, and thus also against Russia, which politically deprive[d] the draft of any realistic prospects'.[130] Prime Minister Sikorski concurred: 'the decree, in [its] final revision, must have an anti-German tone'. The debate originally scheduled for 2 July was moved to the next meeting of the Council of Ministers.

At the turn of June and July 1942, Michał Potulicki, on behalf of the Ministry of Foreign Affairs, submitted reservations concerning the progress of the works on the decree. He was critical of the Ministry of Justice's ending of the works of the inter-ministerial conferences initiated in April 1942, in order to have the text of the decree drafted instead by a narrow circle of employees of the justice ministry and of the LWC, without consultation with the MFA. He emphasized: 'such kind of drafts of [instruments relating to] international law should not go out into the broader forum without the Ministry of Foreign Affairs, (...) all the more because this Ministry handles the matter of punishment to the Germans on inter-Allied level'.[131] In Potulicki's opinion, the stance developed by the Inter-Allied Commission on the Punishment of War Crimes, established by the signatories of the Declaration of St. James's Palace, should have served as the primary frame of reference for the Polish Government on the matter. He emphasized that its members had been 'thus far (...) speaking firmly against the Fascist-Nazi system of retroactive punishment'.[132] In June 1942, the terms of a truce with the German Reich became the focal point of the commission's works, along with the drafting of extradition treaties and determination of the types of courts and procedural tracks for domestic war-crime trials. 'All these matters the draft decree either decides unilaterally or partially frustrates, corralling us into an isolated position for the trifling (...) hope that placarding the decree throughout occupied Poland will deter the Germans from further prosecutions', Potulicki went on to summarize. In giving retroactive force to the decree, he saw the political danger of the Polish Government ending up being perceived as 'concealed ideologues of fascism'.[133] Roman Piotrowski laid out similar arguments but in harsher language:

---

130 Minutes of the meeting of the Council of Ministers, 2 July 1942, IPMS, PRM-K, 102/48a, leaves 2–5, PPRM vol. IV, 352–353.

131 Note by Michał Potulicki, 18 June 1942, attachment to IPMS minutes, PRM-K. 102/48c, leaves 40–41, PPRM vol. IV, 372–373.

132 Note by Michał Potulicki for the Prime Minister and the Minister of Justice, 30 June 1942, IPMS, PRM-K. 102/48 c, leaves 25–27, PPRM vol. IV, 370–372, here 371.

133 *Ibidem.*

> It would be (…) a highly dangerous and inexpedient thing to tarnish one's own legislation after the manner of the German one through the introduction thereto – if only 'by way of retorsion' – of principles contradicting [even] the most primitive sense of justice and rule of law; principles that would tear Polish legislation from the family of the legislations of civilized states, bringing it down to a level with the legislation of Nazi Germany.
>
> The enactment of such a decree would understandably scandalize even our friends in Allied states, Anglophone (United Kingdom, USA) in particular, in which the legal sense and respect for the law are especially highly developed. It would give rise among them also to justified doubts as to the exceptional punish worthiness of the German crimes and equitability of ensuring the extradition of their perpetrators to the domestic courts of the wronged states. We would unquestionably shake their faith in especially the ability of Polish courts to judge impartially and justly the German crimes.[134]

It is worth emphasizing that the main cause of scepticism towards the draft decree was its reception in the international forum and lack of support from the United Kingdom and USA for the very idea of penal repression against war criminals. In a note for Edward Raczyński, Michał Potulicki admitted: 'I understand that a time may come when, after the end of the war, we could introduce the (…) retroactive operation of criminal statutes with regard to the occupying powers anyway, but for that we still have time'.[135] Given the lack of realistic prospects of implementation of the decree before the end of war, he advocated for the publication in Poland of an announcement outlining the key points of the decree but: 'without tying the Prime Minister's hands in the Allied forum and without containing too precise legalese'.[136]

Wacław Komarnicki's response to the critical remarks on the assumptions of the decree arrived in the form of short papers read in the Council of Ministers plenaries on 2 and 15 July and 17 October 1942, and previously the Legislative Works Commission on 23 June 1942.

---

134 Roman Piotrowski, Remarks on the draft Decree of the President of the Republic of Poland on Punishment for War Crimes, submitted on 1 July 1942 to the Minister of Justice in connection with the meeting of the Council of Ministers on 2 July 1942, AAN 2/133/0/6/44, leaves 458–465, here: 459 and 462.

135 Note by Michał Potulicki, PPRM vol. IV, 372–373.

136 *Ibidem*, 371.

In Komarnicki's opinion, the key argument in favour of the promulgation of the Decree of the President of the Republic of Poland on Punishment for War Crimes was the lack of domestic or international provisions covering facts and sanctions that could be applicable to the German crimes. He went on to characterize the German policy of extermination as organized crimes, committed within a 'system of total war' and atrocities carried out 'with such sophistication and on such a scale as we cannot find in any [other] modern war'.[137] Besides the lack of a precise definition of facts in existing provisions of domestic and international law, the application of such provisions in war-crime trials would – in Komarnicki's opinion – have been inexpedient due to the disproportionality of the penalties to the gravity of the crimes: 'The intensification of criminality, the criminal sophistication displayed by the Germans, is so great that the penalties provided in the Conventions and Codes appear manifestly disproportionate'.[138]

Komarnicki emphasized that Poland's unique situation arising from the scale of the crimes committed in the country's territory and their objective – 'destruction of the Polish nation, both deprivation of its material bases of existence and destruction of its cultural heritage accumulated over centuries'[139] – further legitimized Polish authorities' aspirations for the use of all available means to stop the German extermination and lay down the principles to govern the punishment of those guilty of the crimes. These arguments fit in with the parallel ongoing discussion of new types of international crimes – crimes against humanity and crime of genocide. As a result, Komarnicki placed great importance on the form in which the Polish Government's intention to hold war criminals accountable was to be publicly announced. He argued: 'because (…) the gravity of legislative instrument that is a decree of the President of the Republic of Poland and its binding force are paramount, this form must be used as an expression of the Republic's intention to punish the perpetrators of the German crimes'.[140]

On the one hand, the determined position of the Polish Government, expressed in the form of a statute regulating the legal bases of the criminal responsibility of war criminals, would on the one hand have answered the expectations of – and provided moral support to – the population of occupied Poland.[141] On the other hand, it would have been a voice of objection to Ger-

137 AAN, 2/133/0/6/44, leaf 409.

138 Komarnicki's speech of 15 July 1942, AAN, 2/133/0/6/44, leaf 469.

139 AAN, 2/133/0/6/44, leaf 410.

140 AAN, 2/133/0/6/44, leaf 410.

141 The attitudes of Polish society towards the occupiers and concepts of retribution against Germany are discussed by Adam Basak in the *Biuletyn Informacyjny*; see Basak, *Kwestia*.

many's attack on the 'legal sense of civilized nations' (he used the archaic term 'cultivated') and its violations of principles of international law and international relations. Minister Komarnicki started his speech in the Council of Ministers plenary on 2 July 1942 with a reference to the above-quoted excerpt from the February Declaration, makings calls for the 'complete and effective disarmament of [Germany], precluding any future aggression' part of the official policy of the Polish Government-in-Exile, and their implementation recognized as an 'imperative of elementary historical justice'.[142] With that, he argued: 'the Polish government ha[d] placed the matter on the highest level', not contenting itself merely with the compensation of wrongs suffered by Poland but instead taking a 'general position aimed at the fulfilment of the demand of elementary historical justice, and thus the dominance of moral principles in international relations'.[143]

In his speeches, Komarnicki appealed to the axiological sources of international law, especially the principles of equity and justice, recalling that the sources include treaties and conventions and also customary law and the value system arising from the 'legal sense of civilized nations'. He proposed to resolve the issue of normative bases for criminal responsibility for war crimes, in the absence of norms of positive law, by resorting to the philosophy of the law of nature and the discourse proper to it. The danger facing the Government-in-Exile of finding itself in an isolated position, against which Potulicki warned, Komarnicki juxtaposed with being in the 'avant-garde of change'. In his opinion, the Polish concept of accountability was not limited to the protection of Polish-particular interests. Rather, it took a universalist stance seeking to stop 'the German criminality that [had arisen] from a system demolishing international relations and attempting to turn back the entire progress of humanity',[144] and to secure the guarantees of compensation for the victims and punishment for the offenders, as prompted by the 'imperative of historical justice'.

From the very onset of conceptual works on the presidential decree, retroactivity was their single most controversial aspect. Declaring himself in favour of retaining the applicability of the decree, as from 31 August 1939, Komarnicki emphasized that he had remained an adherent of the principles of democracy and rule of law and that the intention of the drafters of the decree in no way had been to emulate the 'Nazi principles of retroactive applicability of a crim-

142 AAN, 2/133/0/44, leaf 405.

143 *Ibidem.*

144 *Ibidem.*

inal statute'.[145] In the opinion of the justice minister, the retention of the proposed temporal applicability was justified as a use of retorsions against the German Reich, constituting a form of retaliation allowed by international law – harmful but lawful measures in response to the harmful actions of another state.[146] In support, he cited the 'trampling by the Germans, with regard to the Polish State and its citizens, of all legal and moral principles', including the use of retroactive criminal legislation. Special criminal legislation for territories occupied by German armed forces was introduced, among others, by the Regulation of 1 October 1939 on the Prosecution of Crimes Committed before 1 September 1939 in Polish territories occupied by German forces.[147] Komarnicki pointed out: 'on the basis of this decree, the Germans sentenced to death tens of thousands of Polish citizens (…); they also extended it to the entire existence of the Polish State, applying it to, e.g. participants of the Greater Polish and Upper Silesian Uprisings'.[148]

Another argument invoked by Komarnicki was the fact that, being a special statute as it was, the decree did not introduce any new definitions but narrowed down acts already recognized as criminal offences by instruments of domestic or international law, only enabling the imposition of penalties proportionate to the degree of harm contained in the act. Accordingly, that was a case of 'retroactivity in the formal sense' and not from the perspective of substantive law.[149] Finally, he emphasized, the enactment of a special statute laying down the rules of criminal responsibility for acts committed under the occupation was the inevitable consequence of the process of bringing justice for German crimes, which the Polish Government had initiated in the international arena by causing the Declaration of St. James's Palace to be signed. Citing the works of the international legal bodies – Inter-Allied Commission on the Punishment of War Crimes, London International Assembly and Cambridge Commission on Penal Law Reconstruction and Development[150] – Komarnicki underscored that the 'necessity of legislative regulation (…) of the justice system for German occupiers' was increasingly gaining trac-

145 *Ibidem*, leaf 406.

146 Cybichowski, *Prawo międzynarodowe*, 298.

147 *Verordnung über die Verfolgung der vor dem 1. 9.1939 in den von deutschen Truppen besetzten polnischen Gebieten begangenen strafbaren Handlungen, 1.10.1939, abbreviation* VOBL. *Polen, 24; Wrzyszcz,* Okupacyjne, *57–58., Nr 24.* See Karol Marian Pospieszalski, *Polska pod niemieckim prawem 1939–1945* (*Ziemie Zachodnie*) (Poznań: Wydawnictwo Instytutu Zachodniego 1946), 136–139 and 266; Wrzyszcz, *Okupacyjne*, 57–58.

148 AAN, 2/133/0/6/44, leaf 471.

149 AAN, 2/133/0/6/44, leaf 406.

150 AAN, 2/133/0/6/44, leaf 469.

tion among British jurists. The implementation of the concept – developed as early as mid-1942 at the London International Assembly – of jurisdiction for war crimes, split among domestic courts for the generality of offenders and international tribunals for the main criminals, was impossible without enacting special laws to define the substantive principles of criminal responsibility. Both cases necessitated the use of retroactive legislation. The exceptionality of the circumstances, Komarnicki went on to conclude, nevertheless justified the use of exceptional means.[151] Arguing that the promulgation of the presidential decree would mark the natural continuity of Polish efforts on behalf of the popularization of the concept of penal repression against war criminals, the Minister of Justice noted that the Polish draft, being the first attempt at domestic codification, would be of 'significant importance to the general development of concepts in th[at] matter'. The principal argument in favour of the fastest possible promulgation of the decree was its anticipated deterrent effect, intended to stop the German policy of extermination, as well as sustaining the 'unrelenting attitude' of the Polish population towards the occupying power. As Komarnicki stressed, towards the conclusion of his speech during the Council of Ministers plenary on 15 July, it was beyond his own competence to answer the question of the most opportune timing for the promulgation of the decree, and for that he passed the voice to the Minister of the Interior and the President of the Council of Ministers.

There was a difference of opinion between Minister Mikołajczyk, in favour of the most expedited promulgation possible, and Prime Minister Sikorski, warning against the potential intensification of the prosecution. Sikorski reiterated that 'the most important goal in [that] matter [wa]s and w[ould] continue to be for the United Kingdom and the USA to offer guarantees of extradition of German criminals'.[152] The vote on the draft in the meeting of the Council of Ministers on 15 July reflected this difference. Ministers Mikołajczyk and Kwapiński voted yea, Seyda and Stańczyk nay, and Raczyński submitted certain reservations relating to Poland's international situation. A 'compromise motion' passed, tabled by Stanisław Stroński, who proposed the adoption of principles of the draft by the Council of Ministers and authorization for Ministers Raczyński, Mikołajczyk and Komarnicki to consult with Allied governments before the promulgation of the decree. The final text was to be drafted by a special committee led by the Minister of Justice and includ-

151 *Ibidem.*

152 Minutes of the meeting of the Council of Ministers on 15 July 1942, IPMS, PRM-K, 102/48 c, leaves 17–21, PPRM vol. IV, 364–365.

ing Ministers Mikołajczyk, Stroński, Seyda, and Raczyński. The committee deliberated at the Ministry of Justice on 8 October 1942.[153]

Amendments submitted by Stanisław Mikołajczyk and Marian Seyda, concerning Articles 1, 3, and 7 of the draft, were made the subject of debate. Seyda's proposal for the modification of Article 1 concerned the expansion of the personal scope of application of the statute. It envisaged the criminal liability of citizens of the German Reich, 'reflecting the current German legislation and persons having another form of German nationality', as well as nationals of 'states allied to the German Reich'.[154] As for Article 3 of the draft, both ministers recommended shortening the period of loss of freedom in the *actus* ('If the act mentioned in Article 2 has caused death, special torment, disability, lasting physical or mental illness, loss of freedom for a period of one month, displacement or resettlement of a Polish national, the perpetrator shall be liable to life imprisonment or death penalty') from one month to 14 days, so as to 'bring [that] provision in line with Polish legislation'.[155] Other remarks concerned the redaction of Article 7, penalizing the destruction or theft of cultural property. In the opinion of Marian Seyda, the use of terms such as 'cultural property' or 'property of historical value' narrowed the applicability of that Article and thus of the decree as a whole. He recommended the use of broader language in outlining the scope of liability for damaging or pillaging cultural property or economic assets, so as to penalize 'cases of pillaging, theft, destruction or significant impairment of public or private property, if such property h [eld] value to the nation as a whole',[156] understood as referring to either economic or cultural property. Stanisław Mikołajczyk recommended the following wording for Article 7: 'Whoever, contrary to norms of international law, appropriates, damages, destroys or removes abroad property holding special value to Polish culture shall be liable to life imprisonment or death penalty'.[157]

Following debate on the suggested amendments, the modification of the time threshold in Article 3 of the draft passed, and the following wordings were adopted for Articles 1 and 7:

---

153 Minutes of the Conference of Ministers for the determination of the definitive text of the Decree on Criminal Responsibility for War Crimes, held at the Ministry of Justice on 8 October 1942, 3.30 hours, IPMS, Kol. 180/30.

154 Amendments to the draft Decree on Criminal Responsibility for War Crimes, IPMS, Kol. 183/30.

155 *Ibidem.* In this case, Art. 5 of the Act of 23 June 1939 on Martial Law (Dz.U.RP.1939.57.366) and Art. 24(6) of provisions implementing the Criminal Code and Law of Infractions (Dz. U.RP.1932.60.573), as well as Art. 248(2) of the Criminal Code (Dz.U.RP.1932.60.571).

156 *Ibidem.*

157 *Ibidem.*

(Article 1) Criminal liability by virtue of the provisions of this decree shall apply to persons belonging to the German Reich or states allied or linked thereto or remaining in the service of the German Reich or of such states in war time, for criminal offences committed after 31 August 1939, irrespective of the place of commission of the act.

(Article 7) Whoever, contrary to the norms of international law, commits the pillaging, theft, destruction or significant impairment of public or private property, if such property holds national value, shall be liable to life imprisonment or death penalty.

Moreover, Article 12 received a modification assigning the competence for the implementation of the decree: 'The implementation of this decree shall be entrusted to the Ministers of the Interior, Justice and Military Affairs'. The remaining articles were left unchanged. In that shape, although under a new title – 'Decree of the President of the Republic of Poland on Criminal Responsibility for War Crimes' – the decree was referred to debate in the Council of Ministers.

The only change proposed by Wacław Komarnicki in the meeting of the Council of Ministers on 17 October 1942[158] was for the competence of the Minister of Foreign Affairs to be added to Article 12 'due to the necessity of consulting on the course of action with other Allied states with regard to the enactment and implementation of the decree'. He emphasized the necessity of reaching an understanding with the governments of Allied states, prior to promulgation. The increasing recognition for the concept of the penal repression of war crimes, expressed in the latter half of 1942 in the speeches of Franklin D. Roosevelt and Winston Churchill of August and September 1942 during the meeting of the Inter-Allied Commission on the Punishment of War Crimes on 20 August 1942, as well Lord Chancellor Simon in the Lords on 7 October 1942, was something the Polish justice minister tended to perceive as connected to some extent with the initiatives of the Polish Government-in-Exile in the international sphere. He emphasized that the promulgation of the statute would give the Polish Government the opportunity to exert continued influence on the Allied position. Komarnicki attached particular importance to the assertion of Viscount Maugham in the forum of the London International Assembly on 28 September 1942 that the retroactive force of statutes was not foreign to English law. Furthermore, he argued that in the case of special statutes dealing with the punishment of war criminals, it was inevit-

158 IPMS PRM-K. 102/51C, 22–27, PPRM, vol. V, 38–51.

able.[159] The international situation, in the opinion of the Minister of Justice, was favourable to the publication of the decree, while the intensification of terror in Poland and the need to oppose the policy of extermination made further deferrals of promulgation no longer an option.

His arguments carried the day. On 17 October 1942, the Council of Ministers adopted the draft Decree of the President of the Republic of Poland on Criminal Responsibility for War Crimes, and by resolution of 3 November of the same, referred it to the National Council of the Republic of Poland for opinion.[160]

3.6 *Deliberations of the Legal–Political Committee of the National Council of the Republic of Poland and Redaction of the Final Text of the Decree*

The last stage of the works on the draft Decree of the President of the Republic of Poland on Criminal Responsibility for War Crimes coincides with the turn of 1942 and 1943. On 7 December 1942 and 5 January 1943, meetings of the Legal–Political Committee of the National Council of Poland were convened to dispose of amendments to the draft.[161] In attendance were the Committee's chair, Stanisław Celichowski, as well as interior minister Władysław Banaczyk, Wacław Komarnicki, Adam Ciołkosz, Stanisław Sopicki, Roman Battaglia, Mieczysław Szerer, and Stefan Glaser.[162]

During the first meeting of the Legal–Political Committee of the National Council, the draft decree was introduced by Adam Ciołkosz – the leader of the Polish Socialist Party – as rapporteur. In his speech, he noted the lack of unanimity among Allied states as to the question of punishment for perpetrators of violations of international law, as well as difficulties arising from the non-accession of the United States and United Kingdom to the Declaration of St. James's Palace:

---

159 Komarnicki noted: 'the diffident position of the British Government concerning this topic arises from other [than legal] reasons: purely political, relating to the British war goals and diplomatic tactic in this regard'. Speech by the Minister of Justice on the draft Decree on Criminal Responsibility for War crimes, delivered in the meeting of the Council of Ministers on 17 October 1942, IPMS PRM-K. 102/51 c, leaves 28–31, reprinted in PPRM, vol. V, 42–47, here: 45.

160 See Minutes of the meeting of the Council of Ministers, 3 November 1942, IPMS, PRM-K., 102/52a, leaves 2–6, PPRM vol. V, 52–56, here: 56.

161 AAN, 2/133/0/44, leaves 348–350. Minutes of the meeting of the National Council on 7 December 1942, see: IPMS, A.5/13/7/2.

162 The list of attendees was reconstructed on the basis of the minutes. Originally attached lists have not been preserved. *Cf.* IPMS, A.5/13/6; IPMS, A.5/13/7.

> The [Inter-Allied] Conference at St James's Palace has resolved that a solution [to the problem of punishment for war criminals] should be found in a spirit of international solidarity. Only 9 states participated in the conference. G[reat] Britain only as an observer. Nor were the U[nited] S[tates], Soviets, China or the Dominions present. In Eden's speech, one cannot find even a single word of commitment. G[reat] Britain does not want to commit. The Soviets are considering the problem on their own. In these circumstances, the question arises whether Poland has been alone in attempting to codify its legal provisions in this area. If it is not possible to do so jointly, someone must begin. Poland has a right to be the first to take up this matter. However, one should ponder together with Mr Min[ister] Komarnicki what the positive effects are going to be of such an individual coming forward and what the negative ones, and what preponderates.[163]

Ciołkosz emphasized the importance of Polish attempts to win Allied support as soon as possible, recalling that failure to put war criminals on trial after the First World War arose from the decision to do so having only been made after the ceasefire. He argued:

> it is important for the oppressors to be warned and for the occupied countries to be reassured that there is no crime without punishment and that retribution will take place. Therefore, it is necessary for suitable legal norms to be established already now on the plane of domestic and international legislation.[164]

Ciołkosz recommended promulgating the decree, following the incorporation of the amendments submitted by the National Council and consideration of potential negative Allied response. According to him, they key concern was to obtain guarantees of extradition from Allied states, without which the implementation of the decree would not be possible.[165]

Both the drafters and the members of the Legal–Political Committee of the National Council responded to his remarks. The reservations surfacing during the debate concerned the potential for criticism from other Allied states and the ability to implement the provisions of the Decree of the President of the Republic of Poland on Criminal Responsibility for War Crimes. In this case,

163 IPMS, A.5/13/6, leaf 3.
164 IPMS A.5/13/6, leaf 1.
165 IPMS, A.5/13/6, leaf 6.

the stake was not only the much-needed support from the governments of Allied states but also the cooperation of the future German government on matters of extradition. The promise of severe punishment, conveyed by the determination and promulgation of the terms on which war criminals were to be brought to justice, was regarded as a necessary response to the expectations of the victims and of the population of occupied Poland. 'The homeland demands punishment and justice immediately. Only this the homeland demands, and not declarations and speeches'.[166]

The second meeting of the Legal–Political Committee of the National Council of the Republic of Poland discussed amendments to the draft. Similarly to what had been the case at the prior stages, the modifications proposed by the National Council dealt primarily with the facts of Article 1 and the matter of the criminal responsibility of collaborationists. Speaking as the rapporteur, Adam Ciołkosz proposed to expand the personal circle by replacing the words: 'persons (…) remaining in the service of the German Reich or of such states' with: 'persons acting in the service and (or) in the interest of the German Reich, as well as (or) on behalf of the German Reich and (or) belonging to the German Reich or states allied thereto'. The purpose was to achieve the criminal liability of those 'who [we]re not formally in the service of the German Reich but acting in its interest and rendering services in the scope covered by the provisions of the decree'.[167] As for Article 3, the proposal was to avoid time thresholds for the loss of freedom (which the previous revision had set to 14 days).

Stefan Glaser advocated for the inclusion of sexual crimes, such as forcing a person to 'submit to a lewd act or forcible insemination', as an additional aggravated form of the offence defined in Article 2 of the decree. He drew attention to acts of rape, various forms of violence against women, as well as gender-based violence, as an element of a systemic policy of extermination maintained by the occupying power. Stanisław Sopicki and Mieczysław Szerer also proposed to modify the sentencing limits in Article 3, which contained two options – either life imprisonment or death penalty. In their opinion, the lack of an alternative, milder penalty significantly curtailed the flexibility of sentencing, and in cases of lesser importance, not qualifying for either life imprisonment or death, the outcome could be the non-imposition of any penalty whatsoever.[168] Such changes were opposed by Adam Ciołkosz, Stanisław Celichowski, and Stefan Glaser, who emphasized the purpose of the decree being to enable the escalation of the penalties envisaged by domestic legisla-

166 IPMS, A.5/13/6, leaf 6.
167 AAN, 2/133/0/44, leaf 348.
168 IPMS. A.5/13/7, leaf 3.

tion, which provided no such option. The opponents argued that in cases of lesser importance, courts could still resort to the corresponding generally applicable provisions of the Criminal Code.[169] Another amendment added a new Article 9: 'Whoever, by action or omission, assists persons guilty of criminal offences covered by this decree to avoid liability shall be liable to imprisonment, life imprisonment or death penalty'.

The debate also explored the matter of jurisdiction – common courts or courts martial – and the procedural track. The recommendation was that the existing Article 11, establishing the jurisdiction of courts martial adjudicating on the wartime track, be replaced with: 'The judicial procedure for cases covered by this decree shall be determined by a separate decree'. Accordingly, the decision was to limit the competence to implement provisions of the decree – originally attributed to the Minister of Justice, Minister of Military Affairs and Minister of Foreign Affairs – to the Minister of Justice alone. The National Council of the Republic of Poland approved the draft Decree on Criminal Responsibility for War Crimes, together with the Legal–Political Committee's amendments, on 8 February 1943. On 14 February, the President of the National Council forwarded it to Prime Minister Sikorski along with Ministers Mikołajczyk and Komarnicki. The LWC Section VI for Legislative Technique completed the final revision on 18 February 1943.[170] On 1 March 1943, in the Council of Ministers, Wacław Komarnicki tabled the motion to adopt the text of the Decree of the President of the Republic of Poland on Criminal Responsibility for War Crimes.

Article 1 stipulated the criminal liability of persons 'belonging to the German Reich or states allied thereto or co-operating therewith, as well as other persons acting in the interest (*w interesie*) of the German Reich or of such states, for criminal offences committed after 31 August 1939, irrespective of the place of commission of the act'. Article 2 provided: 'Whoever, contrary to the norms of international law, commits an act detrimental to the Polish State, a Polish legal person or Polish national shall be liable to the penalty of imprisonment'. By virtue of Article 3, in cases when the act had resulted in the death, special torment, disability, lasting physical or mental illness, lasting incapacity for occupational work, or subjection to a lewd act or displacement of a Polish national, the perpetrator was to be subject to life imprisonment or death penalty. The heightened sentencing limits also featured in the subsequent sections for situations when the act mentioned in Article 2 had caused a public danger to human life or health in Poland (Article 4) and for persons compel-

169 *Ibidem.*
170 AAN, 2/133/0/44/leaf 359.

ling Polish nationals to join foreign armed forces or work for the enemy in violation of international law (Article 5). Article 6 provided:

> (1) Whoever, adjudicating on behalf of the occupation authorities on the basis of legal provisions enacted contrary to provisions of international law, does a wrong to a Polish national shall be liable to imprisonment.
> (2) If such kind of judgment has caused one of the consequences mentioned in Article 3, the perpetrator shall be liable to life imprisonment or death penalty.

Article 7 stipulated life imprisonment or the capital penalty in cases of looting, theft, destruction, or significant impairment of public or private property, if the property held value to the nation as a whole, which – in the drafter's intention – encompassed both cultural property and economic (business) property. Article 8 provided for the additional penalties of confiscation of property and forfeiture of inheritance capacity. In accordance with Article 9, life imprisonment or death was the penalty for assisting 'the perpetrator of a criminal offence covered by this decree to avoid liability' or failure to prevent escape or some other form of avoidance of liability by the perpetrator, if it was preventable. Article 10 stipulated the criminal responsibility of both the giver and the executor of an order to commit a crime specified in the decree. Article 11 mandated for the statutes of limitations set out in Article 86 of the Criminal Code, in cases of war crimes, to begin 6 months after the return of the Supreme Court to operation. Article 12 entrusted the implementation of the decree to the Minister of Justice; Article 13, the last one, provided for the decree to come into effect on the day of publication.

In this shape, the draft was submitted by the Minister of Justice to the Council of Ministers and adopted on 22 March 1943[171] and signed by President Władysław Raczkiewicz on 30 March. The Journal of Laws published the Decree of the President of Poland on Criminal Responsibility on 31 March 1943.

4 The Position of the Department of Justice of the Government Delegation for Poland, and Initiatives from Occupied Poland

One of the most important factors leading to the publication of the Decree of the President of the Republic of Poland on Criminal Responsibility for War

171 Minutes of the meeting of the Council of Ministers of 22 March 1943, IPMS, PRM-K .102/56e, leaves 18–21, PPRM, vol. V, 315–318, here: 315.

Crimes was Polish society's expectations of a strict and just accounting for the crimes committed under the occupations. The resolution of the Cabinet Committee for Home Affairs of 28 December 1939 already commended to the Polish Government the demands of the 'Polish political circles of Warsaw' for Allied guarantees of individual criminal responsibility. The Delegate's report of 12 June 1942 urged the authorities in London to take determined steps for the 'immediate punishment of [German] barbarity' and creation of an international criminal tribunal to judge all the crimes committed by the Germans.[172] Independently from the expectation of such steps to be taken by the government, the underground conspiracy also prepared its own drafts. At the beginning of 1942, the Department of Justice of the Government Delegation for Poland prepared a draft Decree on the Punishment of Certain Criminal Offences Committed While Under Enemy Invasion. The Soviet-backed Polish Committee of National Liberation also promulgated a competing statute on 31 August 1944.

4.1 *Underground Courts and 'Civic Morality Code'*

Both in the military and in the civilian structures of Polish Underground State, there existed branches responsible for the administration of justice and legal aspects of life in occupied Poland, such as the Department of Justice of the Government Delegation for Poland.[173] A particular role in those structures belonged to the underground courts, the principal purpose of which was to repress 'persecutors, traitors, spies and provocateurs'[174] and to halt the spread of wartime criminality and eliminate the various forms of collaboration harmful to the *raison d'état* and social cohesion.[175]

The establishment of two types of 'hooded courts' (*sądy kapturowe* – literal translation; *cf.* Vehmic courts or 'faceless judges') in the military structures of Polish Underground State and under the Government Delegate for Poland, as

172 Report of the Delegate of the Government [for Poland], 12 June 1942, IPMS, A9III/2b/9.

173 The Department of Justice of the Government Delegation for Poland was established in 1941. Its inaugural director was Leon Nowodworski, former dean of Warsaw Bar Council. After Nowodworski's death in December 1941, the headship of the department passed to the vice dean of Warsaw Bar Council and former director of Warsaw Capital City Legal Department, Feliks Zadrowski. The works of the Department of Justice were handled by its three Divisions – Administrative, Legislative and Prisons – as well as a Bar Commission and a Notaries Commission. They included preparations for the organization of the justice system in the post-war period, as well as compilations and translations of German legislative acts.

174 Resolution of the Cabinet Committee for Home Affairs concerning Hooded Courts, 16 April 1940, *Armia Krajowa w Dokumentach* vol. 1, 220.

175 *Ibidem*, 12–13.

well as regional and district delegates, was by the resolution of the Cabinet Committee for Home Affairs of 16 April 1940. The Code and the substantive provisions for the Hooded Courts of the Union of Armed Struggle (ZWZ) were approved by General Kazimierz Sosnkowski on 7 May 1940. The jurisdiction covered crimes against the interests of the Polish state or Polish citizens: treason, provocation, espionage, denunciation, and 'inhuman persecution of or harm to the Polish population'.[176] The list also included new types of crimes, not featured in the Criminal Code of 1932:

– the crime of provocation, i.e. acting in concert with the authorities of a foreign state or on one's own initiative with the intention of provoking: 'acts or activities against a foreign state for the purpose of their exposure';
– the crime of denunciation, i.e. enabling the authorities of a foreign state to prosecute criminal offences committed against that state; and
– the crime of inhuman persecution of the population, and thus wronging the population in a manner deemed 'inhuman, contrary to the natural sense of justice' or enacting legislation or ordinances to achieve the same effect.[177]

From November 1941 onward, Special Courts Martial (literally 'Special Military Courts') operated in occupied territories with jurisdiction for crimes against the Armed Forces. Also from November 1941 onward, investigative work within the structures of the Government Delegation for Poland was handled by investigative–prosecutorial commissions (*kolegia śledzo-oskarżające*) of the Directorate of Civil Resistance. Their task was to 'gather investigative materials on activities hostile or harmful to the Polish nation or state'.[178] Towards the end of 1942, the first Civilian Hooded Courts (Civilian Special Courts) were created for

---

176 Leszek Gondek, *W imieniu Rzeczypospolitej. Wymiar sprawiedliwości w Polsce w czasach II wojny światowej* (Warszawa, PWN 2011), 185–186; Union of Armed Struggle (ZWZ), Hooded Courts Code (*Kodeks Sądów Kapturowych*), 7 May 1940, *Armia Krajowa w Dokumentach* vol. I, 229–234.

177 Substantive Provisions (*Przepisy Materialne*), 7 May 1940, in *Armia Krajowa w Dokumentach* vol. I, 233–234.

178 Waldemar Grabowski, 'Struktury organizacyjne służb bezpieczeństwa i wymiaru sprawiedliwości Polskiego Państwa Podziemnego', in Waldemar Grabowski (ed.), *Organy bezpieczeństwa i wymiar sprawiedliwości Polskiego Państwa Podziemnego* (Warszawa 2005), 89. In the words of Waldemar Grabowski: 'from 1943 onward, the role of the [investigative-prosecutorial] commissions was taken over by the adjudicating commissions of the Directorate of Civilian Resistance (Directorate of Underground Resistance). Their purpose was the elimination of harmful aspects of life under the occupation by stigmatizing the acts of unworthy individuals or groups or groups incompatible with Polish *raison d'état* and national interest'. In accordance with its provisions, by February 1944 there existed 13 Civilian Special Courts and more than thirty adjudicating committees. *Cf.* Grabowski, *Struktury organizacyjne*, 90.

the purpose of 'prosecution of criminal offences set out in criminal provisions, consisting in acting for the benefit (*na korzyść*) of the occupying power or to the detriment (*na szkodę*) of the Polish state (treason, espionage, provocation, persecution, etc.) committed or attempted after 1 September 1939'.[179] Both branches of the underground judiciary were targeted against negative social developments calling for a response from and repression by public authorities. There were two types of those. The first type was repressions against the civilian population and crimes committed by the occupying powers. The second type was any and all forms of collaboration with the occupying powers, acting 'to the detriment' (*na szkodę*) of the Polish state, espionage and denunciation, as well as principles of 'civic morality'. The latter was given much more attention in announcements and instructions addressed to society.

Instructions from the Polish Underground State concerning the acceptable forms of contact with the occupiers, methods of civilian resistance, and forms of civic conduct under the occupation had been published by conspirational press since early 1940.[180] Subsequently, an 'underground ethico-legal code' was drafted and published as a Civic Morality Code. The Code contained 25 Articles grouped in four divisions. Division I dealt with treason against the Polish state and nation, for which the base penalty was death. That could be commuted to imprisonment, loss of public rights, prohibition of exercise of a profession, or complete or partial confiscation of property.[181] This group of criminal offences included disavowing or repudiating Polish nationality, 'active collaboration with the enemy in their struggle', denunciating compatriots, failing to give shelter or refusing to render 'urgent necessary assistance to a person wanted by the enemy on account of service to the Polish State and Nation', or undertaking activities intended to 'weaken of the defensive spirit of the Polish nation'. Criminal offences from Division II, directed 'against membership in the Polish nation', were prohibited on pain of loss of public rights, honorary rights, and loss of the exercise of a profession. Those offences consisted in

179 Statute of Civilian Special Courts (*Statut Cywilnych Sądów Specjalnych*), Art. 1 1, cited after Gondek, *W imieniu*, 204–206.

180 Tomasz Szarota, *Okupowanej Stolicy Dzień Powszedni. Studium Historyczne* (Warszawa: Czytelnik 1978), 562–564. As noted by Tomasz Szarota, the establishment of a catalogue of patriotic and civic norms and methods of their enforcement was a typical element of organized underground conspiracy in the occupied countries: 'The creation of a code of civic morality constituted in occupied Europe one of the manifestations of a crystallizing resistance movement [and] was an element of each society's civilian resistance to the invader'. Concerning this topic see also: Gondek, *W imieniu*, 78–84.

181 Civic Morality Code (*Kodeks Moralności Obywatelskiej*), AAN 2/11325/0/ 202/ IV-1, leaf 200. The document is quoted extensively, with comments, by Tomasz Szarota; *cf.* Szarota, *Okupowanej Warszawy*, 567–573.

'serving the enemy' or failing to take advantage of a position held in the occupation apparatus to assist Polish citizens or act for the benefit of the Polish state, giving passive assistance to the enemy, or making 'use of the enemy's ordinances and impunity in the application thereof for one's own benefit to the detriment of the Polish state and nation'.[182] Divisions III and IV penalized offences against civic morality and dignity, such as maintaining contacts with the enemy, offering public criticism of Polish laws (rights) and customs, refusing to assist Poles who had been 'harmed by the enemy's activities or ordinances', as well as participating in entertainment events organized by the occupying powers, or failure to maintain a 'dignified moral stance'. As the authors of the Code themselves emphasized, its purpose was to:

> inhibit the manifestation of the social process of abandonment of, on the one hand, certain legal norms, of which the violation constitute[d] a criminal offence *stricto sensu*, and, on the other hand, of certain ethical norms that should be binding on any Pole in a day of struggle. (…) The attempt was made to formulate the code in such a manner as to inspire in society the belief in the existence of an authority expressing not only moral values but also force in the sense of strict but just repression'.[183]

4.2 *Draft Decree on the Punishment of Certain Criminal Offences Committed while under Enemy Invasion*

The necessity of opposing negative social developments and the need to emphasize the existence, despite the difficult circumstances of life under the occupation, of effective organs of the administration of justice were matters of key importance to the Polish Underground State. These expectations were clearly formulated by the draft Decree on the Punishment of Certain Criminal Offences Committed While Under Enemy Invasion, prepared by the Department of Justice of the Government Delegation for Poland at the turn of 1941 and 1942 and forwarded to the authorities in London most probably in early 1942.[184] The Department's draft laid the canvas for the legislative works on the Decree of the President of the Republic of Poland on Criminal Responsibility for War Crimes.[185] The drafters were Stanisław Śliwiński, professor of criminal law and head of the Department of Criminal Law at the University of Warsaw,

182 *Ibidem.*

183 Government Delegation for Poland. Department of Justice, 'Civic Morality Code', AAN 2/11325/0/ 202/ IV-1, leaf 202.

184 AAN 2/133/0/6/83.

185 Cyprian and Sawicki, *Prawo norymberskie*, 98.

and Mieczysław Siewierski, Prosecutor to the Supreme Court, Head of the Legislative Division of the Government Delegation for Poland, who went on to serve as a prosecutor before the Supreme National Tribunal after the war.[186]

In the 'Remarks on the London decree on the prosecution of war crimes', the employees of the Department of Justice noted with satisfaction 'that the same thoughts and outlooks the Department had expressed in [its own] draft had caused the enactment of the Decree of 20 March 1943 on Criminal Responsibility for War Crimes'.[187] Despite the consensus on the need to supplement Polish legislation with new fact sets in crime definitions and escalate the penalties for certain criminal offences already defined in the Code, and to enact a spe cial statute for wartime crimes, the decree drafted by the emigration authorities incurred criticism from the Department of Justice. The 'Remarks on the London decree' emphasized its failure to meet the tasks of 'exemplary punishment of the criminals and their accomplices and backers' and demanded 'significant modifications and supplementations (…) or replacement by a new decree'.[188]

The substantive provisions of the Decree on the Punishment of Certain Criminal Offences Committed While Under Enemy Invasion were repeated in the form of recommendations contained in the 'Remarks on the London decree', probably drafted in mid-1943, which is why they will be discussed jointly, as a commentary on the statute of 1943. It is worth noting, however that the Warsaw draft differed significantly from the London decree in volume and structure. The Delegation's draft spanned 54 provisions grouped in three parts. The first one was general provisions (Articles 1–19), listing Criminal Code provisions and special statutes[189] to which the provisions of the decree were to apply, as well as modifications of general provisions of the Criminal Code and statutory definitions. The second part contained special provisions (Articles 20–31), and the most extensive, third part – procedural provisions (Articles 32–54).

---

186 Ryszka, *Norymberga*, 131.

187 Remarks on the London decree on the prosecution of war crimes, AAN 2/133/0/6/90, leaf 36. The erroneous date of promulgation of the London decree is given by the cited source.

188 *Ibidem*.

189 Those were: Regulation of the President of the Republic of Poland of 24 October 1934 on Criminal Offences Against the Security of the State (Dz.U.1934.94.851); Decree of the President of the Republic of Poland of 22 November 1938 on the Protection of Certain Interests of the State (Dz.U.1938.91. 623), Act of 9 April 1938 on the Universal Military Obligation (Dz.U.1938.25.220); Act of 30 March 1939 on Communications in the Service of the Defence of the State (Dz.U.1939.29.195).

The last provision of the draft's general part contained the definition of the term 'enemy' – of key importance to the document as a whole. Article 19 provided:

> The following are to be deemed the enemy within the meaning of the present law:
> states having been at war with Poland from 1 January 1939 to the end of said state;
> states allied thereto in war, as well as states taking part in the occupation of territories of the Polish State;
> members of the armed forces and functionaries of said states, as well as natural and legal persons belonging to said states;
> military and political organizations co-operating with the aforementioned states and members of said organizations;
> irrespective of nationality, persons of German ethnicity and persons liable to punishment on the grounds of Article 22 of the present law.[190]

Out of the eleven articles of the draft's specific part, only one (Article 31) defined criminal offences committed by the subject specified in Article 19.

> Article 31 '(1) Whoever, being the enemy:
> (a) has contributed to the oppression of the Polish Nation, a Polish citizen or legal person, especially committed violence against a person by reason of the victim's belonging to the Polish Nation or State, or the killing, abduction, displacement or imprisonment of the population, forced induction in enemy armed forces or forced labour, or pillage or destruction of cultural heritage or public or private property;
> (b) has reviled or derided the Polish Nation or Polish State;
> (c) has been a leader or member of the government of so-called General Government, headed the administration in the districts established by the occupying powers in the territories of Poland, belonged to the enemy's political policy or collaborated therewith, committing crimes mentioned under letter a of the present article, or directed such activity of said institution or organization or been its executive organ, shall be liable to death penalty.
> (2) In cases of lesser gravity, the perpetrator shall be liable to imprisonment for life for a time no shorter than 10 years.

190 AAN 2/133/0/6/83, leaf 5.

(3) An inciter, aider or abettor in acts mentioned in section 1 of the present article not being an enemy, provided [their] act does not fall under a more severe provision, shall be liable to imprisonment.[191]

The remaining articles of the draft's specific part referred to Polish nationals (Articles 20 and 22–25) or Polish nationals and those of foreign states, as well as various forms of collaboration with or acting for the benefit of the enemy. Article 1 of the draft, defining the scope of the statute,[192] refers – in principle – not to crimes committed by the functionaries of the occupying powers but to collaboration and offences against the security of the state, criminalizing:

> felonies and misdemeanours that contributed or may have contributed to supporting the enemy's intentions or caused or may have caused special torment to the general public or an individual in connection with the circumstances created by the invasion, or where the perpetrator anticipated or may have anticipated impunity or favourable treatment by the enemy, or [where the perpetrator] held themselves out to be an organ of the enemy.[193]

Any activities assisting the operations of the occupying powers or 'acts of treason by outcasts from Polish society' were a topic of central interest to the Department of Justice of the Delegation.[194] Both the draft decree and the remarks on the London decree clearly elucidated the demand for repression against crimes committed by the functionaries of the occupation authorities' military and administrative apparatus. In principle, however, the draft from the Department of Justice covered a broader range of offenders.

The criticism of the Decree of the President of the Republic of Poland on Criminal Responsibility for War Crimes, submitted by the Department of Justice, focused on the excessively narrow definition of the perpetrator and likewise, too narrow list of criminal offences in Articles 2–7, 9, and 10. In the opinion of the Government Delegation for Poland, the restriction of the term 'perpetrator' to 'persons belonging to the German Reich' and 'persons acting

191 AAN 2/133/0/6/83, leaves 8–9.

192 The specific provisions of the Criminal Code of 1932 to which the decree was to apply included (as per Art. 1(a)) Arts. 93–107 CC (crimes of state and offences against the state's external interests), Arts. 154 and 152 from the 'offences against public safety' chapter; Arts. 215–229 from the 'causing a public danger' chapter; and Arts. 258–261 and 263 CC from Chapter XXIX CC 'Offences against property'.

193 AAN 2/133/0/6/83, leaf 1.

194 AAN 2/133/0/6/90, leaf 36.

in the interest of the German Reich or states allied thereto or co-operating therewith' excluded crimes committed by German, Polish, Soviet, or Ukrainian citizens solely in their own self-interest. The Delegation's concept envisaged the adoption of the model of a *delictum commune* – a crime 'open to all' – as opposed to a *delictum proprium*, i.e. a crime requiring the perpetrator to meet specific qualifications. With regard to Articles 3 and 4 of the London decree, it was deemed necessary to emphasize the underlying premises of Nazi crimes and distinguish persecution based on ethnic grounds, aiming at the destruction of the Polish society and its national, cultural and social values, and structures. And thus: 'in particular, the most severe penalty should be imposed on any enemy having contributed to the oppression of the Polish Nation, a Polish national or Polish legal person on account of their Polishness'.[195]

The London Decree incurred criticism for failure to capture facts corresponding to criminal offences committed to the detriment of the Polish state or nation by Polish nationals, and thus broadly understood forms of denunciation or collaboration with the occupying forces. In the view of the Department of Justice, those offences called for 'the most severe repression, for the nation's conscience w[ould] not suffer them to go unpunished or be only liable to the penalty specified by the Code, so it may take recourse to lynching'.[196] In the Warsaw draft, acts 'unworthy of a Polish citizen', listed in Articles 22–26, included renunciation of Polish nationality, public praise of the enemy's conduct, denunciations, providing information in support of enemy propaganda, or giving scandal by one's 'conduct towards the enemy'.[197] It was also recommended that Polish nationals who accepted 'enemy citizenship' face imprisonment, and the same for disavowing or renouncing their Polish nationality, or signing the *Deutsche Volksliste*. In accordance with Article 22 of the draft, the base penalty was five years' imprisonment, and in particularly grave cases, when the defendant had held a high civilian or military office or an 'eminent position in Polish society', the upper limit was 10 years.[198]

Another category of motivations left out of the Decree of 30 March 1943 was self-interest, as opposed to acting to the detriment of the Polish state or for the benefit of the enemy. Crimes of that type included making denunciations or false reports to occupation authorities, 'whereby the perpetrator settle[d] personal scores', as well as intimidation, blackmail, or extortion. Articles 27–30 of

195 AAN 2/133/0/6/90, leaf 41.
196 AAN 2/133/0/6/90, leaf 39.
197 AAN 2/133/0/6/83, leaves 6–7.
198 AAN 2/133/0/6/83, leaf 6.

the Delegation's draft dealt with those in detail.[199] Furthermore, the 'contrary to the norms of international law' qualification was viewed as unduly narrowing the circle of perpetrators and acts falling under the decree. As the Department of Justice argued in its remarks, norms of international law 'd[id] not regulate the obligations of citizens towards the state' and could not apply to offences against the security of the state committed by Poles.[200] An additional difficulty came from the fact that only states were subjects of international law, for which reason the decree would be applicable solely to criminal offences committed by the organs of a state, leaving individuals to be responsible only for incitement, aiding, or abetting. The recommendation was to modify the wording of Article 1 to: 'whoever commits an act to the detriment of the Polish state, etc., shall be liable (…), unless the law of nations authorize[d] them to such act'.[201]

For increased definitional precision, the recommendation was to use narrower language to describe the offences consisting in acting for the benefit of the enemy, worded somewhat vaguely in Article 100 CC: 'Whoever, in a time of war, acts for the benefit of the enemy or to the detriment of a Polish or allied armed force shall be liable to imprisonment for a time no shorter than 10 years or for life'.[202] An official interpretation offered by the drafters themselves would have helped adjudicators interpret the law and made it easier to prevent collaboration by clarifying what constituted a criminal offence.[203] Examples of criminal offences falling under Article 100 CC were given in Article 20 of the draft decree prepared by the Department of Justice:

- collaborating in the intensification of the enemy's armed strength and fruition of the enemy's political and military goals; collaborating with the enemy's political police;
- collaborating in the destruction or pillaging of cultural property, displacement or abduction of the population, appropriation of property and ill-treatment of the population;
- denunciatory activity capable of assisting the enemy's interests;
- editing, producing, publishing or distributing writings, prints or images, recording or displaying films serving the purposes of enemy propaganda;
- reviling the Polish State or Nation, its allies, Polish or allied armed forces, Polish authorities, offices or officials or arrangements;

---

199 AAN 2/133/0/6/90, leaf 40.
200 *Ibidem*, 38.
201 *Ibidem*, leaves 38–39.
202 Art. 100 of the Criminal Code of 1932, Dz.U.1932.60.571.
203 AAN 2/133/0/6/90, leaf 39.

- participation in the enemy's public or private organizations having the purpose of the achievement of the enemy's political and military objectives.[204]

The Department's comments on necessity ('state of higher necessity'), intertemporal law, superior orders (as a defence or plea), and the application of existing legal provisions Of particular interest from the perspective of debates within the government circles on the topic of individualization of culpability during the drafting works on the Decree of the President of the Republic of Poland on Criminal Responsibility for War Crimes and from the perspective of the international debate on the constructs of substantive law used for war-crime trials.

In response to the problem of superior orders and necessity (the latter, a situation when refusal to carry out one's orders could have meant exposure to repressions or death), attention was drawn to the defence offered by Article 22 CC:

> Whoever acts for the purpose of lifting a direct danger threatening their own good or that of another, if the danger cannot otherwise be avoided, shall not be liable to punishment. (...) (3). The good sacrificed must not represent an evidently higher value than the good protected.

The Department of Justice recommended that the Decree on Criminal Responsibility for War Crimes contain a provision with the following wording: 'in the consideration of whether necessity exists, the good of the Polish state, Polish legal person or Polish citizen protected by the law of nations must be regarded as representing always a value evidently higher than any other good of the occupier's'. Moreover, in cases of necessity, Article 22(4)CC, providing for extraordinary commutation in cases of exceeding the limits of necessity, was not to apply.[205] Provisions to that effect were made in Article 7 of the Decree on the Punishment of Certain Criminal Offences Committed While Under Enemy Invasion. The issue of the binding force of Nazi law, legitimizing the crimes committed 'in the majesty of the law' against the population of the occupied territories was disposed of by Article 4 of the draft: 'The unlawfulness of the act shall not be eliminated by provisions or ordinances enacted by the enemy contrary to the law of nations'.[206]

---

204 AAN 2/133/0/6/83, leaves 5–6.

205 *Ibidem.*

206 Draft Decree on the Punishment of Certain Criminal Offences Committed While Under Enemy Invasion, AAN 2/133/0/6/83, leaf 2.

Similarly to the London draft, the purpose of the Delegation's draft was to create legal bases for the aggravation of sentencing, relative to the sentencing limits prescribed by the Criminal Code, and thus creation of a catalogue of penalties proportionate to the degree of culpability and harm found in acts committed during the hostilities and occupation. Against this background emerged an interpretative problem with those criminal offences defined by the Criminal Code, for which the decree raised the sentencing limits. Motivated by justice as the purpose of punishment, the Department of Justice called for the abrogation – in respect of the offences prescribed by the decree – of Articles 1 and 2 of the Criminal Code regulating the temporal applicability of the criminal statute (responsibility for an act prohibited by a statute at the time of commission) and of the principle of applying – where different criminal provisions were in force at the time of adjudication than at the time of commission – whichever ones were more favourable to the perpetrator (Article 2 of the Criminal Code of 1932).[207]

5 The Three Decrees

The draft Decree on the Punishment of Certain Criminal Offences Committed While Under Enemy Invasion, similarly to the Decree of the President of the Republic of Poland on Criminal Responsibility for War Crimes of 30 March 1943, was intended by its authors to fill the lacuna in domestic legislation and create a basis in substantive law for subsequent trials of the perpetrators of crimes committed during the hostilities and occupation. Nevertheless, both the structure and the thematic scope of the two drafts differed. The London decree was the first domestic statute promulgated by an Allied state to lay down the principles of liability for war crimes. It did not contain the statutory definition of a 'war crime' but instead attached criminal penalties to acts mentioned in the statute, in so far as committed, 'contrary to the norms of international law' by nationals of foreign states, or members of the administrative apparatus or armed forces or persons collaborating with them. The principal goal of the statute was to establish in domestic law, individual responsibility for violations of international law, and thus a principle not previously based in treaty-based international law, and in that way, to influence the decision-making of the other Allied states with regard to the determination of the legal bases for the prosecution, trial, and punishment of war criminals. According to the intention of the Polish Government-in-Exile, persons accused of collabor-

207 *Ibidem.*

ation would be tried under the provisions of the Criminal Code or special legislation enacted at a later time.

On the other hand, the purpose of the draft prepared by the Department of Justice of the Delegation of the Government for Poland was to penalize criminal offences committed 'while under enemy invasion' by foreigners and by members of occupation forces (defined by Article 31 of the draft, without, however, use of the term 'war crimes'), as well as Polish nationals acting 'to the detriment of' (meaning 'against the interests of', 'wrongfully doing harm to', etc.) the Polish state and nation.[208] The Delegation's draft particularly emphasized the precise definition of the offences, among them various forms of collaboration or acting 'for the benefit of' (or 'in the interest of') the enemy. That was the effect of the observation of the occupation realities and activities of the Polish Underground State's justice system.

The two instruments were largely complementary to each other, laying down the basis in domestic substantive law for of the prosecution and punishment of war crimes or collaboration. As a matter of historical fact, neither decree, however, would ultimately see application in the post-war trials that actually took place. The draft Decree on the Punishment of Certain Criminal Offences Committed While Under Enemy Invasion did not progress to the later stages of the legislative process, not even in the sole scope of penalizing the collaboration of Polish nationals with the occupation apparatus. The viability of the application of the Decree of the President of the Republic of Poland on Criminal Responsibility for War Crimes, which did constitute a binding source of Polish law, ceased with the loss of political mandate (diplomatic recognition) by the Polish Government-in-Exile. The communist authorities in Warsaw, which were recognized by the Western Allies on 5 July 1945, did not recognize the legality of the Polish Government-in-Exile or its legislation.[209] The basic instrument of substantive law regulating the legal bases for the punishment of perpetrators of crimes committed in occupied Poland was the Decree on the Sentencing Limits for Fascist-Nazi Criminals Guilty of Killings and Ill-Treatment of the Civilian Population and Prisoners of War and for Traitors to the Polish Nation[210] (the 'August Decree'), promulgated on 31

---

208 As emphasized by Franciszek Ryszka, the draft Decree on the Punishment of Certain Criminal Offences Committed While Under Enemy Invasion 'was an interesting manifestation of Polish legal thought and one more witness to the astonishing intellectual activity of the elites of Underground Poland', and the assumptions of the draft 'could be regarded at the very least as intervention clauses for the whole complex of prosecution of war crimes'. *Cf.* Ryszka, *Norymberga*, 131.

209 *Cf.* PKWN Manifesto, 22 July 1944.

210 Dz.U.1944.4.16.

August 1944 by the Polish Committee of National Liberation (PKWN) and applied together with the provisions of the Criminal Code of 1932.

The 'August Decree' was one of the first pieces of legislation enacted by the PKWN, modelled on the USSR Praesidium of the Supreme Soviet Decree No. 39 'On punishment measures for Nazi villains guilty of killing and torturing the Soviet civilian population and captured Red Army soldiers, for spies, traitors to the motherland from among Soviet citizens and for their accomplices' of 19 April 1943.[211] Foreboding severe punishment for crimes against the Polish state and nation, the decree became an instrument of legitimization of the communist government as a 'body fulfilling social needs'[212] with regard to compensation for wartime wrongs. A system of special courts was created to carry out the decree – Special Criminal Courts established by the Decree on Special Criminal Courts for the Cases of Fascist-Nazi Criminals[213] (following the dissolution of the special courts in autumn 1946, their jurisdiction passed to the common judiciary)[214] and the Supreme National Tribunal, established by a decree of 22 January 1946 for the judgment of the main Nazi criminals,[215] modelled, as it were, on the International Military Tribunal.

The 'August Decree' laid down the terms of criminal liability for acts committed after 31 August 1939 by members of German occupation forces and persons suspected of collaboration. Because of the vagueness of the definition

---

211 Adam Lityński, 'Ze studiów nad początkami wojskowego prawa karnego w PRL', in *Problemy Prawa Karnego* vol. 21 (Katowice 1995).

212 Kładoczny, *Prawo jako*, 183.

213 Decree on Special Criminal Courts for the Cases of Fascist-Nazi Criminals, Dz. U.1946.56.324. The first trial of Nazi criminals under the August Decree – the Majdanek trials (of camp staff) – took place before the Special Criminal Court in Lublin in December 1944.

214 Decree of 17 October 1946 Abolishing Special Criminal Courts, Dz.U.1946.59.324.

215 *Cf.* Decree on the Supreme National Tribunal, Dz.U.1946.59.326. By virtue of Art. 6 of the Decree, the jurisdiction of the Supreme National Tribunal (NTN) also extended to trials of the opponents of the communist government – persons responsible for 'the September defeat and fascization of state life' – but, in practice, the NTN's caseload was limited to the cases of Nazi criminals. For more on NTN trials see: Tadeusz Cyprian and Jerzy Sawicki, *Siedem Wyroków Najwyższego Trybunału Narodowego* (Poznań: Instytut Zachodni 1962); Mark A. Drumbl, 'The Supreme National Tribunal of Poland and the History of International Criminal Law', in Morten Bergsmo, Cheah Wui Ling and Yi Ping (eds.), *Historical Origins of International Criminal Law*, vol. 2 (Brussels: Torkel Opsahl Academic Epublisher 2014), 563–602; Patrycja Grzebyk, 'The Role of the Polish Supreme National Tribunal in the Development of Principles of International Criminal Law', in Bergsmo, Ling and Ping (eds.) *Historical Origins*, 603–633; Joanna Lubecka, *Niemiecki zbrodniarz przed polskim sądem. Krakowskie procesy przed Najwyższym Trybunałem Narodowym* (Kraków: IPN, Ośrodek Myśli Politycznej 2021).

of the elements of the offences[216] and severity of the sanctions, as well as the influence of the International Criminal Tribunal in Nuremberg, the decree underwent several amendments, the last one on 10 December 1946.[217] Articles 1 and 2 provided:

> Article 1. Whoever, acting conveniently to the authorities of the German state or of a state allied thereto:
> 1. has taken part in the carrying out of killings among the civilian population or military persons or prisoners-of-war;
> 2. has, by identification or apprehension, acted to the detriment of persons wanted or persecuted by the authorities for political, ethnic, religious or racial reasons, shall be liable to death penalty.
>
> Article 2. Whoever, acting conveniently to the authorities of the German state or of a state allied thereto, has acted in a manner other or in circumstances other than set out in Article 1, to the detriment of the Polish State, Polish legal person or persons from the civilian population, military persons or prisoners-of-war, shall be liable to imprisonment for a term no shorter than 3 years or for life, or death penalty'.

---

216 In the original wording of August 1944, the Decree distinguished three types of criminal offences (Arts. 1 and 2), and, in Art. 4, established the principle of liability for attempt, incitement or aiding and abetting. Art. 3 excluded the defence of necessity. The wording of Art. 1 included the imprecise term 'acting conveniently to the occupation authorities' (*działanie na rękę władzy okupacyjnej*) and also 'participation in the carrying out of killings, (...) ill-treatment or persecution of the civilian population';
  1 Whoever, acting conveniently to the German occupation authority:
    a) has taken or takes part in carrying out the killings of persons from among the civilian population or prisoners-of-war or in the ill-treatment or persecution of the same;
    b) has acted or acts to the detriment of persons staying in the territory of the Polish State, especially through the apprehension or transportation of persons wanted or persecuted by the occupation authorities for any reasons (excluding common crimes) shall be liable to death penalty.
  2 Whoever has extorted or extorts benefits from such persons or their inner circle under the threat of the apprehension of such persons and their delivery to the occupation authorities shall be liable to imprisonment for up to 15 years or for life'.

217 Council of Ministers (People's Republic of Poland), Decree of 10 December 1946 amending the Decree on the Sentencing Limits for Fascist-Nazi Criminals Guilty of Killings and Ill-Treatment of the Civilian Population and Prisoners of War and for Traitors to the Polish Nation, Dz.U.1946.69.376.

The influence of the Nuremberg Charter and of the judgment of the International Military Tribunal can be seen in the amended Article 1(2), with political, religious, racial and, additionally, ethnic prosecution dealt with in a similar manner, as in Article 6(c) of the Nuremberg Charter. Article 3 of the decree established criminal responsibility for the extortion of financial benefits 'under the threat of causing persecution by the authorities of the German state or of a state allied thereto' and for acting to the detriment of persons wanted by occupation authorities. That meant denunciatory activities and threats, motivated by self-interest, of delivering persecuted persons and especially Polish Jews to the occupation authorities. An amendment of December 1946, added a new Article 4, introducing the principle of criminal liability for participation (*udział*, hence not mere passive membership) in organizations deemed to be criminal, as expounded by the judgment of the International Military Tribunal at Nuremberg.[218] However, the provisions of the 'August Decree' employed a broader definition of entities classifiable as a criminal organization, prescribing a sentencing range from three years' imprisonment to life, or death penalty, for participation in a 'criminal organization established or recognized by the authorities of the German state or of a state allied thereto or by a political association acting in the interest of the German state or of a state allied thereto'.[219] The vague definition left the field open for wide interpretation possibilities and for the use of the provisions of the decree not only as a means of repression against Nazi criminals and collaborationists but also against the political opponents of the communist government. The latter, especially included members of the Home Army and of the underground pro-independence conspiracy.[220]

6 Reception in the Legal and Academic Circles of the Émigrés

Discussions and debates concerning the topics of justice for the occupying powers' crimes and reconstruction in post-war Europe were initiated during the Second World War by international legal organizations, ministries of just-

218 The judgment of the International Criminal Tribunal recognized the leadership of the NSDAP, the SS Security Service (*Sicherheitsdienst*, SD), the SS (*Schutzstaffel*, literally 'Protection Squadron') and the Gestapo (literally 'Secret State Police') as criminal organizations. IMT Judgment, paras. 470–485.

219 Art. 4(1) of the restated and final text (after all amendments), Dz.U.1946.69.377.

220 Concerning this topic see Kładoczny, *Prawo jako*, 176–194; Gabriel Finder, Alexander Prusin, *Justice behind the Iron Curtain. Nazis on Trial in Communist Poland* (Toronto–Buffalo–London: University of Toronto Press 2018)

ice of the Governments-in-Exile of the occupied states, and legal associations. The participation of émigré lawyers in that process was not limited to the political sphere or mandate held from the governments of the Allied states. Rather, they acted through informal contact networks, along with the fora of academic and expert debate,[221] often as a continuation of the professional networking of specialists from the various legal fields from the inter-war period.[222] On the international scale, the work of legal associations meeting in 1942–1943 in the United Kingdom – London International Assembly and Cambridge Commission for Penal Reconstruction and Development[223] – serves as a perfect illustration. Their activities paved the way for the United Nations War Crimes Commission, created in 1943. Although the achievements of these organizations have been discovered and discussed by researchers in recent years, such studies give little or no attention to the activities of lawyers and jurists from particular countries in their narrower professional and scholarly circles. A closer look at the Polish case shows another dimension of the debates on accountability for war crimes, along with professional and academic community building.

The works on the text of the Decree of the President of the Republic of Poland on Criminal Responsibility for War Crimes, the new developments in international law and international criminal law, as well as broadly understood legal and political problems arising from the occupation and from the end of the war all found themselves in the centre of the attention of bodies such as the Polish Lawyers' Association in the United Kingdom, Polish Lawyers' Association in the United States of America, Association of Polish Lawyers Refugees in Tel Aviv, and Polish Lawyers' Association in Jerusalem. By publishing scholarly and press articles, organizing specialized lectures and conferences, members of Polish legal associations took an active role in the expert debate on the subject of the punishment of Nazi criminals and elimination of the consequences of the war. They analysed the 'Polish specificity' of the topic and acquainted broader Polish circles with drafts and concepts discussed on the international level.

---

221 Concerning the importance of co-operation in the academic circles of the Second World War era, see: Stefan Glaser, 'Zrzeszenie Profesorów Uniwersytetu Państw Sprzymierzonych w Londynie. Historia Powstania', in Stefan Glaser, *Urywki wspomnień* (London 1978), 196–199; Stefan Glaser, 'Kilka słów o powstaniu w Anglii Zrzeszenia Polskich Profesorów Szkół Akademickich', in *ibidem*, 200–203.

222 Von Lingen, 'Legal Flows', 508–513, and the literature cited therein.

223 Concerning this topic, see Chapter 3 of this book.

6.1 *The Polish Lawyers' Association in the United Kingdom*

The Polish Lawyers' Association in the United Kingdom began to operate on 24 August 1940. Its first president was the legal practitioner from Warsaw, Stanisław Szurlej, who would later resign and be replaced in March 1944 by Dr. Ludwik Krajewski.[224] The Association's tasks included organizing aid for Polish émigré lawyers, legal education for Poles in the field of English law and lectures by its own members, as well as promoting interest in Polish legal and political thought in the United Kingdom and maintaining contacts with other associations of Polish lawyers in exile and other organizations of legal professionals in the world. Providing learning and training opportunities, as well as legal education were important aspects of its works, in cooperation with the Ministry of Justice. On the Association's initiative – in spring 1942 – a Polish organizational unit for legal and administrative studies (*Studium Prawno-Administracyjne*) was established at the University of St. Andrews, followed by training courses for bar trainees and judicial trainees. The first half of 1944 saw the creation of a Polish Law Faculty at the University of Oxford. In the summer, dedicated training sessions were held for prospective civil servants in occupied territories after their liberation. Polish legal minds were given the opportunity to study English law, and the Association's members to participate in programmes delivered by the UK Council of Legal Education. From April to July 1944, Association members attended a course for Polish lawyers at the Westminster Commercial Institute.[225]

One of the contact platforms with British academic and practising circles was the Polish Lawyers Association's conferences of legal scholars and practitioners of Allied states. The idea was promoted in autumn 1941 by Herman Lieberman and Manfred Lachs. The Minister of Justice planned the 'organization of an international convention of lawyers in London' and beginning of specialized work on legislative provisions to be enacted by Central–Eastern European states as part of creating a regional confederation.[226] The legal aspects of the post-war European order and demand for the unification of Euro-

224 The Association inaugural management board included: Stanisław Szurlej (president), Franciszek Wójcicki (vice-president), Stefan Glaser, Jerzy Kuncewicz, Jerzy Kuncewicz, Witold Łęgowski, Zygmunt Nagórski, Rapczewski, Jerzy Rotwand (secretary) and Mieczysław Szerer. Report of the Management Board of Polish Lawyers' Association in the United Kingdom for the 1st operating period (28 September 1940 – 31 December 1941), 1–2, IPMS Kol. 403/15, no pagination. See also: Edward Muszalski, 'Adwokaci polscy w Wielkiej Brytanii w latach 1939–1945: fragmenty'. *Palestra* 308 (1983), 62–65, here: 64.

225 Report of the Management Board of Polish Lawyers' Association in the United Kingdom for 1945, 4. IPMS, Kol. 403/15. The programme was organized by Józef Bloch.

226 Minutes of the Association's general meeting on 27 March 1943, 4, IPMS Kol. 403/2, no pagination.

pean legal systems also found their way to the sketch of an Allied Lawyers Congress, designed by Manfred Lachs and submitted to Stanisław Szurlej and Franciszek Wójcicki in October 1941.[227] Lachs recommended that the Association's authorities organize a conference jointly with the law faculty of the University of London or New Commonwealth Institute, with whom he had been collaborating. He stressed that the Polish initiative 'emphasized in the organization of [that] Congress would evoke a lively resonance as a demonstration of a Poland that ha[d] been and continue[d] to be the victim of the greatest lawlessness in the struggle for law'. To Lachs, the matter of the new legal order implemented in the occupied Polish territories, as well as anticipated post-war European reconstruction being raised by Polish lawyers in the international forum could become the vehicle for 'certain legal concepts in the fight for our rights at the Peace Conference'.[228] Proposed topics focused around the legal aspects of the ongoing war, as well as responsibility for war crimes. The tentative agenda included positions such as: 'Law in the new European order'; 'For a judgment on those who violate the law in this war'; 'Unification of legal systems after the war'; and 'The war goals in the light of the law' (different contemporary translations of the titles may have existed).[229] The preserved documentation of the works of the Polish Lawyers' Association in the United Kingdom is not sufficient to confirm that efforts to organize the conference did in fact begin in autumn 1941. Liebermann's death on 21 October 1941, beginning of the works of the International London Assembly and Cambridge Commission for Penal Reconstruction and Development in autumn 1941, as well as Polish MFA's conference of governments of occupied states in November 1941, may all have contributed to delays or abandonment of the plans.

The idea was revisited at the beginning of 1943 when discussing prospects of a closer cooperation between the Association and British legal circles.[230] In the end, however, the Association did not take upon itself to organize an Allied lawyers' conference on such a large scale. Nevertheless, foreign legal minds, both from the occupied countries and from the United Kingdom, were invited to attend the Association's meetings. The co-ordination of such contracts prompted the establishment, in April 1942, of a 'Section for Inter-Allied Legal Contacts' (*Dział Zbliżenia Prawniczego Międzyalianckiego*) in the

227 Manfred Lachs, Design for convening an Allied Lawyers Congress, IPMS Kol. 403/15.

228 *Ibidem.*

229 *Ibidem.*

230 Minutes of the Association's general meeting on 27 March 1943, 4–5, IPMS Kol. 403/2, no pagination; letter from the management board of the Czechoslovak Advocates Association in the United (*Spolek československých advokátů* ve *Velké Británii*), 26 August 1942, IPMS Kol. 403/16.

Association's Management Board, with Józef Bloch, Feliks Gadomski, Zygmunt Nagórski, Jerzy Rotwand, and Mieczysław Szerer as members.[231] In spring 1942, the Association approached The Law Society for approval for a library search to be carried out by the Association's member, Edward Muszalski, who was working on a treatise dealing with war damages in the light of Polish, French, and German law.[232] In August of the same year, the Association's authorities began cooperation with the newly created Czechoslovak Advocates Association in the United Kingdom (*Spolek československých advokátů ve Velké Británii*).[233]

Contacts with academic circles in the United Kingdom were also established through the mediation of British lawyers of Polish origin. At the beginning of May 1942, the Association's secretary, Jerzy Rotwand, extended an invitation to Professor Hersch Lauterpacht, holder of the Whewell Chair of International Law at the University of Cambridge, to participate in the Association's meeting.[234] Another invitee was Leon Radzinowicz, a prominent expert in criminal law, who had been sent to study the English system at the University of Cambridge through a scholarship funded by Polish Ministry of Justice in 1937.[235] The meeting, with both in attendance, took place at Rubens Hotel in London on 16 July 1942.[236] One month later, on 28 August 1942, the Association celebrated its second anniversary with a special meeting, which Harold Gutteridge – professor of comparative law also at the University of Cambridge – was invited to join. The celebration marked an opportunity to invite 'prominent British and Allied jurists in a hope of establishing closer contacts among the legal circles of the United Nations'.[237] Jerzy Rotwand's suggested lecture topic was Retribution for War Crimes,[238] his explanation being lack of competence in the field of international criminal law. Gutteridge presented a paper titled 'The English Approach to Juristic Problems'. Attend-

---

231 Report of the Management Board of Polish Lawyers' Association in the United Kingdom for 1942, 2. IPMS, Kol. 403/15. Stanisław Szurlej's letter to Michał Potulicki, Władysław Kulski and Karol Poznański, 22 April 1942, IPMS Kol. 403/16.

232 Correspondence between the Polish Lawyers' Association in the United Kingdom and The Law Society, May 1942. IPMS Kol. 403/16.

233 Report of the Management Board for 1942, 4. IPMS, Kol. 403/15.

234 *Cf.* Correspondence between Jerzy Rotwand and Hersch Lauterpacht, May and July 1942, IPMS, Kol. 403/16.

235 Leon Radzinowicz's bio; see Roger Hood, 'Leon Radzinowicz (1906–1999)'. *Proceedings of the British Academy* 111 (2001), 637–655, available at https://www.thebritishacademy.ac.uk/sites/default/files/111p637.pdf (accessed 15 June 2025).

236 Correspondence between Jerzy Rotwand and Hersch Lauterpacht, IPMS, Kol. 403/16.

237 Letter from Jerzy Rotwand to Harold Gutteridge, 7 July 1942, IPMS Kol. 403/16.

238 *Ibidem.*

ing were Polish and British lawyers, as well as representatives of both governments: for the Poles, Wacław Komarnicki and Edward Raczyński; for the Brits, Sir Cecil Dormer, Ambassador to the Polish Government, and Frank Savery, Councillor of the Embassy (also former Consul-General to Poland).[239] Leon Radzinowicz presented a paper titled *Angielska Polityka Kryminalna* ('English Criminal Policy').[240] The Association held a special meeting dedicated to topics of criminal responsibility for war crimes on 9 January 1943, with lectures given by the Prime Minister of Yugoslavia, Serbian constitutionalist, Dr. Slobodan Jovanović, and the Polish Minister of Justice, Wacław Komarnicki.[241]

In the summer of 1943, the Association joined efforts with The Law Society and British Council to hold a series of informal meetings of British and foreign lawyers called 'Allied Lawyers' Foyer'.[242] The Association's representative to the Foyer was Józef Bloch, who on 15 May 1944 delivered a paper titled 'Social Legislation in Poland', which the Association subsequently released in print. Due to the large interest, Bloch's publication went to the printing press twice, for a total of 5000 copies.[243] Moreover, papers discussing Polish law in the Foyer's meetings in 1944 were delivered by W. Fink ('Foreigners before Polish Civil Courts') and Edward Muszalski ('Some aspects of the Polish Constitution').[244]

Polish legal and political institutions were also more closely introduced to the British public opinion by publications printed or promoted through the Association's efforts, such as Jan Jankowski and Antoni Serafiński's 'Polska w liczbach – Poland in Numbers',[245] Józef Bloch's Workers' protective legislation in Poland,[246] and an anthology of twelve essays titled 'Studies in Polish and

---

239 Report of the Management Board of Polish Lawyers' Association in the United Kingdom for 1942, 3–4, IPMS, Kol. 403/15.

240 Radzinowicz's paper was published by the Polish Lawyers' Association in the United Kingdom: Leon Radzinowicz, *Angielska polityka kryminalna: próba wykładni* (Stowarzyszenie Prawników Polskich w Zjednoczonym Królestwie, London 1942).

241 Report of the Management Board of Polish Lawyers' Association in the United Kingdom for 1943, 2. IPMS, Kol. 403/15. Account of Slobodan Jovanović's visit and text of his speech in French: IPMS Kol. 38/7, no pagination.

242 Report of the Management Board, 2. IPMS, Kol. 403/15, no pagination. The Allied Lawyers' Foyer was launched in November 1943 and by the end of December had about 450 members, including 45 Poles. At the beginning of 1945, the numbers were 530 and 65 respectively.

243 Józef Bloch, *Social Legislation in Poland* (London: Polish Lawyers' Association 1944).

244 Report of the Management Board, 2. IPMS, Kol. 403/15.

245 Jan Jankowski, Antoni Serafiński, *Polska w liczbach – Poland in Numbers* (London, Stowarzyszenie Prawników Polskich w Zjednoczonym Królestwie 1941).

246 Jan Stańczyk (preface), *Workers' protective legislation in Poland: 20 years' co-operation with the International Labour Organisation* (London: Liberty Publications 1941).

Comparative Law'. The preface was written by Harold Gutteridge, professor of comparative law at Cambridge and member of the Cambridge Commission on Penal Reconstruction and Development.[247]

The 'Studies in Polish and Comparative Law' give a cross-sectional overview of the main currents of research conducted by selected Polish legal scholars active during the Second World War era in the United Kingdom.[248] Those were largely topics of the policy of the Polish Government-in-Exile, such as the legal grounds for the punishment of war criminals, the shape of post-war international relations, the international security system, or Poland's place in post-war Europe. The history of Polish constitutionalism and development of parliamentary democracy and civil rights were discussed in an article written by Wacław Komarnicki. He emphasized the closeness to those traditions transpiring from the constitutional programme for post-war Poland that the Council of Ministers had adopted in its February Declaration (24 February 1942). In 'Some Remarks on the Polish Criminal Code', Stefan Glaser outlined in English, the characteristic features and basic principles of Polish substantive law. There, he gave a prominent place to the theories of culpability and perpetration adopted in the Criminal Code of 1932, the theory of subjective culpability, the principle of individual responsibility, and the applicability of the twofold principle of *nullum crimen, nulla poena sine lege*.[249] In reference to debates on individual responsibility for acts violating the law of nations, as well as the relationship between domestic and international law, Glaser stressed the importance of the principle of international solidarity, expressed in Polish provisions on the universal repression of *delicta iuris gentium* (Article 9 CC), recognition of foreign court judgments, and criminalization of the propa-

247 The Polish Lawyers' Association in the United Kingdom, *Studies in Polish and Comparative Law with foreword by Professor H. C. Gutteridge* (London: Stevens & Sons Limited 1945).

248 The following articles were also published (under English titles): 'The Spirit of Polish Constitutional Law and its Recent Development' by Wacław Komarnicki, 'Some Remarks on the Polish Criminal Code' by Stefan Glaser; '*Nullum Crimen Sine Poena*' by Stanisław Szurlej; 'Codification of Civil Law in Poland (1918–1939)' by Zygmunt Nagórski; 'The Revision of Treaties and the Interests of Peace' by Włodzimierz Moderow; 'The Status of Consuls in International Law' by Karol Poznański; 'A General Outline of Some Principles of Conflict of Laws in Poland' by Roman Kuratowski; 'Andrew Wolan: Sixteenth Century Polish Calvinist Writer and Philosopher of Law' by Eugeniusz Jarra; 'Marriage Law in Poland: A problem of Comparative Law' by Karol Aleksandrowicz; 'The Principles of Polish Budget Law' by T. Gordyński; 'Certain Aspects of Modern Corporations' by M. Fryde; and 'Labour Legislation and Social Insurance in Poland' by Józef Bloch. *Cf.* The Polish Lawyers' Association in the United Kingdom, *Studies in Polish*.

249 Stefan Glaser, 'Some Remarks on the Polish Penal Code', in *Studies in Polish*, 12–25.

ganda of aggressive war (Article 113 CC).[250] The matter of the legal basis of organization of the international community and guarantees of peace was explored by Włodzimierz Moderow's 'The Revision of Treaties and the Interests of Peace' – an article also published in the English language. Using the example of the invocation of the revision clause contained in Article 19[251] of the Covenant of the League of Nations[252] by the German Reich against Article 228 of the Treaty of Versailles concerning the extradition of war criminals, as well as the revision of Czechoslovakia's borders in Munich Conference. Moderow highlighted the dangers to world peace and security – and especially to the sovereignty of small states – arising from the openness of the formula used for the revision of international treaties.[253] The matter of punishment for the criminals of the ongoing war was his starting point for an analysis of the consequences of the revision of international treaties, including those laying down the rules of individual criminal liability for war crimes.[254] Stanisław Szurlej's article '*Nullum Crimen sine Poena*' delved into the matter of individual responsibility of perpetrators of criminal offences committed during the hostilities and occupation. It discussed the political, social, and moral aspects of punishment for war crimes, analysing different models of court procedure, including the concepts adopted in the Decree of the President of the Republic of Poland on Criminal Responsibility for War Crimes, of 30 March 1943. One of the focal aspects of exacting justice for the crimes of the Third Reich offering full satisfaction to the 'wounded sense of justice' was the re-education of German society.[255]

Legal aspects of the occupation, war crimes and punishment of the criminals, Polish legislation of the transitional period, and directions of development in international law were the focus of interest of Polish lawyers in emigration, frequently featuring as topics of lectures organized by the Polish Lawyers' Association in the United Kingdom. Some examples from 1940–1944: *Polska pod Prawem najeźdźcy Niemieckiego* ('Poland under the German invader's law') by Gustaw Gazda; 'Polish Labour under German

---

250 *Ibidem.*

251 'The Assembly may from time to time advise the reconsideration by Members of the League of treaties which have become inapplicable and the consideration of international conditions whose continuance might endanger the peace of the world'.

252 The Covenant of the League of Nations https://avalon.law.yale.edu/20th_century/leagcov.asp.

253 Włodimierz Moderow, 'The Revision of Treaties and the Interests of Peace', in *Studies in Polish*, 70–97.

254 *Ibidem*, 81.

255 Stanisław Szurlej, '*Nullum Crimen sine Poena*', in *Studies in Polish*, 20–43.

Occupation' by Feliks Gros; *Karta Atlantycka* ('The Atlantic Charter') by Manfred Lachs; *Eksperyment gdański* ('The Gdańsk experiment') by Włodzimierz Moderow; *Zagadnienia federalizmu* ('Topics of federalism') by Bohdan Winiarski; *Prawo odwetu* ('The Right of Retaliation') by Stanisław Szurlej; *Współczesna angielska polityka kryminalna* ('Modern English criminal Policy') by Leon Radzinowicz; *Inkorporacja ziem polskich do Rzeszy w świetle niemieckiego prawa państwowego* ('Incorporation of Polish territories into the Reich in the light of German state law') by M. Litauer; *Polityka gdańska Niemiec w latach 1935–1939* ('Germany's Policy on Gdańsk 1935–1939') by Roman Battaglia; Zagadnienie szkód wojennych ('The problem of war damages') by Aleksander Bramson; *Zagadnienia aneksji ziem wschodnich RP w świetle prawa międzynarodowego* ('Topics of annexation of the eastern territories of the Republic of Poland in the light of international law'); *Administracja sowiecka na ziemiach polskich w pierwszym okresie okupacji* ('Soviet administration in Polish Territories in the initial period of the occupation') by Wiktor Sukiennicki, and *Zagadnienia ustawodawstwa okresu przejściowego* ('Topics of legislation of a transitional period') by Ludwik Krajewski.256 The predominant theme in the Association's lectures were topics of English law: *O sądownictwie angielskim* ('On the English court system') by Józef Bloch; *Organizacja Adwokatury Angielskiej* ('Organization of the English bar') by Jerzy Rotwand; *Współczesna angielska polityka kryminalna* ('Modern English criminal policy') by Leon Radzinowicz, *Ubezpieczenia morskie w Wielkiej Brytanii* ('Maritime insurance in Great Britain') by E. Tomaszewski; *Konflikty między polskim a angielskim prywatnym prawem międzynarodowym* ('Conflicts between Polish and English private international law') by W. Fink; *Odrębność prawa szkockiego* ('The distinctness of Scottish law') by Edward Muszalski; *Prawo gruntowe we współczesnej Anglii* ('Land law in modern England') by M. Śmigielski; and *Siedziba Parlamentu Brytyjskiego* ('The seat of British parliament') by Lord Natham; *Zagadnienie sądów przysięgłych Wielkej Brytanii* ('The Topic of Jury Trials in the United Kingdom') by R. Jackson; *Rola Międzynarodowej Organizacji Pracy w odbudowie świata* ('The role of the International Labour Organization in the reconstruction of the world') by W. Jenks, *Angielska Ustawa o Sojuszniczych Sądach Morskich* ('The Allied Powers (Maritime Courts) Act (UK)'); *Rozwój ochrony pracy i opieki społecznej w Wielkiej Brytanii* ('Development of labour protection and social welfare in Great Britain') by Józef Bloch; *Ubezpieczenia Społeczne w Wielkiej Brytanii* ('Social Insurance in the United Kingdom') and *Spółki z ograniczoną odpowiedzialnością* ('Limited-liability companies') by Aleksander Bramson; *Źródła*

256 IPMS Kol. 403/18.

prawa angielskiego ('Sources of English law'); *O osobliwościach angielskiego cywilnego postępowania sądowego* ('On the Curiosities of the Civil Procedure of English Courts') by Bernard Ziffer; *Przestępczość małoletnich* ('Juvenile crime') by Wanda Grabińska; and *Europa powojenna w literaturze angielskiej* ('Postwar Europe in English literature') by Jerzy Kuncewicz.

In 1943, together with the *Polska Informacja Społeczna* ('Polish Social Information'), the Association issued an English-language publication by Józef Bloch discussing German occupation penal laws discriminating against Poles and Jews, and the German justice system in occupied territories, titled 'Justice Outlawed'.[257] Sir Henry Slesser, Labour politician and former Solicitor General of England and Wales, wrote the preface. On the pages of the *Głos Prawniczy*, a journal published by the Association from mid-1944, the problem of extradition of war criminals was discussed by Kazimierz Rutczyński.[258]

The contacts kept by Polish émigrés with academic and legal circles abroad also served as a platform to disseminate information about living conditions in occupied Poland and the crimes committed by the occupying powers. That was achieved by publications,[259] protest notes and appeals for support for the Polish cause, and condemnation of Nazi crimes. The first in that line of actions was the protest campaign by intellectual circles against the *Sonderaktion Krakau* and the deportation of the professors of Jagiellonian University and of the Mining Academy to the camp in Sachsenhausen in September 1939. In September 1941, members of the Association of Polish Professors and Docents of Academic Schools in the United Kingdom published a protest against the 'destruction of Polish culture by the Nazis'.[260] On the second anniversary of the *Sonderaktion Krakau* – 26 November 1941 – Polish authorities organized a meeting at the Royal Institute with representatives of British universities to commemorate the victims of the persecutions of academia under German occupation.[261]

---

257 Henry Slesser, *Justice Outlawed: administration of law in German-occupied territories, with foreword by* (London: Liberty Publications 1943).

258 Kazimierz Rutczyński, 'Ekstradycja Zbrodniarzy wojennych' ('Extradition of war criminals'). *Głos Prawniczy* 2 (1944), 11–24. The article was part of Colonel Kazimierz Rutczyński's work titled *Zbrodnie Wojenne* ('War Crimes'), from 1944, published in 1946; see: Kazimierz Rutczyński, *Zbrodnie Wojenne. Stdudjum w skali międzynarodowej* ('War crimes. A study on the international scale') (Glasgow: Książnica Polska, 1946).

259 For more on this topic, see Chapter 1 of this book.

260 Polish scholars' protest against the destruction of Polish culture by the Nazis (London: 20 September 1941), in Stanisławska (comp.), *Sprawa polska*, 234–235.

261 Polish Ministry of Information, *Martyrdom of Polish Professors* (London: Stratton House 1942).

In their speeches, members of The Association of University Professors and Lecturers of the Allied Countries in Great Britain, founded on Stefan Glaser's initiative in the spring of 1942, expressed their solidarity with the victims of Nazi crimes.[262]

In a resolution of 17 July 1942, they condemned the German Reich's policy of extermination of the intellectual circles and persecution of science and culture in the occupied territories.[263] Another tragic event commemorated on that occasion was the arrests and executions of Polish professors in Lviv on 4 July 1941, in the immediate aftermath of the Third Reich's aggression against the USSR (the Wzgórza Wuleckie Massacre). In August 1944, the Polish Lawyers' Association in the United Kingdom addressed to British lawyers an open letter concerning the dramatic course taken by the Warsaw Uprising, and in autumn 1944, a joint 'Appeal to the Governments and Citizens of the United Nations' was published by Polish associations active in the United Kingdom.[264]

6.2 *Polish Émigré Legal Associations outside of the United Kingdom*

Members of other Polish émigré legal organizations also discussed the legal and political topics relating to the actions of the occupation authorities, as well as reconstruction of international relations, the place of Poland in Europe, and evolution of international law and international criminal law after the war. February 1941 saw the establishment of the Polish Lawyers' Association in the USA, with Józef Witenberg as its inaugural president. During its initial months, the Association organized a series of lectures on the prospective Central–European Federation and Poland's role in the ongoing war (translating from Polish titles): *Zadania prawnictwa polskiego na uchodźstwie* ('The

262 The Association of University Professors and Lecturers of the Allied Countries in Great Britain was established in London on the initiative of Stefan Glaser on 11 May 1942. Its tasks included the preparation of the assumptions of the reconstruction of academic life in the occupied countries and intensification of co-operation among scholars from Allied states. Stefan Glaser, 'Zrzeszenie Profesorów Uniwersytetu Państw Sprzymierzonych w Londynie. Historia Powstania', in Stefan Glaser, *Urywki wspomnień* (Londyn 1978), 196–199. The following resolution was adopted during the Association's founding meeting: '1. The members of the Association send their heartfelt greetings to all colleagues in the occupied countries and in particular to those who are now suffering in concentration camps and prisons. 2. The Association considers the re-establishment of freedom, liberty and justice in Europe an essential condition for the development of all learning science, humane studies and the progress of civilisation. 3.'. Letters of support for the Association's protests from British universities: Polish Ministry of Information, *Martydrom of Polish Professors*, London, Stratton House 1942, 33–36.

263 *Ibidem*. 199.

264 Report of the Management Board of Polish Lawyers' Association in the United Kingdom for 1944, 8–9, IPMS, Kol. 403/17, no pagination.

tasks of Polish lawyerdom in exile') by Józef Witenberg; *Podstawy Federacji* ('The Foundations of the Federation') by Aleksander Herz; *Stany Zjednoczone Centralnej Europy* ('The United States of Central Europe') by Anatol Muehlstein; *Stosunki gospodarcze w powojennej Europie* ('Economic relations in postwar Europe') by Stefan Ropp; and *Cele wojny a sprawa polska* ('The war goals and the Polish cause') by Oskar Halecki.[265] Topics of administration of the occupied territories, validity of legislation enacted by occupation authorities, and transfers of property in such territories were discussed on the pages of the *Biuletyn Prawniczy* ('Legal Bulletin') – a journal published by the Polish Lawyers' Association in the USA – in July 1943, in articles by Lester Hood Woolsey, titled *The Forced Transfer of Property in Enemy Occupied Territories* (as it would be titled in English in the American Journal of International Law), and by Władysław Józef Szatensztajn titled *Głos w dyskusji nad zagadnieniem zmian w stanie własności, wywołanych zarządzeniami władz okupacyjnych* ('A voice in the discussion on the topic of changes to property caused by the ordinances of occupation authorities').[266] Another issue of the *Biuletyn Prawniczy*, in autumn 1943, published a report of the Pan-American Congress of Jurists concerning the development directions in international law, as well as an article by Charles Warren – an expert in state law and international law, vice-president of the American Society of International Law – titled *Głos w Dyskusji nad zagadnieniem odpowiedzialności karnej za przestępstwa wojenne* ('A voice in the discussion on criminal responsibility for war crimes').[267] Warren communicated the recommendations of the legal committee of the Pan-American Congress of Jurists as to the determination of the legal grounds for the punishment of war criminals, according primacy to international custom and 'moral law'. There were also suggestions for the organization of international relations, after the war, to be founded upon the condemnation of violence, a duty to resolve international disputes by peaceful means, and solidarity of states in the event of aggression. The idea that sanctions 'imposed by the inter-

265 In June 1941, the Association had 38 members. *Cf.* Report on the activities of Polish Lawyers' Association in the USA for the period from 12 February 1941 to 30 June 1941, IPMS Kol. 403/16; IPMS Kol. 213/9, no pagination.

266 Lester H. Woolsey, 'Transfer własności pod przymusem na obszarach okupowanych przez nieprzyjaciela'. *Głos Prawniczy* 5 (1 July 1943), 2–6 (followed by 'Lester H. Woolsey, The Forced Transfer of Property in Enemy Occupied Territories'. *American Journal of International Law* 37 (1943), 282–286; Władysław Józef Szatensztajn, 'Głos w dyskusji nad zagadnieniem zmian w stanie własności, wywołanych zarządzeniami władz okupacyjnych'. *Biuletyn Prawniczy* 5 (1943), 7–12.

267 C. Warren, 'Głos w Dyskusji nad zagadnieniem odpowiedzialności karnej za przestępstwa wojenne'. *Biuletyn Prawniczy* 6 (1943), 2–7.

national community on the aggressor' was in the interest of the international community as a whole[268] gained particular emphasis. Dynamic legal interpretation was proposed by the Congress as a cure to the ailment of insufficiency of norms of positive law in the context of preparing for the trials of war criminals: 'Existing provisions of positive law must be understood, not as aimed at the maintenance of the *status quo* but as the indispensable foundation of the international order and stabilization in the course of the introduction of new provisions, more compatible with the new needs of the international community'.[269]

On behalf of the Polish Government, the Ministry of Foreign Affairs responded to the recommendations of the Pan-American Congress of Jurists near the end of 1943, emphasizing that their viability would depend on the clear and unequivocal stipulation of sanctions for violations of international law.[270] New development directions in international law and the topic of an individual's subjecthood in it became the centre of the interest of the Polish Lawyers and Economists Circle in Rio de Janeiro, existing since July 1941. Polish Government's envoy to Rio, Dr. Tadeusz Skowroński, assisted the Pan-American Congress of Jurists in an expert capacity.[271] As part of the Circle's works in 1942, Advocate (legal practitioner) Henryk Szulc wrote a paper titled 'Human rights as the principle of the future world order'.[272]

Polish lawyers' associations in the Middle East also showed significant activity in the areas of education, publishing, and cooperation with local legal circles. Those were the Legal–Political Section of the Society for Iranian Studies in Tehran (*Sekcja Prawno-Polityczna Towarzystwa Studiów Irańskich w Teheranie*); Polish Lawyers Circle in Tehran (*Koło Prawników Polskich w Teheranie*); (Polish) Judges and Prosecutors Association in Jerusalem (*Stowarzyszenie Sędziów i Prokuratorów w Jerozolimie*); Polish Lawyers Association in Jerusalem (*Stowarzyszenie Prawników Polskich w Jerozolimie*); and Association of Polish Lawyers Refugees in Tel Aviv (*Zrzeszenie Prawników Uchodźców Polskich w Tel Awiwie*). The legislative works of the Polish Government-in-Exile were discussed in their studies by members of the Society for Iranian Studies – the chairman of the Society's Legal-Political Section, Wiktor Turek, published a series of articles in Iranian academic press about the codification of law in

268 *Ibidem.*

269 *Ibidem.*

270 Letter from Minister Gwiazdowski to the Ministry of Preparatory Works, 21 December 1943, IPMS A.21.6/5.

271 Letter from Tadeusz Skowroński to the MFA, 24 July 1942, IPMS A 21. 6/5, no pagination.

272 Report of the works of the Polish Lawyers' and Economists Circle in Rio de Janeiro, 17 July 1942, IPMS Kol. 403/16,

reborn Poland. On the Section's initiative in 1943, the Delegation of the Ministry of Labour and Social Welfare in Tehran published a study by Dr. Józef Auber under the title 'Polish legislation in emigration' (*Ustawodawstwo polskie na Emigracji*).[273] The Association of Polish Lawyers Refugees in Tel Aviv, founded in November 1941, with Dr. Julian Golczewski as inaugural president and Dr. Bertold Rappaport as secretary, organized lectures for its members, where Polish constitutional and criminal law, as well as post-war international relations, were the topics of discussion.[274] The Association launched a study programme in English and Palestinian law, as well as lectures in Polish law as part of the Higher Academic Courses organized in Tel Aviv by Dr. Kazimierz Rouppert, a botanist from Jagiellonian University. The subjects of lectures in Polish included substantive criminal law, military criminal law, and offences against the security of the state, with topics such as 'Evolution of English Legal Thought on the Co-Existence of Nations'; 'Several Remarks on State Confederation'; 'Homeland Security'; and 'The Role of Law in Post-war Reconstruction'.

More in-depth studies into topics of war crimes and legal bases for the punishment of war criminals were conducted in 1942–1943 by members of the Polish Lawyers' Association in Jerusalem. The fruit of the labours was the first extensive Polish-language publication of the Second World War era dealing with responsibility for war crimes, titled *Zbrodnie wojenne. Szkic prawny*[275] ('War crimes. A legal outline'), completed in the summer of 1943 and published

---

273 Józef Auber (ed.), *Ustawodawstwo polskie na Emigracji* ('Polish legislation in emigration'), preface by Wiktor Turek (Delegation of the Ministry of Labour and Social Welfare in Tehran, Cultural-Educational Division 1943). The Legal-Political Section of the Society for Iranian Studies was established in December 1942 (and the Society itself in November of the same year) by Wiktor Sukiennicki, who served as its first chair. The Society published a journal titled *Studia Irańskie* ('Iranian Studies'). Members of the Society's Legal-Political Section included Dr. Wiktor Turek, assistant professor at the Department of Private International Law of John Casimir University in Lwów (nowadays Lviv in Ukraine), counsellor of the General Counsel to the Republic of Poland; Dr. Józef Auber, Regional Court Judge in Cracow; Dr. Józef Brzeski, Head of Division of the General Counsel to the Republic of Poland in Lviv; Dr. Kazimierz Jaworski, counsellor of the General Counsel to the Republic of Poland in Lviv; Dr. Jerzy Lenczowski, attaché of the Polish Mission in Tehran; Bronisław Minc – referendary of the General Counsel to the Republic of Poland; and Dr. Adolf Tilles, advocate in Cracow. *Cf.* Wiktor Turek's letter to the Polish Lawyers' Association in the United Kingdom, 13 May 1943, IPMS Kol. 403/17, no pagination.

274 *Cf.* Report on the activities of the Association of Polish Lawyers Refugees in Tel Aviv, 13 February 1943, IPMS Kol. 403/17.

275 Zenon Goryński, *Zbrodnie wojenne. Szkic prawny* (Jerusalem: Kurs Administracyjny na Bliskim Wschodzie 1944).

in early 1944. The authors' names, unfortunately, could not be ascertained. Due to fears of Nazi retaliation against their family members in occupied Poland, the authors – three members of the Polish Lawyers' Association in Jerusalem – used the name 'Zenon Goryński' as their collective *nom de plume*.[276]

6.3 *Selected Publications*

The *Zbrodnie wojenne. Szkic prawny* ('War crimes. A legal outline') was compiled in 1943 by members of the Polish Lawyers' Association in Jerusalem and made part of a publishing series by the Polish Administrative Course in the Middle East. It is a discussion – supported by an extensive source base – of the international debate unfolding in the initial decades of the twentieth century on the development of international law, the theories of the law of war, state subjecthood and individual subjecthood under the law of nations, as well as scholarly disputes around criminal responsibility for war crimes. The study comes in two parts. The first part quotes from the most important statements made by the Polish Government-in-Exile and international declarations concerning the punishment of war criminals, published since 1939 (Chapter II). Chapter III discusses the types of sources of international law applicable to war-crime trials. The study explores the jurisdiction of domestic and international courts on war-crime cases (Chapter IV), the relationship between domestic and international law, as well as interpretation of the principle of *nullum crimen sine lege* in the context of violations of international law (Chapter V). With much detail, it discusses the liability of the direct perpetrator, instigator, aider and abettor, as well as defences of necessity and superior orders as applicable (or not) to war crimes (Chapter VI).[277]

The second part of the study is wholly dedicated to the Decree of the President of the Republic of Poland on Criminal Responsibility for War Crimes, of 30 March 1943.

It quotes the full text of the decree along with the most important stages of the legislative process (Chapter I) and a detailed commentary, the only one ever to come out in print (Chapter II). The gloss on Article 1 comments on the personal scope of its application, the liability of Polish nationals and foreigners for war crimes, and the applicability of the decree to Polish nationals participating in a criminal offence as instigators, aiders and abettors or co-perpet-

276 Tadeusz Cyprian's letter to the Polish Lawyers' Association in the United Kingdom, 4 August 1944, IPMS Kol. 403/18, no pagination.

277 Goryński, *Zbrodnie*, 5–84.

rators.[278] The commentary on Articles 2 and 3[279] is also noteworthy, in defining the 'detriment' in Articles 2, 3, and 6 as material, physical or moral harm. Attention is drawn to the central position taken by the norm of international law in the drafters' entire concept of legal bases for the punishment of war criminals.[280] Following the footsteps of Ludwik Ehrlich, the authors of the commentary define a norm of international law as a 'notion arising from international agreements, conventions and universally adopted customs, jurisprudence and doctrines'.[281] They also appreciate the difficulty of foreigners and foreign legal persons not caught by the hypothesis of Article 2 of the decree – in the case of war crimes, their cases could be decided on the basis of the general provisions of Polish Criminal Code or special statutes enacted for the punishment of war crimes by their own states of nationality.[282] The commentary on Article 6, regulating criminal responsibility for harm ('detriment') done by handing down judgments on behalf of the occupation authorities on the basis of legal provisions enacted contrary to norms of international law, emphasizes the applicability of this provision both to judicial and to administrative decisions and rulings.

From the perspective of ideas of unification of criminal law and sentencing guidelines for war crimes, the commentary lays out an interesting proposal in the context of the additional penalties (*kara dodatkowa*, nowadays *środek karny* – 'punitive measure') of confiscation of property and forfeiture of inheritance capacity. Under Polish law, their imposition could only affect holders of

---

278 *Cf.* Goryński, *Zbrodnie* – paras. 6, 9, and 12 of commentary on Art. 1 of the Decree of the President of the Republic of Poland on Criminal Responsibility for War Crimes, 95–98.

279 Art. 2: 'Whoever, contrary to the norms of international law, commits an act detrimental to the Polish State, a Polish legal person or Polish national shall be liable to the penalty of imprisonment'.

280 'Out of all principles at its disposal, the Polish drafter chose the most humanitarian one and theoretically the most equitable. The concept of the perpetrators' culpability is construed as the violation of a norm of international law. This is a very significant step forward for compelling compliance with international law. It also has momentous significance from the perspective of general prevention. (…) The Polish drafter has resolved in the affirmative the existing doctrinal dispute as to the very existence of a norm of international law. (…) It accepts that the judicature may operate on a norm of international law and determine that a given act is either compatible or incompatible with it. And in this consists the merit of the Polish drafter's courage of thought'. Goryński, *Zbrodnie*, 89–90.

281 Goryński, *Zbrodnie*, 28 and 101. The definition was taken from Ludwik Ehrlich, 'Rozwój prawa międzynarodowego i zagadnienie kolektywnego bezpieczeństwa', in *Collective Security, a Record of the Seventh and Eighth International Studies Conferences 1934–1935* (Paris 1936).

282 *Ibidem*, 104.

property or right of inheritance in Poland, significantly curtailing their *de facto* severity to everyone else. In the light of the above, it was deemed expedient:

> to secure the inclusion 'in an international criminal code or any other international act, of an additional provision enabling the enforcement of [such an] additional penalty also beyond the borders of Poland and its inclusion in the criminal statutes of other states. That would make it impossible for the war criminals to enjoy such pillaged property as they were hiding in other countries, as one would readily expect them to do if they were judged elsewhere'.[283]

In this context, the authors also ponder the question of inheritance of property obtained by pillaging, and of investigations in such cases in the event of the defendant's decease before judgment.[284]

Another Polish-language publication exploring criminal liability for war crimes, and supplementing the studies presented in the work of the members of the Polish Lawyers' Association in Jerusalem, is Colonel Kazimierz Rutczyński's *Zbrodnie wojenne. Studjum w skali międzynarodowej*[285] ('War crimes. A study on international scale'), completed in 1944 and published in 1946. It elucidates on international declarations concerning the punishment of war criminals, the principles of territorial and personal jurisdiction in Polish law and in the legislation of other states, as well as points of substantive law and procedure.. The former include definitions and lists of war crimes. The latter refer to the necessity to guarantee the impartiality of the trials of war criminals. There are also mixed points, such as the limits of the applicability of the *respondeat superior* defence, and the establishment of an international criminal tribunal. The problem of asylum for political criminals and its potential conflict with the extradition of war criminals are discussed extensively. The main source material is the Report of Committee Concerned with Crimes against International Public Order by International Commission for Penal Reconstruction and Development. Thus, the study has the effect of introducing the Polish audience to the Commission's legacy and the contributions of its Polish members.[286]

---

283 *Ibidem*, 112.

284 *Ibidem*, 112–113.

285 Rutczyński, *Zbrodnie wojenne*.

286 *Ibidem*, 7 and 23.

Manfred Lachs's *War Crimes an Attempt to Define the Issue*,[287] in turn, summarizes the debates of the 1942–1945 period in Allied legal circles on topics relating to war-crimes policy. Lachs's work covers the definitions of war crimes, their victims and perpetrators, as well as the legal grounds for the individual responsibility of those guilty of violations of international law. Lachs recounts written and unwritten sources of international law, acts of key importance to the law of armed conflicts dating from 1856 to 1945, examples of application of domestic law to war-crimes cases, and declarations made by Allied states in 1941–1945 concerning the criminal responsibility of offenders against international law.

He distinguishes two facets of war crimes: 'crimes committed during the war' and 'crimes committed in connection with war' in 'specially favourable conditions'. The latter refers primarily to command responsibility and the liability of persons entitled to immunity under the act of state theory ordering or inciting their subordinates to commit a crime. As defined by Lachs, a war crime is any violent act meeting the following conditions cumulatively:

a) classified as a criminal offence;
b) committed during and in connection with the war, in specially favourable wartime conditions facilitating its commission;
c) committed against the other belligerent state, its interests or its nationals, or stateless persons and their interests.[288]

War crimes cannot be regarded as political crimes, which means that their perpetrators were not eligible for asylum. Any member of the armed forces, government, administration or security apparatus, any holder of a political, legal or business position linked to the war or member of an organization acting on orders from a belligerent party (whether a national of that party or not), can be held criminally responsible. The work is a development upon Lachs's earlier article on several topics relating to the extradition of war criminals and asylum, titled 'War Crimes and Political Offences'.[289]

---

287 M. Lachs, *War Crimes. An Attempt to define the Issues* (London: Stevens & Sons 1945).
288 *Ibidem.*
289 Mander Lachs, 'War Crimes and Political Offences'. *Juridical Review* 56 (1944) (Edinburgh).

CHAPTER 6

Cooperation between the Polish Government-in-Exile and the United Nations War Crimes Commission

A breakthrough moment in the formative process of Allied policy on bringing war criminals to justice came in October 1943 with the establishment of the United Nations War Crimes Commission – a multinational organization, supporting and coordinating the international effort to track and document Nazi crimes in occupied territories and gathering legal experts from Allied countries. Until that time, the sole Allied body dealing with the topic of war crimes had been the Inter-Allied Commission for War Crimes. With neither the United Kingdom nor the United States participating in its work, the earlier commission had limited options for exerting political influence. Nevertheless, it unquestionably paved the way to the creation of the subsequent United Nations Commission.

The unofficial organizations bringing together legal experts from the United Kingdom and from the occupied countries whose work would later inform the UNWCC were the London International Assembly and the International Commission for Penal Reconstruction and Development – the Cambridge Commission.[1] Both expert groups explored key aspects of the issue of accountability for international crimes: the sources and principles of the law of nations; scope of individual responsibility for violations of international law including jurisdictional immunity, as well as the defences of necessity and superior orders. They also addressed the definitions of war crimes and procedural issues relating to the establishment of a domestic or international jurisdiction over international crimes. Prior to the establishment of the UNWCC, Polish experts actively participated in the work of the London International Assembly and Cambridge Commission, presenting their own ideas developed in the course of government work and the issue of accountability for discussion in an international forum.

1 Daniel Marc Segesser, 'On the Road to Total Retribution? The International Debate on the Punishment of War Crimes 1872–1945', in Roger Chickering, Stig Förster and Bernd Greiner (eds.), *A World at Total War. Global Conflict and the Politics of Destruction, 1937– 1945* (Cambridge 2005); Julia Eichenberg, '*Crossroads in London on the Road to Nuremberg: The London International Assembly, Exile Governments and War Crimes'*. Journal of the History of International Law / Revue d'histoire du droit international 24 (2022), 334–353.

1 The Works of the Cambridge Commission on Penal Development and Reconstruction and of the London International Assembly

The Cambridge Commission on Penal Development and Reconstruction was established on 14 November 1941 during a conference on war crimes and the organization of the post-war justice system in Europe,[2] titled 'Rules and Procedure to Govern the Case of Crimes against International Public Order'. The inaugural lecture under the same title was delivered by Arthur Goodhart, professor of international law at the University of Cambridge, who organized the event together with Hersch Lauterpacht. The works were presided over by Professor Arnold McNair (later Lord McNair), Vice-Chancellor of the University of Liverpool and Lauterpacht's predecessor in the chair of international law at Cambridge. The principal task laid before the Commission was to design 'rules and procedures to govern the case of crimes against international public order'. Participating on behalf of the Polish government were Professors Stefan Glaser – chairing the Commission's Committee on the Rights to be Accorded to Persons Suspected or Accused of Crimes – and Bohdan Winiarski.

Glaser also delivered a speech during the Commission's inaugural meeting. In it, he emphasized the importance of the cooperation among Allied legal experts to post-war reconstruction, to the human-rights system, and especially to the rebuilding of the population's trust in the legal system in the occupied countries:

> This meeting of jurists today has a special significance. We are witnesses of and we take part in the most horrible struggle against law and order the world has ever encountered in the past. Our common enemy intend to build so-called New Order on the ruins of right and justice. War has been declared on all traditional conceptions of the law as they were understood by the Stoics, the Roman jurists, the Fathers, and by medieval and modern thinkers up to present time. (…).
>
> In addition, and perhaps above all, the duty of the jurists will be to restore and to defend for the future the dignity and the respect of man. Those who scheme to introduce in Europe their New Order would base it on an improved slave system with the most effective degree of cruelty and injustice.[3]

2 International Commission for Penal Reconstruction and Development. Report of Committee concerned with Crimes against International Public Order, TNA LCO 2/2973.

3 Stefan Glaser's speech in the inaugural meeting of the Cambridge Commission on Penal Reconstruction and Development, 14 November 1941, TNA/ LCO 2/2973.

The Cambridge Commission on Penal Reconstruction and Development comprised three committees: Committee I, led by Belgian lawyer General Marcel de Baer, dealt with the definition of war crimes, and points of procedure to be used in the trials of war criminals, Committee II, for the defence of superior orders, under the Dutch delegate, Johannes M. de Moore, and Committee III, for the extradition of war criminals, under the representative of the Czechoslovak government, Václav Beneš.[4] The Commission's studies were based on questionnaires distributed to all the representatives. In April 1942, Arnold McNair circulated a survey on the principles to govern the punishment of crimes committed during the ongoing war, including questions about such topics as: types of crimes; the period investigated (acts committed after the German invasion of Poland or before); substantive and procedural law applied in cases of war crimes; organization of the works of an international criminal tribunal; opinion on the defence of superior orders (*respondeat superior*); and sovereign immunity.[5] Following in October were questions from Marcel de Baer's Committee on the applicable law and existing court decisions in cases of war crimes ('National Laws and Jurisdictions' questionnaire) and definitions and classifications of international crimes.[6]

On behalf of Poland, responses concerning the organization of the justice system for war crimes and analyses of Polish law in the Commission's area of interest were prepared by Stefan Glaser. He advocated for the adoption of the principle of jurisdiction of domestic courts for cases of war crimes, and in exceptional cases – such as acts committed in the territory or against the nationals of more than one state – the jurisdiction of an international tribunal. Concerning trials before domestic courts, Glaser stressed the need for a greater level of precision in the criminal statutes of Allied states whose relevant provisions did not capture facts corresponding to the new forms of crimes committed by the occupation forces. The basic problem was the lack of sanctions proportionate to the gravity of the act – necessary, according to him, for the judgment and severe punishment of the new types of crimes committed by officials of the German Reich. Among the new forms of violence against the civilian population of the occupied territories, needing regulation and specific sanctions, Stefan Glaser mentioned:

> compelling young women to become pregnant against their will, physical and mental torture, transfer of population, establishment of ghettos,

4 *History of the UNWCC*, 94–95.

5 Questionnaire of 28 April 1941, TNA/ LCO 2/2973.

6 International Commission for Penal Reconstruction and Development, Report of Committee concerned with Crimes against International Public Order, TNA/LCO 2/2973.

> causing mass starvation, illegal judgments, plunder or destruction of cultural property, privation of medical assistance (help) and of medicaments.[7]

In his reports, Glaser discussed the potential scope of application of the Polish Criminal Code of 1932 for the trials of perpetrators of international crimes. He referenced the publications of the Government-in-Exile and the works on the Decree of the President of the Republic of Poland on Criminal Responsibility for War Crimes.[8]

The result of the Commission's comparative analysis of the legislative systems of the Allied states in respect of jurisdiction and substantive law applicable to crimes committed in war time, as well as crimes against the security of the state, were reports on the current state of international law and domestic legislative systems. The efforts were summarized in a memorandum titled 'Punishment of War Crimes' by Hersch Lautepacht. It expounded the definition of war crimes adopted by the Cambridge Commission:

> War Crimes may properly be defined as such offences against law of war as are criminal in the ordinary and accepted sense of fundamental rules of warfare and of general principles of criminal law by reason of their heinousness, their brutality, their ruthless disregard of the sanctity of human life and personality, or their wanton interference with rights of property unrelated to reasonably conceived requirements of military necessity.[9]

The second organization whose work on the development of international law preceded those of the UNWCC was the London International Assembly (LIA). The LIA was established on 20 October 1941 under the auspices of the League of Nations Union, a British pacifist organization of lawyers promoting international justice and led by Robert Cecil, 1st Viscount Cecil of Chelwood (known for most of his life as Lord Robert Cecil).[10] LIA's vice-presidents were Thanassis Aghides, the Ambassador of Greece to the United Kingdom; the head of the legal services of the Free French, René Cassin; the Czechoslovak

7 TNA/LCO 2/2973. Glaser's response to the 'National Laws and Jurisdictions' questionnaire, 22 October 1942.

8 *Ibidem*. For more on the Cambridge Commission's works, see: History of the UNWCC, 94–99; Segesser, *Recht statt*, 318–329; v. Lingen, *Crimes against Humanity*, 239–245.

9 *History of the UNWCC*, 95.

10 Concerning the formation and composition of the LIA see: London International Assembly, The Form and Function of the World Organisation Proposed by the LIA, undated,

Minister of Foreign Affairs, Jan Masaryk; and the Polish representative – head of the Civilian Chancery of the President of the Republic of Poland – August Zaleski. Participants in the discussions included representatives of British authorities, members of the League of Nations Union and of the International Law Association, as well as delegates from the majority of the United Nations. Those were experts in a varied range of disciplines, taking part in the meetings of the LIA's nine committees and working on the various aspects of post-war organization of international relations in legal, political, economic, and cultural fields.[11] The LIA was subdivided into nine committees: I. Liquidation of the War and Punishment of War Criminals; II. Political and Colonial; III. Legal; IV. Collective Security, V. The Place of Education, Science and Learning in Post-War Reconstruction; VI. Economic & Financial, VII. Social and Labour, VIII. International Organisation; and IX. The Place of Religion in the Post-War Reconstruction. Representing Poland were Jan Baliński-Jundziłł, Adam Ciołkosz, Witold Czerwiński, Tytus Filipowicz, Witold Kulerski, Tadeusz Nieduszyński, Professor Maria Skalińska, Professor Henryk Tennenbaum, Antoni Wójcicki, Professor Bohdan Winiarski, August Zaleski, and K. Załuski.[12]

Topics relating to justice for war criminals were the purview of Committee I (Liquidation of the War and Punishment of War Criminals), headed by Marcel de Baer. The Polish government was represented by the deputy head of the Supreme Audit Office (alternatively: Supreme Audit Chamber; *Najwyższa Izba Kontroli*), Zygmunt Nagórski, and Professor Bohdan Winiarski. The fruit of Committee I's labours were the 'Reports on the Punishment of War Crimes', published in 1943, counting 450 pages and covering – on the basis of the achievements of the scholarship of international law, as well as domestic and international legal instruments – the key legal aspects of investigating and prosecuting war crimes.

Discussions in the LIA concentrated on the definition of war crimes and crimes of international law, as well as the difficulty in defining a *numerus clausus* of acts included in the category. The list developed by the Commission of Fifteen in 1919 was used as the basis, with the proviso that it was not to be regarded as exhaustive. In calling attention to the mass persecutions of civilians, recommendations were made to supplement that list with racially or politically motivated acts of extermination, even where committed against

1–2; London International Assembly, The Punishment of War Criminals; Recommendations of the LIA, London 1944/45.

11 London International Assembly, The Form and Function of the World Organisation Proposed by the LIA, undated. IPMS Kol. 133/76.

12 *Ibidem.*

Axis nationals, thus opening the path to the protection of stateless persons and German Jews victimized by the Nazis within the territory of the German Reich.[13] Out of that concept, the notion of crimes against humanity would later be developed.[14] In the front and centre of the LIA's interest stood the question of aggressive war, and thus violation of Kellogg-Briand Pact, as an international crime. The matter of penalization of aggressive war was pressed primarily by the Czechoslovak representatives in the LIA – Bohuslav Ečer and Václav Beneš. In a memorandum titled 'The Crime of Aggressive War', Ečer asserted that the unequivocal condemnation of aggressive war in the Kellogg-Briand Pact – of which both Germany and Italy were signatories – provided, despite the lack of a penal sanction in the text of the Pact, the basis for the punishment of the Axis leaders guilty of violations of the Pact.[15] Furthermore, Ečer strongly advocated for the prosecution of heads of states and for the limitation of the doctrine of sovereign immunity, arguing 'that leaders should be held criminally responsible as individuals for launching an aggressive war'.[16]

One of the most important topics discussed by LIA was international criminal jurisdiction and the respective competence of domestic courts. In 1942, Marcel de Baer prepared the draft statute of an International Criminal Tribunal, citing the League of Nations Convention for the Prevention and Punishment of Terrorism (1937), providing for the establishment of an international criminal jurisdiction. The determinations of the International Law Association conference of 1926 in respect of the need of a Permanent International Criminal Court, and recalling that the fiasco of the penal provisions of the Treaty of Versailles had resulted from the non-existence of any structures of international justice at the time.[17] Following more than a year of deliberations on the draft statute, with the participation of Lord Maugham, Lord Cecil, Sheldon Glueck, Johannes M. de Moore, René Cassin, Bohdan Winiarski, and Victor Bodson, the decision was made in favour of the most expansive definition of the scope of *ratione materiae* jurisdiction of the Court. That was to be: 'crimes committed in Germany against Jews and stateless persons and possibly against

13 *History of the UNWCC*, 100.

14 *Ibidem*, 101–102. Von Lingen, *Crimes against,* 296–316.

15 Bohuslav Ečer, 'The Crime of Aggressive War'; LIA, Reports of the Punishment of War Crimes, TNA LCO 2/2973, 172(a–h). More on this see Segesser, *Recht statt*, 319–320, *History of the UNWCC*, 100–101.

16 Jessie Barton Hronešová, Adam B. Lerner, 'Bohuslav Ečer, the UN War Crimes Commission, and the Intellectual History of the Nuremberg Charter'. *Modern Intellectual History.* Published online 2025:1–26, doi:10.1017/S1479244325000010.

17 London International Assembly, Reports of the Punishment of War Crimes, TNA LCO 2/2973, 324–339.

Allied nationals'; those committed in the territory or against the nationals of more than one state; or by political leaders and persons in leading positions in the armed forces or in the administration of occupied territories, especially persons responsible for the preparation of aggressive war, racial extermination, acts of terror, mass killings, deportations, economic violence, or establishment of concentration camps.[18] The responsibility of civilian and military leaders for violations of international law was thus recognized, leading to limitations on sovereign immunity and the immunity of state leaders arising from the act-of-state theory.[19] The jurisdiction of the International Criminal Court was, however, to be subsidiary in relation to domestic court systems.

Therefore, the necessity of guaranteeing the effective administration of justice on domestic level was emphasized. In its resolution of 2 June 1943, the LIA recommended supplementing national legislations with provisions needed for putting war criminals on trial, especially by extending domestic courts' jurisdiction to cover 'crimes committed abroad against their own nationals'. As shown by the results of the Cambridge Commission's survey of October 1942 ('National Rules and Jurisdiction'), out of all Allied states, only the Criminal Code of Poland, in its general part, stipulated the jurisdiction of domestic courts to try foreigners 'having committed abroad a criminal offence direct against the welfare or interests of the Polish State, of a Polish national or Polish legal person'.[20]

The LIA's suggestions also addressed the matter of the defence of superior orders (*respondeat superior*), available in all Allied legal systems with the effect of excluding the criminal liability of persons carrying out the orders of their superiors. The decision was that the fact alone of having been ordered to commit a criminal offence ought not to constitute a defence for the person executing an unlawful order, but compulsion might offer a mitigating circumstance to be considered in sentencing. The latter was to be barred in two situations – 'when the act was so obviously heinous that it could not be accomplished without revolting the conscience of an average human being' and 'when the accused, at the time, was a member of an organisation whose membership implied the execution of criminal orders'.[21] Articles 8, 9 and 10 of the IMT Charter, dealing with the principle of *respondeat superior* (Article 8)

18 *Ibidem*, 340, *History of the UNWCC*, 103.

19 Hersch Lautetpacht, 'The Problem of Jurisdictional Immunities of Foreign States'. *British Yearbook for International Law* 1951.

20 Art. 5 of the Criminal Code of 1932, Dz.U.1932.60.571. See fn. 132 and *History of the UNWCC*, 97.

21 *History of the UNWCC*, 101.

and the criminal responsibility of members of a criminal group, penalizing membership itself in such a group, later reflected the above concept.[22]

The outcome of the deliberations of the London International Assembly made an important contribution to those of the UNWCC and the representatives of Governments-in-Exile in the LIA or in the Cambridge Commission participated in UNWCC meetings as delegates of their governments and heads of the various sections within the UNWCC.

Having examined the work of the International London Assembly and Cambridge Commission, as well as the contributions made by the legal minds of the occupied states to the codification of the principles of international criminal law in the era of the Second World War, especially the definition of crimes against humanity, Kerstin von Lingen concluded: 'without the engagement of exiled lawyers (…) there would never have emerged a self-consciously "global" project of penalizing war crimes on a planetary scale, linking contemporaneous realities with future horizons'.[23]

2 The Establishment and Works of the United Nations War Crimes Commission

The UNWCC was inaugurated on 20 October 1943 at the Foreign Office in London, nearly two years after the announcement of the Declaration of St. James's Palace, whose signatories had prioritized documenting the occupants' crimes in preparation for the anticipated trials of war criminals. The delay in the establishment of the Commission is attributable to conceptual differences on war-crimes policy between the United Kingdom and the USSR and the low priority placed by the Western Powers on it.[24]

After the announcement of plans for the creation of a Fact Finding Commission in the Lords on 7 October 1942, the Foreign Office approached the governments of China, United States, and the USSR to negotiate the terms of organization of the UNWCC – its seat, composition, and selection of the president. The proposal was to entrust the presidency to the American repre-

22 Arts. 8, 9 and 10 of the IMT Charter, 82 UNTC. 280.

23 Kerstin von Lingen, 'Legal Flows: Contributions of Exiled Lawyers to the concept of crimes against humanity during the Second World War'. *Modern Intellectual History* 17 (2020), 507–525, here: 509. See also: Sabina Ferhadbegović, Kerstin von Lingen and Julia Eichenberg (eds.), 'The United Nations War Crimes Commission UNWCC, 1943–1948, and the Codification of International Criminal Law' (2022) 24 Journal of the History of International Law / Revue d'histoire du droit international 305.

24 Kochavi, *Prelude*, 27 and 36–62; *History of the UNWCC*, 111–112.

sentative, with a view to achieving the impartiality of the works. The Department of State responded only in summer 1943, which is when the selection of the US candidate to the UNWCC took place. That came out to be Herbert C. Pell, former ambassador to Portugal and Hungary, as well as close associate of President Roosevelt's. His lack of a law degree provoked objections from members of the Department of State, contributing to the delay. The Secretary of State, Cordell Hull, suggested the appointment of the British candidate to lead the Commission.[25] During the planning stage of the Commission's organization, the Soviet Union withdrew its interest. Several factors contributed, but the decisive one was probably the British government's objection to mandates for delegates of the Soviet Socialist Republics – Ukrainian, Belarusian, Moldavian, Lithuanian, Latvian, Estonian, and Karelo-Finnish – due to the lack of international recognition of territorial cessions to Russia and annexations of the Baltic states.[26]

The USSR's non-accession to the international organization tasked with investigating war crimes was not, however, a sign of Moscow's disinterest in cooperation with London and Washington, D.C., on cases involving the prosecution of the Nazis. The conference of ministers of foreign affairs of the USSR, United Kingdom, and USA in Moscow (19–30 November 1943) resulted in the publication of the so-called Moscow Declaration of atrocities. It was the first resolution of the Great Powers announcing that those guilty of crimes in the occupied territories would be 'sent back to the countries in which their abominable deeds [had been] done, in order [to] be judged and punished according to the laws of these liberated countries'. The determination of the terms on which the leading criminals were to be judged and of the organization of the justice system was left to be decided by the Allies at a later time.[27] The Moscow Declaration proclaimed:

> At the time of granting of any armistice to any government which may be set up in Germany, those German officers and men and members of the Nazi party who have been responsible for or have taken a consenting part in the above atrocities, massacres and executions will be sent back to the countries in which their abominable deeds were done in order that they may be judged and punished according to the laws of

---

25 Segesser, *Recht statt*, 350–351.

26 Kochavi, *Prelude*, 44–50.

27 *Cf.* Moscow Declaration of Atrocities, 30 October 1943, A Decade of American Foreign Policy: Basic Documents, 1941–1949 (Washington, DC: Government Printing Office 1950), via Avalon Project: https://avalon.law.yale.edu/wwii/moscow.asp, accessed 17 June 2024.

> these liberated countries and of free governments which will be erected therein. Lists will be compiled in all possible detail from all these countries (…).

Being the first official agreement among the Great Three concerning the form to be taken by responsibility for war crimes, the Moscow Declaration was essential to the whole process of the development of Allied policy on war crimes, as well as to the works of the newly established UNWCC, which became one of the tools for the implementation of its assumptions.

The UNWCC was the first international body established by Allied governments to collect and verify the evidence of war crimes committed during the Second World War. The charge files and dossiers of war criminals gathered for the Commission's purposes supplied the material for the official lists of names of suspects and evidence for use at Nuremberg, as well as in almost 2,000 criminal cases tried before the domestic courts of Allied states after the war. By the UNWCC's efforts, reports from selected domestic trials of war criminals were translated into English and published in 1947–1949 in 15 volumes of its Law Reports.[28] The Commission's achievement was the co-ordination of investigations and cooperation among the member states in respect of the documentation of the crimes of the Axis and identification of the perpetrators. The Commission developed a harmonized documentation and reporting system and acted as an advisory and consultative body to Allied governments. It played an important role in the promotion of international justice during the years of the Second World War and in the development of concepts of international criminal law prevailing until the present day: the concepts of crimes against peace and crimes against humanity; individual criminal responsibility for international crimes; cooperation of domestic and international investigative bodies on international crimes; and principle of the subsidiary nature of international jurisdiction relative to the domestic justice system.[29]

The UNWCC was an organization of global reach, with experts from 17 Allied states participating in the works: Australia, Belgium, China, Czechoslovakia, France, Greece, Yugoslavia, Canada, Luxembourg, Norway, New Zealand, Poland, United States, Union of South Africa, and the United Kingdom. On 11 January 1944, the British delegate – Sir Cecil Hurst, former legal advisor to the Foreign Office and judge of the Permanent Court of International Just-

---

28 UNWCC, Law Reports of Trial of War Criminals, vols. I–XV (London: HMSO 1947–1949), available at https://www.loc.gov/item/2011525464/ (accessed 11 October 2023).

29 Mark Ellis, 'Assessing the Impact of the UNWCC on the Principle of Complementarity'. *Criminal Law Forum* 25 (2014), 191–222.

ice in The Hague and president of that court in 1934–1936 (afterwards vice-president until 1945) – was elected President. In January 1945, he was replaced by the Australian representative, Lord Wright of Durley. Another British representative, Hugh Mc Kinnon Wood, former counsellor at the League of Nations legal section, became the Commission's Secretary General. With the expansion of the secretariat at the beginning of 1945 came the employment of two additional legal officers – Egon Schwelb of Czechoslovakia and Jerzy Litawski of Poland.[30] In February 1944, a special Far Eastern and Pacific Sub-Commission was created in Chongqing.

The Polish delegate starting from October 1943 was Stefan Glaser, who would resign in connection with his appointment as Polish minister to Belgium and his work at the Polish Faculty of Law at the University of Oxford in autumn 1944. His successor, Tadeusz Cyprian, held the post until July 1945, when the Polish Government-in-Exile ceased to be recognized by the Western Powers.[31] In August 1945, Mieczysław Szerer became the delegate of the Provisional Government of National Unity in Warsaw, with Tadeusz Cyprian as his deputy.

The UNWCC's organization and scope of mandate were discussed already in the inaugural meeting on 20 October 1943, with Lord Chancellor Simon presiding and recalling the Commission's responsibilities as defined in the autumn of 1942:

(1) It should investigate and record the evidence of war crimes, identifying where possible the individuals responsible; and

(2) It should report to the Governments concerned cases in which it appeared that adequate evidence might be expected to be forthcoming.[32]

Lord Simon emphasized that the UNWCC had been established to co-ordinate the investigations and documentation works of the Allied governments, whereas points of law relating to the criminal procedure and organization of the trials were to be agreed upon by the governments at a later time.[33] The British authorities recommended the establishment of a special Technical Committee, independent from the Commission and filled by experts in international law. It was to be responsible for topics relating to the legal and organizational aspects of proceedings involving war crimes, for giving recommendations and making decisions binding on Allied governments in that regard.[34] The decision to exclude from the Commission's purview the creation and inter-

30 History of the UNWCC, 119.

31 The full list of delegates is provided in the Commission's official report; see: *History of the UNWCC*, 112–123.

32 History of the UNWCC, 3.

33 UNWCC, Minutes of a Meeting at the Foreign Office on October 20th, 1943, 4.

34 *Ibidem.*

pretation of the law to be used in trials for international crimes was viewed as motivated by a desire to undermine the UNWCC's authority and position.[35] The vote on the establishment of the Technical Committee was postponed to another meeting, and the idea was ultimately abandoned.

On 26 October 1942, an informal meeting of UNWCC members took place to discuss the scope of the Commission's responsibilities. The initiative came from the representatives of the exiled governments, whose ambitions and expectations for the UNWCC's role exceeded a role limited to gathering information on crimes committed in occupied territories and assembling lists of suspects.[36] The following were regarded as crucial tasks instead: to define the term 'war crimes'; decide on the type of courts or tribunals; identify the perpetrators and record their personal information and evidence; and decide on the method of evaluating the documentation submitted by the governments, as well as principles of substantive and procedural law to the used in the trials. Marcel de Baer's recommendation was to create a separate section to act as a 'Technical Committee' within the Commission. Lawyers from the occupied states – especially Bohuslaw Ečer as the delegate of Czechoslovakia, Stefan Glaser for Poland and Marcel de Baer for Belgium – advocated for the transformation of the Commission into a consultative expert body also empowered to resolve points of law.[37] On 17 December 1943, Ečer addressed the members of the Commission with a memorandum concerning the scope of its responsibilities. He was firmly in favour of the inclusion of legal analysis and of a consultative role towards Allied governments, emphasizing the high level of expertise possessed by the Commission's members in the area of international law, as well as the fundamental importance of their cooperation to the development of international justice, being 'the most effective weapon in the struggle against international anarchy'.[38]

Recapitulating the discussion among the UNWCC members on the shape and scope of the Commission's tasks and powers, Ečer's memorandum recommended setting up three committees to organize the works: I. Facts and Evidence – responsible for the examination of the evidence submitted by the states and providing guidelines and recommendations for the national war-crimes offices; II. Enforcement – for technical and executive aspects of the preparation and handling of the trials (extradition, organization of the justice

35 Kochavi, *Prelude*, 59–60.

36 UNWCC, Notes of Unofficial Preliminary Meeting on 26th October 1943, at the Royal Courts of Justice, London.

37 Von Lingen, *Crimes*, 277–278.

38 UNWCC, Minutes of Sixth Meeting held on 25th January 1944, 4. Concerning this topic: Kochavi, *Prelude*, 93; v. Lingen *Crimes against Humanity*, 278–280.

system); III. Legal Committee – for work on points of law relevant to the punishment. In a vote held on 25 January 1944, the motion passed.[39]

The primary importance belonged to the works of Committee I (Facts and Evidence), chaired by the Belgian representative, General Marcel de Baer. Committee I was created to evaluate the dossiers of suspects and charge files submitted by Allied governments, give recommendations to governments on the structuring of the charges, and provide support with regard to evidence taking. Once the verification of the materials was complete, the Secretariat of Committee I – acting as the central bureau for the gathering of information about crimes and perpetrators – assembled official lists of suspects.[40]

The evidence was graded by Committee I on a four-tier scale. Categories A and B1 were used for evidentially complete charge files and suspects whose names would automatically be added to the list of war suspects justifying extradition requests. Category B2 applied to cases with sufficient grounds to indict the suspects but demanding more evidence. Disqualified charge files were assigned to category C.[41]

Contacts between Committee I and the authorities of a given state were mediated by delegates of governments and national offices, which the member states were obligated to establish in early 1944. Representatives of the national offices were invited to weekly meetings of the Committee to discuss the charges files submitted by them. The cooperation of the national offices with the Commission focused on national charges and took a variety of forms – analysis and evaluation of evidence, exchange of information, legal positions, knowledge, and practices. The charge files were forwarded on behalf of the governments to the Commission's Secretariat via the heads of the national offices and presented in the UNWCC forum by the delegate of the relevant government, who was simultaneously responsible for communication among the UNWCC, the national offices, and the government.

As a condition of admissibility, charges submitted to the UNWCC had to be accompanied by *prima facie* evidence, which posed a great challenge to the national offices due to the lack of established practices with regard to the documentation of war crimes, as well as difficulties with access to evidence in territories still under occupation. Especially during the first stage of the Commission's works, the result of the above was only a small number of charge files with a positive evaluation and consequently a small number of names on suspect lists. With a view to developing a methodology for file processing,

39 *Ibidem.*

40 For the full list of members of the UNWCC's Committee I, see: *History of the UNWCC*, 123.

41 AIPN GK 159.1, leaf 119.

effective cooperation and exchange of information between the Commission and the national offices, a special conference was held from 31 May to 2 June 1945 between the national offices and the UNWCC. The conference enabled national agencies to cooperate more closely on the identification of perpetrators, evidence gathering, and drafting of charges in cases of acts committed in multiple countries, with materials originating from different national offices or in an incomplete state.[42]

As a result of the cooperation between Committee I and Allied governments, the Commission examined a total of 8,178 charge files in cases of war crimes and compiled 80 lists of persons charged, to a total of 36,529 suspect names, of whom 34,270 were Germans.[43]

The tasks of Committee II (Enforcement) included procedural and technical preparation of the trials – extradition clauses, draft statute of an international tribunal, and procedures for the taking of evidence from occupied territories. The works of Committee II were presided over by the American delegate, Herbert Pell, and, following his resignation, by the US delegate to the UNWCC, Lieutenant Colonel Joseph Hodgson.

One of the Commission's main tasks was to evaluate and systematize the evidence of war crimes gathered by the Allied states. The Commission did not, however, have its own investigative bodies. To streamline the documentation works at Committee II, the suggestion was offered – in spring 1944 – of establishing a special section at the Supreme Headquarters Allied Expeditionary Force (SHAEF) for the gathering and examination of the evidence of war crimes. That was supposed to be either a delegation of the UNWCC in the occupied territories or a separate SHAEF unit for cooperation with the Commission.[44] Neither the Foreign Office, nor SHAEF leadership responded favourably to the initiative. Nevertheless, in the spring of 1945, SHAEF created within its own structure a cell tasked with responsibilities similar to those

---

42 The members of the UNWCC presented the following papers: 'Cooperation between National Offices and the War Crimes Commission with a view to preparing evidence and charges against enemy key-men who have not yet been indicted by National Offices' – Marcel de Baer; 'Establishment of closer connections between the United Nations War Crimes commission and the National Offices and the strengthening and assisting of these offices' – Radomir *Živković*; and 'The establishment and maintenance of a central recording office, the pooling of information on war crimes, and the establishment of a uniform indexing system and use of uniform machine records' – Joseph Hodgson. In attendance on behalf of Poland were Jerzy Litawski, Manfred Lachs and Tadeusz Cyprian. UNWCC, National Offices Conference, 31 May to 2 June, 1945.

43 *History of the UNWCC*, 509–510.

44 UNWCC, C. 24, 30 May 1944: Establishment in Enemy Territory of War Crimes Offices, Kochavi, *Prelude*, 104–105

contemplated by the UNWCC's scuttled plan: Central Registry of War Criminals and Security Suspects (CROWCASS),[45] in which the UNWCC's lists of war criminals were viewed as sufficient grounds of arrest of a suspect without requiring any additional evidence of guilt. For the prosecutions to be effective, some procedures had to be implemented with regard to arrest and extradition. On the basis of the draft extradition convention prepared in autumn 1943 by the ministers of justice of the Allied states from Belgium, Luxembourg, the Netherlands, Norway, and Poland,[46] the UNWCC Committee II prepared a Draft Convention for the Surrender of War Criminals and other Offenders. As the Commission failed to win the British government's support for the extradition convention, the latter was not signed. However, draft armistice articles were prepared in the summer of 1944 with provisions for the 'surrender by the axis Powers of persons wanted for trial as war criminals'.[47]

Also in the spring of 1944, Committee II began work on a Draft Convention on the Trial and Punishment of War Criminals, leading the Commission to approve – on 26 September 1944 – a Draft Convention for the Establishment of a United Nations War Crimes Court. The Court was to be established by treaty among the Allied states as a permanent international court with subsidiary jurisdiction relative to the domestic courts adjudicating on international crimes.[48] Irrespective of its activities, the recommendation was to establish military tribunals in Allied states with jurisdiction for the group of war criminals mentioned in the Moscow Declaration.[49] As a result of the British and American governments' rejection of the idea of a United Nations War Crimes Court and the ensuing conflict over the scope of the UNWCC's competence,[50] Sir Cecil Hurst resigned as Chairman in January 1945.

---

45 *Ibidem.* Concerning demands for the Commission's responsibilities to include the conduct of investigations, as well as expansion of the investigative structures, see: Narrelle Morris and Aden Knaap, 'When Institutional Design is Flawed: Problems of Cooperation at the United Nations War Crimes Commission, 1943–1948'. *The European Journal of International Law* 28 (2017), 521–523; *History of the UNWCC*, 344–390.

46 Draft Convention for the surrender of war criminals drawn up by the Ministers of Justice of certain of the occupied countries; United States, Department of State: Foreign Relations of the United States: Diplomatic Papers, vol. 1, 1354ff.

47 UNWCC, Surrender by the axis Powers of persons wanted for trial as war criminals, C.34, 18 July 1944.

48 William Schabas, 'The United Nations War Crimes Commission's Proposal for an International Criminal Court'. *Criminal Law Forum* 25 (2014), 171–189, here: 183–186.

49 *Ibidem*, Kochavi, *Prelude*, 110–118.

50 Arieh Kochavi, 'The British Foreign Office versus the UNWCC during the Second World War'. *Holocaust and Genocide Studies* 1 (1994), 28–49, here: 38.

Committee III (Legal Questions) assisted Allied governments in an opinion-giving capacity on matters of substantive law and procedure to be used for the trials. It also assisted Committee I in a similar way with regard to the examination of the charge files, evaluation of the evidence, and classification of the acts. The first chairman of Committee III was Stefan Glaser, serving in that role from February to September 1944; his successor was the Czechoslovak delegate, Bohuslav Ečer. Shortly after the works of Committee III commenced, its members were appointed as reporters on the following questions: definition of war crimes, the plea of superior orders; the gaps in national legislations concerning war crimes, collective criminal responsibility.[51] The works of Committee III also focused on defining with more precision the legal principles underlying the Allied states' war-crime policy, previously discussed in meetings of the Cambridge Commission and LIA. They made a significant influence on the concepts of individual responsibility for international crimes that would be adopted by the Nuremberg Tribunal – crime against humanity, aggressive war, criminal organization, and individual responsibility for membership in an organization deemed criminal.

In May 1944 – on the basis of Marcel de Baer's memorandum – Committee III defined the following types of crimes that, in its opinion, the Commission's jurisdiction should cover:

> (1) crimes committed for the purpose of preparing or launching the war, irrespective of the territory where the crimes have been committed;
> (2) crimes perpetrated in the Allied countries and crimes committed against members of the armed forces or civilian citizens of the UN abroad, in the air or on the sea;
> (3)crimes committed against any persons without regard to nationality, stateless persons, because of race, nationality, religious, or political belief, irrespective of where the crimes have been committed;
> (4) crimes that might be perpetrated in order to prevent the restoration of peace.[52]

The deliberations of the UNWCC paid special attention to the unprecedented level of organized violence against civilians in occupied territories, as well as persecutions potentially having affected Axis nationals and citizens of areas incorporated into the Reich. The first use of the term 'crimes against humanity'

51 UNWCC, M.12, Minutes of Twelfth Meeting, 7 March 1944.

52 UNWCC, Scope of the Retributive Action of the United Nations according to their Official Declarations, C. 20, 16 May 1944; *History of the UNWCC*, 173–175. Kochavi, 97.

in international legal debate was in that forum.[53] In spring 1944, the UNWCC oversaw the drafting of a report exploring a new category of crimes of international law, of which prosecution should fall under United Nations jurisdiction, being organized persecution motivated by race, religion, or political convictions, irrespective of the victim's nationality.[54] In the related debate, Marcel de Baer argued for universal jurisdiction: 'any member of the War Crimes Commission shall be entitled to bring before Committee I the case of any person accused of a war crime irrespective of the nationality of the victim or the place where the crime was committed'.[55] The consequence would be for the jurisdiction of the UNWCC – and, in a more distant perspective, also the jurisdiction of domestic courts competent in cases of war crimes – to be extended to crimes against Axis nationals, German and Austrian Jews, as well as inhabitants of territories annexed to the German Reich. The UNWCC sought the British authorities' approval for the extension of its jurisdiction onto cases of that type but never obtained it. Crimes against humanity were placed in the Commission's jurisdiction on 30 January 1946,[56] already after the adoption of the London Agreement for the prosecution and punishment of the major war criminals of the European Axis,[57] and commencement of the proceedings before the IMT. Crimes against peace, defined by Article 6(a) of the IMT Charter, also were assigned to the Commission's jurisdiction on the same day.

The matter of the criminalization of aggressive war – arising from the Kellogg-Briand Pact of 1928 and from the Geneva Protocol – and the addition of the launching and waging of a war of aggression to the list of international crimes were discussed in the UNWCC simultaneously with the term 'crimes against humanity'. In spring 1944, Bohuslav Ečer submitted a report on that topic for debate in Committee III. He called for the recognition of aggressive war as a war crime, entailing responsibility for the preparation and implementation of a plan of aggressive war, and thus the responsibility of heads of state and members of cabinets for developing plans of total war, where '[t]he aims were to enslave foreign nations, to destroy their civilisation and physically

53 Von Lingen, *Crimes against*, 287–289.

54 UNWCC Archive, Reel 36, Main File of Committee I – Facts and Evidence, leaf 50: 21 April 1944, Extension of the Commission's Competence to War Crimes not Committed against United Nations Nationals; *History of the UNWCC*, 174–180. On this topic see: Kochavi, *Prelude*, 138–143; Segesser, *Recht statt*, 353–357.

55 UNWCC Archive, Reel 33, C. 12; Extension of the Commission's Competence to War Crimes not Committed against United Nations Nationals of 21 April 1944. Proposal by the Chairman of Committee I.

56 Commission's meeting of 30 January 1946; UNWCC's report on crimes against humanity adopted on 22 January 1947.

57 London Agreement, Art. 6(c).

annihilate a considerable section of the population on racial, political or religious grounds'.[58] Committee III initially concurred with Ečer's arguments and with the demand for the inclusion of the crime of aggression in the scope of the UNWCC's works. Nevertheless, because of differences of opinion, a special subcommittee was established to examine the matter; it did not manage to develop a unified position by the end of war.[59] Committee III's recommendations also included individual responsibility for membership in a group regarded as a criminal organization, following a report and proposal submitted to the Commission by the French representative, Professor André Gros, who argued that 'the membership of an association of criminals is a crime in itself'.[60] That principle was the fruit of reflection on the responsibility of members of the Third Reich's government for acts committed by their subordinates or resulting from the implementation of the law of the Third Reich and its policy of extermination with regard to the populations of occupied territories and prisoners-of-war. When compiling the lists of suspects and drafting the charges, Committee III recommended the adoption of the principle that membership in such a group (SA, SS, or Gestapo) would constitute *prima facie* evidence providing Allied states with grounds to indict their own nationals for acceding to such an organization, as well as any Germans or other foreigners having served in that country's territory as members of such organizations.[61] Despite the existence of contrary solutions in the legal systems of Allied states, the UNWCC also formulated some recommendations concerning the defence of superior orders. The attribution of culpability would in each case require the examination of the circumstances of the case and: 'that the mere fact of having acted in obedience to the orders of a superior does not of itself relieve a person who has committed a war crime from responsibility'.[62]

58 *History of the UNWCC*, 180.

59 *Ibidem*, 181–182; Kochavi, *Prelude*, 100. More broadly on this topic see: v. Lingen, *Crimes against.*

60 UNWCC, Reel 34, C.85, 28 March 1945, Memorandum by [P]rofessor Andr[é] Gros on the Problem of collective responsibility for war crimes.

61 History of the UNWCC, 291; UNWCC Archive, Reel 33,C. 105 (1), 17 May 1945, Collective Responsibility for War Crimes. Recommendation to the Governments.

62 UNWCC, Reel 33, C. 86, Report to the Governments on the plea of superior orders. Submitted by [D]r Liang and adopted by the Commission on 28th March 1945.

3 Cooperation between the Polish Government-in-Exile and the United Nations War Crimes Commission

Polish authorities' efforts to document Nazi crimes and identify suspects since the first months of war had reached an advanced stage by the time the UNWCC was established. This resulted in a high number of charges and dossiers of alleged criminals submitted to the Commission in early 1944. In February 1944 11 Polish charges were registered by Committee I, and by the end of June there were 25 charges against a total of 372 suspects. In August 1944 Polish cases made up over fifty percent of all cases classified by the Commission in category B1 (sufficiently documented cases). Until the end of the Commission's work in spring 1948, Polish War Crimes Office – since August 1945 operating under the communist government in Warsaw – had submitted 7,805 charges against 7,715 suspects.[63] The documentation collected by the Polish Government-in-Exile was also used in large part for the indictments submitted to the UNWCC by the representatives of the communist Government between January 1946 and early 1948.

The cooperation between the Polish Government-in-Exile and the UNWCC was also evident in the active participation of Polish representatives across various areas of the Commission's work. Poland's first delegate to the UNWCC was Stefan Glaser, who served from October 1943 to the end of September 1944. Glaser was succeeded by Tadeusz Cyprian, who held the position from the autumn of 1944 to August 1945. In September 1945, Mieczysław Szerer took over with Cyprian as his deputy. In February 1944, during the first meeting of Committee III (Legal), Glaser was elected to serve as its chairman. In spring 1945, Jerzy Litawski was employed as a legal officer in the Commission's Secretariat General and later as secretary of Committee I,[64] in which role he continued until the end of the UNWCC's works. He was responsible for coordinating crime documentation, managing case records, and overseeing cataloguing. After 1945, he participated as an observer in Nazi trials in Europe. Litawski was one of the inspiratory contributors to the compilation of the Commission's documents published in 1949, *History of United Nations War Crimes Commission and the Development of the Laws of War* and of 14 volumes of the *Law Reports.*[65]

---

63 D. Plesch, op.cit., p. 91.

64 *History of the UNWCC*, 119–126. See correspondence concerning the appointment of Litawski to the position of legal officer at the UNWCC Secretariat, AIPN GK 159.125 / leaves 76–77. UNWCC, Reel 41 (Poland. Correspondence with national offices).

65 UNWCC, Law Reports of Trial of War Criminals, vols. I–XV (London: HMSO 1947–1949), available at https://www.loc.gov/item/2011525464/.

An important aspect of the cooperation between the War Crimes Office of the Polish Government-in-Exile and the UNWCC were consultations on the drafting of the charges, opinions on the collected evidence, and works on evidence-gathering methods. Through national offices and delegates to the UNWCC, the governments of all member states had the opportunity to supplement the lists of suspects or their personal information. In addition to processing the already existing reports on Nazi atrocities and listing war criminals, shortly after its establishment the Polish War Crimes Office expanded its structures to improve its investigative work and collaboration with the UNWCC. In spring 1944, a special 'Jewish section' was established under the direction of Dr. Manfred Lachs to process materials gathered since the beginning of the war and to obtain new evidence..[66] In August 1944 a branch of the Polish War Crimes Office was created in Scotland and conducted interrogations of Polish prisoners of war or soldiers forcibly drafted into the Wehrmacht, who in summer 1944 had been emancipated from German capture.[67] Many of them were formerly imprisoned in the concentration camps in occupied Poland and Germany. Their accounts provided valuable testimonies and lists of victims and perpetrators. Jerzy Litawski prepared the interrogation questionnaire, which was later adopted by the UNWCC for its 'Recommendations for the interrogation of enemy prisoners of war' of 17 January 1945.[68] In these recommendations the Commission noted the existing practice of interrogations done by the military authorities of the Allied states, during which attention was not paid to whatever information about war crimes the prison-

---

66 AIPN 159.2/203–207.

67 AIPN 159.1/ k. 62.

68 On 1 December, Litawski reported to de Baer on the first weeks of the delegation's works, providing a translated 'Screening Interrogation Form'. The questionnaire served as a model for the UNWCC's own recommended form for the same purpose, approved in a meeting on 17 January 1945. The form contained seven questions. Compared to the Polish version of the document, questions concerning the identification of the person testifying were changed, and questions from third to fifth from the Polish 'Screening Interrogation Form' were moved directly to the Commission's form. The following points were added:
1. Have you been garrisoned in an occupied country, where and when?
2. Have you been a member of the police (state unit, etc. ... with particular reference [,] in the case of Germans, to the Gestapo, the S.S.and the S.A.)?
3. Have you been employed in the civil or military administration of an occupied country (state place and time)?
4. Have you belonged to the personnel of a camp for prisoners of war, of a concentration camp, of a forced labour camp, and the like (for Germans add the Todt Organisation)? UNWCC, Interrogation of enemy prisoners of war. Recommendation adopted by the Commission on 17th January, 1945, Minutes of the 44th Meeting held on 17 January 1945, UNWCC, Reel 33, 371–372.

ers-of-war or former camp prisoners may have had. Allied governments were encouraged to use the UNWCC standard form to streamline the procedure and gain access to eyewitness information, which was highly valuable for fulfilling the Commission's mandate.[69]

Agencies of the Polish Government-in-Exile also collected documentation of Nazi crimes and evidence for UNWCC charges outside the United Kingdom, through special Investigation Commissions, at the Polish Ministry of Justice, operating in Jerusalem, Tehran (with a branch in Istanbul), Nairobi, Paris, and Stockholm. Investigative work was limited by lack of access to occupied territories and the ability to secure evidence at the crime scene. One way to overcome these obstacles was by reaching eyewitnesses through cooperation among government agencies gathering war-crime documentation and the military authorities responsible for the supervision of prisoner of war camps in which German prisoners were kept, as well as Allied nationals inducted into German armed forces or deported to German prisoner-of-war camps. Another solution was for the UNWCC to send delegates to occupied territories. As the Red Army offensive in the eastern territories of the Second Republic proceeded in 1944, Polish government in London expected to gain access to these regions. In the UNWCC plenary on 19 September 1944, Glaser tabled a motion to establish an international investigative group for war crimes, delegated by the Commission to gather and secure the evidence of Nazi crimes in Polish territories. Glaser submitted the most up-to-date information from national reports about the situation at Majdanek and Auschwitz and requested that the UNWCC's delegates set to work as soon as possible and start investigations in the Lublin district, which was liberated in the summer of 1944.

> The members of this commission are aware of the unbelievable cruelties which the Germans have committed in Poland. (…) The extermination of about 3 million Jews in Poland and of hundreds of thousands of Poles, including, in particular, our intellectuals, is a fact known to all of you today. In the last few days it has been disclosed what has happened in only one of the concentration camps in Poland – at Majdanek, near Lublin (…) Bearing this state of affairs in mind our Government will submit to the Commission in the very near future information as detailed as possible about these acts of criminality and will ask the Commission at the same time writing to appoint a delegation composed of competent members of the Commission to go to Poland and to see on the spot the true

69 *Ibidem.*

situation, to collect trustworthy information and to secure evidences [*sic*] there where the abominable crimes have been perpetrated.[70]

Glaser's motion opened the deliberations of the Commission on 19 September 1944. Neither the minutes nor the preserved documents of the Polish delegate's office mention whether a debate on it took place. In October 1944, the Polish government sent an official letter concerning the appointment of a delegation by the UNWCC to investigate the war crimes committed in concentration camps in Polish territories.[71] No UNWCC delegation to investigate war crimes in Polish territories was formed within the timeframe requested by the Polish government, i.e. autumn 1944. The matter of dispatching delegates from the Commission to inspect the concentration camps became current in the spring of 1945, with the SHAEF, under the command of General Eisenhower, organizing a visit to Buchenwald. On 26–27 April 1945, the Commission's delegates took part in the inspection of the camp (the Polish government was represented by Tadeusz Cyprian).[72] After the delegation's return to London, in meetings on 3 and 10 May 1945, the Commission decided to establish a delegation to examine investigate *in situ* the principal camps in the Reich. It was to include representatives from Poland (Tadeusz Cyprian), Czechoslovakia (Bohuslav Ečer), Belgium (Marcel de Baer), Greece (M. Stavropoulos), Yugoslavia (M. Marković), and the United States (Col. Hodgson).[73] Due to the great number of victims from Poland and Czechoslovakia, the delegation was to include four experts from each of the two countries, and representatives of the governments at the UNWCC, and two each from other states.[74]

The Polish Government-in-Exile contributed to the UNWCC through its advocacy for the establishment of the Commission and active, multifaceted engagement in its operations. This included the practical dimension of conducting investigations, identifying the suspects, collecting and verifying evidence, as well as the conceptual discussions on the terms of individual liability

70 AIPN GK 159.125, leaves 176–177.

71 AIPN GK 159. 63a, leaves 10–11.

72 The delegation's report was presented in a meeting of the UNWCC on 3 May 1945. Visit of Delegation to Buchenwald Concentration Camp in Germany. UNWCC, Minutes of Fifty-ninth Meeting held on 3rd May, 1945, Minutes of Meetings, 500–505.

73 UNWCC, Minutes of Fifty-ninth Meeting held on 3rd May, 1945, 497–501.

74 In a meeting of the Council of Ministers on 11 May 1945, the following list of Polish delegates was approved: Tadeusz Cyprian; Czesław Meissner, member of the 2nd National Council; Jerzy Litawski and Edward Snop as representatives of the War Crimes Office; and Judge Roman Haiman of the Ministry of Justice. See Visit of the Inter-Allied War Crimes Commission Subcommittee to the principal camps in Germany, IPMS, PRM-K. 103/17a, leaves 9–10. Reprinted in PPRM, vol. VIII, 486–487.

for international offences and on the definitions of war crimes, with particular focus on the organized nature of Nazi violence and new types of criminality targeting civilian population.

4 Definition of War Crimes and Principles of Individual Liability

Polish proposals submitted to the UNWCC resulted from four years of experience in documenting crimes, systematizing evidence for official publications and future trials, and work and the Decree of the President of Polish Republic on Criminal Responsibility for War Crimes.

The scale, systematic nature, and methods of violence against the civilian population required, in the opinion of Polish lawyers, an extension of the catalogue of war crimes recognized by the Commission and establishment of principles of individual liability for these acts. On 2 December 1943, the Commission decided that crimes listed in the charge files should align with the list developed by the Commission of Fifteen in preparation of the peace treaty with Germany in 1919, counting 32 types of crimes. The first Polish initiative in the plenary of the UNWCC, tabled by Stefan Glaser, was to extend this list by two crimes: 1. 'taking hostages'/'indiscriminate mass arrests' and 2. persecution of population in occupied territories through discriminatory laws.[75] The discussed motion was prompted by the experiences suffered by civilians in occupied Poland, widespread application of collective responsibility, and the need for the incrimination of crimes committed in a systematic manner.

The first of the two crimes proposed was the use of 'indiscriminate mass arrests for the purpose of terrorising the population, whether described as taking hostages or not'.[76] It was emphasized that 'taking hostages' by the German military and occupation forces, killing, or threatening to kill seized civilians was a consistent practice not only during active hostilities but also under German administration in occupied Poland.[77] Indiscriminate arrests and shootings were a commonly used means of everyday terror and retaliation against civilians applied from the very beginning of the war. The victims of that form of persecution (mass arrests, denial of civil rights, deportation to concentration

75 Draft motion submitted (with insignificant changes) by Jerzy Litawski on 15 March 1944. *Cf.* AIPN GK 159.125, leaves 234–238.

76 UNWCC, Proposal by the Polish representative for adding new items to the list of war crimes. Report of Committee 3 (As amended by the Committee on 8 May 1944.), C.15(1).

77 AIPN GK 159.125/230.

camps, death sentences handed down by the special courts and military or police summary courts) were thousands of civilians, starting from the intellectual circles, local social and political leaders and their families. Thus it was considered as an instrument of elimination of individuals 'posing a particular threat to the Reich' and of persecution directed against Polish cultural, social and political life.[78] Glaser emphasized the use of special proscription lists by the occupation authorities, prepared even before outbreak of the war by the Gestapo and SS. The *Sonderfahdungsbuch Polen* (Special Prosecution Book Poland) of 1939 listed over 61,000 names of individuals from Polish western territories (destined according to the *Generalplan Ost* for Germanization) to be apprehended and arrested. The proscription lists were used for extermination of thousands of Polish civilians within the *Intelligenzaktion* between September 1939 and summer 1940.[79] Since autumn 1943, as a result of the intensification of repressive measures against civilians and Hans Frank's decree of 2 October 1943, so-called 'death placards' were published in all districts of the General Government. They contained lists of names of hostages and prisoners who were sentenced to death for acts committed against the occupying authorities and the 'German Restoration Plan'. As means of repression and intimidation of Polish society they increased the psychological effect of the practice of mass arrests and hostage-taking.

Another type of the occupation forces' activities targeting the civilian population deserving of inclusion in the list of war crimes, was the implementation of discriminatory and degrading procedures and legislation ('procedures aimed at lowering human dignity').[80] In support of the motion, Glaser provided examples of German legislation discriminating against Polish and Jewish people in the occupied territories, such as special criminal laws for Poles and Jews,[81] prohibition from entering public transport or public buildings, bans on the use of the Polish language in public spaces, stigmatization of the Jewish population, bans on religious practices, restrictions of marriage law, as well as persecution of cultural life, and systemic emaciation

---

78 (Katowice–Warszawa: *IPN* 2019).

79 It is estimated that about 50,000 people died as a result of the Intelligenzaktion in occupied Poland in 1939 alone; another 50,000 were sent to concentration camps. The total number of Intelligenzaktion deaths (through June 1940) is estimated at 30,000–40,000 in Pomerania, 60,000 in the Greater Poland region, over 6,000 in General Government and around 1,500 in Silesia. Maria Wardzyńska, *Był rok 1939. Operacja niemieckiej policji bezpieczeństwa w Polsce. Intelligenzaktion* (Warszawa: IPN 2009)

80 UNWCC, Proposal by the Polish representatives; AIPN GK 159.125/232.

81 *Cf.* Regulation of 4 December 1941 concerning criminal proceedings against Poles and Jews in incorporated eastern territories (so-called *Polenstrafrechtsverorndung*, RGBI. 1941 I 759ff).

by food rationing.[82] In all that, he saw the violation of basic human rights motivated by ethnic and cultural identity or membership in a group. Such persecutions constituted an element of a policy aimed at the destruction of the cultural and spiritual sphere of life of the individual as a member of a community. The methods used to analyse German terror and draw conclusions, emphasizing the complexity of Nazi violence aiming at the physical and spiritual destruction of persecute group are close to the argumentation developed by Raphael Lemkin on the pages of the *Axis Rule in Occupied Europe*. As emphasized by Glaser, discriminatory legislation and enforcement methods were marked by exceptionally severe forms of 'moral and psychological violence' against the population of the occupied territories and deserved to be viewed as an independent war crime.[83]

Requesting the addition of the two offences to the UNWCC's catalogue of war crimes, Stefan Glaser underlined that they constituted planned and systemic activities targeted against the civilian population. He stressed that these acts were incompatible with the reasonable administration of occupied territory and violated the preamble of the Hague Convention, guaranteeing that 'the inhabitants and the belligerents remain under the protection and the rule of the principles of the law of nations'.[84]

Glaser's additions were approved. Mass arrests of the inhabitants of occupied territories were included in the war-crimes list under the number 33 as 'Indiscriminate mass arrests'.[85] Concerning the crime of enacting and implementing discriminatory legislation intended to abase the dignity of the inhabitants of the occupied territories, the Commission adopted the principle that offences belonging to that type also could be charged and would be considered by Committee I, and that the passage from the preamble of the Hague Convention cited by Glaser could be invoked in the relevant cases. Both of the new types were included in the charge files submitted by Polish national office to the UNWCC, some examples will be discussed below.

Polish proposals to the UNWCC plenary also addressed the individualization of culpability for war crimes, a topic that was thoroughly discussed during

82 On this topic see: Witold Kulesza, *Crimen laesae iustitiae. Odpowiedzialność karna sędziów i prokuratorów za zbrodnie sądowe według prawa norymberskiego, niemieckiego, austriackiego i polskiego* (Łódź: Wydawnictwo Uniwersytetu Łódzkiego 2013), 26–28.

83 Polish War Crimes Office. Addition of items to the list of War Crimes, AIPN GK 159.125/leaves 237–238.

84 Preamble of The Hague Convention (IV) Respecting the Laws and Customs of War on Land, https://www.refworld.org/legal/agreements/hague/1907/en/31788, (accessed 17 June 2024).

85 UNWCC, Proposal by the Polish representative.

the works on the Decree of the President of the Republic of Poland on Criminal Responsibility for War Crimes, of 30 March 1943. The resulting rules for the establishment of individual liability in cases of war crimes, deviating from the assumptions of the act-of-state theory, which would have guaranteed jurisdictional immunity, and from the principle of exclusion of the responsibility of persons acting on superior orders (*respondat superior*) were presented by Stefan Glaser in the UNWCC plenary on 7 April 1944.

The first of the principles addressed the criminal responsibility of both the person issuing a criminal order and the person executing it. It stipulated the responsibility of all of the officials belonging to the occupation apparatus who issued or signed illegal legislation incompatible with international law or gave orders to commit criminal offences. The second principle established the individual responsibility of administrative superiors for acts committed within their districts. The third principle stipulated the of judges for judicial crimes and for adjudicating on the basis of legal provisions violating international law. Glaser wrote:

> 1. We should establish the responsibility of all those who have issued or signed dispositions or regulations which are in fact illegal, i.e. contrary to international law, and which involve the perpetration of crimes (dispositions of taking or executions of hostages, establishment of ghettos or their liquidation, confiscation of property etc.). Such a rule would only be a consequence of the principle that the responsibility should lie on both: those who ordered the perpetration or a crime, and those who execute such an order.
> 2. Secondly, those who are in charge of the administration of a district should be responsible for all crimes committed within their territorial authority (competence). It should be assumed that such crimes have been committed with their knowledge and consent, or at any rate that they were able to prevent them, therefore their guilt consists at least in omission.
> 3. Thirdly, we should establish the responsibility of the judges who pronounce sentences, the basis of which are illegal, i.e. laws or regulations which have been issued in violation of international law (in other words, such laws, which occupying power was not entitled to issue). Condemnation on the basis of such laws should be considered a crime. This conception follows the above mentioned rule that those who execute illegal order are also responsible.[86]

86 Stefan Glaser's paper of 7 April 1944, AIPN GK 159.125, 220–221.

The first charges submitted by the Polish government to the Commission in spring 1944 already reflected these principles.

Charge no. 12 of March 1944 addressed the victims of the *Intelligenzaktion* (*Aktion AB*) in General Government and persecution of Polish academic and cultural life – arrests of 174 professors of Jagiellonian University and Mining Academy in Cracow in November 1939 and their imprisonment in Sachsenhausen and Dachau concentration camps. The principal defendants were the commandant of the Gestapo in Cracow, and the Governor General ('Chief of the General Gouvernement'), Hans Frank, as well as his deputy, Otto Wächter:

> Apart from the responsibility of the offender Dr. Mayer who was the principal executor in carrying out the arrest of the professors, the following representatives of the German authorities in Poland should be prosecuted in view of their official position; Dr, Hans FRANK, Governor General of Poland, Dr, Wächter (…). All these persons are responsible for the whole line of policy in the General Government and for the systematic extermination of the Polish intellectual class. There can be no doubt at all that the arrest of so many prominent scholars was carried out not only with the full knowledge of these persons but even following their joint decision which must have been taken after the consultation with the heads of all the principal authorities of occupation the representatives of which were at the time of the arrest the above mentioned offenders.[87]

Hans Frank and Ludwig Fischer also opened the list of persons accused of the extermination of the Jews at KL Treblinka, in charge no. 15, submitted to the UNWCC on 24 April 1944. The heads of seven districts within the General Government were charged with responsibility for the liquidation of the ghettoes and establishment of KL Treblinka for the purpose of extermination of the Jewish population. In the particulars of the charge we read:

> The accused Dr. FRANK Hans as Chief of the General Government, and the accused Dr. Fischer Ludwig as Chief of the District of Warsaw, established in March 1942 in connection with the liquidation of the Jewish ghettos in Poland death's camp at Treblinka intended for a mass-killing of Jews. (…)
>
> The above mentioned offences were committed by the accused I and II partly on their own initiative, partly in carrying out the Reich's general

87 UNWCC, Reel 14 [Polish Charge against German war criminals], 68/P/G/12.

> policy of persecution of Jews aiming at their complete extermination in Poland.[88]

Charge No 18 of 22 May 1944 concerned the liability for the enforcement of the German racial ideology and colonial policy in the Polish western territories incorporated into the ReichsGau Wartheland by means of persecution, expropriation, and mass deportations of Polish civilians. The main focus of this charge was on the Germanization of the Poznań region, on the enforced transfer of over 100,000 civilians into the General Government and colonization of these territories by German settlers.[89] However, it addressed 'a whole system of deportations applied by the Germans in Poland (…)' that had been 'planned long before the war started'. Thus, the individuals accused of ordering and carrying out the deportations and 'pursuing a policy strengthening the German element in the occupied country (…) to the detriment of the native population' included heads of the local administration: Arthur Greiser, the Gauleiter of Wartheland, his deputy Kurt Schaltz and *Kreisleiters* in smaller towns in the region (Ostrów, Mogilno, Kalisz, and Leszno), as well as heads of police, gendarmerie, and SS in the Reichsgau Wartheland. The suspect list demonstrated the systemic, organized nature of the crime:

> While considering the problem of the responsibility for deportations as a war crime it must be stressed that they represent a whole system and not an isolated case and were carried out in a huge scale.
>
> At the highest peak of the German official hierarchy in the provinces of the incorporated part of Poland [are placed] the Reichtstatthalters, who took the leading part in the realisation of the above mentioned system and were assisted in doing so by German administrative officials of lower ranks such as Kreisleiters and Landrats. The formations of Gestapo, SS, Police and G[e]ndarmerie with their Chiefs represent the executive power to the system. All these officials took active part in the deportations and in consequence should share responsibility implied in committing this war crime.[90]

88 UNWCC, Reel 14, 79/P/G/16.

89 Over 80,000 civilians were deported from the Poznań region (Wartheland) between September and December 1939.

90 UNWCC, Reel 14, Polish Charge No 18, 110/P/G/19.

Not only did these charges discussed here set the example for further Polish indictments concerning organized violence, persecutions of civilians, and execution of a policy of extermination in the occupied territories (including crimes in concentration camps, enforced transfer of population, expropriations and forced labour),[91] but also played a significant role in the UNWCC's internal discussions about the responsibility of Reich officials for acts committed by their subordinates and crimes arising from membership in a criminal organization. The topics were analysed by the UNWCC in spring and summer 1944 in connection with the drafting of guidelines for Allied states concerning the compilation of lists of suspects and the need to gather evidence against the Nazi leadership (the 'arch-criminals') responsible for designing and implementing the policy of extermination and persecution, whose direct involvement in the crimes was often difficult to prove.

During the UNWCC meeting on 26 September 1944, Johannes de Moore recommended the adoption of the principles of individual responsibility presented in the Polish charges. Referring to the Treblinka case, he stated that 'in regard to the systematic barbarities in concentration camps, the guilt could not be limited to the camp officials; the Polish National Office – in the case of camps in Poland – had rightly extended it to the Governor, Dr. Frank'. His recommendation for the Commission was to 'go further and declare the whole German Government responsible for these atrocities'.[92] As a result of additional discussions, the Commission agreed to recognize the government of the Third Reich as a criminal organization, which was confirmed in May 1945. Nevertheless, the principle of individual responsibility of the members of the Reich's government, including Adolf Hitler, had already been invoked in the charges submitted to the Commission at the end of 1944 and beginning of 1945. Apart from the charges already mentioned, those were also Polish charge no. 34 against Adolf Hitler and members of the Reich's government concerning the enactment of discriminatory legislation, charges no. 6–16 from the Czechoslovak government, and Belgian charge no. 4 of March 1945, naming Adolf Hitler and Hermann Göring among those responsible for the crimes at KL Auschwitz-Birkenau.

---

91 *Cf.* Table 1 on p: 306.

92 UNWCC, Minutes of Meetings, 26 September 1944.

5 Characteristic of Polish Indictments

Between February 1944 and July 1945, the Polish War Crimes Office submitted 41 charges to the UNWCC, listing over 1,000 suspects, which represented only a small portion of all expected indictments. In October 1943, the 'German Archive' at the Ministry of Interior included approx. 4,000 names of alleged war criminals and in May 1945 about 10,000 records. Along with reports and evidence obtained since the autumn 1939, this list was the basis for the compilation of the UNWCC charge files, which presented a broad spectrum of Nazi crimes committed in occupied Poland. They highlighted the systematic nature of German crimes, their previously unprecedented scale, and the methods of persecution of the civilian population, its racial and political motivations, and the sufferings of the vulnerable victims – women, children, elderly, and disabled persons. The new forms of criminality targeting civilians were highlighted, such as concentration camps, mass executions of civilians, extermination by labour, destruction of the persecuted group's culture, and acts of sexual violence such as rape, forced abortions, forced inseminations, and the extermination of disabled persons. As the WCO's capacity was limited by time and lack of access to the occupied territories, the first Polish complaints concerned the groups of crimes for which the most complete documentation was available: crimes committed in concentration camps; persecution and extermination of the Jewish population; forced labour; terror against civilians, taking hostages; destruction of cultural heritage and persecution of the Polish intelligentsia; deportations and expropriation of civilians; ill-treatment and murders of prisoners of war; judicial crimes; and the institutionalization of Nazi violence through binding legislation.[93]

Until July 1945, the Polish War Crimes Office submitted to the UNWCC 11 charges documenting crimes committed in concentration camps in Ravensbrück, Treblinka, Auschwitz-Birkenau, Stutthof, Organinburg-Sachsenhausen, Majdanek, Piła, Mauthausen-Gusen, Bełżec, Kosów Podlaski, Kulmhof, and their sub-camps. The names and official ranks of more than 400 suspects were identified. The complaints, in many cases supported by reports, maps, and witness accounts, presented details on the camp staff, facts about the organization and purposes of the camps, the forced-labour system, the inhumane living conditions, and the methods used to torture and exterminate the inmates. Among the first charges submitted to the Commission in March 1944, was charge 13 on medical experiments in KL Ravensbrück against Karl Gephard (physician conducting experimental surgical operations) and Max

---

93 See: Table 1 on page 306.

Koegel (the camp's commander). In October 1944 it was supplemented by charge 31, providing names of 18 further suspects along with details on crimes committed in Ravensbrück. Deportations, tortures, and killings at the Auschwitz-Birkenau concentration camp were covered by charges 30 (of 18 September 1944) and 38 (of 2 May 1945). These charges against a total of 141 suspects (chiefs of administration in occupied territories, commanders of the SS, police and Gestapo, camp guards, doctors, and kapos) described the layout and operation of the camp, along with the methods of 'systematic extermination' of the internees – Jews, civilians, and POWs from different European countries. This included the murders in gas-chambers, mass executions of prisoners, system of disciplinary punishments, tortures performed in the so-called penal squad, medical experiments conducted in block 10, killings of disabled persons by phenol injections, or acts of sexual violence against women and minors.[94] The number of Jewish and Polish prisoners of KL Auschwitz of the camp between 1940 and 1943 was estimated at around one million, and the number of Jewish victims murdered in the camp at around 520,000.[95]

While most Polish charges concerning the persecution of civilians highlighted acts of violence against the Jewish population and all cases relating to concentration camps also dealt with the extermination of Jews, the 'Jewish section' of the Polish War Crimes Office prepared a group of charges devoted particularly to anti-Semitic offences. These included, for example, charges 33 and 34 dealing with expropriation and legal discrimination of Jewish population in occupied Poland; charge 29 concerning the crimes of the Wehrmacht on Jews in September 1939, and charge 20, submitted to the UNWCC on 3 June 1944, devoted to the execution of the plan of the 'Final Solution to the Jewish Question'. The latter charge described the liquidation of ghettos in General Government in 1942–1943 (so-called Operation Reinhardt) and the deportations and extermination of Polish and European Jews at Bełżec, Majdanek, Kosów Podlaski, Kulmhof, and Auschwitz death camps.[96] In April 1944, Jerzy Litawski drafted a list of charges being prepared by his office covering 'the entire scope of the persecution and extermination of Jews in Poland from the earliest days of the German occupation'.[97] The following crimes were to be covered: 1. the legal position of Jews in occupied Poland as created by discriminatory German regulations; 2. regulations offending the human dignity of Jews; 3. the treatment of Jewish women and children; 4. restrictions on Jewish

94 UNWCC, Reel 14, *Charges* Nos. 30, 38.

95 Fleming, *In the Shadow*, 176–181.

96 UNWCC, Reel 14.

97 Litawski's letter to Lord Wright of 29 April 1944, AIPN GK 159.125, leaf 218.

occupational activities; 5. confiscation of Jewish property; 6. persecution of religion; 7. compulsory labour for Jews; 8. expulsions and deportations of the Jewish population; 9. establishment of ghettos and concentration camps for Jews; 10. murders, massacres, brutalities and tortures inflicted upon the Jewish population; and 11. biological mass extermination of Jews.[98] Similarly to other complex cases investigated by the Polish War Crimes Office, not all charges on this list were submitted to the UNWCC as complete charges before July 1945. This, however, illustrates the priority given by Litawski's office to the documentation and prosecution crimes of the Holocaust.[99] Of particular significance was charge 34, presenting the systemic nature of the persecution of Jews and its ideological foundations, which also contains many cross-references to the aforementioned charges addressing selected types of crimes.

Charge 34 against Adolf Hitler and 23 members of the Reich government and administrative heads in occupied Poland concerned the legal situation of the Jewish population and the crime of enacting and applying discriminatory laws against the civilian population in the occupied territories. By referring to the term of *capitis diminution maxima*, institution of the Roman law indicating a loss of legal status, citizenship, and personal liberty this case presented the discriminatory legislation and policy against Jews in the incorporated territories and the General Government. The texts of the respective legal acts were quoted and analysed in the following chapters: 'the legal definition of Jews', 'curtailment of freedom', 'the Jewish labour', 'the fight against the Human Dignity of the Jews', 'The punishment of Jews and legal murder'. The suspects were accused of:

> having signed and issued, during the years 1939 to 1943, numerous laws, decrees and regulations which were designed to outlaw persons defined as Jews and eventually became an instrument which, through complete *capitis diminutio* of such persons facilitated the achievement of the German Reich's final aim: the biological extermination of Jews in Poland.[100]

The use of binding legal frameworks to legitimize Nazi violence in occupied territories was considered by the Polish Government-in-Exile as a measure of a policy of humiliation and extermination, which should constitute a separate war crime. The Polish motion of April 1944 to extend the UNWCC's list of war crimes by the crime of the 'persecution of population in occupied territories by

98 *Ibidem.*
99 Fleming, *In the Shadow*, 176–178.
100 UNWCC Polish Charge against German war criminals, charge No. 34, RN 473/P/G/34.

means of discriminatory laws' was followed by indictments devoted to the issue of the use of law and judiciary to pursue German policy of discrimination and extermination. These cases drew attention to the systemic and organized nature of German crimes, the 'statutory lawlessness' of Nazi laws regulating the situation of civilians in the occupied territories and to the problem of individual liability for issuing and executing this type of regulations. The premeditated nature of Nazi crimes led to charges against members of the German government and in conspiracy charges against the NSDAP, formulated i.e. in charge 34:

> All of the accused are distinguished German lawyers and high administrative officials. Being the authors of these decrees they are, without exception, members of the National Sozialistische Deutsche Arbeiter Partei (NSDAP) the bearer of the official German policy.
>
> The NSDAP has had an openly proclaimed aim: to deprive the Jews of their property in order to transfer it to the German people, and the termination of Jews both as individuals and community. These criminal aims make the NSDAP a criminal conspiracy. The man who was the head of the German Reich and the creator and head of the NSDAP – Adolf Hitler – inspired his fellow conspirators hereby accused to crime. On that ground he is the chief criminal.
>
> The use of legislative measures for the preparation and, at the same time, formal justification of monstrous crimes, shows clearly the assassins' premeditation and their *mens rea*. They prepared already the defence when committing the crime. They misused laws, the instrument of maintaining order and protecting human life, to commit crimes unprecedented in the history of mankind.[101]

Polish UNWCC charges addressing crimes committed by the German judiciary and the persecution of population in occupied territories by means of discriminatory laws also include charge 31 of October 1944, titled 'Violation of State Sovereignty with regard to the organisation of the judiciary and the administration of justice'; 33, regarding the German expropriation legislation against the Jews; 36, of May 1945, on the expropriations targeted against the Polish population; and 37, concerning executions of Polish forced labourers on the

101 Ibidem.

basis of the racist legislation of the Third Reich.[102] Charge 37, dated 1 April 1945, concerned the execution of Polish forced labourers in Alsace and Baden-Württemberg in 1941–1942 by the SS for 'disgracing the race' on the basis of the *Polen-Erlasse* regulations. The charge drew attention to the use of the criminal repression against Polish forced labourers suspected of having sexual relations with German women on the basis of the racist law of the Third Reich – execution as a result of direct orders from the Reichsführer SS, Heinrich Himmler, and SS-Gruppenführer Kurt Kaul, without even the semblance of a criminal trial. From the descriptive section of this indictment, the problem of judicial crimes of the Sondergerichte and Volksgeichtshof committed on Polish forced labourers was the focus of another case drafted by the Polish War Crimes Office for submission to the UNWCC. Its aim was to show the scale of judicial murders 'committed in occupied Poland on the grounds of so-called 'racial superiority'" and to charge German judges and other functionaries with 'murders of Polish citizens committed by means of sham trials'.[103] The WCO's agenda for 1945 also included the drafting of additional charges linked to the enactment of discriminatory legislation: 'The occupying power's policy and laws aimed at the abasement of human dignity'; 'Food rationing as an element of a policy of extermination'; and 'Discriminatory labour legislation in respect of Polish labourers in the Reich'.[104]

Polish UNWCC charges concerning systemic violence and criminal repression against the civilian population also applied the principles discussed above for determining the responsibility of direct perpetrators and those who ordered the commission of a crime or issued legal regulations that justified particular act of repression. A separate category represents cases dealing with the means of everyday terror inflicted on the civilians in the occupied territories raised on the charges of systemic terrorism, murders, and massacres and of the new crime, added to the UNWCC war-crimes list at Polish request – mass arrests/taking hostages. The latter charge was among the first ones filed with the Commission's Secretariat on 12 February 1944, thus before the expansion of the catalogue of crimes in the UNWCC plenary on 6 May 1944.

Charge no. 1, of February 1944, concerned the massacre on civilians committed in the Lublin District (Józefów and neighbouring localities) in spring 1940 as part of the AB Aktion (…) – aiming at the persecution and extermination of

102 UNWCC, Reel 14, Charge No. 36, RN 850/P/G/39; charge No. 37, RN 721/P/G/36.
103 UNWCC, Reel 14, Charge No. 37, RN 721/P/G/36.
104 AIPN 159.2, leaf 348.

intellectuals and social leaders in the General Government. The individuals charged of mass killings of civilians in Józefów, burning down houses, and applying retaliatory measures, were not only Ludolf Jakob von Alvensleben,[105] the commander of the Selbstschutz, carrying out the executions but also the heads of police and administration in the Lublin District. Odilo Globocnik, chief of SS and Police, and Ernst Zoerner, Governor of Lublin District were to be held responsible as the 'representatives of the authorities which ordered and [we]re responsible for sending out the punitive expedition'.[106] Another example is charge 4, concerning mass reprisals against the population of Warsaw and the execution of 17 hostages in March 1941 in retaliation for the killing by members of the Polish military resistance (ZWZ) of Igo Sym, a Warsaw actor and Gestapo agent sentenced to death by a judgment of the Military Special Court of the Polish Underground State. One of the first mass executions of Polish civilians in the GG (in Wawer near Warsaw) was the subject of charge 14, documenting in detail the arrests and execution of 107 Polish civilians on 26–27 December 1939 in retaliation for the killing of two German soldiers. The suspects were the commander of the police detachment Landesschutz Warschau (Major Friedrich Wilhelm Wenzel, whose personal details were not provided in the charge) and Ludwig Fischer, the governor of the Warsaw district. Fischer's liability was established on the ground of his capacity as the Governor of Warsaw District. 'Being the head of the administration he had the right and duty to issue regulations concerning the public order and security in the whole district and is therefore responsible for the methods applied at Wawer'.[107] The persecution of civilian population and the *Intelligenzaktion* in the Wartheland and Pomerania (the Western territories incorporated into the Reich) were the subject of, for example, 2 concerning the murders and tortures of civilians in Leszno in September 1939, 3 dealing the killings of Polish landowners in Kownaty near Konin in September 1939,[108] and 5, 6, 10, and 19 concerning the shooting and torture of hostages in Inowrocław, Pisatoszyn, Kościany, and Nowe Miasto Lubawskie. Mass arrests, tortures, and killings of civilians from the Pomerania region were addressed by charge 25 against Albert Forster, the head of administration at Reichsgau Danzig-Westpreußen; Max Pauly, the commandant of KL Stutthof, and 12 staff members. KL Stutthof was established in the territory of the Free City of Danzig on 2 September 1939,

105 The charge file provides the name of Graf Werner von Alvensleben, Selbstschutz commander in Lublin District.
106 UNWCC, Reel 14, Charge No 1, 17/P/G/1.
107 UNWCC, Reel 14, Charge No 14, 70/P/G/III.
108 UNWCC, Reel 14, Charge No. 3, RN 19/P/G/3.

immediately after the German invasion. The structure and functions of the concentration camp expanded over time – in the summer of 1944 it became one of the extermination sites as part of the final solution to the Jewish question. However, until 1942 KL Stutthof had operated as a detention camp mostly for Polish civilians, intellectuals, and social and political leaders from the Pomerania region and Wartheland, who were arrested on the basis of proscription lists – which was the main subject of the case no 25.[109] The charges no. 21 and 24 of June 1944 were devoted to the persecution and extermination of the catholic clergy in the Poznań region and Danzig-Westpreußen and Oberschlesien regions. Detention in concentration camps, forced labour, deportations, and killings of priests were considered part of 'ruthless (...) German activities aiming at the suppression of the Polish element irrespective of religion and birth.'[110]

The persecution of religion, educated classes and social leaders, as well as the devastation of cultural and scientific goods, were strongly emphasized in the Polish indictments to the UNWCC.[111] Cases concerning the material losses of Polish culture were prepared by the Bureau for the Recovery of Cultural Losses, which documented the looting of artworks, archives, and libraries in occupied Poland in close cooperation with the Department of Education and Culture at the Government Delegation for Poland, chaired by Professor Stanisław Lorenz. Over the five years of war, this unit collected an extensive photographic documentation of the destruction of Polish culture under the German and Soviet occupation and compiled a list of approximately 2,000 individuals suspected of destroying and looting artworks. In 1944, the Bureau for the Recovery of Cultural Losses published a detailed summary of its works: *Cultural Losses of Poland: Index of Polish cultural losses during the German occupation, 1939– 1944*.[112] This report provided important documents for Polish recovery efforts and evidence for the criminal prosecution of crimes against or affecting cultural heritage. The first charges built upon this material were the Polish UNWCC charges 7 of February 1944 (Destruction of the monument of the first king of Poland, Bolesław Chrobry in Gniezno in September 1939) and 40 of July 1945 (Suppression of Polish culture).[113] A strong emphasis in these charges was placed on the aim of the German occupation of 'weakening Polish national spirit and power of resistance' and on its colonial approach

109 UNWCC, Reel 14, Charge No 25, 150/P/G/25.

110 UNWCC, Reel 14, Polish Charge No 21.

111 UNWCC, Reel 14, Charges Nos 7, 12, 21, 26 and 40.

112 K. Estreicher (ed.), *Cultural losses of Poland: index of Polish cultural loses during the German occupation, 1939– 1944* (London: 1944).

113 S. Nahlik, *Grabież dzieł sztuki. Rodowód zbrodni międzynarodowej* (Ossolineum: 1958), 286.

that used the destruction of Polish cultural heritage as a tool of Germanization and exploitation of the population in the occupied territories. This line of argument was also shown in charge 12 of 30 March 1944, concerning the arrest of 174 professors of Jagiellonian University and of the Mining Academy in Cracow in November 1939 and their imprisonment at Sachsenhausen and Dachau camps. The file provided the full list of names and titles of imprisoned scholars (including the father of Karol Estreicher – Stanisław Estreicher, professor of law and former rector of Jagiellonian University, who died in Sachsenhausen in December 1939) and details of the torture inflicted on the internees. It underlined the organized and systemic character of Nazi policy aimed at the 'destruction of the Polish intellectual classes' and culture:

> Nowhere is the real aim of the German authorities in Poland shown so clearly as in the field of culture. … [it is] the transformation of the Polish nation into a community of slaves deprived of their own culture and national tradition and forming a reservoir of labour for the benefit of the German Reich. One of the methods employed to attain this end is the destruction of Polish intellectual classes: i.e. scholars, professors, teachers, writers, artists, lawyers, engineers and doctors by torturing them to death in concentration camps and by depriving the reminder of their lifehood.[114]

6 Evaluation of the Work of Litawski's Office

The authorities of the UNWCC, and especially members of Committee I, responsible for the evaluation of charge files and evidence, often spoke approvingly of the work of the Polish War Crimes Office and Polish achievements in documenting the occupiers' crimes and identifying the perpetrators. During a little more than the UNWCC's first year of operation, the Polish side filed the largest number of charges (*cf.* Chart 2 and Table 1),[115] the majority of which were assigned by Committee I to categories A or B.1 – indicating no further evidence was required. Poland also submitted the greatest number of names of war criminals with the required supporting documentation (in August 1944, the breakdown of B.1 inflow was as follows: 139 charges from Poland, 35 from the United Kingdom, 16 from the Netherlands, 14 from Belgium, and 9 each

114 UNWCC, Reel 14, Polish Charge no 12.

115 Table 1 provides a breakdown of Polish charges submitted by Polish authorities to the UNWCC between February 1944 and July 1945.

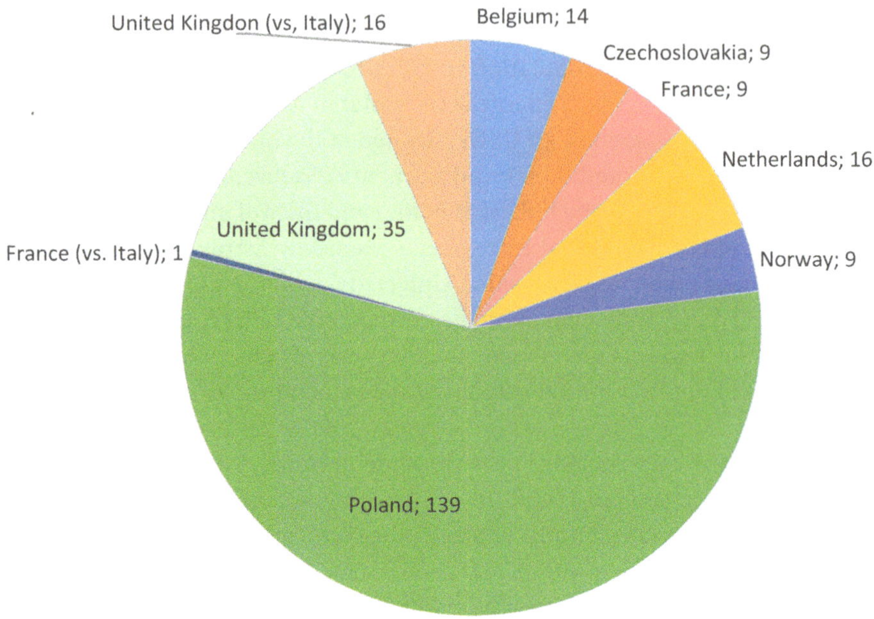

CHART 6.1 UNWCC, B.1 caseload as at August 1944

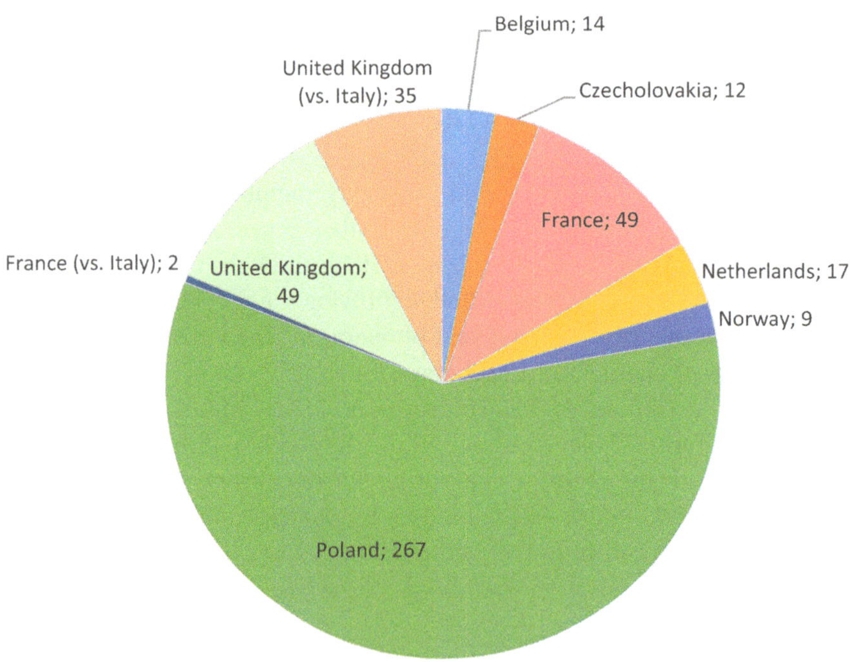

CHART 6.2 UNWCC, total number of accused persons as at 1 August 1944

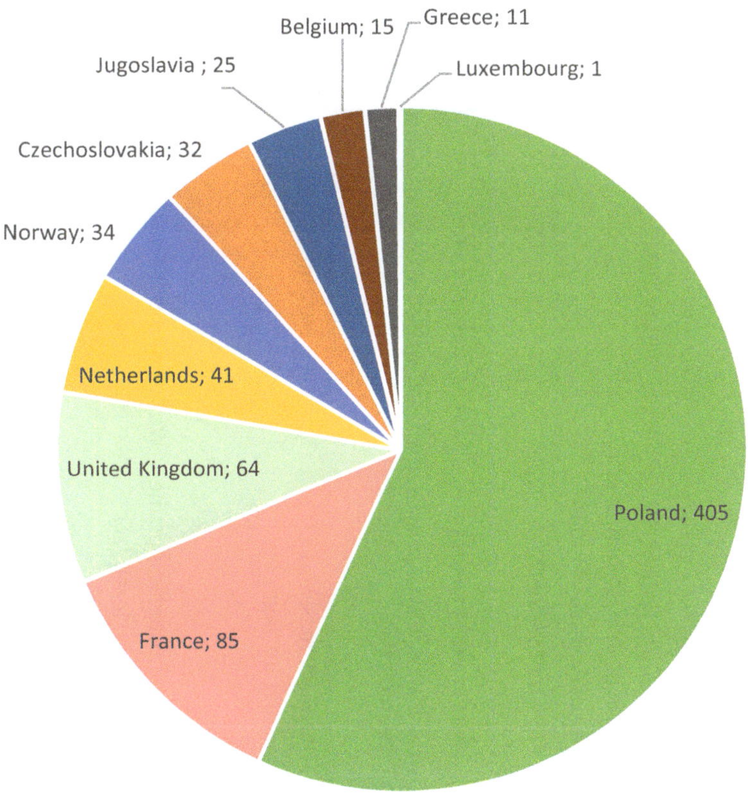

CHART 6.3 UNWCC's first list of category A German criminals. As at 22 November 1944

from France, Czechoslovakia, and Norway).[116] The first list of German criminals – marked 'A' – published by the UNWCC in November 1944 contained 711 names, out of which 405 submitted by the Polish side (*Cf.* Chart 3).[117]

In early September 1944, Jerzy Litawski and his colleagues received praise from Marcel de Baer, who was particularly appreciative of the WCO's work products and Litawski's management of operations.

> I hope you realise how much Committee I appreciates the excellent work which has been done by the Polish War Crimes Office which has

116 UNWCC, Committee I, Statistics of Cases Classified as B.1. down to 1st August 1944, AIPN GK 159.1, leaf 119. The Commission's report of August 1944 gives the number of defendants implicated in the charges. The total number of defendants in the 27 charges filed by the Polish governments in the period from July to August 1944 was 267, provided that some names appear in more than one charge. See Chart 1.

117 AIPN GK 159.2, leaf 347.

TABLE 6.1 List of cases concerning German war criminals, submitted to the UNWCC by the Polish War Crimes Office from January 1944 to July 1945.

Charge no.	Submission date	Title	Number of accused	Charges	Place and date of crime	Case category
1.	12.02.1944	Punitive expedition at Józefów, massacres of civilians	1	Murder and massacres (I), wanton destruction of property, imposition of collective penalties (XVII)	Józefów, June 1940	A
2.	12.02.1944	Massacres, murders, and infliction of tortures upon civilian population of Leszno	4	Murder and massacres (I), tortures of civilians(III)	Leszno, September – October 1939	B1
3.	12.02.1944	Shooting of Polish civilians and seizing hostages in Kownaty (near Konin)	2	Murders, massacres (I); seizing hostages	Kownaty, November 1939	B1, A
4.	12.02.1944	Shootings of hostages in Warsaw	1	Seizing hostages, putting hostages to death (II)	Warsaw, March 1941	A

TABLE 6.1 List of cases concerning German war criminals, submitted to the UNWCC by the Polish War Crimes Office from January 1944 to July 1945. (*cont.*)

Charge no.	Submission date	Title	Number of accused	Charges	Place and date of crime	Case category
5.	12.02.1944	Shooting of hostages	3	Murders, massacres (I); putting hostages to death (II), tortures of civilians (III)	22 October 1939	B.1
6.	12.02.1944	Shootings of hostages in Piastoszyn, near Tuchola	1	Murder and massacres (I), imposition of collective penalties (XVII)	Piastoszyn, 21–22 October 1939	B.1
7.	23.02.1944	Destruction of the historic monument of the Polish King Bolesław Chroby at Gniezno	14	Wanton destruction of religious, charitable, educational, and historic buildings and monuments (XX)	Gniezno, December 1939	B.1.
8.	23.02.1944	Shooting at and wounding Polish officers (POW s) at Oflag II E, Neu Brandenburg	1	Ill-treatment of POW s and wounded prisoners (XXIX)	Neu Brandenburg, Germany, April 1944	B.1.

TABLE 6.1 List of cases concerning German war criminals, submitted to the UNWCC by the Polish War Crimes Office from January 1944 to July 1945. (*cont.*)

Charge no.	Submission date	Title	Number of accused	Charges	Place and date of crime	Case category
9.	23.02.1944	Tortures in the forced labour camp Unterbuchsbau near Gdańsk	2	Murders, massacres (I); tortures of civilians (III)	Unterbuchsbau September-October 1939	B.2./A
10.	23.02.1944	Mass imprisonments and tortures of civilians, execution of hostages at Kościany	1	Murders, massacres (I); putting hostages to death (II), tortures of civilians (III), plunder of property (XIII)	Kościany September-November 1939	B.1.
11.	23.02.1944	Shooting of prisoners of war	1	Murders, massacres (I); Ill-treatment of POW s and wounded prisoners (XXIX)	Bielsk, Silesia October 1939	B.1.

TABLE 6.1 List of cases concerning German war criminals, submitted to the UNWCC by the Polish War Crimes Office from January 1944 to July 1945. (*cont.*)

Charge no.	Submission date	Title	Number of accused	Charges	Place and date of crime	Case category
12.	30.03.1944	Arrestment of 167 professors and assistants of the University of Cracov and their deportations to concentration camps in Germany	2	Tortures of civilians (III), deportations of civilians (VII); systematic terrorism internment under inhuman conditions (VIII) Arts.	November 1939 – April 1940; Kraków, Breslau; Sachsenhausen, Dachau	B.1.
13.	30.03.1944	Experimental surgical operations upon Polish women and girls at Ravensbrück concentration camp (1942–1943),	2	Murder, massacres (I) systematic terrorism, torture of civilians (III), internment under inhuman conditions (VIII);	Ravensbrück 1942–1943	B.1
14.	30.03.1944	Punitive expedition at Wawer and Anin near Warsaw; arrestment and shootings of civilians	2	Murder, massacres (I); torture of civilians (III); imposition of collective penalties (XVII)	Wawer and Anin December 1939	B.1.

TABLE 6.1 List of cases concerning German war criminals, submitted to the UNWCC by the Polish War Crimes Office from January 1944 to July 1945. (*cont.*)

Charge no.	Submission date	Title	Number of accused	Charges	Place and date of crime	Case category
15.	24.04.1944	Treblinka death camp	8	Murder and massacres (I), systematic terrorism, torture of civilians (III) Art.225,246,248 CC; 2,3,4,10 of the 1943 Decree	Treblinka 1942–1943	B.1.
16.	12.04.1944	Massacre of civilians at Częstochowa in September 1939	92	Case details missing	Częstochowa September 1939	B.1
17.	26.04.1944	Ill-treatment of POW s at the temporary camp for Polish prisoners of war at Radom	1	Murder, massacres (I), ill-treatment of wounded and POW s (XXIX); arts. 225 i 226 CC; arts. 2, 3 of the 1943 Decree	Radom September-December 1939	B.1
18.	22.05.1944	Deportations of about 100,000 civilians from Wartheland	15	Deportations of civilians (VII), 217 c, 248§2, 251 CC; 2,3,4, 10 of the 1943 Decree	Poznań, Kalisz, Mogilno, October 1939 - December 1941	B.1, A

TABLE 6.1 List of cases concerning German war criminals, submitted to the UNWCC by the Polish War Crimes Office from January 1944 to July 1945. (*cont.*)

Charge no.	Submission date	Title	Number of accused	Charges	Place and date of crime	Case category
19.	24.04.1944	Shooting of 15 Poles in Nowe Miasto Lubawskie on the plea of collective responsibility.	1	Murder, massacres, systematic terrorism (I) putting hostages to death (II) arts. 225, 217 c) CC; arts. 2, 3, 4 of the 1943 Decree	Nowe Miasto Lubawskie (Pommerania) November 1939	B.1.
20.	3.06.1944	Extermination of Jews in concentration camps in Bełżec, Majdanek, Sobibór, Koszów Podlaski, Chełmno, Auschwitz January 1942 - December 1943	21	Murder, massacres, systematic terrorism (I) tortures of civilians (III), internment under inhuman conditions (VIII), pillage Arts. 225, 246, 248§2 CC; 2, 3, 10 of the 1943 Decree	Bełżec, Majdanek, Sobibór, Kosów Podlaski, Chełmno, Auschwitz January 1942 - December 1943	B.1

TABLE 6.1 List of cases concerning German war criminals, submitted to the UNWCC by the Polish War Crimes Office from January 1944 to July 1945. (*cont.*)

Charge no.	Submission date	Title	Number of accused	Charges	Place and date of crime	Case category
21.	22.05.1944	Persecution and extermination of the Polish Catholic clergy in Wartheland	94	Murder, massacres, systematic terrorism (I) tortures of civilians (III), deportations (VII); internment under inhuman conditions (VIII), pillage Arts. 225, 230§2, 235§1a,b, 246, 248, 257 CC, arts. 2, 3, 4, 10 of the Decree	September 1939 - January 1942	B.1 B.2
22.	21.06.1944	Concentration Camp at Piła	2	Tortures of civilians (III), deportations (VII); internment under inhuman conditions (VIII), Arts. 235, 236, 248§2 CC arts. 2, 3 of the 1943 Decree	Piła (Schneidemuhl)near Bydgoszcz September – December 1939	B.1.

TABLE 6.1 List of cases concerning German war criminals, submitted to the UNWCC by the Polish War Crimes Office from January 1944 to July 1945. (*cont.*)

Charge no.	Submission date	Title	Number of accused	Charges	Place and date of crime	Case category
23.	21.06.1944	Tortures of prisoners-of-war at war-prisoners camp at Kunau	20	Ill-treatment of POW s (XXIX), 22§2 i 235§1 CC, arts. 2 and 3 of the 1943 Decree	Kanau, Germany September-December 1939	A
24.	29.06. 1944	Persecution and extermination of the Polish Catholic Clergy in the districts so-called Gau Danzig-Westpreussen, Provinz Oberschlesien, and Gau Oberschlesien	73	Murder, massacres (I), putting hostages to death (II); tortures of civilians (III), deportations (VII); internment under inhuman conditions (VIII), Arts. 225, 235, 246, 248 CC 2, 3, 10 of the 1943 Decree	Gau Danzig-Westpreussen, Ostpreussen, Oberschlesien; September 1939–1942	B.1., B.2.

TABLE 6.1 List of cases concerning German war criminals, submitted to the UNWCC by the Polish War Crimes Office from January 1944 to July 1945. (*cont.*)

Charge no.	Submission date	Title	Number of accused	Charges	Place and date of crime	Case category
25.	29.06.1944	Stutthoff Concentration Camp	14	Murder, massacres, systematic terrorism (I), putting hostages to death (II); tortures of civilians (III), deportations (VII); internment under inhuman conditions (VIII), Arts. 225, 246, 248 CC 2, 3, 4, 10 of the 1943 Decree	Stutthof, near Gdańsk September 1939-April 1941	B.1.

TABLE 6.1 List of cases concerning German war criminals, submitted to the UNWCC by the Polish War Crimes Office from January 1944 to July 1945. (*cont.*)

Charge no.	Submission date	Title	Number of accused	Charges	Place and date of crime	Case category
26.	16.08.1944	Persecution and extermination of the Polish Catholic Clergy in General Gouvernement	72	Murder, massacres(I), putting hostages to death (II); tortures of civilians (III), deportations (VII); internment under inhuman conditions (VIII), Arts. 225, 246, 248 CC 2, 3, 10 of the 1943 Decree		B.1, B.2
27.	7.08.1944	Murder of approx. 1,000 patients and staff of the Public Hospital for Mental Diseases at Świecie	5	Murder, massacres(I); tortures of civilians (III) arts. 225§1 kk, arts. 2, 3 of the 1943 Decree	Świecie, Gau Danzig-Westpreussen 10–17 September 1939	B.1.

TABLE 6.1 List of cases concerning German war criminals, submitted to the UNWCC by the Polish War Crimes Office from January 1944 to July 1945. (*cont.*)

Charge no.	Submission date	Title	Number of accused	Charges	Place and date of crime	Case category
28.	28.08.1944	Ill-tratment of prisoners of war at the Norderney Camp	5	Murders and massacres (I), ill-treatment of wounded and POW s (XXIX) arts. 225§1, 236 cc, arts. 2, 3, 10 of the 1943 Decree	Norderney, Channel Islands April-May 1942	A
29.	20.09.1944	Atrocities of the German army on the Jewish population (during the September campaign)	28	Case details missing	September 1939	A
30.	18.09.1944	Concentration Camp at Oświęcim (Auschwitz), Rajsko, Brzezinka (Birkenau).	93	Murder and massacres, systematic terrorism (I), tortures of civilians (III), deportations (VII), pillage of property (XIII); 225, 230§2, 235§1a,	Auschwitz, Birkenau June 1940 - December 1943	A

TABLE 6.1 List of cases concerning German war criminals, submitted to the UNWCC by the Polish War Crimes Office from January 1944 to July 1945. (*cont.*)

Charge no.	Submission date	Title	Number of accused	Charges	Place and date of crime	Case category
				b, 246, 248, 257 CC, 2, 3, 4, 10 of the 1943 Decree		
31.	25.10.1944	Violation of state sovereignty in the organization of the judiciary and the administration of justice	18	Case details missing		A
32.	23.10.1944	Concentration Camp at Ravensbrück (additional charge)	18	Murder and massacres, systematic terrorism (I), tortures of civilians (III), deportations (VII), internment under inhuman conditions (VIII), pillage of property (XIII); 225, 230§2, 235§1a,b, 246, 248 CC, 2, 3, 4, 10 of the 1943 Decree	Ravensbrück, Germany 1941–1942	A

TABLE 6.1 List of cases concerning German war criminals, submitted to the UNWCC by the Polish War Crimes Office from January 1944 to July 1945. (*cont.*)

Charge no.	Submission date	Title	Number of accused	Charges	Place and date of crime	Case category
33.	29.11.1944	Expropriation of Jewish property	17	Case details missing		A
34.	5.01. 1945	Legal situation of the Jewish population	24	Art. 43 of the 4th Hague Convention 2, 3, 4, 10 of the 1943 Decree	General Gouvernement, Polish territories incorporated into the Reich 1939–1944	A
35.	8.02.1945	Concentration Camp at Majdanek	100	Murder and massacres, systematic terrorism (I), tortures of civilians (III), deportations (VII), internment under inhuman conditions (VIII), pillage of property (XIII); 225, 230§2, 235§1a,b, 246, 248,, 257 CC; 2, 3, 4, 10 of the 1943 Decree	Majdanek 1940–1944	

TABLE 6.1 List of cases concerning German war criminals, submitted to the UNWCC by the Polish War Crimes Office from January 1944 to July 1945. (*cont.*)

Charge no.	Submission date	Title	Number of accused	Charges	Place and date of crime	Case category
36.	23.05.1945	Expropriation of Polish population	214	Confiscation of property (XIV); 2 and 6 of the 1943 Decree	1939–1944	
37.	1.04.1945	Executions of Polish forced labourers in Alsace, Baden-Würtemberg for "Rassenschande"	7	Murders, massacres (I), 2, 3, 6, 10 of the 1943 Decree	Alsace, Baden-Würtemberg	A
38.	2.05.1945	Auschwitz Concentration Camp (supplementary case)	47	Murder and massacres, systematic terrorism (I), tortures of civilians (III), deportations (VII), internment under inhuman conditions (VIII), pillage of property (XIII); 225, 230§2, 235§1a,b, 246, 248CC, 2, 3, 10 of the 1943 Decree	June 1940 – January 1945	A

TABLE 6.1 List of cases concerning German war criminals, submitted to the UNWCC by the Polish War Crimes Office from January 1944 to July 1945. (*cont.*)

Charge no.	Submission date	Title	Number of accused	Charges	Place and date of crime	Case category
39.	16.05.1945	Oranienburg-Sachsenhausen Concentration Camp	85	Murder and massacres, systematic terrorism (I), tortures of civilians (III), deportations (VII), internment under inhuman conditions (VIII); 225, 230§2, 235§1a,b, 246, 248CC, 2, 3, 10 of the 1943 Decree	Sachsenhausen, November 1939–1945	A
40.	21.07.1945	Destruction and suppression of Polish culture	129	Attempts to denationalize the inhabitants of occupied territory (XII), wanton devastation and destruction of property	September 1939– 1944	B1, B2

TABLE 6.1 List of cases concerning German war criminals, submitted to the UNWCC by the Polish War Crimes Office from January 1944 to July 1945. (*cont.*)

Charge no.	Submission date	Title	Number of accused	Charges	Place and date of crime	Case category
				(XVIII); wanton destruction of religious, charitable, educational, and historic buildings and monuments (XX); 2, 6, 7 of the 1943 Decree		
41.	19.07.1945	Concentration Camp Mauthausen-Gusen	61	Murder and massacres, systematic terrorism (I), tortures of civilians (III), deportations (VII), internment under inhuman conditions (VIII); 225, 230§2, 235§1a,b, 246, 248CC, 2, 3, 10 of the 1943 Decree	Mauthausen, Gusen (Austria) 1940–1944	A

> provided the Committee with a greater number of accused than all the other countries taken together. The Polish office can really be cited as a model in this respect, and I am sure that I am expressing the feeling of Committee I, when I say that we are most grateful to you for conducting this business in such an efficient way'.[118]

Litawski was congratulated on the high quality of the Polish WCO's work under his leadership in a meeting of Committee I, on 17 January 1945, stressing the excellent preparation of the Polish charge files, both in form and substance, which allowed the Commission to examine them without difficulty.[119] The Chairman of the Commission, Lord Wright, also spoke favourably about the organization of the Office's work.[120] At Lord Wright's request, following his visit to the Office in late February 1945, Jerzy Litawski shared with the UNWCC the WCO's press archives titled *The British Press on War Crimes*. The collection had been managed by employees of the Office since 1943, and previously, from 1940, by the Ministry of the Interior.[121]

Jerzy Litawski's involvement in the UNWCC's work led to his nomination as candidate for the position of legal officer in the UNWCC Secretariat General by the American delegate, Joseph Hodgson, in March 1945.[122] Despite the American support and the highly positive evaluation of his work to date, Litawski took the position only in May 1945, losing the first round of the competition to the Czechoslovak candidate, Dr. Egon Schwelb. Nominating the Czech, who was only at the stage of gaining his first experience of working with the UNWCC, was dictated by purely pragmatic considerations and the leadership's attempt to co-operate with the USSR to gain access to information and materials available to the Soviets. The talks were mediated by the Czechoslovak delegate to the UNWCC, Dr Bohuslav Ečer.[123] Moreover, another key factor that cast a shadow over the cooperation of the Polish Government-in-Exile

---

118 Copy – Marcel de Baer's letter to Jerzy Litawski, 6 September 1944, AIPN GK 159.1/ leaf 85.

119 Note by Jerzy Litawski from the meeting of Committee I of the UNWCC, 17 January 1945, AIPN GK 159.125/ leaf 119.

120 Letter from Lord Wright to Tadeusz Cyprian, of 12 April 1945, IPMS A.11.E/124, leaf.

121 Letter from Jerzy Litawski to UNWCC Secretary McKinnon Wood, 26 March 1945, AIPN 159.125/leaf 81; IMPS, A11.E/124, leaves 45–77.

122 The decision to create a new position in the Secretariat was made in early 1945. Due to the great number of charge files inbound, the UNWCC intended to hire a lawyer for the evaluation of the new arrivals before forwarding them to Committee I. Hodgson suggested the nomination of Litawski to Tadeusz Cyprian towards the end of February 1945. *Cf.* Note by Tadeusz Cyprian, 5 March 1945, IMPS A.11.E/124/ leaf. 409. Letter from Lord Wright to Tadeusz Cyprian, 28 February 1945, IMPS A.11.E/124., leaf 401.

123 AIPN GK 159.125/leaf 76; Note by Jerzy Litawski, 26 March 1945, IPMS A.11.E/124, leaf 423.

with the UNWCC in spring 1945 – including the delays with Litawski's nomination as legal officer at the UNWCC Secretariat General – was the 'unfavourable general political climate attending Polish affairs in the international area'.[124] Following the government's intervention with Lord Wright through Tadeusz Cyprian, emphasizing Litawski's achievements in the field of war-crime documentation and the close cooperation between the Polish delegates and the UNWCC, Litawski was eventually appointed legal officer in the Secretariat by the UNWCC's resolution of 4 May 1945.[125] The political situation unfolding at the time thwarted any hopes Polish authorities may have previously harboured of being allowed to take an active role in Allied trials of war criminals, such as by delegating a judge to the anticipated international tribunals in cases of acts committed against Poles or in the territory of the Polish state.[126]

In May and June 1945, Polish investigators intensified their efforts even as British and American authorities distanced themselves from the Polish Government-in-Exile. The lack of prospects for the inclusion of Polish representatives in the judicial panel or prosecutorial team in the event of an Inter-Allied Tribunal being established by the Great Powers was communicated to Władysław Kulski in a meeting on 22 May 1945 by the Undersecretary of State at the Foreign Office, Christopher Werner. The participation of any representatives of the Polish government in London was reportedly blocked by Moscow, while the Western Allies would not allow anyone from the government in Warsaw.[127] Neither were Polish representatives invited to the June session of the United Nations Relief and Rehabilitation Administration..[128] The Polish government's efforts to interrogate Hans Frank following his capture by the American forces at the beginning of May 1945 were also futile. The request was apparently made on behalf of the Polish government by the Minister of Foreign Affairs, Adam Tarnowski.[129] In a meeting of the Council of Ministers on 11 May, the Minister of Justice was tasked with appointing a special investigative commission to oversee the interrogation of Hans Frank and for the conduct of investigations into cases involving him. The rationale for the decision stated:

> Dr Frank [is] one of the main war criminals whose activities have chiefly affected Poland. The Government of the Republic of Poland has the right

---

124 *Ibidem.*

125 Letter from A. Demidecki to Jerz Litawski, 11 May 1945, IPMS, A.11.E/124, leaf 436.

126 IPMS A.11.E/124/ leaf 448.

127 Letter from Władysław Kulski to Józef Marlewski, 22 May 1945, IPMS, A.11.E/124, leaf 274.

128 *Cf.* Minutes of the meeting of the Council of Ministers, 5 June 1945 and 12 June 1945, PPRM vol. VIII, 543 and 557.

129 Minutes of the meeting of the Council of Ministers, 11 May 1945, PPRM, vol. VIII, leaf 485.

> and duty to address to the Allied Governments a request for remanding (…) Dr Frank to the judicial authorities of the Republic of Poland. The Minister of Justice as the Prosecutor General of the Republic of Poland has the jurisdiction to conduct the investigation and secure the evidence in this matter.[130]

As late as the end of May, plans were still being made for Polish prosecutors to interrogate the main individuals from the Polish list of suspects apprehended by SHAEF in Reich territory – the Reichsstatthalter of Wartheland, Arthur Greiser, and the holder of the corresponding position for Danzig (Gdańsk)-West Prussia, Albert Forster. Despite the enormous importance that the spread of information had always had to Poland's campaign for the popularization of the idea of individual criminal responsibility for war crimes ever since the end of 1939, the decision was made during the final stages of trial preparations to avoid media publicity.[131] Not only did the difficulties encountered by the Polish government with the investigations call into question the active participation of Poland in the trials of the main criminals of the Third Reich, they also cast doubt on the possibility of holding domestic trials. In such circumstances, the exiles focused on processing as many charge files as possible, supplementing the materials already available and forwarding the Polish lists to the British and American governments and to the UNWCC in the hope that action would be taken on them. Michał Potulicki verbalized that pragmatic position as follows:

> Our duty is to prevent the culprits from escaping punishment. The only practical thing, therefore, for us to do is duly prepare the dossiers and submit them to the United Nations War Crimes Commission.[132]

The Polish diplomats' fears did not prove to be unfounded. On 25 July, during the first meeting of Committee I of the UNWCC after the Western Allies' recognition of the government in Warsaw, when the most recently arrived Polish charge files (submitted on 17 and 21 July, concerning Mauthausen and Gusen camps and persecution and destruction of Polish culture), the decision was made to defer their consideration, citing 'difficulties of diplomatic nature'. With that, the Polish War Crimes Office – by then operating under the Interim

130 *Ibidem*, leaves 485–486.
131 Inter-Ministerial Conference on War Crimes, 13 June 1945.
132 Letter from Michał Potulicki to Józef Marlewski, 3 June 1945, IPMS A.11.E/124, leaf. 270. In his letter to Józef Marlewski, of 22 May 1945, Władysław Kulski struck a similar tone, IPMS, A.11.E/124, leaf 274.

Treasury Committee for Polish Affairs – lost its ability to submit charge files to the UNWCC.[133] The first Polish charge file submitted by the delegate of the Provisional Government of National Unity, Mieczysław Szerer, took until 31 January 1946 to arrive in the Secretariat.[134] In July 1945, following the loss of diplomatic mandate by the Polish Government-in-Exile, Tadeusz Cyprian resigned from the position of delegate to the UNWCC, as a result of which the Polish side was unrepresented at the time of drafting of the indictment brought in October 1945 before the International Military Tribunal at Nuremberg – a fact later cited to explain the limited inclusion of Nazi crimes committed in Poland in the indictment before the IMT.[135]

7 Towards Nuremberg

The loss of diplomatic recognition by the Government-in-Exile on 5 July 1945 closed the door to implementing the objectives of its war-crimes policy developed between 1939 and 1945, including the creation of a justice system for Nazi criminals on domestic and international levels. Nevertheless, the work of the Polish émigré legal circles involved in the Government-in-Exile's efforts to bring perpetrators of war crimes to justice was not without its own impact on the preparation and conduct of the trial ultimately held before the IMT. Their post-war publications are an interesting source of commentary on the trials that have so far remained largely unexplored.

In line with the stipulations of the London Agreement and IMT Charter of 8 August 1945, the signatory states were empowered to nominate judges and deputy judges (Article 2), as well as prosecutors (Article 14) to be responsible for the drafting of the bill of indictment and the preparation of evidence for the trials.[136] The indictment was drafted by prosecutorial teams from the United Kingdom led by Hartley Shawcross; United States, led by Robert H. Jackson; Soviet Union, led by Roman Rudenko; and France, led by François de Menthon and subsequently Auguste Champetier de Ribes. The representatives of the four great powers agreed on the draft and selected the individuals to be charged. According to the recommendations of the London Conference, each

133 Note by Jerzy Litawski, 26 July 1945, AIPN 159.125, leaf 16.

134 UNWCC, Polish Charges against German war criminals, Polish Charge No 42, RN 2244/P/G/42.

135 Tadeusz Cyprian and Jerzy Sawicki, *Sprawy polskie w Procesie Norymberskim* (Poznań: Instytut Zachodni 1956).

136 Charter of the International Military Tribunal of 8 August 1945, A/CN.4/5, available at https://legal.un.org/ilc/

of the delegations was responsible for working out the details of assigned counts of the indictment. Robert Jackson's team handled the first count of the indictment, referring to the criminal offence of conspiracy to commit crimes listed in Article 6 of the IMT Charter; the British delegation prepared the counts pertaining to crimes against peace; the teams from France and the Soviet Union were responsible for charges relating to war crimes and crimes against humanity in the Western (France) and Eastern (USSR) fronts.[137] As the Charter did not provide for the participation of judges or prosecutors from the Allied states occupied by the Third Reich, the Nazi crimes committed in Poland, Czechoslovakia, Yugoslavia, and other countries of Central and Eastern Europe were covered by the Soviet prosecutorial team. Under the wording of Article 21 of the IMT Charter, however, the Tribunal was required to 'take judicial notice of official governmental documents and reports of the United Nations', dealing with war crimes, as well as the "records and findings of military or other tribunals of any United Nations member".[138]

The Nazi crimes committed during the Second World War in Poland were included in the indictment submitted to the IMT, albeit in a degree reflecting neither the scale and consequences of the German policy of terror in occupied Poland nor the scope of damage inflicted. References to the Third Reich's crimes in Poland in the indictment included preparation for the military aggression against Poland; the attack on 1 September 1939; violation of the provisions of Kellogg-Briand Pact and Polish–German declaration of non-violence of 1934; pursuit of an aggressive policy of territorial expansion; deportation of Polish nationals for forced labour; extermination in Auschwitz and Majdanek camps; and murder and prosecution of Polish populations.[139] Moreover, at the request of the Soviet prosecutors, the third part of the indictment incorporated – among acts committed by members of German armed forces on prisoners-of-war – the charge of murdering 11,000 Polish officers in the Forest of Katyń in September 1941, in an attempt to shift the blame for the NKVD's crime onto the leaders of the Third Reich. The IMT's judgment, however, made no reference to Katyń.[140] The fact itself of the inclusion of the Katyń Massacre demonstrates not only a lack of conceptual cohesion among the four prosecutorial teams[141] but also a relative disregard for Polish casualties and the extent of war damage suffered by the country.

137 Priemel, *The Betrayal*, 102.

138 *Cf.* Art. 21 of the IMT Charter.

139 Nuremberg Trial Proceedings Vol. 1. Indictment: Count One: https://avalon.law.yale.edu/imt/count1.asp Count Two: https://avalon.law.yale.edu/imt/count2.asp

140 Judgment of the IMT, A/CN.4/5, https://legal.un.org/ilc/; Mackiewicz, *The crime*, vi–viii; Hirsch, *Soviet Judgment*, 372.

141 On this topic, see Priemel, The Betrayal, 102.

The haphazard selection of cases for inclusion in the indictment – not representative of the scale of war damage suffered by Poland – is something Tadeusz Cyprian explained with the absence of a Polish representative in the UNWCC at the time of the drafting of the IMT Charter and the fact that the communist authorities in Warsaw accepted the London Agreement and IMT Charter of 8 August 1945 with some delay, on 26 September 1945.[142] Cyprian himself, whose appointment to the UNWCC by the Government-in-Exile effectively expired with the latter's loss of diplomatic mandate, remained in London throughout the summer of 1945, and on 31 August 1945 he took the position again but this time as a nominee of the Communist government in Warsaw.[143]

Having no opportunity to influence the shape taken by the indictment in the hands of the prosecutorial teams from the United States, United Kingdom, France, and the USSR, the Provisional Government of National Unity in Warsaw took the decision – at the beginning of October 1945 – to send a delegation of four members to Nuremberg to represent Poland and prepare and submit evidence to the Tribunal concerning the Nazi crimes in Poland.[144] The delegates were: Tadeusz Cyprian, Supreme Court prosecutor and Poland's representative in the UNWCC; Stanisław Piotrowski, former treasury counsel with the General Counsel to the Republic of Poland; Jerzy Sawicki, Head of International Law Section at the Ministry of Justice and Supreme Court prosecutor; and lawyer Stefan Kurowski as chair (future head prosecutor before the Supreme National Tribunal).[145] The presence of the Polish delegation in Nuremberg, having arrived in mid-November 1945, was an unprecedented development. The delegation was initially given only a few weeks to examine the available evidence gathered by the Allies at the Document Centre in Nuremberg and Heidelberg. Through the agency of Tadeusz Cyprian, they were allowed to stay and cooperate in the selection of evidence of German crimes in Poland. Efforts to gain recognition of their legal status were to no avail, however, and they were not allowed to participate in the trial as prosecutors

142 Cyprian, *Faktyczna i prawna sytuacja delegacji polskiej na proces norymberski*, 3–4, Archive of the Polish Academy of Sciences, Poznań Office, Tadeusz Cyprian's Materials.

143 Among the delegates appointed by the Warsaw government to the UNWCC were two of the lawyers having previously worked for the Government-in-Exile –Tadeusz Cyprian and Mieczysław Szerer – whose new nominations came from the Minister of Justice of the Warsaw Government, Henryk Świątkowski, on 31 August 1945; *cf.* Cyprian, *Faktyczna i prawna*, 8.

144 Cyprian, *Ibidem*; Tadeusz Cyprian and Jerzy Sawicki, *Sprawy polskie w Procesie Norymberskim* (Poznań: Instytut Zachodni 1956); Finder and Prusin, *Finder, Prusin.*

145 Cyprian and Sawicki, *Sprawy polskie*, 710.

or in any similar procedural role, or participate in the interrogation of defendants such as Hans Frank. As reminisced by Tadeusz Cyprian himself:

> To a great extent, the matter was one of prestige. Poland had been the first to defy Hitler; her military personnel fought on the Allied side on all the fronts of the world, always as the armed forces of a country having a lawful government belonging to the Allies; the resistance movement in the homeland gained in strength throughout the war, to reach approximately 400,000 armed combatants by the end of hostilities. (...) Moreover, through the war and occupation, Poland lost approximately six million citizens. In that situation, being denied official participation as co-equal prosecutors was deeply difficult to accept.[146]

Polish lawyers examined and translated the evidence, then forwarding it to the American, British, or Soviet delegations. During those works, Stanisław Piotrowski reviewed 38 volumes of Hans Frank's journals, of which a digest was translated during the trial and used as key evidence in the proceedings.[147] At the beginning of 1946, Jerzy Sawicki, in his capacity as a Polish prosecutor, secured Robert Jackson's approval to interrogate German generals and other military personnel suspected of having committed crimes in Poland. Those were SS-Obersturmbannführer Alfred Naujocks, field marshal and army Commander-in-chief during the German invasion of Poland, Walter von Brauschitsch, Chief of the General Staff of the German Army High Command. Heinz Guderian, SS-Obergruppenführer Erich von dem Bach-Zelewski, who was responsible for the suppression of the Warsaw Uprising in summer 1944, SS-Brigadeführer Ernst Rode and the Deputy to the Governor General in General Government Joseph Bühler.[148] In December 1945, a 'Polish indictment' was submitted to the IMT as a supplement to the Allied indictment. It was an official report depicting the Nazi crimes in Poland, compiled by members of the Polish delegation working together with Manred Lachs and Mieczysław Szerer studying the archives of the Polish War Crimes Office in London.[149]

---

146 Cyprian, *Faktyczna i prawna*, 16.

147 Stanisław Piotrowski (ed.), *Dziennik Hansa Franka* (Warszawa: Wydawnictwo Prawnicze 1956).

148 Jerzy Sawicki, *Zburzenie Warszawy. Zeznania generałów niemieckich przed polskim prokuratorem członkiem polskiej delegacji przy Międzynarodowym Trybunale w Norymberdze* (Warszawa: Instytut Wydawniczy Kolumna 1949).

149 The Republic of Poland, *German Crimes against Poland. Official Report of the Polish Government to be submitted to the International Military Tribunal* (London-Nuremberg: December 1945).

Pursuant to the aforementioned Article 21 of the IMT Charter, the report, given the title 'German Crimes against Poland. Official Report of the Polish Government to be submitted to the International Military Tribunal',[150] was admitted into evidence by the Tribunal.

The Polish indictment submitted to the Nuremberg Tribunal in December 1945 counted 120 pages and, following the structure outlined in Article 6 of the IMT Charter, included: (1) crimes against peace and crime of conspiracy to commit such crimes; (2) war crimes (violation of the provisions of the Hague Convention during the September Campaign; crimes committed on prisoners-of-war; policy of Germanization of Polish society; usurpation of sovereign power in occupied territories; resettlements; destruction of culture, works of art, libraries, and public and private property; persecutions of the intelligentsia; deportations for forced labour); and (3) crimes against humanity (policy of terror; mass reprisals; hostage taking; judicial crimes; concentration camps).[151] An additional, voluminous count of the Polish indictment concerned Nazi crimes against Polish and European Jews, including ethnic persecution, violence and legal discrimination, forced resettlements, creation of ghettoes, deportation to concentration camps, and extermination in death camps.[152]

It is worth emphasizing that a substantial part of the 'Polish indictment' presented on behalf of the communist authorities had been written in autumn 1945 in London on the basis of evidence gathered and systematically arranged during the war by the Government-in-Exile. Especially the documents of the War Crimes Office, its publications, and Polish white books and charges submitted to the UNWCC were among the materials used.[153] Not only did the documentation rely on the Government-in-Exile's publications and files on the German crimes, it was built by lawyers formerly working for that government in preparation of post-war trials. For example, Mieczysław Szerer had been a member of Section V of Criminal Procedure and Prisons in the Legislative Works Commission of the Ministry of Justice and participated in the works on the Decree on Criminal Responsibility for War Crimes, whereas Manfred Lachs had since spring 1944 been in charge of the works of Jewish section of the Polish War Crimes Office. Tadeusz Cyprian had served as a member of the LWC and, in 1943–1945, represented the Polish Government-in-Exile in the UNWCC.

150 *Ibidem.*

151 *Ibidem.*

152 More extensively on this topic see: Finder, Prusin, *Justice behind*, 62–69.

153 Cyprian, *Faktyczna i prawna*, 14–15.

The documentation prepared by Polish lawyers was used by the IMT prosecutorial teams, and, at the Polish delegation's request, Seweryna Szmaglewska and Samuel Rajzman –former prisoners of Auschwitz-Birkenau and Treblinka camps – were interrogated at the trial.[154] Hans Frank's journals; Jürgen Stroop's reports on the liquidation of the Warsaw Ghetto; transcripts of interrogations of German military personnel at Nuremberg by Jerzy Sawicki, and many other documents obtained by Polish delegates were subsequently admitted into evidence in Polish trials before the Supreme National Tribunal and ordinary courts.

Thanks to the Polish delegates' endeavours, the problem of Nazi crimes in Poland was more forcefully emphasized at Nuremberg than would have been possible based on the 6 October 1945 indictment alone. Nevertheless, Polish casualties and war damage sustained by Poland were not the focus of the Tribunal's attention. The trials of the heads of the Third Reich's military and civil administration in Poland and of KL Auschwitz staff took place in Poland before the Supreme National Tribunal (*Najwyższy Trybunał Narodowy*) in 1946–1948.[155] Members of the delegation dispatched to Nuremberg – Tadeusz Cyprian, Jerzy Sawicki and Stefan Kurowski – would go on to serve as prosecutors before that Tribunal.

The majority of the members of the Polish Government-in-Exile and of the legal circles involved in the development of its war-crimes policy remained in the West after the war, disputing the Great Four's decisions from Yalta and Potsdam. Their scepticism was also roused by the IMT Charter of 8 August 1945 and the Nuremberg Trials themselves. They took a critical position on Article 2 of the Charter, which reserved the judicial appointments to representatives of the Great Four, thus burying the prospect of the inclusion of any Polish judges in the panel. The lack of a Polish prosecutor and the incorporation of German crimes committed in Poland and against Poles in one joint indictment filed on behalf of all of the states of Eastern Europe by the Soviet Union were perceived as marginalizing the importance and extent of the crimes committed in Poland. A booklet titled *Poland Accuses. An Indictment of the Major German War*

---

154 See Seweryna Szmaglewska, *Niewinni w Norymberdze* (Warszawa: Prószyński i S-ka 2020).

155 See Oktawian Kuc, *The Supreme National Tribunal and International Criminal Law Polish Perspectives on Prosecuting War Criminals* (Routledge 2026); Drumbl, *The Supreme*, 563–602; Grzebyk, *The Role*, 603–633, Lubecka, *Niemiecki zbrodniarz*. Cyprian and Sawicki, *Siedem*; Drumbl, *The Supreme*, 563–602; Grzebyk, *The Role*, 603–633, Lubecka, *Niemiecki zbrodniarz*.

Criminals,[156] published in spring of 1946 by the Council of Polish Political Parties in London and providing some commentary on the structure of the trial itself and of the indictment negotiated by the great powers, was an attempt to respond to the exclusion of representatives of the Polish Government-in-Exile from the Nuremberg Trials, as well as Polish judges and prosecutors.[157]

In the preface, Bronisław Kuśnierz, Minister of Justice in the Government-in-Exile, recounted the extent of war damage suffered by Poland, the number of civilian casualties and the nature of the German crimes, committed with 'savage brutality' as a 'medium to the cultural, economic and physical destruction of the Polish nation'. And in spite of all that, as the justice minister emphatically remonstrated:

> the Indictment presented to the International Military Tribunal at Nuremberg by the four accusing Powers has almost entirely omitted the German crimes committed against Poland. During the trial itself in Nuremberg, these crimes were also treated very cursorily and glossed over as if of secondary importance, whereas in reality they were, both in quality and quantity, so enormous that to have shown them in their true perspective would have placed Poland in the forefront as the main victim of the war crimes.[158]

---

156 The Council of Polish Political Parties, *Poland Accuses. An Indictment of the Major German War Criminals* (London: The Montgomeryshire Printing & Stationery Co., Limited 1946). Typescript titled 'Polska Oskarża', IPMS, Typescripts & Manuscripts, B.1766.

157 The Council of Polish Political Parties was a representative body of Polish authorities and political parties in exile, formed on 17 September 1945. Its objectives were to 'combine the efforts of Polish political parties for the reconstruction of a fully independent and truly democratic Polish State and assurance of self-determination to the Polish Nation' and included 'co-operation with democratic political organizations from other nations'. Cited after Anna Siwik, 'Próby utworzenia reprezentacji ugrupowań politycznych na emigracji w latach 1946–1949'. *Dzieje Najnowsze* XXXVIII (1996), 71–87, here: 71.

158 The preface made no mention of the Decree of the President of the Republic of Poland on Criminal Responsibility for War Crimes or of the Polish government's initiatives to win support for bringing the war criminals to justice as a matter of their personal responsibility. Komarnicki (his predecessor as Minister of Justice) wrote to Kuśnicki a letter with the following reproach: 'the publication *POLAND ACCUSSES* paints a counterfactual picture of the Polish Government's wartime works on criminal responsibility for war crimes. The publication ignores the role of the highest powers of the state, as expressed by the Decree [of the President of the Republic of Poland on Criminal Responsibility for War Crimes]. [It] is, therefore, out of accordance with the applicable legislation' – Wacław Komarnicki's letter to Bronisław Kuśnierz, 1 November 1946, 3; IPMS, Kol. 38/39.

The 'Polish indictment' followed the structure of the charges brought before the IMT and covered three categories of crimes: crimes against peace (part I), war crimes (part II), and crimes against humanity and mass murder (part III). A succession of subchapters detailed the criminal nature of the activities of the military and civil administration of the German Reich and offered a synthesis of available information on the crimes committed in Poland, previously published in Polish white books and charge files submitted to the UNWCC.[159] The structure of the brochure reflects the following taxonomy of crimes: I. Crimes against peace: subversive activities in Poland; denunciation of the Polish-German declaration of non-aggression of 26 January 1934; the accomplice in the crime; II. War crimes: 1. violation of the laws and customs of war during the Polish-German campaign in 1939 (bombardment of open towns and the civilian population; atrocities committed on soldiers, prisoners of war and civilians); 2. violation of the laws and customs of war during the German occupation of Poland (usurpation of sovereignty; Germanization); and 3. common crimes (murders and ill-treatment of the population; murders and Ill-treatment of prisoners of war; deportation of the population for forced labour; expulsion of the population and pillage of property; wanton destruction of towns and villages; looting of works of art and destruction of culture; the economic plundering of Poland; looting of public property; looting of private property; and looting of properties under the special protection of the law of nations); III. Crimes against humanity and mass murders: 1. concentration camps, 2. extermination of the Jews; 3. the fight against religion; and 4. the fight against youth and children.

The purpose of *Poland Accuses* was to bring the most egregious German crimes into daylight, emphasizing their systematic and large-scale nature, aimed at extermination. Hence, one of its noticeable shortcomings was that the names of specific perpetrators are included only in some cases. For example, the publication fails to incorporate the data from the Polish charges to the UNWCC, such as the names of the commandants and personnel of the concentration camps described in the booklet.

An important novel quality compared to the Government-in-Exile's prior publications on the crimes committed in occupied Poland is the inclusion of crimes against peace (violation of the principle of *pacta sunt servanda*; military aggression) and war crimes committed by the Soviet Union.[160] *Poland Accuses* mentions Adolf Hitler's speech of 22 August 1939, announcing the conclusion of a German-Soviet non-aggression pact of 23 August 1939 along

159 *Poland Accuses*, v (list of contents).

160 *Poland Accuses*, 1–8.

with a secret protocol dividing zones of interest in Central and Eastern Europe – clearly revealing premeditated preparations 'for this plot against peace and against the integrity and independence of the Polish state'.[161] In the view of Polish lawyers, the signing of the Molotov-Ribbentrop Treaty was the final stage of preparation for German aggression against Poland involving persecution and planned extermination of the population of the occupied territories (the description uses the term 'genocide'):

> The signing of the Soviet-German Agreement (...) was the last link in the German preparations. This act made possible the attack on the existence of the Polish State and nation, on which, in consequence, the crime of genocide was systematically committed throughout the German occupation of Poland.[162]

It was argued that the adoption, on 28 September 1939, of additional provisions to the Molotov-Ribbentrop Treaty – known as a 'friendship and frontier treaty' – established the commitment, by the two powers acting in collusion, of a war crime in the form of usurpation of sovereignty in the occupied territory (in violation of Articles 42 and 55 of the Hague Convention).

The Soviet crimes are described in much more detail in the context of the Nuremberg Trials in Wiktor Sukiennicki's 100-page typescript 'Poland Accuses Russia' (1947).[163] Sukiennicki's core assumption in his work was the recognition of the catalogue of crimes stipulated in the IMT Charter and reflected in the IMT's Nuremberg judgment of 1 October 1946 as principles of international law applicable *erga omnes*, in keeping with the resolution of the United Nations General Assembly of 11 December 1946.[164] Accordingly, he argued that if the commission of similar crimes by persons holding the reins of power in a sovereign state organization were to have been established by evidence, the court would not have hesitated to convict.[165] Sukiennicki's indictment included crimes defined in the IMT Charter: crimes against peace (criminal conspiracy, responsibility for causing the Second World War), war crimes (murder, ill-treatment and deportation of civilian population; policy of terror

161 'Polska Oskarża' typescript, 8.
162 *Poland Accuses*, 4.
163 W. Sukiennicki, *Poland Accuses Russia*, IPMS, Kol. 214, vol. 16.
164 'Principles of International Law Recognized in the Charter of the Nuremberg Tribunal and in the Judgment of the Tribunal'. *The Yearbook of the International Law Commission* II (1950), par. 97, available at http://legal.un.org/ilc/texts/instruments/english/draft_articles/7_1_1950.pdf (accessed: 15 June 2025).
165 Sukiennicki, *Poland Accuses*, 2.

in occupied territories; murder and ill-treatment of prisoners of war; the Katyń Massacre), crimes against humanity (extermination of the civilian population, enslavement, mass deportations, the Gulag). It also added two further chapters: 'Common crimes' and 'Pillaging of public and private property'. The accusation of acts committed 'against the Polish Nation and State in (...) 1939–1947' was levied against the leaders of the Communist Party exercising the "autocratic rule of the Soviet State', the leadership of Soviet Armed Forces and NKVD and secret or open agents dependent on those authorities and taking orders and instructions from them.[166] Sukiennicki's work has never been published, but a large part of his arguments is cited in Bronisław Kuśnierz's *Stalin and the Poles. An indictment of the Soviet Leaders* (1949).[167]

Both of the 'Polish indictments' – penned while the Nuremberg Trials were already in progress – demonstrate that the problem of justice for war crimes and the need to highlight in the international forum the dramatic fate suffered by the Polish state and nation in the Second World War remained important points on the Government-in-Exile's agenda even after the loss of diplomatic recognition.[168] The critical analysis of the provisions of the IMT Charter precluding the participation of representatives of the occupied states and their judiciaries and prosecution services, the treatment of the German crimes committed in Poland as though they had been of secondary importance in the Nuremberg indictment, and of the omission of the Soviet crimes from the Allied designs of a justice system for war crimes, is an important voice in the debate on the history and legacy of the Nuremberg Trial.

The caesura of 1945 did not mark the end of the commitment of lawyers affiliated with the Polish Government-in-Exile to the pursuit of justice for victims of crimes committed during the Second World War and to the development of international criminal law. The political upheaval at the end of the war and the new reality divided by the Iron Curtain, personal choices to return to communist Poland or to remain in exile had a significant impact on their postwar destinies. However, the paths of their careers and research were significantly marked by their war-time experiences and involvement in developing the principles of accountability for international crimes. Manfred Lachs, Stefan Glaser, Wacław Komarnicki, and Tadeusz Cyprian continued their studies

166 Sukiennicki, *Poland Accuses*, 5.

167 Bronisław Kuśnierz, *Stalin and the Poles. An indictment of the Soviet leaders*. With a foreword by August Zaleski (London 1949).

168 Concerning the endeavours of the Polish Government-in-Exile to establish the criminal responsibility of the perpetrators of Soviet crimes in 1945–1956 and the use of Polish government documentation on the Katyń Massacre in Nuremberg Trials, see Wolsza, *'Katyń'*, 50ff.

on the Nuremberg Principles and the directions of development of international criminal law and the human-rights system.[169] Cyprian co-authored with Jerzy Sawicki a significant number of publications devoted to the legacy of the IMT and Nuremberg successor trials, Polish wartime losses in light of the trials of Nazi criminals, and coined the term 'Nuremberg law'(*prawo norymberskie*).[170] After the war, Stefan Glaser continued his studies in international criminal law as a lecturer in international law at the universities of Liège and Louvain and was one of the initiators of the Convention on the Non-Applicability of Statutory Limitations to War Crimes and Crimes Against Humanity.[171] Bohdan Winiarski and Manfred Lachs served as judges and presidents of the International Court of Justice at The Hague. Bohdan Winiarski served as a judge of the International Court of Justice in 1946–1967, including in 1961–1964 as its President. He was succeeded in that position by Professor Manfred Lachs, who served as a judge until 1993, and in 1973–1976 was the

---

169 Among others see: Stefan Glaser, 'La Charte du Tribunal de Nuremberg et les nouveaux principes du droit international'. *Revue pénale suisse* 63 (1948), 13–38; *idem*, 'La guerre d'agression à la lumière des sources du droit international'. *Revue Generale de Droit International Public* 3 (1953); *idem*, 'La Responsabilité de l'individu devant le droit international'. *Revue pénale suisse* 1949; *idem*, 'Infraction internationale, ses éléments constitutifs et ses aspects juridiques', in *Revue internationale de droit comparé* (Paris: Librairie générale de droit et de jurisprudence 1957); idem, *Droit International Pénal Conventionnel* vol. I (Brussels: Etablissements Emile Bruylant 1970); idem, *Droit International Pénal Conventionnel* vol. II (Brussels: Etablissements Emile Bruylant 1978); Manfred Lachs, *War Crimes. An attempt to define the issue* (London 1945); *idem*, 'The Unwritten Laws of Warfare'. Reprinted from *Tulane Law Review* XX (1945) 120–128; *idem*, 'Le Jugement de Nuremberg'. *Revue Internationale de Droit Penal* 3–4 (1946); Stefan Glaser, 'La Charte du Tribunal de Nuremberg et les nouveaux principes du droit international'. *Revue pénale suisse* 63 (1948), 13–38; Manfred Lachs, 'Walka o definicję agresji'. *Wojskowy Przegląd Prawniczy* 3 (1952); Wacław Komarnicki, 'La définition de l'agresseur dans le droit international moderne (Volume 75)', in Académie de Droit International, *Collected Courses of the Hague Academy of International Law* (Paris 1949).

170 Tadeusz Cyprian and Jerzy Sawicki, *Prawo Norymberskie: Bilans i perspektywy* (Warszawa: 1948); Cyprian and Sawicki, *Sprawy polskie*; 'Zur Nichtverjährbarkeit von Verbrechen gegen das Völkerrecht'. *Staat und Recht* (Berlin Jg, 18, 1969); Tadeusz Cyprian, Marian Muszkat and Jerzy Sawicki, *Le droit polonais au service de la paix dans la lutte contr les criminels de guerre: rapports présentés au Congrés International de juristes-democrates et á l'Association Internationale de droit pénal* (Warszawa: GKBZHP 1947), Tadeusz Cyprian and Jerzy Sawicki, *Procesy wielkich zbrodniarzy wojennych w Polsce: Najwyższy Trybunał Narodowy* (Warszawa: Czytelnik 1949); Tadeusz Cyprian and Jerzy Sawicki, *Walka o zasady norymberskie (1945– 1955)* (Warszawa: 1956).

171 Wierczyńska, Wierczyński, 'Stefan Glaser'; Convention on the Non-Applicability of Statutory Limitations to War Crimes and Crimes against Humanity, 26 November 1968, UNTS v. 754 (p. 73) (no. 10823).

President of the ICJ.[172] Tadeusz Cyprian played, as a prosecutor of the Supreme National Tribunal, a leading role in the formation of the Polish justice system for Nazi criminals.

The Polish legal minds involved in the making of the Government-in-Exile's policy on bringing war criminals to justice made lasting contributions to the development of international criminal law, earning for themselves a place in its history. Their legacy and their works themselves unquestionably deserve to be revisited and made the subject of further study and reflection.

---

172 Manfred Lachs also served as a member of the Polish delegation to the UN General Assembly, several times chairing the UNGA's Legal Committee. See Marta Sobiecka and Mikołaj Ślęzak (eds.), *Manfred Lachs, „W podróży, którą nazywamy życiem"* (Warszawa: IKMP Sapere Aude 2015).

Conclusion

The presented research confirms that the problem of prosecution and punishment of war criminals belonged to the political priorities of the Polish Government-in-Exile. The key directions of the Sikorski Cabinet's war-crimes policy were determined as early as at the turn of 1939/1940 and included international information campaigns on the atrocities committed in Poland and Europe, documentation of crimes, gaining Allied support for the demand to punish individuals violating the laws and customs of war and developing a legislative and institutional framework for future criminal trials. These objectives were pursued consistently, with involvement from almost all government departments, throughout the war.

Poland's war-crimes policy stood out due to its systematic approach, that included collecting evidence, developing communication channels with the homeland, and establishing specialized structures responsible for securing documentation. In autumn 1943, the 'German Archive' at the Ministry of Interior included approx. 4,000 names of alleged war criminals and in May 1945 about 10,000 records. Along with reports on all aspects of life under the occupation and war crimes evidence obtained since the autumn 1939, this was the basis for the compilation of the Polish UNWCC charge files. In effect, between February 1944 and July 1945, the Polish War Crimes Office submitted 41 charges to the UNWCC, listing over 1,000 suspects.

The shape of the war-crimes policy of General Sikorski's Cabinet was determined by both international policy factors and internal political ones. Of key importance was the reserve on the part of the Western powers towards the demand for punishing war criminals, tense relations between Poland and the USSR, and the weakening of the international position of General Sikorski's Cabinet after Stalin broke off diplomatic relations with Poland, as well as the strong involvement of the representatives of European governments of occupied countries in exile. The cooperation between the Polish and Czechoslovak governments in 1940–1943 around the issue of security and maintaining the European balance of power after the war could not succeed due to the USSR's interference, but it gave rise to development of a strong common position on the question of accountability for Nazi crimes. Polish and Czechoslovak lawyers drafted the first inter-allied declaration on the punishment of war criminals, which was adopted by representatives of nine Governments-in-Exile on 13 January 1942 at St. James's Palace in London and implemented by the work of Inter-Allied Commission on the Punishment of War Crimes and United Nations War Crimes Commission. Through their advocacy for accountability for crimes committed under Nazi rule, coordinated information strategies and diplomatic campaigns, and contribution to London International Assembly and Cambridge Commission representatives of the small states developed a political forum and tools to influence the decision-making of the Great Powers, independently from the constrains of power politics.

At the domestic policy level, an important factor was the expectations of the Polish society for severe punishment of the perpetrators and the strong involvement of the underground movement in occupied Poland in documenting German and Soviet crimes, and in the discussion on criminal liability of the perpetrators. Thanks to the cooperation with the London government of legal scholars and experts in criminal, constitutional and international law from the universities of the Second Polish Republic, e.g. Wacław Komarnicki, Stefan Glaser, Tadeusz Cyprian, Bohdan Winiarski, Wiktor Sukiennicki, or Władysław Kulski, the assumptions of the Polish doctrine of accountability for war criminals constituted a critical elaboration of the debate on the development of the law of nations from the inter-war period. That doctrine was predicated on the assumption of holding violators of international law personally accountable by putting them on trial. Under the Polish concept, an effective justice system for war crimes would require a division of jurisdiction between domestic and international courts, guarantees of extradition, and adaptation of substantive law on international and domestic level.

The development of Polish war crimes policy culminated with the drafting of the Decree of the President of the Republic of Poland on Criminal Responsibility for War Crimes in 1942 and its promulgation on 30 March 1943, half a year before the establishment of the UNWCC. The Decree was the first domestic enactment of an Allied power during the Second World War laying down the rules of individual responsibility for violations of international law as well as the basics of substantive law with a view to domestic criminal trials after the war. The arguments presented by Polish lawyers in the course of works on this law touched upon essential questions in debate on the national and international jurisdiction over war criminals and provided possible solutions. They emphasized the significance of effective jurisdiction over war criminals, which required a sound legal foundation imposing penalties proportionate to the severity of the crimes and underlined the importance of distinguishing the new forms of criminal activities, committed by the German Reich in occupied territories against the civilian population (such as organized mass executions, concentration camps, torture, expulsion of civilians, slavery, starvation, enforced sterilization, or insemination) from offences defined in national penal codes. New legislation and definitions of war crimes were thereby to overcome the legal gap in this respect and address the new genre of criminality imposed in occupied territories. The systemic and organized character of the crimes, committed within the legal and administrative systems, legitimizing the policy of discrimination and annihilation was another distinction of Nazi violence. Therefore, the question of personal liability for war crimes, along with the grounds for excluding criminal responsibility such as pleas of superior orders, higher necessity or the question of the binding force of unjust positive law imposed by the German Reich, were of key importance in the debate on the Presidential Decree on the Individual Liability for War Crimes. The rules and arguments underlying the Polish war crimes policy were also applied in the Polish UNWCC charges and Commission's conceptual work, thus providing important contribution to the international discussion on the definitions of international offences, including crimes against humanity and on the principles of accountability for war crimes.

Due to the comprehensiveness, broad scope and early starting point of work aimed at bringing war criminals to justice, the policy of the Polish authorities in the discussed area distinguished itself significantly from the conservative stance of the Great Powers. The example of the work of the Polish government proves that the process of formulating the Allied states' position on the problem of accountability for war crimes had reached an advanced stage long before the signing of the Moscow Declaration (30 October 1943) or the drafting of the Charter of the International Military Tribunal (8 August 1945). This process was characterized by two dynamics, with a fundamental role played by the governments of the occupied countries, which already at the turn of 1941/1942 began international cooperation in the field of documenting war crimes and drafting principles for punishing their perpetrators. The contribution of the Polish government as the initiator of these efforts deserves special emphasis.

The accomplishments of Polish lawyers involved during the Second World War in preparing a legal and institutional framework for the effective prosecution of war criminals undoubtedly require further research. A valuable extension would be an in-depth study of their biographies considering both their contribution to the development of international criminal law in the interbellum period and the impact of the experiences gained during the war on their careers after 1945. Little-explored topics from this area include the cooperation between the government and the organs of the national judiciary operating within the structures of the underground movement in occupied Poland, as well as the significance of the concepts developed by them for the course of trials of war criminals in Poland based on the provisions defined by the PKWN Decree of 31 August 1944. An analysis of the records of trials before the Supreme National Tribunal and common courts would allow determining to what extent the results of the investigative and documentary work of the Polish authorities in exile were used in the trials of Nazi criminals in Poland after 1945. A similar analysis could be made for the case of war-crimes trials held before the American, British, and French tribunals in occupied Germany. A critical study of the Polish charges submitted to the United Nations War Crimes Commission and of the forms of cooperation between UNWCC members between 1945 and 1948 can also provide valuable knowledge about the enforcement of the Allied war-crimes trial programme in the initial phase of the Cold War, when the strong polarisation between East and West threatened to jeopardize the goals set in 1943 by UNWCC's founders who suddenly found themselves on two sides of the Iron Curtain. The contributions provided by the lawyers from occupied countries, in particular from Eastern Europe, to the wartime efforts of the Allies to establish accountability for international crimes, extends past the caesura of 1945. Exploring this body of work, the histories of efforts made by actors with less political agency and the individual commitment of lawyers, diplomats, and intellectuals shall allow us to complement existing narratives and compile a more comprehensive understanding of the history and legacy of the Nuremberg Trial.

Bibliography

Abbreviations

AAN	Polish Modern Archives (*Archiwum Akt Nowych*)
AIPN	Archives of the Institute of National Remembrance (*Archiwum Instytutu Pamięci Narodowej*)
CROWCASS	Central Registry of War Criminals and Security Suspects
Dz. U.	Journal of Laws of the Republic of Poland (*Dziennik Ustaw*)
Dz.U.R.P.	Journal of Laws of the Republic of Poland (*Dziennik Ustaw Rzeczypospolitej Polskiej*)
GG	General Government (*Generalne Gubernatorstwo*)
IPMS	Polish Institute and Sikorski Museum (*Instytut Polski i Muzeum im. gen. Sikorskiego w Londynie*)
LWC	Legislative Works Commission (*Komisja Prac Ustawodawczych*)
(C)CHA	(Cabinet) Committee for Home Affairs (*Komitet Ministrów dla Spraw Kraju*, KMSK, KSK)
LIA	London International Assembly
MoI	Ministry of the Interior (*Ministerstwo Spraw Wewnętrznych*, MSW)
MoID	Ministry of Information and Documentation (*Ministerstwo Informacji i Dokumentacji*, MIiD)
MoND	Ministry of National Defence (*Ministerstwo Obrony Narodowej*, MON)
MFA	Ministry of Foreign Affairs (*Ministerstwo Spraw Zagranicznych*, MSZ)
IMT	International Military Tribunal
NKVD	People's Commissariat of Internal Affairs (USSR)
SNT	Supreme National Tribunal (*Najwyższy Trybunał Narodowy*, NTN)
UN	United Nations
PISM	Polish Institute and Sikorski Museum
PTA	Polish Telegraphic Agency (*Polska Agencja Telegraficzna*, PAT)
PCK	Polish Red Cross (*Polski Czerwony Krzyż*)
PKWN	Polish Committee of National Liberation (*Polski Komitet Wyzwolenia Narodowego*)
RGBl	Reich Law Gazette (*Reichsgesetzblatt*)
SA	*die Sturmabteilungen der NSDAP* (NSDAP Storm Troopers)
SHAEF	Supreme Headquarters Allied Expeditionary Force
SS	*die Schutzstaffel der NSDAP* (NSDAP Protection Squadrons)
STGB	*Strafgesetzbuch* (The German 1871 Penal Code)
TNA	The National Archives in Kew (United Kingdom)

TRJN	Provisional Government of National Unity (*Tymczasowy Rząd Jedności Narodowej*)
UNWCC	United Nations War Crimes Commission
ZWZ-AK	Union of Armed Struggle/Home Army (*Związek Walki Zbrojnej – Armia Krajowa*)

Universities

JCU	John Casimir University in Lviv (Lwów in Polish, Lemberg in German) (Uniwersytet Jana Kazimierza we Lwowie)
JU	Jagiellonian University, (Uniwersytet Jagielloński)
SBU	Stephen Báthory University in Vilnius (Wilno at the time, in Polish) (Uniwersytet Stefana Batorego w Wilnie)

Sources

Archives

Polish Institute and Sikorski Museum, London (PISM)

PISM	Polish Institute and Sikorski Museum
PRM	Praesidium of the Council of Ministers (Prezydium Rady Ministrów), miscellanea
PRM-K	Chancellery of the Praesidium of the Council of Ministers (Kancelaria-laria prm)
PRM-l	Stefania Liebermanowa's Materials
A.5	National Council of the Republic of Poland
A.9	Ministry of the Interior
A.10	Ministry of Information and Documentation
A.11	Ministry of Foreign Affairs
A.12	Polish Embassy in London
A.20	Ministry of Justice
A.21	Ministry of Preparatory Works
AXII.1	Cabinet of the Commander-in-Chief
Kol. 38	Wacław Komarnicki Collection
Kol. 133	Adam Ciołkosz Collection
Kol. 183	Stanisław Stroński Collection
Kol. 213	Polish Lawyers' Association (Stowarzyszenie Prawników Polskich) in the USA
Kol. 214	Wiktor Sukiennicki Collection
Kol. 252	Stefan Glaser Collection
Kol. 403	Polish Lawyers' Association (Stowarzyszenie Prawników Polskich) in the United Kingdom

Polish Modern Archives

Collection of the Ministry of Justice of the Government-in-Exile.
Collection of the Ministry of Information and Documentation of the Government-in-Exile.
Collection of the Ministry of Foreign Affairs.
Collection of the Government Delegation for Poland.

Hoover Institution Archives

800/42/0 Ministry of Foreign Affairs

Archives of the Institute of National Remembrance

AIPN BU 159 MoI London, Polish War Crimes Office
AIPN BU 160 Ministry of Justice London
AIPN BU 1804 Activities of the Government-in-Exile

Archives of the United Nations War Crimes Commission

UNWCC, Reel 14–15 Polish Charges against German War Criminals.
UNWCC, Reel 33–34 Minutes of Meetings.
UNWCC, Reel 41 Poland. Correspondence with national offices.

The National Archives KEW

FO 371 Foreign Office: Political Departments, General Correspondence
PRO, PREM1 Public Record Office. Prime Minister's Office: Correspondence and Papers
PRO PREM 4 Public Record Office. Prime Minister's Office: Confidential Papers
TNA LCO 2 Lord Chancellor's Office and Lord Chancellor's Department
Archive of the Polish Academy of Sciences, Poznań Office (Archiwum Polskiej Akademii Nauk Oddział w Poznaniu) Tadeusz Cyprian's Materials

Printed Sources

Source Editions Published by the Polish Government-in-Exile

Extermination of the Polish People and Colonisation by German Nationals (New York: Polish Information Centre 1941).
German Exploitation of Polish Forests (New York: Polish Information Centre 1941).
German Destruction of Cultural Life in Poland (New York: Polish Information Centre: 1941).

German Organisation of Distribution in Poland (New York: Polish Information Centre 1941).

German Iron and Steel Policies (New York: Polish Information Centre 1941).

German Organisation of Courts in General Government of Poland (New York: Polish Information Centre 1941).

German Persecution of Religious Life in Poland (New York: Polish Information Centre).

German Withdrawal in the East: A Study in Vital German and Polish Statistics (London: Polish Research Centre 1941).

German Failures in Poland. Natural Obstacles to Nazi Population Policy (London: Polish Research Centre 1942).

L'invasion allemande en Pologne: documents, témoignages authentifiés et photographies / recueillis par le Centre d'Information et de Documentation du Gouvernement Polonais; av.-prop. par Édouard Herriot (Paris: Flammarion 1940).

L'Occupation Allemande et Sovietique de la Pologne. Note adressée en date du 3 Mai 1941 aux Gouvernements des Puissances alliées et neutres au sujet de l'occupation allemande et soviétique de la Pologne (London: République de Pologne Ministère des Affaires Étrangères 1941).

Polish Ministry of Information, *The German Fifth Column in Poland* (London, Melbourne: Hutchinson & Co 1941).

Polish Ministry of Information, *The German New Order in Poland* (London: Hutchinson & Co. 1942).

Poland and Danzig (London: Polish Research Centre 1941).

Poland and the USSR, 1921–1941 (London: Polish Research Centre 1941).

Polish Ministry of Information, *Poland's Martyrdom: The German Invasion in Photographs and Facts.* Introduction by P. J. Noel-Baker (London: M.I. Kolin 1940).

Polish Ministry of Information, *Martyrdom of Polish Professors* (London 1942).

Polish Ministry of Information, *The Quest for German Blood: Policy of Germanization in Poland* (London 1943).

Polish Ministry of Information, *The Legal Position of Jews in Poland* (London 1942).

Polish Ministry of Information *The Protestant Church in Poland* (London 1942).

Polish Ministry of Information, *The Nazi Kultur in Poland* (London: Hutchinson 1945).

The Mass Extermination of Jews in German occupied Poland: note addressed to the Governments of the United Nations on December 17th, 1942, and other documents (New York: Republic of Poland. Ministry of Foreign Affairs 1943).

The Orthodox Eastern Church in Poland. Past and Present (London: Polish Research Centre 1942).

The Persecution of Jews in German-occupied Poland (London: Free Europe 1940).

The Council of Polish Political Parties, *Poland Accuses: An Indictment of the Major German War Criminals* (London: The Montgomeryshire Printing & Stationery Co, Limited 1946).

The German Invasion of Poland: Polish Black Book Containing Documents, Authenticated Reports and Photographs. Preface by the Archbishop of York (1940). Published by the authority of Polish Ministry of Information (London, Melbourne: Hutchinson & Co.(Publishers) LTD 1940).

The Story of Wilno (London: Polish Research Centre 1942).

The Truth about Poland (New York: Polish Information Centre 1944).

The Protestant Churches in Poland (London: Polish Research Centre 1944).

The Soviet Occupation of Poland (New York: Polish Information Centre 1941).

Source Editions

Armia Krajowa w dokumentach 1939–1945, vols. I–VI (London: Studium Polski Podziemnej 1970–1989).

Auber J., (comp.), *Ustawodawstwo polskie na Emigracyi*, foreword by Wiktor Turek (Tehran: Delegatura Ministerstwa Pracy i opieki Społecznej w Teheranie, Wydział Kulturalno-Oświatowy 1943).

Auswärtiges Amt, *Die polnischen Greueltaten an den Volksdeutschen in Polen*, (Berlin 1939).

Auswärtiges Amt, *Polnische Dokumente zur Vorgeschichte des Krieges* (Berlin 1940).

Bartoszewski W., Zofia Lewinówna (comps.), *Ten jest z ojczyzny mojej: Polacy z pomocą Żydom 1939–1945*, third supplemented edition (Warszawa: Stowarzyszenie ŻIH – Świat Książki 2007).

Central Welfare Council (*Rada Główna Opiekuńcza*), *Likwidacja skutków wojny w dziedzinie stosunków prawnych i ekonomicznych w Polsce* (Warszawa 1917).

Czechoslovak Ministry of Foreign Affairs Department of Information, German Massacres in Occupied Czechoslovakia Following the Attack on Reinhard Heydrich (London 1942).

Długołęcki P. (ed.), *W obliczu Zagłady. Rząd RP na uchodźstwie wobec Żydów* (Warszawa: PISM 2021); English edition: Długołęcki, P. (ed.) et al., *Confronting the Holocaust. Documents on the Polish Government-in-Exile's policy Concerning Jews 1939–1945*, (Warszawa: PISM 2022).

Grabowski W. (comp.), Protokoły Posiedzeń Komitetu Ministrów dla Spraw Kraju, (Warszawa: IPN 2008).

Hułas M. (ed.), *Polskie Dokumenty Dyplomatyczne 1940* (Warszawa: Polski Instytut Spraw Międzynarodowych 2010).

Inter-Allied Information Centre, *Punishment for War Crimes. Collective Notes Presented to the Governments of Great Britain the USSR and the USA and Relative Correspondence* (London: His Majesty's Stationery Office 1942).

Kulski W. M. Potulicki (comps.), *Współczesna Europa polityczna: zbiór umów międzynarodowych 1919–1939* (Warszawa: Księgarnia Powszechna 1939).

Mackiewicz J. (ed.), Władysław Anders (Preface), *The crime of Katyn: Facts & Documents* (London: Polish Cultural Foundation 1965–1982). Polish edition: *Zbrodnia katyńska w świetle dokumentów* (London: Gryf Publications 1948).

The Molotov Notes on German Atrocities. Notes Sent by V. M. Molotov, People's Commissar for Foreign Affairs, to All Governments which the U.S.S.R. Has Diplomatic Relations (London: H.M. Stationery Office 1942).

Pilichowski C. (ed.), *Ściganie i karanie sprawców zbrodni wojennych i zbrodni przeciwko ludzkości: wybór dokumentów* (Warszawa: GKBZHWP 1978).

Pospieszalski K. M. (ed.), Crawford G., Anessi Thomas, Kotowski Krzysztof (transl.), *Documenta Occupationis* (vol. V): *Nazi Occupation „Law" in Poland. Part I: Incorporated Territories* (Poznań: Institute for Western Affairs 2019). Polish Edition: Pospieszalski, K. M. (ed.) *Documenta Occupationis*: *Hitlerowskie "prawo" okupacyjne w Polsce* Cz. 1 Ziemie wcielone: wybór dokumentów (Poznań: Instytut Zachodni 1952).

Pospieszalski K. M. (ed.), Crawford G., Anessi Thomas, Kotowski Krzysztof (transl.), *Documenta Occupationis* (vol. VI): *Nazi Occupation „Law" in Poland. Part II: General Government* (Poznań: Institute for Western Affairs 2019). Polish Edition: Pospieszalski, K. M. (ed.) *Documenta Occupationis*: *Hitlerowskie "prawo" okupacyjne w Polsce*. Cz. 2: *Cz. 2.* Generalna Gubernia: wybór dokumentów i próba syntezy (Poznań: Instytut Zachodni 1958).

The Republic of Poland, *German Crimes against Poland. Official Report of the Polish Government to Be Submitted to the International Military Tribunal* (London-Nuremberg: December 1945).

Rojek W. (ed.), *Polskie dokumenty dyplomatyczne wrzesień–grudzień 1939* (Warszawa: PISM 2007).

Sontag R. J., James S. Beddie (eds.), *Nazi–Soviet Relations 1939–1941: Documents from the Archives of the German Foreign Office* (Washington: U.S. Department of State 1948).

Stanisławska S. (comp.), *Sprawa polska w czasie drugiej wojny światowej na arenie międzynarodowej. Zbiór dokumentów* (Warszawa: PWN 1965).

UNWCC, *History of United Nations War Crimes Commission and the Development of the Laws of War* (London: His Majesty's Stationery Office 1948).

UNWCC, *Law Reports of Trial of War Criminals*, vols. I–XV (London 1947–1949), available at https://www.loc.gov/item/2011525464/ (last accessed 11 October 2024).

Winiarski B., *Wybór źródeł do nauki prawa międzynarodowego* (Warszawa 1938).

Zgórniak M. (ed.), Wojciech Rojek, Andrzej Suchcitz (comps.), *Protokoły posiedzeń Rady Ministrów Rzeczypospolitej Polskiej*, vols. I–VIII (Kraków: Wydawnictwo Secesja 1994–2008).

National Laws (Poland)

Declaration of the Government of National Unity (*Deklaracja Rządu Jedności Narodowej*), 24 February 1942, Dz.U.RP 1943.8.40.

Decree of the President of the Republic of Poland – Law on the System of Courts Martial (*Dekret Prezydenta RP – Prawo o ustroju sądów wojskowych*), 29 September 1936, Dz.U.1936.76.536.

Decree of the President of the Republic of Poland on the Nullity of the Occupation Authorities' Legal Acts (*Dekret Prezydenta RP o nieważności aktów prawnych władz okupacyjnych*), 30 November 1939, Dz.U.1939.102.1006.

Decree of the President of the Republic of Poland on Criminal Responsibility for War Crimes (*Dekret Prezydenta RP o odpowiedzialności karnej za zbrodnie wojenne*), 30 March 1943, Dz.U.RP.1943.3.6.

Decree of the President of the Republic of Poland on Gathering and Securing the Evidence in Cases of Common Crimes (*Dekret Prezydenta RP o zbieraniu i zabezpieczaniu dowodów w sprawach o przestępstwa pospolite*), 29 April 1940, Dz. U.1940.9.23.

Decree of the President of the Republic of Poland on the Appointment of a Commission in Connection with the Outcome of the Defensive War in 1939 (*Dekret Prezydenta Rzeczypospolitej o powołaniu Komisji w związku z wynikiem kampanii wojennej 1939 roku*), Dz.U.1940.10.27.

Decree of the President of the Republic of Poland on the Protection of Certain Interests of the State (*Dekret Prezydenta RP o ochronie niektórych interesów państwa*), 22 November 1938, Dz.U.1938.91.623.

Decree of the President of the Republic of Poland on the Polish Faculty of Law at the University of Oxford (*Dekret Prezydenta RP o Polskim Wydziale Prawa w Uniwersytecie w Oksfordzie*), 14 April 1944, Dz.U.1944.5.11.

Regulation of the President of the Republic of Poland – Military Criminal Code (*Rozporządzenie Prezydenta RP – Kodeks karny wojskowy*), 21 October 1932, Dz. U.1932.91.765.

Regulation of the President of the Republic of Poland – Criminal Code (*Rozporządzenie Prezydenta RP – Kodeks karny*), 11 July 1932, Dz.U.1932.60.571.

Regulation of the President of the Republic of Poland on Certain Criminal Offences Against the Security of the State (*Rozporządzenie Prezydenta RP o niektórych przestępstwach przeciwko bezpieczeństwu państwa*), 24 October 1934, Dz.U.1934.94.851.

Act on the Universal Military Obligation (*Ustawa o powszechnym obowiązku wojskowym*), 9 April 1938, Dz.U.1938.25.220.

Act on Communications in the Service of the Defence of the State (*Ustawa o komunikacjach w służbie obrony państwa*), Dz.U.1939.29.195.

National Laws (the German Reich)

Decree on the Possession of Weapons (*Verordung des Oberbefehlshabers des Heeres über Waffenbesitz*) 12 September 1939 VOBl. Polen, 8–9.

Decree of 4 December 1941 on criminal law for Poles and Jews of 4 December 1941 (*Verordnung über die Strafrechtspflege gegen Polen und Juden in den eingegliederten Ostgebieten* vom 4. Dezember 1941), RGBl. 1941 I, 759.

The Law for the Protection of German Blood and German Honour (*Gesetz zum Schutze des deutschen Blutes und der deutschen Ehre*), 15 September 1935, RGBl. I, 1147.

The Penal Code of the German Empire (*Strafgesetzbuch für das Deutsche Reich*), 15 May 1871, RGBl. 1871, 127.

Reich Citizenship Law (*Reichsbürgergesetz*) 15 September 1935, RGBl. I, 1146.

Regulation on the Introduction of the Nuremberg Laws in the Incorporated Eastern Territories (*Verordnung über die Einführung der Nürnberger Rassengesetze in den eingegliederten Ostgebieten*) 31 May 1941, RGBl. I, 1941.

Special Wartime Military Decree of 17 August 1938 (*Kriegssonderstafrechtsverordnung*), RGBl 1939 I, 1455.

Treaties

Geneva Convention Relative to the Treatment of Prisoners of War (Third Geneva Convention), 12 August 1949.

Convention (III) relative to the Opening of Hostilities. The Hague, 18 October 1907.

Convention on the Prevention and Punishment of the Crime of Genocide, 9 December 1948.

International Agreement for the Prosecution and Punishment of the Major Criminals of the European Axis and Charter of the International Military Tribunal (London Agreement), 8 August 1945.

Treaty of Peace between the Allied and Associated Powers and Germany, signed at Versailles, 28 June 28, [1919] UKTS 4 (Cmd. 153); [1920] ATS 1.

UN General Assembly, Universal Declaration of Human Rights, Resolution 217 A (III), 10 December 1948.

Studies

Books

Allen, P., *Katyń: The Untold Story of Stalin's Polish Massacre* (New York: C. Scribner's Sons 1991).

Ambos K., *National Socialist Criminal Law. Continuity and Radicalization* (Nomos: Baden-Baden 2019).

Bałtruszajtys, G. (ed.) *Profesorowie Wydziału Prawa i Administracji Uniwersytetu Warszawskiego 1808–2008* (Warszawa: LexisNexis 2008).

Bałtruszajtys G. (ed.), *Zarys dziejów Wydział Prawa i Administracji Uniwersytetu Warszawskiego* (Warszawa: Wolters Kulwer 2016).

Basak A., *Historia pewnej mistyfikacji: zbrodnia katyńska przed Trybunałem Norymberskim* (Wrocław: Wydawnictwo Uniwersytetu Wrocławskiego 1993).

Bass, G., *Crimes against Humanity: Historical Evolution and Contemporary Application* (Cambridge: Cambridge University Press 2011).

Bass G. J., *Stay the Hand of Vengeance: The Politics of War Crimes Trials* (Princeton: Princeton University Press 2002).

Batowski H., *Walka dyplomacji hitlerowskiej przeciw Polsce 1939–1945* (Kraków-Wrocław: Wydawnictwo Literackie 1984).

Bębnik, G. (ed.), *Sonderfahndungsbuch Polen. Specjalna księga gończa dla Polski* (Katowice–Warszawa: IPN 2019).

Becker, M., *Mitstreiter im Volkstumskampf, Deutsche Justiz in den eingegliederten Ostgebieten 1939–1945* (München 2014).

Berezowski C., *Powstanie państwa polskiego w świetle prawa narodów*, (Warszawa: Themis Polska 1934).

Berezowski C., *O polskim projekcie międzynarodowego prawa karnego* (Warszawa 1927).

Biegański, W., M. Juchniewicz, P. Matusak, S. Okęcki (eds.), *Polish Resistance Movement in* Poland and Abroad (Warszawa: PWN 1987).

Bieńczyk-Missala A., (ed.), *Civilians in Contemporary Armed Conflicts: Rafał Lemkin's Heritage* (Warszawa: Wynawnictwo Uniwersytetu Warszawskiego 2017).

Bieńczyk-Missala A. and Sławomir Dębski (eds.), *Rafał Lemkin: A Hero of Humankind*, Warszawa: Polski Instytut Spraw Międzynarodowych 2010.

Bloch, J. *Social Legislation in Poland* (London: Polish Lawyers' Association 1944).

Bloxham, D., and A. Dirk Moses (eds.), *The Oxford Handbook of Genocide Studies* (Oxford: University Press 2010).

Bloxham D., *Genocide on Trial. War Crimes Trials and the Formation of History and Memory* (Oxford University Press 2001).

Viscount Bryce, *The Treatment of Armenians in the Ottoman Empire* (London: HMSO 1916), available at https://archive.org/details/treatmentofarmen001963mbp/page/n4 (accessed 20 October 2019).

Chinciński T. and Paweł Machcewicz (eds.), *Bydgoszcz 3–4 września 1939: studia i dokumenty* (Warszawa: IPN 2008).

Cooper J., *Raphael Lemkin and the Struggle for the Genocide Convention* (Palgrave Macmillan 2008).

Crowe D. M., *War Crimes, Genocide and Justice: A Global History* (Palgrave Macmillan 2014).

Cybichowski Z., *Międzynarodowe prawo wojenne z uwzględnieniem przesilenia bałkańskiego* (Lwów 1914).

Cybichowski Z., *Międzynarodowe prawo karne: kompetencja sądów do ścigania przestępstw zagranicznych* (Warszawa 1927).

Cybichowski Z., *Prawo międzynarodowe publiczne i prywatne* (Warszawa 1928).

Cyprian T., Stanisław Kosiński and Mieczysław Siewierski, *Proces ludobójcy Amona Leopolda Goetha przed Najwyższym Trybunałem Narodowym* (Warszawa-Łódź-Kraków: Centralna Żydowska Komisja Historyczna w Polsce).

Cyprian T., and Jerzy Sawicki, *Ludzie i sprawy Norymbergi* (Poznań: Wydawnictwo Poznańskie 1967).

Cyprian T., and Jerzy Sawicki, *Nieznana Norymberga, Dwanaście procesów norymberskich* (Warszawa 1965).

Cyprian T., and Jerzy Sawicki, *Prawo Norymberskie. Bilans i Perspektywy* (Warszawa 1947).

Cyprian T., and Jerzy Sawicki, *Procesy wielkich zbrodniarzy wojennych w Polsce: Najwyższy Trybunał Narodowy* (Warszawa: Czytelnik 1949).

Cyprian T., and Jerzy Sawicki, *Walka o zasady Norymberskie* (Warszawa: PWN 1956).

Cywiński J. W., Tadeusz S. Rojewski and Wiesław Toporowski, *Monografia polskiego wydziału prawa 1944–1947* (London: Polska Fundacja Kulturalna 1997).

David G. Williamson, *Poland Betrayed. The Nazi-Soviet Invasions 1939* (Barnsley: Pen & Sword Military 2009).

Duraczyński E., *Polska 1939–1945. Dzieje Polityczne* (Warszawa: Bellona – Wiedza Powszechna 1999).

Duraczyński E., *Rząd Polski na uchodźstwie 1939–1945: organizacja, personalia, polityka* (Warszawa: Książka i Wiedza 1993).

Duraczyński E. and Romuald Turkowski, *O Polsce na uchodźstwie. Rada Narodowa Rzeczypospolitej Polskiej 1939–1945* (Warszawa: Wydawnictwo Sejmowe 1997).

Drywa D., *Poselstwo RP w Bernie. Przemilczana historia* (Warszawa-Oświęcim 2020).

Ehrlich L., *Prawo narodów* (Lwów 1932).

Engel D., *Facing a Holocaust. The Polish Government-in-Exile and the Jews, 1943–1945* (Chapel Hill & London: The University of North Carolina Press 1993).

Epstein, C., *Model Nazi: Arthur Greiser and the Occupation of Western Poland* (OUP 2010).

Estreicher K. (ed.), *Cultural losses of Poland: Index of Polish Cultural Loses during the German Occupation, 1939–1944* (London 1944).

Estreicher K., *Dziennik wypadków*. Vol. 1, 1939–1945, edited by Anna Maria Joniak (Kraków: Pałac Sztuki Towarzystwa Przyjaciół Sztuk Pięknych 2001).

Estreicher K., *Dziennik wypadków*. Vol. 1, 1939–1945, edited by Anna Maria Joniak (Kraków: Pałac Sztuki Towarzystwa Przyjaciół Sztuk Pięknych 2001).

Finder, G. and Alexander Prusin, *Justice behind the Iron Curtain. Nazis on Trial in Communist Poland* (Toronto–Buffalo–London: University of Toronto Press 2018).

Fleming M., *In the Shadow of the Holocaust. Poland, the United Nations War Crimes Commission and the Search for Justice* (Cambridge: Cambridge University Press 2022).

Garliński, J., *Poland in The Second World War*, (Basingstoke: Macmillan 1985).

Gardocki L., *Zarys prawa karnego międzynarodowego* (Warszawa: PWN 1985).

Gerrard, A., *The Path to Lidice: And the Legacy of the Lidice Shall Live Campaign* (Independent Publishing Network 2022).

Gilbert, M., *Auschwitz and the Allies: A Devastating Account of How the Allies Responded to the News of Hitler's Mass Murder* (London: Michael Joseph 1981).

Glaser S., *La guerre d'aggression a la lumiere des sources du droit international* (Paris: A. Pedone 1953).

Glaser, S. and Aleksander Mogilnicki, *Kodeks karny. Komentarz. Prawo o wykroczeniach. Przepisy wprowadzające, tezy orzeczeń Sądu Najwyższego* (Kraków 1934).

Górecki D., *Polskie naczelne władze państwowe w latach 1939–1990*, (Warszawa: Wydawnictwo Sejmowe 2002)

Glaser, S., *Przestępstwa polityczne a prawo ekstradycji* (Lwów 1925).

Glaser S. and Przemysław Dąbkowski (eds), *Okupacja niemiecka na Litwie w latach 1915–1918: stosunki prawne* (Lwów 1929).

Glaser, S., *Infraction internationale, ses éléments constitutifs et ses aspects juridiques: exposé sur la base du droit pénal comparé* (Paris: Librairie générale de droit et de jurisprudence 1957).

Glaser S., *Przestępstwa polityczne a prawo ekstradycyi* (Lwów 1925).

Glaser S., *L'uniformisation du droit d'extradition: rapport présenté au Congrès International de Droit Comparé à La Haye – 1932* (Warszawa 1932).

Glaser S., *Urywki wspomnień* (London: Odnowa 1978).

Gmitruk, J., Arkadiusz Indraszczyk and Adam Koseski (eds.), *Pro memoria (1941–1944). Raporty Departamentu Informacji Delegatury Rządu RP na Kraj o zbrodniach na narodzie polskim* (Warszawa: Muzeum Historii Polskiego Ruchu Ludowego 2005).

Gmitruk, J. and Jerzy Mazurek, *Działalność władz okupacyjnych na terytorium Rzeczypospolitej w okresie od 1 IX 1939 – 1 XI 1939. Raport z archiwum politycznego prof. Stanisława Kota* (Warszawa: Muzeum Historii Polskiego Ruchu Ludowego 1999).

Grzebyk, P., Bartłomiej Krzan and Karolina Wierczyńska *Polish Contributions to International Criminal Law* (Leiden-Boston: Brill 2025), Polish edition: (Warszawa: IWM 2023).

Glueck S., *War Criminals: Their Prosecution and Punishment* (New York: Knopf, 1944).

Goryński Z., *Zbrodnie wojenne. Szkic prawny* (Jerusalem: Kurs Administracyjny na Bliskim Wschodzie 1944).

Górecki D., *Polskie naczelne władze państwowe w latach 1939–1990*, (Warszawa: Wydawnictwo Sejmowe 2002).

Górka O., Konstanty Jeziorański and Paweł Skwarzyński, *The Polish Spirit of Freedom* (London: Polish Ministry of Information 1942).

Grabowski W., *Delegatura Rządu Rzeczpospolitej Polskiej na Kraj 1940–1945* (Warszawa 1995).

Grabowski W., *Polska Agencja Telegraficzna 1918–1991* (Warszawa: PAP 2005).

Grabowski W., *Polska tajna administracja cywilna 1940–1945* (Warszawa: IPN 2003).

Greene, J. M., *Justice at Dachau – The Trials of an American Prosecutor* (Broadway: 2003).

Grzankowski W., *Zagadnienie sankcyj międzynarodowych Ligi Narodów* (Warszawa 1930).

Grzebyk P., *Criminal responsibility for the crime of aggression* (New York: Routledge 2013).

Grzebyk P., Rafał Tarnogórski (ed.), *Siła prawa zamiast prawa siły. Ludwik Ehrlich i jego wkład w rozwój nauki prawa międzynarodowego i stosunkach międzynarodowych* (Warszawa: PISM 2020).

Grześkowiak A. (ed.), *Prawo karne w poglądach Juliusza Makarewicza* (Lublin: KUL 2005).

Hankel G., *Die Leipziger Prozesse. Deutsche Kriegsverbrechen und ihre strafrechtliche Verfolgung nach dem Ersten Weltkrieg* (Hamburg: Hamburger Edition 2003).

Heller K. J, *The Nuremberg Military Tribunals and the Origins of International Criminal Law* (Oxford: OUP 2011).

Hirsch, F., *Soviet Judgment at Nuremberg. A New History of the International Military Tribunal after World War II* (New York: OUP 2020).

Hodža, M., *Federation in Central Europe. Reflections and Reminiscences* (London: Jarrolds 1942).

Hułas, M., *Goście czy intruzi? Rząd polski na uchodźstwie wrzesień 1939–lipiec 1943* (Warszawa: IH PAN 1996).

Ilgiewicz, H. *Instytut Naukowo-Badawczy Europy Wschodniej oraz Szkoła Nauk Politycznych w Wilnie (1930–1939)* (Warszawa: Scholar 2019).

Iwanek T., *Zbrodnia ludobójstwa i zbrodnie przeciwko ludzkości* (Warszawa: Wolters Kulwer Polska 2015).

Jankiewicz A., *W poszukiwaniu idei państwa prawa. Koncepcje Komisji Prac Ustawodawczych Rządu RP (1942–1945)* (Warszawa: Wydawnictwo Sejmowe 1992).

Jankowski J. and Antoni Serafiński, *Polska w liczbach* (London: Stowarzyszenie Prawników Polskich w Zjednoczonym Królestwie 1941).

Jardim, T., *The Mauthausen Trial: American Military Justice in Germany* (Harvard University Press: 2012).

Jedlicki M. Z., *Przeobrażenia ustrojowe i polityczne dzisiejszych Niemiec* (Kraków: Koło Uczniów i Absolwentów Szkoły Nauk Politycznych 1939).

Jordan, J. – Jan Lanicek (eds.), *Governments-in-Exile and the Jews during the Second World War* (Middlesex: Vallentine Mitchell 2013).

Karol M. Pospieszalski (ed.), *Documenta Occupationis. Nazi occupation 'law' in Poland, Selected Documents*, Part I: The incorporated territories; Part II: The Government General (Poznań, Instytut Zachodni 2019).

Karski, K., M. Szonert-Binienda (eds.), *Katyń: State-Sponsored Extermination. Colelction of Essays* (Ohio 2013).

Karski, J., *Story of a Secret State* (Boston: Houghton Mifflin Co. 1944).

Kaufmann, A., *Gustav Radbruch. Rechtsdenker, Philosoph, Sozialdemokrat* (München: Piper 1987).

Kelly J. M, *Historia zachodniej teorii prawa.* Original title: *A Short History of Western Legal Theory.* Translated by Dorota Pietrzyk-Reeves (et al.) (Kraków: WAM 2006).

Kisielewski T., *Federacja środkowoeuropejska. Pertraktacje polsko-czechosłowackie 1939–1943* (Warszawa: Ludowa Spółdzielnia Wydawnicza 1991).

Kochavi A., *Prelude to Nuremberg: Allied War Crimes Policy and the Question of Punishment* (University of North California Press 1998).

Kodź S., *Zasada narodowości w prawie międzynarodowem.* With a foreword by Wacław, Komarnicki (1933).

Komarnicki W., 'La Définition de L'Agresseur Dans Le Droit International Moderne', in Academie de Droit International, *Collected Courses of the Hague Academy of International Law* (Paris 1949).

Komarnicki W., *Geneza terytorium państwa Polski ze stanowiska prawa narodów* (Wilno 1925).

Komarnicki W., *Nowy ustrój państwowy Związku Sowietów* (Wilno 1938).

Komarnicki W., *Polskie Prawo po lityczne: geneza i system* (Warszawa: F. Hoesick 1922).

Komarnicki W., *Likwidacja mienia niemieckiego w Polsce (polemika z prof. Kaufmannem)* (Warszawa 1925).

Komarnicki W., *Liga Narodów. Skrypt wg wykładów Wacława Komarnickiego 1935–1936* (Wilno 1936).

Komarnicki W., *Powstawanie państw ze stanowiska nauki o państwie i prawa Międzynarodowego* (Warszawa: Gebethner i Wolf 1916).

Kornat M., Mikołaj Morzycki-Markowski, *W rumuńskiej pułapce. Internowanie Józefa Becka i Edwarda Śmigłego-Rydza w dokumentach rumuńskich służb specjalnych* (Gdańsk: Muzeum II Wojny Światowej 2011).

Koskenniemi, M., *The Gentle Civilizer of Nations The Rise and Fall of International Law 1870–1960* (Cambridge: Cambridge University Press 2001).

Krajewski, L., *Podstawy ustroju Trzeciej Rzeszy* (Warszawa: Księgarnia F. Hoesicka 1935).

Król M., *Próby kodyfikacji zasad międzynarodowej odpowiedzialności państw* (Wilno 1936).

Królikowski M., *Odpowiedzialność karna jednostki za sprawstwo zbrodni międzynarodowej* (Warszawa: Wydawnictwo Sejmowe 2011).

Kubicki, L., *Zbrodnie wojenne w świetle prawa polskiego* (Warszawa: PWN 1963).

Kuc, O. *The Supreme National Tribunal and International Criminal Law Polish Perspectives on Prosecuting War Criminals* (Routledge 2026).

Kulesza W., *Crimes laesae iustitiae. Odpowiedzialność karna sędziów i prokuratorów za zbrodnie sądowe według prawa norymberskiego, niemieckiego, austriackiego i polskiego* (Łódź: Wydawnictwo Uniwersytetu Łódzkiego 2013).

Kulski W., *Anthology of Crime* (London 1945).

Kulski W., *Liga Narodów* (Warszawa 1938).

Kulski W., *Le problème de la sécurité depuis le pacte de la Société des Nations (1918–1926)* (Paris 1927).

Kulski W., *Przed I powszechną konferencją rozbrojeniową* (Warszawa 1931).

Kulski W., *Odpowiedzialność międzynarodowa państw. Wykład Wygłoszony dnia 28 maja 1938 r. na kursie naukowym dla urzędników służby zagranicznej* (Warszawa: MSZ 1938).

Kumoch J. (ed.), *Lista Ładosia* (Warszawa: Instytut Pileckiego 2019).

Kumoch, J. (ed.), *The Ładoś List*, transl. by Julia Niedzielko, Ian Stephenson (Warszawa: Instytut Pileckiego 2020).

Kunert, A. K. (ed.), *Rzeczpospolita Polska czasu wojny: Dziennik Ustaw RP i Monitor Polski 1939–1945* (Warszawa: Kopia 1995).

Kunert A. K., Zygmunt Walkowski, *Kronika kampanii wrześniowej 1939* (Warszawa: Wydawnictwo Edipresse Polska 2005).

Kuśnierz B., *Stalin and the Poles: An Indictment of the Soviet Leaders*. With a foreword by August Zaleski (London 1949).

Kwiatkowski M., *Rząd i Rada Narodowa RP w świetle faktów i dokumentów od września 1939 do lutego 1942 r.* (London 1942).

Lachs M., *War Crimes. An Attempt to Define the Issues* (London: Stevens 1945).

Lachs M., *The Ghetto of Warsaw* (London 1942).

Laqueur W., *The Terrible Secret. An Investigation into the Suppression of Information about Hitler's "Final Solution"* (Boston: Little, Brown 1980).

Lemkin R., *Axis Rule in Occupied Europe: Laws of Occupation – Analysis of Government – Proposals for Redress* (Washington: Carnegie Endowment for International Peace. Division of International Law 1944).

Lemkin R., *Nieoficjalny: autobiografia Rafała Lemkina*. Edited by Donna-Lee Frieze. Translated by H. Jankowska (Warszawa: Instytut Solidarności i Męczeństwa im. W. Pileckiego 2018).

Lemkin R., *Rządy państw Osi w okupowanej Europie. Prawa okupacyjne, analiza rządzenia, propozycje zadośćuczynienia*. Translated by Agnieszka Bieńczyk-Missala, Patrycja Grzebyk, Bogusław Lackoroński, Marek Madej (Warszawa: Wydawnictwo Naukowe Scholar 2013).

Lewis M., *The Birth of the New Justice. The Internationalisation of Crime and Punishment, 1919–1950* (Oxford: Oxford University Press 2014).

von Lingen K., *"Crimes against Humanity". Eine Ideengeschichte der Zivilisierung von Kriegsgewalt 1864–1945* (Padeborn: Ferdinand Schöningh 2018).

Lityński A., *Wydział karny Komisji Kodyfikacyjnej II Rzeczypospolitej: dzieje prac nad częścią ogólną kodeksu karnego* (Katowice: Uniwersytet Śląski 1991).

Lubecka J., *Niemiecki zbrodniarz przed polskim sądem. Krakowskie procesy przed Najwyższym Trybunałem Narodowym* (Kraków: IPN, Ośrodek Myśli Politycznej 2021).

Mackiewicz, J., *The Katyn Woods Murders* (London: Hollis&Carter 1951).

Madajczyk, Cz., *Polityka III Rzeszy w okupowanej Polsce*, vols. 1–2 (Warszawa: PWN 1970).

Majer, D. *'Non-Germans' Under the Third Reich: The Nazi Judicial and Administrative System in Germany and Occupied Eastern Europe, with Special Regard to Occupied Poland, 1939–1945* (Washington, D.C: Texas Tech University Press 2014).

Makarewicz J., *Kodeks karny z komentarzem, wydanie piąte* (Lwów: Wydawnictwo Zakładu Narodowego im. Ossolińskich 1938).

Makiłła, D., *Historia prawa w Polsce* (Warszawa: Wydawnictwo Naukowe PWN 2013).

Makowski, J., *Rozwój i przyszłość prawa międzynarodowego. Przyczynek do teorii prawa narodów* (Warszawa 1926).

Makowski J., *Współczesne formy sądownictwa międzynarodowego* (Warszawa 1922).

Maciejewski M. and Maciej Marszał (eds.), *Pod znakiem swastyki: polscy prawnicy wobec Trzeciej Rzeszy 1933–1939* (Kraków: Ośrodek Myśli Politycznej 2005).

Marrus M. R., *Nuremberg War Crimes Trial, 1945–1946: a Documentary History* (Boston: Bedford Books 1997)

Matelski D., *Karol Estreicher Jr 1906–1984: biografia wielkiego Polaka*, vols. 1–2, 1939–1945, (Kraków: Pałac Sztuki Towarzystwa Przyjaciół Sztuk Pięknych).

Matthäus J., Jochen Böhler, Klaus M. Mallmann (eds.), *War, Pacification, and Mass Murder, 1939: The Einsatzgruppen in Poland,* (Lanham: Alta Mira Press 2014).

Mazower M., *No Enchanted Place: The End of Empire and the Ideological Origins of the United Nations* (Princeton: Princeton University Press 2009).

Mazur G., *Biuro Informacji i Propagandy SZP -ZWZ-AK 1939–1945* (Warszawa: Pax 1987).

Mégret F., Immi Tallgren (ed.), *The Dawn of a Discipline: International Criminal Justice and Its Early Exponents* (Cambridge: Cambridge University Press 2020).

Mettraux G. (ed.), *Perspectives on the Nuremberg Trials* (Oxford: Oxford University Press 2008).

Mosakowski M., Marta Sobiecka, Jarosław Ślęzak, Mikołaj Ślęzak (eds.), *Manfred Lachs. Zbrodnie wojenne w 60. Rocznicę wydania. Uwagi Źródła* (Warszawa: Wydawnictwo Interdyscyplinarnego Koła Myśli Prawnej Sapere Aude 2017).

Moorhouse, R., *The Devils' Alliance: Hitler's Pact with Stalin, 1939–1941* (New York: Basic Books 2014).

Moorhouse, R., *The Forgers. The Forgotten Story of the Holocaust's Most Audacious Rescue Operation* (London: Vintage Digital 2023).

Moorhouse, R., *First to Fight: The Polish War 1939* (London: The Bodley Head 2019).

Muszalski E. (comp.), *Prawo Narodów. Skrypt*, vols. 1–3 (London: Studium Prawno-Administracyjne 1944–1945).

Pachowicz A., *Komitet Ministrów dla Spraw Kraju 1939–1945* (Warszawa: DiG 2010).

Pachowicz A., *Komitet Ministrów dla Spraw Kraju 1939–1945* (Warszawa: DiG 2010).

Person, S., *Escape from the Third Reich: Folke Bernadotte and the white buses* (Barnsley: Frontline Books 2019).

Pendas D., Democracy, Nazi Trials and Transitional Justice in Germany (Cambridge University Press 2020).

Peszke, M. A., *The Armed Forces of Poland in the West, 1939–1946 Strategic Concepts, Planning, Limited Success but No Victory!* (Helion 2015).

Peszke, M. A., *The Polish Underground Army, the Western Allies, and the Failure of Strategic Unity in World War II* (Jefferson: McFarland 2009).

Piotrowski J. (ed.), *Dziennik czynności Prezydenta RP Władysława Raczkiewicza 1939–1947* (Wrocław: Wydawnictwo Uniwersytetu Wrocławskiego 2004).

Plesch D., *Human Rights after Hitler. The Lost History of Prosecuting Axis War Crimes* (Washington, DC: Georgetown University Press 2017).

The Polish Lawyers' Association in the United Kingdom, *Studies in Polish and Comparative Law with foreword by professor H. C. Gutteridge* (London: Stevens & Sons Limited 1945).

Pospieszalski K. M., *Polska pod niemieckim prawem 1939–1945 (Ziemie Zachodnie)* (Poznań: Wydawnictwo Instytutu Zachodniego 1946).

Priemel K. C., *The Betrayal: The Nuremberg Trials and German Divergence* (New York: OUP 2016).

Puławski A., *W obliczu Zagłady. Rząd RP na uchodźstwie, Delegatura Rządu RP na Kraj, ZWZ–AK wobec deportacji Żydów do obozów zagłady (1941–1942)* (Lublin: IPN 2009).

Rabiński J., *Stronnictwo Pracy we władzach naczelnych Rzeczypospolitej Polskiej na Uchodźstwie w latach 1939–1945* (Lublin: KUL 2012).

Raczyński E., *W sojuszniczym Londynie. Dziennik ambasadora, 1939–1945* (London: Polska Fundacja Kulturalna 1997).

Radzinowicz L., *Angielska polityka kryminalna: próba wykładni* (Londyn: Stowarzyszenie Prawników Polskich w Zjednoczonym Królestwie 1942).

Rappaport E. S., *Zagadnienie unifikacji międzynarodowej prawa karnego* (Warszawa: Polski Związek Prawników Kresowców 1929).

Rappaport E. S., *Actes de la conférence internationale d'unification du droit pénal. Publ. avec le concours de Vespasien V. Pella par Michel Potulicki* (Paris: Librairie du Recueil Sirey 1929).

Rappaport, E. S., *Prawo Karne międzynarodowe*, copy from the *Encyklopedia Podręczna Prawa Karnego*, vol. XIV (Warszawa: Biblioteka Polska 1936).

Rappaport E. S., *Propaganda wojny zaczepnej jako delictum iuris gentium* (Warszawa 1929).

Rappaport, E. S., *Tendencje rozwojowe prawa karnego międzynarodowego*, copy from *Ruch Prawniczy Ekonomiczny i Socjologiczny* (Poznań 1934).

Redzik A., *Rafał Lemkin (1900–1959) Co-creator of International Criminal Law: Short Biography* (Warszawa 2017).

Rostocki W., *Stosowanie konstytucji kwietniowej w okresie drugiej wojny światowej 1939–1945* (Lublin: KUL 1988).

Rostworowski M., *Wojna i traktat pokojowy. Jak powstaje państwo w naszych czasach?* (Kraków: Księg. G. Gebethner i Sp. 1916).

Rostworowski M., *Prawo dyplomatyczne. Poprawione i uzupełnione na podstawie wykładów 1936–1937* (Kraków 1938).

Rotshild, J., *Piłsudski's coup d'état* (New York, London: Columbia University Press 1966).

Rutczyński, K., *Zbrodnie Wojenne. Stdudjum w skali międzynarodowej* (Glasgow: Książnica Polska, 1946).

Saliger, F., *Radbruchsche Formel und Rechtsstaat* (Heidelberg: Müller, Jur. Verl. 1995).

Sands P., *East West Street: On the Origins of Genocide and Crimes Against Humanity* (London: Orion Publishing 2017).

Sands P. (ed.), *From Nuremberg to the Hague: The Future of International Criminal Justice* (Cambridge: Cambridge University Press 2003).

Schabas, W., *Genocide in International Law: The Crime of Crimes* (Cambridge: Cambridge University Press 2010).

Schabas W., *Unimaginable Atrocities. Justice, Politics and Rights at the War Crimes Tribunals* (Oxford: Oxford University Press 2012).

Schenk, D., *Die Post von Danzig. Geschichte eines deutschen Justizmords* (Reinbek bei Hamburg: Rowohlt 1995).

Segesser D. M., *Recht statt Rache oder Rache durch das Recht. Die Ahndung von Kriegsverbrechen in der internationalen und wissenschaftlichen Debatte 1872–1945* (Paderborn: F. Schöningh 2010).

Seyda M., *Poland and Germany and the Post-War Reconstruction of Europe* (New York: Polish Information Centre 1943).

Slesser H. (foreword), *Justice Outlawed: Administration of Law in German-Occupied Territories* (London: Liberty Publications 1943).

Smith B., *The Road to Nuremberg* (New York: Basic Books, Inc. Publishers 1981).

Smolar E. (ed.), *Memory and Responsibility: The Legacy of Jan Karski* (Warszawa: Fundacja Edukacyjna Jana Karskiego, Polish History Museum 2015).

Sobczak J., *Polska w propagandzie III Rzeszy w latach 1939–1945* (Poznań: Instytut Zachodni 1998).

Stańczyk, J., Preface in International Labour Organization, *Workers' Protective Legislation in Poland: 20 years' Co-operation with the International Labour Organisation* (London: Liberty Publications 1941).

Stanuch Z. (ed.), *Golgota kobiet: relacje więźniarek Ravensbrück i innych obozów koncentracyjnych ze zbiorów Polskiego Instytutu Źródłowego w Lund* (Szczecin, Warszawa: IPN 2018).

Stola D., *Nadzieja i Zagłada: Ignacy Schwarzbart – żydowski przedstawiciel w Radzie Narodowej RP, 1940–1945* (Warszawa: Oficyna Naukowa 1995).

Štovíček, I., Jaroslav Valenta (eds.), *Czechoslovak-Polish Confederation of the Estabilishment of Confederation and Aliance* (Prague: The Institute of History, Academy of Sciences of the Czech Republic 1995).

Stroński, S., *Polityka Rządu RP na uchodźstwie 1939–1942*. Edited by J. Piotrowski (Nowy Sącz 2007).

Sukiennicki W., *La souveraineté des états en droit international moderne* (Paris 1927).

Sukiennicki W., *Podstawy obowiązywania prawa narodów* (Warszawa-Wilno 1929).

Szmaglewska, S., *Niewinni w Norymberdze* (Warszawa: Prószyński i S-ka 2020).

Tarka K., *Emigracyjna dyplomacja. Polityka zagraniczna rządu RP na uchodźstwie w latach 1939–1990* (Warszawa: Rytm 2002).

Taylor T., *The Anatomy of the Nuremberg Trials. A Personal Memoir* (New York: Skyhorse Publishing 2013).

Tusa, A. and John Tusa, *The Nuremberg Trial* (London: Macmillan 1984).

United Nations War Crimes Commission, *History of the United War Crimes Commission and the Development of the Laws of War* (London 1948).

Vansittart R. G., *Black Record: Germans Past and Present* (London: Hamish Hamilton 1941).

Waciórski J., *Le terrorisme politique*. With a foreword by H. Donnedieu de Varbes (Paris: A. Pedone 1939).

Wandycz, P., *Czechoslovak-Polish Confederation and the Great Powers, 1940–1943* (Westport: Greenwood Press 1979.

Wandycz, P. S., *The United States and Poland* (Harvard University Press 1980).

Wardzyńska, M. *Był rok 1939. Operacja niemieckiej policji bezpieczełstwa w Polsce. Intelligenzaktion* (Warszawa: IPN 2009).

Weinke A., *Die Nürenberger Prozesse* (München: C.H. Beck Verlag 2006).

Weitbrecht D., *Der Exekutionsauftrag der Einsatzgruppen in Polen* (Filderstadt: Markstein Verlag 2001).

Werle G. and Florian Jessberger, *Principles of International Criminal Law, third edition* (Oxford: Oxford University Press 2014).

Winiewicz J., *Aims and Failures of the German New Order*, London 1943; *German Withdrawal in the East: A Study in Vital German and Polish Statistics* (London: Polish Research Centre 1941).

Winstone, M., *The Dark Heart of Hitler's Europe: Nazi Rule in Poland under the General Government* (London: L.B. Tauris & Co. Ltd 2015).

Willis J., *Prologue to Nuremberg: The Politics and Diplomacy of Punishing War Criminals of the First World war* (Westport: Greenwood Press 1982).

Winiarski B., *Bezpieczeństwo, arbitraż, rozbrojenie* (Poznań 1928).

Winiarski B., *„Obrona konieczna" w prawie narodów* (Lwów 1936).

Wolsza T., *Encounter with Katyn: The Wartime and Postwar Story of Poles Who Saw the Katyn Site in 1943* (Durham: Carolina Academic Press 2018).

Włodarski, B. *Szkoła Nauk Politycznych Uniwersytetu Jagiellońskiego 1920–1949* (Kraków: Księgarnia Akademicka 2015).

Wolsza, T., *„Katyń to już zawsze katy i katowani". W „polskim Londynie" o sowieckiej zbrodni w Katyniu (1940–1956)* (Warszawa: IH PAN 2008).

Wood, E. T., Stanisław M. Jankowski, *Karski, How One Man Tried to Stop the Holocaust* (New York: John Wiley & Sons 1994).

Wrzyszcz A., *Okupacyjne sądownictwo niemieckie w Generalnym Gubernatorstwie. 1939–1945. Organizacja i funkcjonowanie* (Lublin: Wydawnictwo Uniwersytetu Marii Curie-Skłodowskiej w Lublinie 2008).

Zabiełło S., *Na posterunku we Francji* (Warszawa: Instytut Wydawniczy Pax 1967).

Zajadło J., *Formuła Radbrucha: filozofia prawa na gruncie pozytywizmu prawniczego i prawa natury* (Gdańsk: Arche 2001).

Ziembiński Z., *O pojmowaniu pozytywizmu oraz prawa naturalnego* (Poznań: Ośrodek Wydawnictw Naukowych 1993).

Zimmerman, J., *Jozef Pilsudski. Founding Father of Modern Poland* (Harvard University Press 2022).

Zmierczak M. (ed.), *Prawo natury w doktrynach polityczno-prawnych Europy* (Poznań: Wydawnictwo Naukowe UAM 2006).

Book Chapters

Balcerzak, M. 'O wileńskiej szkole prawa międzynarodowego (1919–1939)', in Anna Przyborowska-Klimczak Anna et al. (eds.) *Polska nauka prawa międzynarodowego : dziedzictwo przeszłości i wyzwania współczesności* (Lubllin: Towarzystwo Naukowe KUL), 177–208.

Bień-Kacała, A. and Anna Tarnowska, 'Wacław Komarnicki (1891–1954)', in Andrzej Szmyt, Paweł Sarnecki, Ryszard Mojak, (eds.) *Konstytucjonaliści Polscy 1918–2011. Sylwetki uczonych* (Warszawa: Wydawnictwo Sejmowe 2012), 202–209.

Cyprian, T., 'Faktyczna I Prawna Sytuacja Delegacji Polskiej Na Procesie Norymberskim', in *Norymberga – nadal otwarty rozdział historii: w XXX rocznicę wyroku Międzynarodowego Trybunału Wojskowego* (Warszawa: GKBZHP 1977), 110–121.

Douglas L., 'Was Damals Recht War... *Nulla Poena* and the Prosecution of Crimes against Humanity in Occupied Germany', in Elizabeth Edenberg and Larry May (eds.), *Ius Post Bellum and Transitional Justice* (Cambridge: Cambridge University Press 2013), 44–73.

Drumbl M. A., 'the Supreme National Tribunal of Poland and the History of International Criminal Law', in Morten Bergsmo, Cheah Wui Ling, Yi Ping (eds.), *Historical Origins of International Criminal Law*: Volume 2 (Brussels: Torkel Opsahl Academic EPublisher), 563–602.

Dubicki T., Andrzej Suchcitz, 'Walka Dyplomacji Polskiej Z Propagandą Niemiecką W Latach 1939–1945', in Waldemar Michowicz (ed.), *Historia dyplomacji polskiej (połowa X–XX w.)*, vol. V (Warszawa: PWN 1999), 640–665.

Ehrlich L., 'Zarys Historii Nauki Prawa Narodów W Polsce', in Ludwik Ehrlich, Stefan Langrod, *Zarys historii nauki prawa narodów, politycznego i administracyjnego w Polsce* (Kraków 1949), 5–43.

Grabowski W., 'Struktury Organizacyjne Służb Bezpieczeństwa I Wymiaru Sprawiedliwości Polskiego Państwa Podziemnego', in Waldemar Grabowski (ed.), *Organy bezpieczeństwa i wymiar sprawiedliwości Polskiego Państwa Podziemnego* (Warszawa: IPN 2005).

Grzebyk P., 'Emil Stanisław Rappaport: His Road from Abolition to Prosecution of Nations', in Mégret and Tallgren (eds.), *The Dawn*, 93–117.

Grzebyk P., 'The Role of the Polish Supreme National Tribunal in the Development of Principles of International Criminal Law', in Bergsmo, Ling and Ping (eds.) *Historical Origins*, 603–633.

Hułas M., 'Rząd Gen. Władysława Sikorskiego Czerwiec 1940–Lipiec 1943', in Zbigniew Błażyński (ed.), *Władze RP na Obczyźnie podczas II wojny światowej, 1939–1945* (Londyn: Polskie Towarzystwo Naukowe na Obczyźnie 1994), 172–274.

Kamiński M. K., 'Zarys Polityki Zagranicznej Rządu Rp Na Obczyźnie 1939–1945', in Błażyński (ed.), *Władze*, 636–773.

Komarnicki, W., 'Określenie Napastnika We Współczesnym Prawie Narodów', *Księga pamiątkowa ku czci Leona Pińskiego*, vol. 1 (Lwów 1936) 431–442.

Lanicek, J., 'To Get a Refusal Would Result in an Unfortunate Loss of Prestige the Czechoslovak Government-in-Exile and the Holocaust'. *Holocaust Studies: A Journal of Culture and History* 13 (2008), 119–141.

Loehning, M., 'Germany: The Reichsgericht 1933–1945.', in: D. Venema (ed.), *Supreme Courts under Nazi Occupation* (Amsterdam University Press 2022), 65–68.

Mamolea A., 'Vespesian V. Pella: International Criminal Justice as a Safeguard of Peace, 1919–1952', in Mégret and Tallgren (eds.), *The Dawn*, 49–92.

Michowicz W., 'Organizacja Polskiej Służby Dyplomatycznej W Okresie Ii Wojny Światowej', in Michowicz, *Historia*, 9–105.

Moses A. D, 'Raphael Lemkin, Culture and the Concept of Genocide', in Donald Bloxham and A. Dirk Moses (eds.), *The Oxford handbook of genocide studies* (Oxford: Oxford University Press 2010), 19–41.

Puławski, A. 'The Polish Government-in-Exile 1 in London, the Delegatura, the Union of Armed Struggle-Home Army and the Extermination of the Jews', in James Jordan, Jan Lanicek (eds.), *Governments-in-Exile and the Jews during the Second World War* (Middlesex: Vallentine Mitchell 2013), 111–134.

Puławski A., 'Polityka informacyjna Polskiego Państwa Podziemnego w odniesieniu do Zagłady', w: T. Chinciński (ed.), *Przemoc i dzień powszedni w okupowanej Polsce*, (Gdańsk: Muzeum II Wojny Światowej 2011), 365–387.

Redzik A., 'Rozwój Nauk Prawnych W Latach 1871–1939. Prawo Narodów', in Adam Redzik„*Academia militans". Uniwersytet Jana Kazimierza we Lwowie* (Kraków: Wydawnictwo Wysoki Zamek 2015), 506–512.

Redzik A., 'Ludwika Ehrlicha Koncepcja Kształcenia Dyplomatów I Jej Realizacja – Studium Dyplomatyczne Uniwersytetu Jana Kazimierza We Lwowie', in Patrycja Grzebyk and Rafał Tarnogórski (eds.), *Siła*, 255–281.

Redzik A., 'Ludwik Ehrlich (1899–1968) – Zarys Życiorysu', in: Grzebyk and Tarnogórski (eds.) *Siła*, 339–362.

Segesser D. M., 'Hugh H. L. Bellot: A Life in the Service of the Prevention and Punishment of War Crimes and Crimes against Humanity' in Mégret and Tallgren (eds.), *The Dawn*, 24–48.

Segesser D. M., 'On the Road to Total Retribution? the International Debate on the Punishment of War Crimes 1872–1945', in Roger Chickering, Stig Förster and Bernd Greiner (eds.), *A World at Total War. Global Conflict and the Politics of Destruction, 1937–1945* (Cambridge: Cambridge University Press 2005), 355–374.

Stola D., 'Dyplomacja Polska Wobec Zagłady Żydów', in Michowicz (ed.), *Historia*, vol. v, 666–689.

Schabas, W., 'The Law and Genocide' in Donald Bloxham and A. Dirk Moses (eds.), *The Oxford handbook of genocide studies* (Oxford: Oxford University Press 2010), 123–141.

Uczkiewicz D., 'Transitional Justice before Nuremberg. The Polish Contribution to the Works of United Nations War Crimes Commission 1943–1945', in: Wolfgang Form and Dominika Uczkiewicz (eds.), *Polish and German Perspectives on Transitional Justice. World War Two and its Aftermath* (Wrocław: Wydawnictwo CSNE 2021), 50–65.

Walther M., 'Hat der Juristische Positivismus Die Deutschen Juristen Wehrlos Gemacht?', in Redaktion Kritische Justiz (ed.), *Die juristische Aufarbeitung des Unrechts-Staats* (Baden-Baden 1998) 299–322.

Wierczyńska K., Grzegorz Wierczyński, 'Stefan Glaser: Polish Lawyer, Diplomat and Scholar', in Mégret and Tallgren (eds.), *The Dawn*, 306–334.

Wróbel P., 'Dziennik Polski, the Official Daily Organ of the Polish Government in Exile, and the Holocaust', in Robert Moses Shapiro (ed.) *Why Didn't the Press Shout? American & International Journalism During the Holocaust* (Yeshiva University Press 2003) 507–535.

Wyrwa T., 'Odbudowa Władz Rzeczypospolitej W Paryżu I Angers Wrzesień 1939–Czerwiec 1940', in Błażyński (ed.), *Władze*, 1–83.

Journal Articles

Basak A., 'Kwestia ukarania zbrodni niemieckich na łamach „Biuletyu Informacyjnego" Armii Krajowej 1940–1945'. *Acta Universitatis Wratislaviensis* 543 (1981), 59–84.

Bassiouni M. Ch., 'Crimes Against Humanity: The Case for a Specialized Convention'. *Washington Global Studies Law Review* 9 (2010), 575–593.

Birt, M., 'Dekret sierpniowy PKWN z 1944 roku jako instrument legalizacji władzy komunistycznej w Polsce'. *Studia nad Autorytaryzmem i Totalitaryzmem* 41(2020), 65–85.

de Baer M., 'Prace przygotowawcze nad represją zbrodni wojennych 1941–1945'. *Państwo i Prawo* 3 (1948), 5–13.

Bojarski T., 'Tradycja i postęp w nowelizacji prawa karnego – od Makarewicza do stanu obecnego'. *Teka Komisji Prawniczej PAN OL* 2008 v. 1, 7–15.

Cassese A., 'The Martens Clause: Half a Loaf or Simply Pie in the Sky?'. *European Journal of International Law* 11 (2000), 187–216.

Chinciński T., 'Niemiecka dywersja w Polsce w 1939 r. w świetle dokumentów policyjnych i wojskowych II Rzeczypospolitej oraz służb specjalnych III Rzeszy, część 2 (sierpień–wrzesień 1939 r.)'. *Pamięć i Sprawiedliwość* 9 (2006), 159–195.

'Commission on the Responsibility of the Authors of the War and on Enforcement of Penalties. Report presented to the preliminary peace conference'. *The American Journal of International Law* Vol. 14, No. 1/2 (1920), 95–154.

Cybichowski Z., 'Niepodległość Polski a Liga Narodów'. *Prawo* 4/5 (1929).

Dahl I. A., '… this is material arousing interest in common history … Zygmunt Lakocinski and Polish Survivors' Protocols'. *Kwartalnik Historii Żydów* 223 (2007), 319–338.

Drąg Korga I., 'The Information Policy of the Polish Government-in-Exile Toward the American Public During World War II'. *Polish American Studies* 64 (2007), 27–45.

Earl H., 'Prosecuting Genocide before the Genocide Convention. Raphael Lemkin and the Nurnberg Trials, 1945–1949'. *Journal of Genocide Research* 15 (2013), 317–337.

Ellis M., 'Assessing the Impact of the UNWCC on the Principle of Complementarity'. *Criminal Law Forum* 25 (2014), 191–222.

Glaser S., 'La Charte du Tribunal de Nuremberg et les nouveaux principes du droit international'. *Revue penale suisse* 63 (1948), 13–38.

Glaser S., 'La guerre d'agression a la lumiere des sources du droit international'. *Revue Generale de Droit International Public* 3 (1953).

Glaser S., 'Nullum Crimen Sine Lege'. *Journal of Comparative Legislation and International Law* 24 (1942), 29–37.

Glaser S., 'La Responsabilité de l'individu devant le droit international'. *Revue pénale suisse* 3 (1949).

Goldman A., 'Germans and Nazis: The Controversy over 'Vansittartism' in Britain during the Second World War'. *Journal of Contemporary History* 14 (1979), 155–191.

Góras, M.T., 'Profesor Wacław Komarnicki, poseł na sejm RP, jeniec obozu w Kozielsku, ocalony'. *Dzieje Najnowsze* 51 (2019) 2, 265–286.

Grabowski W., 'Nieznany rząd Polski Walczącej 1939–1945. Przegląd badań', *Dzieje Najnowsze* XLIV (2012), 153–156.

Graczyk, K., H. Mielnik, *Special Courts (Sondergerichte) in the General Government (1939–1945)*, The Legal History Review 91 (2023) 271–308.

Groniowski K., 'Poland Fights (1941–1946)'. *Kwartalnik Historii Prasy Polskiej* XXIX (1990), 67–93.

Habielski R., Polityka informacyjna i propagandowa rządu RP na emigracji 1939–1945. *Dzieje Najnowsze* XIX (1987), 53–73.

Hood, R., 'Leon Radzinowicz (1906–1999)'. *Proceedings of the British Academy* 111 (2001), 63–55, available at https://www.thebritishacademy.ac.uk/sites/default/files/111p637.pdf.

International Law Commission, 'Principles of International Law Recognized in the Charter of Nuremberg Tribunal and in the Judgment of the Tribunal'. *Yearbook of the International Law Commission* II (1950), par. 97.

Jończa K., 'Dylematy prawa natury Trzeciej Rzeszy'. *Studia nad Faszyzmem i Zbrodniami Hitlerowskimi* 17 (1994), 5–22.

Kałduński M., 'Immunitet państwa w prawie międzynarodowym w kontekście zbrodni wojennych i zbrodni przeciwko ludzkości'. *Zeszyty Prawnicze Biura Analiz Sejmowych Kancelarii Sejmu* 58 (2018), 67–95.

Kelsen H., 'Will the Judgment in the Nuremberg Trial Constitute a Precedent in International Law?'. *International Law Quarterly* 1 (1947), 153–171.

Kobierska-Motas E., 'Rząd polski na emigracji wobec problemu dokumentowania niemieckich przestępstw wojennych'. *Pamięć i Sprawiedliwość* 38 (1995), 175–202.

Kochavi A., 'The British Foreign Office versus the UNWCC during the Second World War'. *Holocaust and Genocide Studies* 8 (1994), 28–49.

Komarnicki W., 'La Définition de L'Agresseur', in *La sécurité collective. Mémoires présentés par le Comité Central des Institutions polonaises des Sciences Politiques à la VIII-e Conférence des Hautes Études Internationales à Londres, 3–8 juins 1935* (Lwów 1935).

Koredczuk J., 'Znaczenie kodeksu karnego z 1932 r. dla rozwoju nauki i prawa karnego w Polsce w XX wieku'. *Zeszyty Prawnicze UKSW* 11.2 (2011), 45–60.

Kornat M., 'Barbarzyństwo – wandalizm – terroryzm – ludobójstwo: o Rafale Lemkinie i idei zdefiniowania zbrodni w obliczu prawa narodów'. *Polski Przegląd Dyplomatyczny* 3 (2008), 79–100.

Kornat M., 'Rafał Lemkin (1900–1959) – studium biograficzne'. *Zeszyty Historyczne* 147 (2004), 107–156.

Kowalski W., 'From May to Bereza: A Legal Nihilism in the Political and Legal Practice of the Sanation Camp 1926–1935'; *Studia Iuridica Lublinensia* XXIX (2020), 133–145.

Kowalski W., 'Udział Karola Estreichera w alianckich przygotowaniach do restytucji dzieł sztuki zagrabionych w czasie II wojny światowej.' *Muzealnictwo* 30 (1986).

Kroll B., 'Struktura polskich naczelnych władz emigracyjnych w latach 1939–1945'. *Czasopismo Prawno-Historyczne* 28 (1976).

Król M., 'Odpowiedzialność państw w prawie międzynarodowem'. *Rocznik Prawniczy Wileński* 1929.

Krzoska M., 'Der *Bromberger Blutsonntag* Kontroverse und Forschungsergebnisse.' *Vierteljahreshefte für Zeitgeschichte* 60 (2012), 237–248.

Lachs M., 'Le Jugement de Nuremberg'. *Revue Internationale de Droit Penal* 3–4 (1946), 398–404.

Lachs M., 'the Unwritten Laws of Warfare'. Reprinted from *Tulane Law Review* 120–128 (XX) (1945), New Orleans, Louisiana, 120–128.

Lachs M., 'Walka o definicję agresji'. *Wojskowy Przegląd Prawniczy* 3 (1952).

Lachs M., 'War Crimes and Political Offences'. *Juridical Review* (Edinburgh) 56 (1944), 27–41.

Laskowski J., 'Radiostacja *Świt*'. *Zeszyty Historyczne* 6 (1966), 101–130.

Lautetpacht H., 'The Problem of Jurisdictional Immunities of Foreign States'. *British Yearbook for International Law* 1951.

Lemkin R., *Akte der Barbarei und des Vandalismus als* delicta iuris gentium. *Internationales Anwaltsblatt* 19. Jahrgang, Heft 6, S. 117–119.

Librach J., 'Nota o Akcji Kontynentalnej'. *Zeszyty Historyczne* 23 (1973), 159–171.

Lingen von K., 'Setting the Path for the UNWCC: the Representation of European Exile Governments on the London International Assembly and the Commission for Penal Reconstruction and Development, 1941–1944'. *Criminal Law Forum* 25 (2014), 45–76.

von Lingen K., 'Legal Flows: Contributions of Exiled Lawyers to the Concept of "Crimes Against Humanity" during the Second World War'. *Modern Intellectual History*, 17.2 (2020), 507–525.

Łakociński Z., '*Folke Bernadotte* i akcja Szwedzkiego Czerwonego Krzyża'. *Przegąd Lekarski* 1968, 145–152.

Łubieński L., 'Ewakuacja władz polskich we wrześniu 1939 roku'. *Zeszyty Historyczne* (1986), 76.

Maciejewski M., 'Doktrynalne ujęcia relacji prawo naturalne – prawo stanowione od starożytności do czasów oświecenia'. *Krakowskie Studia z Historii Państwa i Prawa* 8 (2015), 107–132.

Maciejewski M., 'Polscy uczeni prawnicy międzywojenni o ustroju i prawie Trzeciej Rzeszy'. *Miscellanea Historico-Iuridica* 2 (XV) (2016), 85–126.

Mierzwa J., 'Działalność Polskiego Wydziału Prawa w Oksfordzie raz organizacji zrzeszających polskich prawników na terenie Zjednoczonego Królestwa w latach 1940–1947'. *Niepodległość i Pamięć* 63 (2018), 77–94.

Muszalski E., 'Adwokaci polscy w Wielkiej Brytanii w latach 1939–1945: fragmenty'. *Palestra* 308 (1983), 62–65.

Pugacewicz T., 'Nauka o stosunkach międzynarodowych w koncepcji Ludwika Ehrlicha'. *Stosunki Międzynarodowe – International Relations* 54 (2018), 231–266.

Radbruch G., 'Gesetzliches Unrecht und übergesetzliches Recht', *Süddeutsche Zeitung* 5 (1946), 105–108.

Redzik A., 'Lwowska szkoła dyplomatyczna. Zarys historii Studium Dyplomatycznego przy Wydziale Prawa Uniwersytetu Jana Kazimierza we Lwowie (1930–1939)'. *Polski Przegląd Dyplomatyczny* 33 (2006), 121–149.

Roszkowski G., 'O Sankcyi Wykonawczej Dla Konwencji Genewskiej'. Copy from *Przegląd prawa i administracyi* (Lwów 1894).

Rudny P., '*Polski Instytut Źródłowy w Lund (PIZ) The Polish Research Institute in Lund. A Presentation of the Archives*'. University of Lund website at http://www3.ub.lu.se/ravensbruck/piz-eng-presentation.pdf (accessed 30 August 2025).

Ryszka F., 'U progu Norymbergi. Ściganie zbrodni wojennych w projektach polskich władz emigracyjnych'. *Czasopismo Prawno-Historyczne* XXX (1978), 155–186.

Salomonowicz, S., `The Legal Status of Poles under German Occupation (1939–1945). Some Remarks on the Need for Research.` *Krakowskie Studia z Historii Państwa i Prawa* 10 (2017), 95–110.

Sandorski J., 'Nauka prawa w życiu i działalności Bohdana Winiarskiego'. *Ruch Prawniczy, Ekonomiczny i Socjologiczny* LXI (1999), 15–32.

Schabas W., 'The United Nations War Crimes Commission's Proposal for an International Criminal Court'. *Criminal Law Forum* 25 (2014), 171–189.

Schmitt M. N., 'Military Necessity and Humanity in International Humanitarian Law: Preserving the Delicate Balance'. *Virginia Journal of International Law* 50 (2010), 795–839.

Segesser D. M., 'Die historischen Wurzel des Begriffs Verbrechen gegen die Menschlichkeit'. *Jahrbuch der Juristischen Zeitgeschichte* 8 (2006), 75–101.

Siwik A., 'Próby utworzenia reprezentacji ugrupowań politycznych na emigracji w latach 1946–1949'. *Dzieje Najnowsze* XXXVIII (3–4) (1996), 71–87.

Skubiszewski K., 'Bohdan Winiarski jako sędzia międzynarodowy'. *Ruch Prawniczy, Ekonomiczny i Socjologiczny* 3–4 (1999), 1–14.

Stola D., '*Early News on the Holocaust from Poland*'. Holocaust and Genocide Studies 11 (1997) 1, 1–27.

Szatensztajn W. J., 'Głos w dyskusji nad zagadnieniem zmian w stanie własności, wywołanych zarządzeniami władz okupacyjnych'. *Biuletyn Prawniczy* 5 (1945), 7–12.

Szawłowski R., 'R. Lemkin. Warszawski adwokat (1934–1939), twórca pojęcia „genocyd" i główny architekt konwencji z 9 grudnia 1948 r. (*Konwencji Lemkina*). W 55-lecie śmierci'. *Palestra* 9 (2014), 288–311.

Tarkowski M., 'Prawo Publiczne na Uniwersytecie Stefana Batorego w Wilnie'. *Zeszyty Prawnicze* 9 (2009), 191–217.

Warren C., 'Głos w Dyskusji nad zagadnieniem odpowiedzialności karnej za przestępstwa wojenne'. *Biuletyn Prawniczy* 6 (1943), 2–7.

Woolsey L. H., 'Transfer własności pod przymusem na obszarach okupowanych przez nieprzyjaciela'. *Głos Prawniczy* 5 (1945).

Wyrwa T., 'Wojskowa misja francuska a internowany rząd polski w Rumunii i odbudowa armii we Francji'. *Zeszyty Historyczne* 64 (1983), 223–236.

Zięba A., 'Michał Rostworowski', Andrzej Zięba (ed.), *Jubileuszowa Księga Nauk Politycznych* (Kraków: Wydawnictwo Uniwersytetu Jagiellońskiego 2015), 113–123.

Index

Index of Subjects

www.ingramcontent.com/pod-product-compliance
Ingram Content Group UK Ltd.
Pitfield, Milton Keynes, MK11 3LW, UK
UKHW021422091026
15624UKWH00010B/405

9 789004 758698